PIER 2
Progress in Electromagnetics Research

Finite Element and Finite Difference Methods in Electromagnetic Scattering

 **Progress in Electromagnetics Research**

Jin Au Kong, *Chief Editor*

Massachusetts Institute of Technology, Cambridge, Massachusetts

PIER 1
Progress in Electromagnetics Research

Jin Au Kong

PIER 2
Finite Element and Finite Difference Methods in Electromagnetic Scattering

Michael A. Morgan

PIER 2
Progress in Electromagnetics Research

Finite Element and Finite Difference Methods in Electromagnetic Scattering

Editor:

Michael A. Morgan

Naval Postgraduate School
Monterey, CA U.S.A.

Elsevier
New York · Amsterdam · London

Elsevier Science Publishing Co., Inc.
655 Avenue of the Americas, New York, New York 10010

Sole distributors outside the United States and Canada:
Elsevier Science Publishers B.V.
P.O. Box 211, 1000 AE Amsterdam, The Netherlands

© 1990 Elsevier Science Publishing Co., Inc.

This book is printed on acid-free paper.

ISBN 0-444-01518-3

ISSN 1043-626-X

Current printing (last digit):
10 9 8 7 6 5 4 3 2 1

Manufactured in the United States of America

ADVISORY BOARD

PREFACE

This second volume of PIER considers recent advances in computational electromagnetics, with emphasis on scattering, as brought about by new formulations and algorithms which use finite element or finite difference techniques. Within the past few years, there has been a growing interest in using these "finite methods" within the electromagnetics research and development communities. A major reason for this new emphasis has been the need to solve ever more complex problems, requiring very large numbers of discrete unknowns.

Until recently, most open-region problems involving antennas and scattering have been approached using integral equations, which implicitly incorporate the far-field radiation conditions. On the other hand, numerical approximation of an integral equation usually results in global interactions between each and every discrete unknown. For the time-harmonic case, this gives fully populated system matrices, while time-domain solutions require causal updating of each unknown, as influenced by all other unknowns at each time-marching step.

In contrast, finite methods result in only local, nearest-neighbor, type interactions between discrete field values at the nodes of the spatial mesh or grid. Finite method use in solving closed-region boundary value problems in the frequency domain yields highly sparse system matrices. This can result in dramatic reductions in solution and fill times, as well as in required computer memory, when compared to dealing with a full matrix of the same rank. In the time-domain, similar efficiency is observed because explicit coupling only exists between nearest spatial nodes.

Although finite methods excel in numerical efficiency for field solutions in closed spatial regions, additional consideration is needed for the open-region case, in order to bound the spatial mesh while enforcing proper radiation conditions at infinity. This mesh termination problem is being approached by a variety of contemporary techniques, most of which are presented in detail in the eight chapters of this volume.

In Chapter 1, Morgan presents a comprehensive and fundamental overview of finite methods and their associated mesh termination techniques, both in the frequency- and time-domains. This first chapter is meant to provide basic reference and a tutorial review. A powerful finite element algorithm is discussed by Fleming in Chapter 2 where, using the unimoment method to enforce the far-zone radiation conditions, scattering by composite (metallic and dielectric) axisymmetric structures is considered. The boundary element method is used to terminate a 2-D finite element mesh and solve several complex scattering problems in Chapter 3, as authored by Wu, Delisle, Fang and Lecours. In Chapter 4, Mittra and Ramahi derive a variety of absorbing boundary conditions and then investigate their performance in bounding finite method meshes in 2-D and axisymmetric 3-D scattering problems. McCartin, Bahrmasel and Meltz develop a finite method, called the Control Region Approximation, in Chapter 5 and apply it to 2-D scattering problems using asymptotic boundary conditions to enforce proper radiation field behavior. In Chapter 6, Morgan presents a new finite element based formulation for representing time-harmonic vector fields in 3-D inhomogeneous media using two coupled scalar potentials. Transient field problems involving corners and wedges in 2-D and 3-D are considered by Cangellaris and Mei in Chapter 7, using conforming boundary elements and leap-frog time-marching. The finite-difference time-domain method is developed by Taflov and Umashankar in Chapter 8, where further consideration is given to the Yee algorithm, radiation boundary conditions and a wide variety of applications and validations.

Finite methods (so named by Professor K. K. Mei over a decade ago) will continue to evolve as problem complexity and computational resources both increase. It is hoped that this volume will serve as a useful reference for students and practitioners of computational electromagnetics who are, or will be, involved in this evolution.

Acknowledgments are given by individual authors at the end of their respective chapters. In addition, special thanks are given to Mrs. Karen Charnley for typesetting most of the book, to Mrs. Sue Syu for detailed editorial comments, and to Professor J. A. Kong, who suggested the creation of this volume.

Michael A. Morgan

Monterey, California
May 22, 1989

CONTRIBUTORS

M. A. Morgan, *Naval Postgraduate School*
Monterey, California 93943, USA

A. H. J. Fleming, *Telecom Australia Research Laboratories*
Clayton, Victoria 3168, Australia

K. L. Wu, *Laval University*
Quebec, Canada, G1K 7P4

G. Y. Delisle, *Laval University*
Quebec, Canada, G1K 7P4

D. G. Fang, *Laval University*
Quebec, Canada, G1K 7P4

M. Lecours, *Laval University*
Quebec, Canada, G1K 7P4

R. Mittra, *University of Illinois*
Urbana, Illinois 61801, USA

O. Ramahi, *University of Illinois*
Urbana, Illinois 61801, USA

B. J. McCartin, *The Hartford Graduate Center*
Hartford, Connecticut 06120, USA

L. J. Bahrmasel, *United Technologies Research Center*
East Hartford, Connecticut 06108, USA

G. Meltz, *United Technologies Research Center*
East Hartford, Connecticut 06108, USA

A. C. Cangellaris, *University of Arizona*
Tucson, Arizona 85721, USA

K. K. Mei, *University of California at Berkeley*
Berkeley, California 94720, USA

A. Taflove, *Northwestern University*
Evanston, Illinois 60201, USA

K. R. Umashankar, *University of Illinois at Chicago*
Chicago, Illinois 60680, USA

CONTENTS

1

PRINCIPLES OF
FINITE METHODS IN
ELECTROMAGNETIC SCATTERING

M. A. Morgan

1.1 Introduction

This book deals with the theory and applications of differential equation based numerical methods in the realm of electromagnetic scattering. To prepare the reader for the advanced discussions of this topic that will follow in subsequent chapters, it is appropriate to begin the book with a tutorial review of the underlying concepts and terminology. Such a review will form the heart of this chapter. In addition, some examples of applications that are not otherwise covered in this text will be considered. It will be assumed that the reader is familiar with the fundamental physical and mathematical aspects of electromagnetic theory at the graduate level. Some excellent references for this knowledge are those by Stratton [1], Harrington [2], Van Bladel [3] and Kong [4].

The International System (SI for the French equivalent) is used in this text. This is a form of meter-kilogram-second (mks) system, with electrical quantities being expressed in the units actually measured: volts, amperes, coulombs, ohms, watts, etc. Using our mathematical notation, vector quantities, including $N \times 1$ and $1 \times N$ arrays, will usually appear with an overbar, e.g. $\overline{V}$. Dyadics and $M \times N$ matrices are most often denoted by a double overbar, e.g. $\overline{\overline{G}}$ for a Green's dyadic. Other symbolism will sometimes appear, at the discretion of individual chapter authors. Examples are the use of an underbar to indicate a row vector of unknowns (e.g. $\underline{a}$), or brackets to represent arrays, as in $[A]$. Such chapter dependent notation will be defined locally, either formally or by way of an obvious context. Unit vectors are uniformly designated by a circumflex; for example, a unit normal vector on a surface is written as $\hat{n}$.

As is customary in electrical engineering, sinusoidally time-varying quantities (known as time-harmonic or frequency-domain) are represented by complex phasor quantities having assumed temporal variation of $e^{j\omega t}$. The conversion from a complex phasor, say $\overline{E}(\overline{r})$, to the corresponding time-harmonic function, $\overline{\mathcal{E}}(\overline{r}, t)$ is effected by the operation $\overline{\mathcal{E}} = Re\{\overline{E}e^{j\omega t}\}$, where Re denotes the real part. Time-harmonic fields will be considered in Chapters 2 through 6, with the time-domain case appearing in Chapters 7 and 8. In this introductory chapter, both frequency- and time-domain cases will be covered.

Numerical approximations will be considered in the next section for the solutions of differential equations using either finite differences or finite elements. These techniques will henceforth be referred to as the "finite methods". When continuous systems are discretized using finite methods, *local* interactions result between unknowns. Thus, unknowns at discrete spatial points (nodes) are explicitly related only to their nearest neighbors in space. This results in highly sparse matrices for the case of time-harmonic fields, while requiring causal updating due only to nearest spatial neighbors in time-domain applications. In contrast, integral equation formulations typically produce global interactions between discrete unknowns, thus generating full system matrices for the time-harmonic case and all-inclusive connectivity in the transient evolution of the time-domain equations. As a result of the numerical efficiency brought about from local, versus global, interactions, the finite methods have the potential to solve larger and more complex electromagnetic problems than can be handled by *volume* integral equations, given the same constraints on computer time and available memory.

Although the finite methods offer numerical efficiency they are, by necessity, formulated as boundary-value and initial-value problems. As such, the solution of scattering and radiation problems in unbounded (open) spatial regions requires a mechanism for coupling closed region numerical solutions to the exterior space. This procedure must also ensure that the proper radiation conditions on the scattered field are satisfied. With the exception of the "infinite element" approach [5], a closed region is used to bound the spatial mesh employed in the finite methods. Various procedures for properly terminating, at least in an approximate numerical sense, the outer boundary of the mesh are employed in the subsequent chapters of this book. We will consider these methods from a basic conceptual point of view, in section 1.3.

1.2   Finite Methods

The finite methods may be classified as the numerical techniques that provide local interaction discretization for solving continuous boundary-value and initial-value problems [6]. As such, the finite methods offer a means to approximate the solution of specified differential equations in one or more spatial dimensions, as well as in time.

We will first consider the general idea of polynomial interpolation, followed by its application to finite-differences, as supported by examples incorporating phasor and time-domain concepts. This will be followed by a discussion, with examples, of the finite element method. A particular point of view will be developed that unifies the finite methods by identifying finite differences as a special case of finite elements.

a. Finite Difference Approximation

The most common finite method has been that of finite differences, where discrete approximations to partial derivatives are obtained by differentiating a piecewise polynomial, or other approximating function, which has been *point-matched* to the actual unknown function at

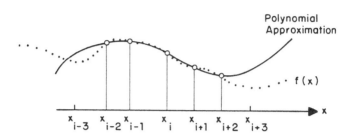

Figure 1   Point matched polynomial approximation around $x=x_i$.

the *nodes* of the problem. As a simple example, consider the finite difference (FD) approximation of the various derivatives, up to the n-th order, of an unknown function, $f(x)$, in one-dimension. The domain of x is partitioned into generally unequal segments, separated by ordered nodes, x_k, for $k = 1, 2, 3, \cdots, M$, as is illustrated in Fig. 1. In the region of x that contains the i-th node, at which point $x = x_i$, let $f(x)$ be approximated by an n-th order polynomial,

$$f(x) \approx a_n\, x^n + a_{n-1}\, x^{n-1} \cdots + a_1\, x + a_0 \tag{1}$$

The $n+1$ unknown coefficients can be found as linear functions of $n+1$ of the unknown nodal values of $f(x)$. Usually, these particular matching nodes are taken to bracket the i-th node except near the $i = 1$ and $i = M$ endpoints of the domain on x. The linear relationship between the coefficients and the nodal values of $f(x)$ is developed by point matching the polynomial in (1) at the $n+1$ nodes, resulting in the linear system defined by

$$\sum_{p=0}^{n} (x_k)^p\, a_p = f(x_k) \quad \text{for } n+1 \text{ values of } k \tag{2}$$

After inverting this system, the resultant linear functional form for each a_p can be substituted into (1). The FD formulas for each derivative up to the n-th order can then be obtained by analytically differentiating (1), followed by an evaluation at $x = x_i$. This procedure will yield a formula for each of the derivatives which is expressed as a linear function of the $n+1$ nodal values of $f(x)$.

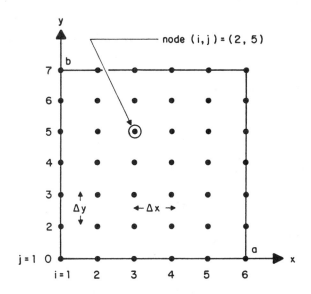

Figure 2 Finite difference grid in a rectangular region.

For example, if $n = 2$ with equal segments $x_i = i\,\Delta x$, then (1) results in a quadratic expression. By enforcing (1) at the three points $k = i - 1$, $k = i$ and $k = i + 1$, a 3×3 linear system,

$$
\begin{bmatrix}
1 & x_{i-1} & x_{i-1}^2 \\
1 & x_i & x_i^2 \\
1 & x_{i+1} & x_{i+1}^2
\end{bmatrix}
\cdot
\begin{bmatrix}
a_0 \\
a_1 \\
a_2
\end{bmatrix}
=
\begin{bmatrix}
f(x_{i-1}) \\
f(x_i) \\
f(x_{i+1})
\end{bmatrix}
\tag{3}
$$

is obtained. After inverting this system, we substitute the a_p's into (1) and differentiate once and then twice to obtain the well-known finite difference formulas for the first and second derivatives,

$$
\frac{d\,f(x_i)}{dx} \approx \frac{f(x_{i+1}) - f(x_{i-1})}{2\Delta x}
\tag{4a}
$$

$$
\frac{d^2 f(x_i)}{dx^2} \approx \frac{f(x_{i+1}) - 2\,f(x_i) + f(x_{i-1})}{(\Delta x)^2}
\tag{4b}
$$

Extensions of this idea can be made to higher order polynomial approximations and to multiple dimensions. As an example, consider overlaying a 2-D rectangular region, defined by $0 \leq x \leq a$ and $0 \leq y \leq b$, with a regular grid of nodes located at (x_i, y_j) for $i = 1, 2, \cdots, 6$ and $j = 1, 2, \cdots, 7$, as per Fig. 2. About a given point (x_i, y_j) in this mesh, we will approximate a continuous function, $f(x, y)$, by a 2nd-order polynomial form

$$f(x, y) \approx c_0 + c_1 x + c_2 y + c_3 x^2 + c_4 y^2 \qquad (5)$$

The five coefficients are found by equating the expansion to the function at the five nodes: (x_{i-1}, y_j), (x_i, y_j), (x_{i+1}, y_j), (x_i, y_{j-1}), and (x_i, y_{j+1}), followed by an inversion of the resultant 5×5 linear system. Finite difference approximations to the partial derivatives are then found by differentiating (5). All of this work results in formulas which are identical in form to (4), e.g.

$$\frac{\partial^2 f(x_i, y_j)}{\partial x^2} \approx \frac{f(x_{i+1}, y_j) - 2 f(x_i, y_j) + f(x_{i-1}, y_j)}{(\Delta x)^2} \qquad (6)$$

This approach can be applied as well to irregular meshes, having non-rectangular and non-equispaced nodal arrangements. As will be shown in subsection 1.2d, the finite difference method can be thought of as a special case of a more generic technique, called the finite element method.

b. Simple Finite Difference Example

The finite difference solution of a boundary-value problem is set up by replacing the analytical derivatives contained in the differential equation by finite difference formulas at each nodal point where the solution function is to be found. Thus, there results a system of linear equations relating the unknown nodal values of the solution function to both the known excitations (drivers) of the differential equation and the known boundary-values of the solution function.

To illustrate this, let us set up the finite-difference frequency domain (FD-FD) solution to the Helmholtz equation in the same rectangular region, defined by $0 \leq x \leq a$ and $0 \leq y \leq b$, as depicted in Fig. 2. The partial differential equation (PDE) being considered is the inhomogeneous Helmholtz equation,

$$\{\nabla^2 + \kappa^2\} f(x,y) = g(x,y) \tag{7}$$

where the Laplacian operator is $\nabla^2 = \partial^2/\partial x^2 + \partial^2/\partial y^2$. The forcing function, $g(x,y)$, is to be specified and the solution, f, is assumed to satisfy homogeneous *Dirichlet* boundary conditions (BC's) on the perimeter: $f(x,0) = f(x,b) = f(0,y) = f(a,y) = 0$. This problem could be found, for instance, in solving for the TM eigenmodes of a metallic rectangular waveguide whose cross section encloses the solution region. In such a case, $f = E_z$, $g = 0$ and the eigenvalues of κ are assumed to have been found through a separate procedure.

The discrete unknowns are the nodal values of $f(x_i, y_j)$ for $i = 2, \cdots, 5$ and $j = 2, \cdots, 6$. We will denote the approximate numerical solution for these nodal values as $f_{i,j} \approx f(x_i, y_j)$. A five node "star" finite difference approximation to the ∇^2 operator can be constructed from the sum of (6) and the corresponding form for $\partial^2/\partial y^2$. Applying this to (7) at each interior node yields

$$\frac{\{f_{i+1,j} + f_{i-1,j}\}}{(\Delta x)^2} + \frac{\{f_{i,j+1} + f_{i,j-1}\}}{(\Delta y)^2}$$

$$+ \{\kappa^2 - \frac{2}{(\Delta x)^2} - \frac{2}{(\Delta y)^2}\} f_{i,j} = g(x_i, y_j) \tag{8}$$

Enforcement of this equation at the interior nodes leads to a linear set of equations. To cast these equations into a matrix form, we need to define arrays for the unknowns, $f_{i,j}$ and the known nodal values of the driver, $g(x_i, y_j)$. By ordering these column vectors as

$$\overline{F} = [f_{2,2}, f_{3,2}, \cdots, f_{2,3}, \cdots, f_{5,6}]^T \tag{9}$$

and

$$\overline{G} = [g(x_2, y_2), g(x_3, y_2), \cdots, g(x_2, y_3), \cdots, g(x_5, y_6)]^T \tag{10}$$

where the T superscript indicates transpose, the linear system is given by

$$\overline{\overline{A}} \cdot \overline{F} = \overline{G} \tag{11}$$

The 30×30 matrix is symmetric, sparse and banded

$$
\overline{\overline{A}} =
\begin{bmatrix}
a_{11} & a_{12} & 0 & 0 & a_{15} & 0 & 0 & 0 & \cdots \\
a_{21} & a_{22} & a_{23} & 0 & 0 & a_{26} & 0 & 0 & \cdots \\
0 & a_{32} & a_{33} & a_{34} & 0 & 0 & a_{37} & 0 & \cdots \\
& \ddots & \ddots & \ddots & & & & \ddots & \\
a_{51} & 0 & 0 & a_{54} & a_{55} & a_{56} & 0 & 0 & a_{59} \\
& \ddots & & & \ddots & \ddots & \ddots & & & \ddots
\end{bmatrix}
\tag{12a}
$$

with

$$
a_{m,n} = a_{n,m} \tag{12b}
$$

$$
a_{n,n} = \kappa^2 - \frac{2}{(\Delta x)^2} - \frac{2}{(\Delta y)^2} \tag{12c}
$$

$$
a_{n,n+1} = a_{k,k-1} = \frac{1}{(\Delta x)^2} \tag{12d}
$$

$$
a_{n,n+4} = a_{k,k-4} = \frac{1}{(\Delta y)^2} \tag{12e}
$$

Note that the m-th row of $\overline{\overline{A}}$ represents the equation defined by enforcing (8) at the node (i,j) corresponding to $f_{i,j}$ of the m-th element of $\overline{F}$ in (9). Inversion of (11) can be accomplished by exploiting the sparsity and block-matrix nature of $\overline{\overline{A}}$. Such procedures will allow the practical solution of very large systems, as will be discussed further in subsection 1.2e and in Chapters 2 and 6.

c. A Brief Visit with the FD-TD Approach

In the example of the previous subsection we considered the finite difference solution of a simple boundary problem centered about the Helmholtz equation in 2-D. This approach can be extended to higher dimensions, including the time-variable. Such is the case in Chapter 8, where Taflove and Umashankar begin by constructing a finite-difference time-domain (FD-TD) discretization of Maxwell's equations in 4-D space-time. To set the stage for this development, we will consider a simple example of FD-TD as applied to the solution of an initial-value problem involving the 2-D (1-D space plus time) wave equation.

In particular, the wave equation for the scalar field $u(x,t)$ in a lossless, uniform and *non-dispersive* medium is given by the PDE,

$$\frac{\partial^2 u}{\partial x^2} - \frac{1}{c^2}\frac{\partial^2 u}{\partial t^2} = 0 \tag{13}$$

where c represents the frequency-independent (hence non-dispersive) propagation velocity of the field u. In the electromagnetic case, this field can represent, for instance, the voltage or current on a uniform TEM x-directed transmission line. Another example is the transverse (to $\hat{x}$) electric or magnetic fields in an ideal plane wave propagating in the $\pm x$ direction. There are similar examples in acoustics and mechanical vibration.

To continue the example, let us first define the domain of the solution as $0 \leq x \leq a$ and $t \geq 0$. This domain is illustrated in Fig. 3. For the domain defined, (13) is to be solved subject to the following *mixed* initial-value and boundary-value conditions:

$$u(x,0) = q(x) \quad \text{for } 0 \leq x \leq a \tag{14a}$$

$$u(0,t) = 0 \qquad \text{for } t \geq 0 \tag{14b}$$

$$u(a,t) = 0 \qquad \text{for } t \geq 0 \tag{14c}$$

where $q(x)$ is specified so that $q(0) = q(a) = 0$. These conditions could define such phenomena as the deflection of a string which is pinned at $x = 0$ and $x = a$ or the $\mathcal{E}_y(x,t)$ electric field in a planar resonator model with conductor plates at $x = 0$ and $x = a$. The analytical solution can be obtained through a variety of elementary methods [7].

Since the wave equation is classified as a hyperbolic PDE, [8], the solution at any point will propagate along outbound "characteristics" which, for the example case, are lines in 2-D space-time defined by $\Delta x/\Delta t = \pm c$. Characteristic lines for the endpoints of the initial-values

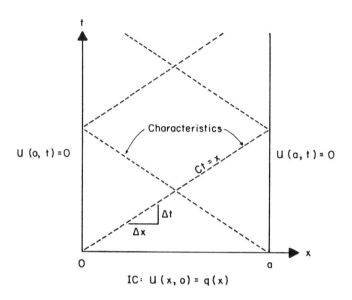

Figure 3 Space-time domain for wave equation solution.

are shown in Fig. 3. For problems in 3-D and 4-D the characteristics become, respectively, space-time cones and expanding spheres. The characteristics can be thought of as bounding the region of space-time which is causally influenced by an "event" at a given $(\bar{r}, t)$ point.

Characteristics play an important role in the numerical solution of processes defined by *hyperbolic* and *parabolic* (e.g. heat transport) PDE's. These processes are set up as equations of evolution and their numerical solution proceeds using a "marching in time" algorithm, with time step Δt. It was recognized as early as 1928, by Courant, Friedrichs and Lewy [9], that the ratio of spatial segmentation distance to time step size should be constrained so as *not* to violate the bounds defined by the characteristics. The result of ignoring the CFL criterion (also referred to as the "Courant limit") is the production of an ill-posed and unstable numerical solution, with rapidly diverging accuracy. This constraint applies not only to the finite method discretization of the original PDE problem but also to the time-stepping solution of the corresponding integral equation formulation for the same physical process. The Helmholtz equation is an example of an *elliptic* PDE. These do not have any characteristics in real space and, hence, we did not concern ourselves with this issue in setting up the previous example in subsection 1.1b. The Courant limit will be discussed further in the advanced time-domain applications considered in Chapters 7 and 8.

Let us return now to the problem at hand: discretizing (13) and (14) using finite differences. In analogy with the Helmholtz equation example, we first define a mesh to overlay the space-time region in Fig. 3. This is shown in Fig. 4. The node positions are located at $(x_i, t_j) = (i\Delta x, j\Delta t)$, where $\Delta x = a/N$. The numerical solution for the (x_i, t_j) nodal values are denoted as $u_{i,j}$. We next apply three-point central difference formulas for the partial derivatives in (13), at node (x_i, t_j). This is similar to what was done in (8) for the Helmholtz equation. The result, after rearranging terms, is the time-marching equation

$$u_{i,j+1} = \gamma^2 \left(u_{i+1,j} + u_{i-1,j} \right) + 2(1 - \gamma^2) u_{i,j} - u_{i,j-1} \qquad (15)$$

where the dimensionless constant is

$$\gamma = c \, \frac{\Delta t}{\Delta x} \qquad (16)$$

The CFL condition for stability is that $\gamma \leq 1$. If c is not a spatial or temporal constant then the CFL condition on γ must be satisfied *locally* in space-time. To begin the evolution of (15) at $i = 1$ we note that the initial condition (IC) is given by $u_{i,0} = q(x_i) = q_i$, with $u_{i,-1}$ assumed to be zero. This yields

$$u_{i,1} = \gamma^2 \left(q_{i+1} + q_{i-1} \right) + 2(1 - \gamma^2) q_i \qquad (17)$$

where we note that $q_0 = q_N = 0$, as assumed in (14). After initiating the $j=1$ step using (17), the updating continues with (16).

An alternate approach, [10], is to use two first-order "state equations" to represent the wave equation in (13). This is done by defining two *state variable* functions: the original unknown $u(x, t)$, plus a new function, $w(x, t)$, where

$$\frac{\partial w}{\partial t} = c \, \frac{\partial u}{\partial x} \qquad (18a)$$

$$\frac{\partial u}{\partial t} = c \, \frac{\partial w}{\partial x} \qquad (18b)$$

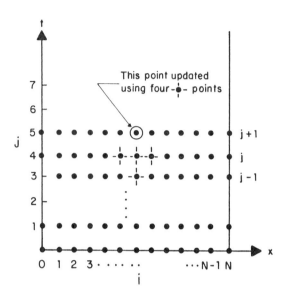

Figure 4 Finite difference mesh for the wave equation showing forward stepping evolution point.

This first-order coupled PDE system may be recognized as the well-known "telegrapher's equations" from transmission line analysis. The wave equation can be generated by differentiating (18a) with respect to x and (18b) with respect to t, followed by equating the resultant 2nd-order cross derivatives of w.

To discretize these equations, we will use a "leapfrog" mesh, [11: 489–496], as shown in Fig. 5. A key feature of this mesh is the space-time offset of the nodes for defining u and w. In particular, let us define

$$w_{i,j} = w(x_i, t_j) \quad \text{for } i = 0, 2, 4, \cdots, N\text{-}1; \quad j = 1, 3, 5, \cdots \quad (19a)$$

$$u_{i,j} = u(x_i, t_j) \quad \text{for } i = 1, 3, 5, \cdots, N \; ; \; j = 0, 2, 4, \cdots \quad (19b)$$

Using central differences, we will enforce (18a) at (even,even) (i,j) nodes and (18b) at (odd,odd) (i,j) nodes. For $i = 2, 4, 6, \cdots, N$ and $j = 0, 2, 4, \cdots$, this procedure produces

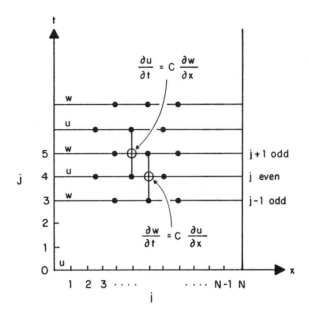

Figure 5 Nodal topology for the leapfrog method showing central difference points to enforce coupled first-order PDE's.

$$\frac{w_{i,j+1} - w_{i,j-1}}{2\,\Delta t} = c\,\frac{u_{i+1,j} - u_{i-1,j}}{2\,\Delta x} \tag{20a}$$

while for $i = 1, 3, 5, \cdots, N$, and $j = 1, 3, 5, \cdots$, it gives

$$\frac{u_{i,j+1} - u_{i,j-1}}{2\,\Delta t} = c\,\frac{w_{i+1,j} - w_{i-1,j}}{2\,\Delta x} \tag{20b}$$

where we have assumed N is odd for terminating the i-index. To begin the *leapfrog* evolution, we start by enforcing (20a) for $j=0$, with $w_{i,-1}$ assumed to be zero, resulting in

$$w_{i,1} = \frac{\Delta x}{\Delta t}\,(q_{i+1} - q_{i-1}) \tag{21}$$

The notation, $q_i = q(x_i) = u(x_i, 0)$ for the nodal values of the specified IC, was employed in (17). After the startup in (21), the relationship in (21b) is used to obtain $u(i,2)$, followed by alternating applications of (21a) and (21b). This leapfrog process has the same stability constraint as the original second-order system, namely the Courant limit:

$\Delta x/\Delta t \leq c$. To get around having double $2\,\Delta x$ and $2\,\Delta t$ increments in defining the central differences, a *half-index* scheme is often used. This will be the case in the time-marching algorithms presented in Chapters 7 and 8. There are numerous other methods for applying the finite-difference method to create time-stepping solutions to hyperbolic and parabolic PDE's. A comprehensive reference on this topic is given in [11].

An extension of this 2-D space-time leapfrog concept to Maxwell's curl equations in 4-D will result in the original *Yee algorithm* [12]. This early (1966) FD-TD method employs two interleaved 3-D rectangular spatial lattices, one for the vector $\overline{E}$-field and one for the vector $\overline{H}$-field. The details of the Yee algorithm are discussed in Chapter 8.

d. Weighted Residual Method

The finite element method can be approached for elliptic, hyperbolic or parabolic PDE's through the "weighted residual method", which we will henceforth call WRM [11]. Let us begin in a very general manner by considering the numerical solution of a specified PDE in an M-dimensional spatial region or space-time region, to be denoted in either case as V_0. Points in the M-D region are given by the ordered vector, $\overline{r} = (r_1, r_2, ..., r_M)$. For example, the Helmholtz equation example in part 1.2b had $M=2$, where $\overline{r}$ was (x, y), while for the wave equation example in the last subsection, M was also 2 and $\overline{r} = (x, t)$.

The generalized PDE can be written as

$$\overline{\overline{\mathcal{D}}}(\overline{r}) \cdot \overline{f}(\overline{r}) = \overline{g}(\overline{r}) \quad \text{for } r \in V_0 \tag{22}$$

where $\overline{\overline{\mathcal{D}}}(r)$ is the given dyadic differential operator, $\overline{f}$ is the unknown vector function and $\overline{g}$ is the known driving vector. Essential boundary data concerning $\overline{f}$ are known on a surface, S_0, which encloses V_0. An example is the scalar Helmholtz equation in 2-D, which we previously considered in (7).

To find the approximate numerical solution of (22), we use a *basis function* expansion to represent $\overline{f}$,

$$\overline{f}_a(\overline{r}) = \sum_{n=1}^{N} \overline{\overline{U}}_n(\overline{r}) \cdot \overline{C}_n \tag{23}$$

where the diagonal dyadic functions,

$$\overline{\overline{U}}_n(\overline{r}) = u_{n,1}\,\hat{r}_1\,\hat{r}_1 + u_{n,2}\,\hat{r}_2\,\hat{r}_2 + \cdots + u_{n,M}\,\hat{r}_M\,\hat{r}_M \qquad (24)$$

are members of the basis set. Each basis function should, ideally, have the same order of differentiability as does the exact solution. As N is increased, the approximate expansion in (23) should converge in a *pointwise* sense to $\overline{f}(\overline{r})$. This last condition depends upon how completely the set of basis functions spans the subspace of functions occupied by the various solutions to (22). This quality is reflected in the linear independence of the function set.

Upon substituting (23) into (22), there results,

$$\overline{\overline{D}} \cdot \overline{f}_a(r) = \sum_{n=1}^{N} \{\overline{\overline{D}}(\overline{r}) \cdot \overline{\overline{U}}_n(\overline{r})\} \cdot \overline{C}_n = \overline{g}(\overline{r}) \qquad (25)$$

To solve for the N vector coefficients, $\overline{C}_n$, we enforce this equation with respect to a succession of N weighted vector integrations over V_0,

$$\langle \overline{\overline{W}}_k(\overline{r}), \overline{\overline{D}} \cdot \overline{f}(\overline{r}) \rangle = \sum_{n=1}^{N} \langle \overline{\overline{W}}_k(\overline{r}), \overline{\overline{D}}(\overline{r}) \cdot \overline{\overline{U}}_n(\overline{r}) \rangle \cdot \overline{C}_n \qquad (26)$$

$$= \langle \overline{\overline{W}}_k(\overline{r}), \overline{g}(\overline{r}) \rangle \text{ for } k = 1, N$$

with

$$\langle \overline{\overline{W}}(\overline{r}), \overline{\overline{G}}(\overline{r}) \rangle = \int_{V_0} \overline{\overline{W}}(\overline{r}) \cdot \overline{\overline{G}}(\overline{r})\, d^M \overline{r} \qquad (27)$$

indicating an integration of the inner (dot) product of the two indicated functions over V_0.

The set of diagonal dyadics,

$$\overline{\overline{W}}_k(\overline{r}) = w_{k,1}\,\hat{r}_1\,\hat{r}_1 + w_{k,2}\,\hat{r}_2\,\hat{r}_2 + \cdots + w_{k,M}\,\hat{r}_M\,\hat{r}_M \qquad (28)$$

is termed the "weighting functions" in WRM. This set is called the "testing functions" in the MoM. There are N vector equations in (28), each of which contains M scalar equations for the M components of each $\overline{C}_n$. Thus, the linear system has rank $N \cdot M$. By using a certain class of basis and weighting functions, this matrix system can be made very sparse. This will be demonstrated in the next subsection.

Before continuing with the development of the WRM, let us pause briefly to consider some of the terminology presented here. The procedure just considered could just as well have been applied to an integral operator equation having the form of (22). In fact, when applied to integral equations in electromagnetics, the WRM concept has historically been termed both the moment method and the method of moments (MoM), [2]. The reference to "moments" is due to the similarity of the inner product integral terms in (27) to statistical moments found in probability theory. Origins of the WRM terminology are in the area of finite elements, as applied to structural and fluid dynamics problems.

Let us now return to the details of the WRM. In setting up the linear system in (26) there are some additional considerations that need to be addressed. One of these concerns the support region of the basis functions: either *full-range* (over all of V_0) or *compact* (each being nonzero over only a portion of V_0). An example of full-range basis functions is the set of complex exponentials employed in Fourier series, where the set of $\overline{C}_n$'s are termed the "spectrum" of the expansion. Compact basis functions are common to finite element applications, as well as MoM solutions of integral equations. Usually, these basis functions are selected so that at each node of the discretized problem all basis functions, *except one*, are zero. At its associated node, where it is nonzero, the basis function will usually be set to unity. In such a case, the coefficients in (23), $\overline{C}_n$'s, represent the solution values of $\overline{f}(\overline{r})$ at the N nodes.

Another consideration involves the set of weighting functions. There is obviously an unlimited selection available. Three of the more common types are:

(1) *Point Collocation*, (also known as simply "collocation") uses a delta function, $w_{k,m} = \delta(\overline{r} - \overline{r}_k)$ for each diagonal component of $\overline{\overline{W}}_k$ in (28). The effect of this is to reduce the integration moments in (27) to simple point-matching at the respective nodes, resulting in nothing more than a special case of the finite difference method where the polynomial approximation in (1) and (2) is replaced by the basis function representation being employed to construct the $\overline{\overline{U}}_n$. Thus, point collocation can be viewed as equivalent to finite differences. An advantage of this approach is its relative simplicity in generating the matrix elements from (26), since integrations are reduced to enforcing the approximation at the node points. On the other hand, there is no control on the behavior of the solution

in-between the nodes, at least in the sense of solving the differential equation. This usually results in the least-accurate solution of the three methods being considered here, where we are assuming a similar node density and computer word-length in each case.

(2) *Subdomain Collocation*, (also known as the "subdomain method") which employs a set of mutually exclusive, unit-amplitude pulse functions, $w_{k,m}(\bar{r}) = 1$, in a defined region around the k-th node. These regions enclosing each node are non-overlapping and usually are directly adjacent to one another, without unfilled space. This approximation is usually more accurate than Point Collocation, but not as accurate as Galerkin's method, when self-adjoint operators are involved.

(3) *Galerkin Method*, which uses the same set of functions for both basis and testing, $\overline{\overline{W}}_k(\bar{r}) = \overline{\overline{U}}_k(\bar{r})$. For the case of a *self-adjoint* operator, $\overline{\overline{\mathcal{D}}}(\bar{r})$, it can be shown that the functional defined by

$$Q(\bar{f}) = \langle \bar{f}, \overline{\overline{\mathcal{D}}} \cdot \bar{f} \rangle - 2\langle \bar{f}, \bar{g} \rangle$$

is stationary about the solution to the original operator equation, in (22), [13].

The variational principle considered above, when applied to the basis function expansion in (23), is termed the *Rayleigh-Ritz Method* and yields the Galerkin's result for the weighted residual approach. This procedure usually provides the most accurate solution and forms the foundation for most of the FEM work that has been done. Another means of achieving this same result (the Galerkin equations, with $\overline{\overline{W}}_k = \overline{\overline{U}}_k$) is by way of the classical Euler-Lagrange variational formulation. This has the advantage of reducing the order of differentiation on the basis functions, *vis-a-vis* a direct Galerkin approach, and will be demonstrated in the following section. Error bounds for the above three methods are considered in detail in [13]. We will also briefly consider this topic in subsection 1.2f.

A hybrid approach is often taken in applying the WRM to time-domain solutions, whereby a finite-element basis function expansion is used to represent the spatial variations of the solution while time derivatives are approximated using finite-differences. If interpreted in the WRM sense, this translates into using space-time weighting functions having delta function temporal variation, thus *sifting out* the

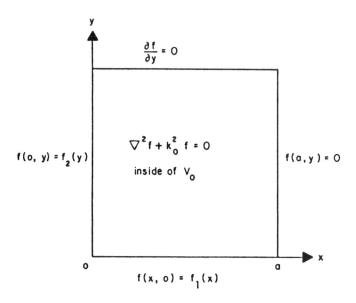

Figure 6 Helmholtz equation with mixed boundary conditions.

discrete time steps of the computational process. Such a procedure is used implicitly in the technique described in Chapter 7, resulting in time-domain leap-frogging of spatial basis function expansions for $\overline{E}$ and $\overline{H}$. A "boundary element" approach is also used in Chapter 7 for restricting irregularities in the space-time lattice (mesh) to the interfaces between dissimilar materials.

e. Simple Finite Element Example

Consider the simple problem of the undriven Helmholtz equation $(g = 0)$ with free space wavenumber $k_0 = \omega/c$ (where ω is the radian frequency and $c = 3 \times 10^8$ m/s),

$$\{\nabla^2 + k_0^2\} f(x, y) = 0 \tag{29}$$

within the rectangular region of Fig. 6, with *mixed* (both Dirichlet and Neumann) BC's,

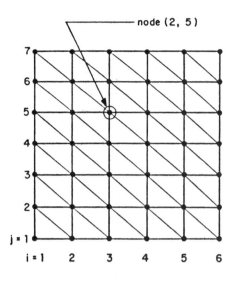

Figure 7 Rectangular region finite element mesh.

$$f(x,0) = f_1(x) \tag{30a}$$

$$f(0,y) = f_2(y) \tag{30b}$$

$$f(a,y) = 0 \tag{30c}$$

$$\frac{\partial f}{\partial y}(x,b) = 0 \tag{30d}$$

The rectangular region is discretized into the same grid of doubly-ordered nodes, as in Fig. 2. As before, the nodal values of the solution will be denoted as $f_{i,j} \approx f(x_i, y_j)$. The Dirichlet boundary condition nodes are specified for $i=1$, $i=6$ and $j=1$. Note that the nodal values along the top row $(j=7)$ are now unknowns since the Neumann BC is specified there.

Proceeding with the FEM approach, triangular "finite elements" are used to divide up the space, as per Fig. 7. These elements are used

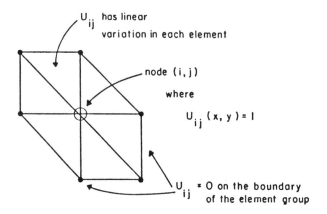

Figure 8   Node with surrounding element group.

to define support regions for the (compact support type) basis functions that will be used to approximate the solution around each node. We will employ piecewise linear *pyramid* basis functions, $U_{i,j}(x, y)$, to represent the solution. Following the general procedure indicated by (23), but for the simpler scalar function case, gives the basis function approximation to $f(x, y)$,

$$f_a(x, y) = \sum_{i=1}^{6} \sum_{j=1}^{7} f_{i,j} \, U_{i,j}(x, y) \tag{31}$$

The support region for a given $U_{i,j}$ is all elements which share the (i, j) node, as illustrated in Fig. 8 for an interior node. In the ℓ-th element, we will locally number the associated 3 nodes, $(k=1,2,3)$ as shown in Fig. 9. Within this ℓ-th element, the linear basis function associated with the k-th node is given by the matrix product

$$U_k(x, y) = [x, \, y, \, 1] \cdot \overline{L}_k \tag{32}$$

where $\overline{L}_k$ is the k-th column of the element coordinate matrix,

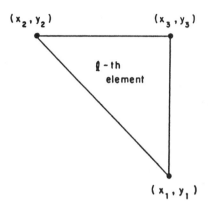

Figure 9   Local coordinates in an element.

$$\overline{\overline{L}} = \frac{1}{\Delta_\ell} \begin{bmatrix} (y_2 - y_3) & (y_3 - y_1) & (y_1 - y_2) \\ (x_3 - x_2) & (x_1 - x_3) & (x_2 - x_1) \\ (x_2 y_3 - x_3 y_2) & (x_3 y_1 - x_1 y_3) & (x_1 y_2 - x_2 y_1) \end{bmatrix} \qquad (33)$$

The Δ_ℓ term is the determinant of the 3×3 matrix within the square brackets in (33). This determinant also equals twice the area of the ℓ-th triangle.

Employing the Euler-Lagrange formulation, we seek the nodal values in (31) about which the quadratic functional below is stationary,

$$Q(f) = \langle \nabla f, \nabla f \rangle - k_0^2 \langle f, f \rangle \qquad (34)$$

Note that this functional has only first order derivatives inside of the $\langle *, * \rangle$ dot-product integrals over x, y. The proof that $Q(f)$ is stationary about the solution to (29), with BC's in (30), follows directly from the Euler equation, [14: pp.275–280],

$$\frac{\partial}{\partial x}\left[\frac{\partial Q}{\partial(D_x f)}\right] + \frac{\partial}{\partial y}\left[\frac{\partial Q}{\partial(D_y f)}\right] - \frac{\partial Q}{\partial f} = 0 \qquad (35)$$

The stationary functional in (34) can also be obtained through applying Green's theorem (or multiple integration by parts) to the Galerkin equations considered in the previous subsection. The numerical approximation to the stationary solution is found by first substituting (31) into (34), to give

$$Q_a = \sum_{i=1}^{6} \sum_{j=1}^{7} \sum_{m=1}^{6} \sum_{n=1}^{7} f_{i.j} \, f_{m,n} \left\{ \langle \nabla U_{i,j}, \nabla U_{m,n} \rangle - k_0^2 \, \langle U_{i,j}, U_{m,n} \rangle \right\}$$

(36)

We then differentiate this quadratic form with respect to each of the *unknown* nodal values of $f_{i,j}$ and $f_{m,n}$, setting the result to zero in each case. Each differentiation of the quadratic form will yield a linear equation representing the stationary requirement for the particular nodal value of f being considered. A linear system results, with one equation for each unknown nodal value as given by

$$\sum_{i=1}^{6} \sum_{j=1}^{7} f_{i,j} \left\{ \langle \nabla U_{i,j}, \nabla U_{m,n} \rangle - k_0^2 \langle U_{i,j}, U_{m,n} \rangle \right\} = 0 \qquad (37)$$

for $m=2$ to 5 and $n=2$ to 7. The terms in the summation involving *known* nodal values for $f_{i,j}$ can be transferred to the right hand side of (37) to put the equations in standard form. Note that for a given (i, j) node, only (m, n) nodes sharing at least one common element will provide a nonzero contribution to the moment integrations in (37). Thus, the resultant system matrix will be quite sparse, with most array elements being zero. As previously mentioned, this sparse matrix feature is produced by all finite methods when using basis and testing functions having compact support.

To put (37) into a block matrix form, let us denote the nodal unknowns across the j-th horizontal row of the mesh in Fig. 7 by the column vector (the T superscript indicates transpose)

$$\overline{F}_j = [f_{2,j}, f_{3,j}, f_{4,j}, f_{5}, j]^T \qquad (38)$$

The matrix equation in (37) can then be written as a linear matrix-vector relationship between adjacent row vectors

$$\overline{\overline{A}}_j \cdot \overline{F}_{j-1} + \overline{\overline{B}}_j \cdot \overline{F}_j + \overline{\overline{C}}_j \cdot \overline{F}_{j+1} = \overline{P}_j \qquad (39)$$

where the *block-matices* each have a banded structure

$$\overline{\overline{A}}_j \sim \begin{bmatrix} \times & \times & & \\ & \times & \times & 0 \\ 0 & & \times & \times \\ & & & \times \end{bmatrix} \tag{40a}$$

$$\overline{\overline{B}}_j \sim \begin{bmatrix} \times & \times & & \\ \times & \times & \times & 0 \\ 0 & \times & \times & \times \\ & & \times & \times \end{bmatrix} \tag{40b}$$

$$\overline{\overline{C}}_j \sim \begin{bmatrix} \times & & & \\ \times & \times & & 0 \\ 0 & \times & \times & \\ & & \times & \times \end{bmatrix} \tag{40c}$$

The nonzero "×" matrix elements as well as the components of the boundary condition vector, $\overline{P}_j$, are obtained in terms of the element integrals within the curly brackets in (37). Inside of the ℓ-th element, having $\overline{\overline{L}}$−matrix defined by (33), the integrands can be obtained directly from (32). Denoting the relationship between local (in element ℓ) and global node coordinates by $k = (m,n)$ and $q = (i,j)$, there results

$$U_k U_q = \overline{L}_k^T \cdot \begin{bmatrix} x^2 & xy & x \\ xy & y^2 & y \\ x & y & 1 \end{bmatrix} \cdot \overline{L}_q \tag{41a}$$

$$\nabla U_k \cdot \nabla U_q = \overline{L}_k^T \cdot \begin{bmatrix} 1 & 0 & 0 \\ 0 & 1 & 0 \\ 0 & 0 & 0 \end{bmatrix} \cdot \overline{L}_q \tag{41b}$$

The matrix entries are thus assembled from element integrations of the type

$$I_{r,s} = \iint_\Delta x^r y^s \, dx \, dy \tag{42}$$

which are available in tabular form in a number of references on finite elements, e.g. [11].

Having loaded the block matrices relating adjacent row vectors of unknowns, the global matrix structure will have a tri-block form

$$
\begin{bmatrix}
\overline{\overline{B}}_2 & \overline{\overline{C}}_2 \\
\overline{\overline{A}}_3 & \overline{\overline{B}}_3 & \overline{\overline{C}}_3 & & 0 \\
& \overline{\overline{A}}_4 & \overline{\overline{B}}_4 & \overline{\overline{C}}_4 \\
& & \cdot & \cdot & \cdot \\
& 0 & & \cdot & \cdot & \cdot \\
& & & & \cdot & \cdot & \cdot \\
& & & & & \overline{\overline{A}}_7 & \overline{\overline{B}}_7
\end{bmatrix}
\begin{bmatrix}
\overline{F}_2 \\ \overline{F}_3 \\ \overline{F}_4 \\ \cdot \\ \cdot \\ \cdot \\ \overline{F}_7
\end{bmatrix}
=
\begin{bmatrix}
\overline{P}_2 \\ \overline{P}_3 \\ \overline{P}_4 \\ \cdot \\ \cdot \\ \cdot \\ \overline{P}_7
\end{bmatrix}
\qquad (43)
$$

The finite element solution thus comes down to inverting a matrix. As was the case for the finite difference example, the global array is mostly filled with zeros. This is in contrast to integral equation methods, which produce full matrix structures. A sparse matrix allows highly economical inversion, for even very large matrix order, by any of a number of different algorithms [15]. In addition, by properly ordering the nodes, as was done here, the matrix can often be made to have a block structure. A block structured matrix can be efficiently inverted by way of the Riccati transform algorithm [16] (also see Chapters 2 and 6 of this book).

In developing the theory and examples for the finite methods, there was no discussion concerning expected accuracy. We will now briefly address this topic at an introductory level. Additional developments will be made in the following chapters for the specific cases to be considered.

f. Basics of Error Analysis

Let us now consider some of the concepts and terminology associated with computational error in numerical solutions. We will begin by using the simple example of the finite difference approximation of the Helmholtz equation as a vehicle to illustrate some of these ideas. The discussion could readily be expanded to include all finite and integral methods, as applied in both the frequency- and the time-domains.

In general, the "pointwise error" in a numerical solution at each node is simply the difference between the exact and computed values of the solution at the node. Referring back to Fig. 2, the pointwise error at node (x_i, y_j) becomes $\delta f_{i,j} = f(x_i, y_j) - f_{i,j}$. There are a number of ways to use the pointwise errors to attain some measure of the "global error" in the whole numerical solution. Some of the most popular and meaningful ways of defining global error are through "energy", "mean-square", and "root-mean-square" (RMS). The energy in the exact solution at the nodes would be defined, for the FD-FD example first considered, as

$$\Omega_f = \sum_{i=2}^{5} \sum_{j=2}^{6} |f(x_i, y_j)|^2 \tag{44}$$

where $|f(x,y)|^2 = f(x,y) \cdot f^*(x,y)$ indicates magnitude squared. Using the vector definition in (9) for the ordered nodal values of f, the energy becomes $\Omega_f = \overline{F} \cdot \overline{F}^*$.

Extending this energy definition to the pointwise error at each node gives

$$\Omega_{\delta f} = \sum_{i=2}^{5} \sum_{j=2}^{6} |\delta f_{i,j}|^2 \tag{45}$$

The *relative* mean-squared error is then defined as the ratio of error energy over solution energy. This leads to the definition for RMS error, which is often expressed as a percentage,

$$\varepsilon_{RMS} = \sqrt{\frac{\Omega_{\delta f}}{\Omega_f}} \times 100\% \tag{46}$$

Errors in the numerical solution result from two sources: discretization and roundoff. The net effect of these error sources depends upon several interrelated factors, including:

(1) Properties of the physical system being modeled,
(2) The basis and weighting functions being used,
(3) The level of segmentation being employed (number and spacing of nodes and/or time-steps) and

(4) The numerical resolution (wordlength) of the computer's numeric data processor and/or co-processor.

Physical system properties affect the *conditioning* (for frequency domain formulations) or the *stability* (for time-domain representations) of the numerical solution. Poorly conditioned or marginally stable physical systems tend to be intolerant of small errors in either the discretized model or the numerical roundoff of the solution process.

For frequency domain problems, this is manifested as error amplification in the linear system solution, as is reflected in the "condition number" of the system matrix [17]. Consider the FD-FD solution for the Helmholtz equation, which resulted in $\overline{\overline{A}} \cdot \overline{F} = \overline{G}$, as presented in (11). Relative errors in the solution for $\overline{F}$ will involve an amplification of the relative errors in computing both $\overline{\overline{A}}$ and $\overline{G}$. This amplification factor is the condition number of the A-matrix.

To be more specific we need to define an appropriate *norm*, denoted by $|| \quad ||$, for the arrays involved. The usual Euclidean vector norm just equals the RMS value of the vector (square-root of the energy). As an example, for the vector $\overline{F}$, as defined by the ordered nodal values in (9), we have $||F|| = \sqrt{\Omega_f}$. The norm of a square matrix, denoted by $||A||$, is generated in terms of the maximum norm of all vectors found from the product $\overline{\overline{A}} \cdot \overline{x}$, where $||x|| = 1$. The condition number of $\overline{\overline{A}}$ is then defined by $C(A) = ||A|| \cdot ||A^{-1}||$. Using this definition for the condition number, it can be shown [18] that the relative error in the solution is bounded by:

$$\frac{||\delta F||}{||F||} \leq \frac{C}{1 - C||\delta A||/||A||} \left[\frac{||\delta A||}{||A||} + \frac{||\delta G||}{||G||} \right] \tag{47}$$

where $\delta\overline{\overline{A}}$ and $\delta\overline{G}$ are the respective arrays formed from the cumulative numerical errors in the evaluation of $\overline{\overline{A}}$ and $\overline{G}$. The condition number is thus seen to amplify the errors in both matrix and driving vector approximations.

As mentioned earlier, the conditioning of a physical system is related to the sensitivity of the solution function to small changes in the input data. A closely related term is "ill-posed", which refers to a mathematical problem whose solution is not unique, at least not from the way it was specified. An example of a poorly conditioned physical problem would be in computing the field strength and modal configuration internal to a low-loss metal cavity with a small excitation port.

As a resonant frequency is approached, large relative changes in the internal field will be produced by small relative changes in the physical system, such as the cavity and excitation port geometry. This is a physical case which results in a poorly conditioned numerical solution, accompanied by a large condition number.

An additional factor which adversely influences the condition number is the rank of the numerical solution matrix. As the mesh density is increased for a fixed physical problem, an increasing matrix size results which is accompanied by a growing condition number. There is a two-fold reason for this. First, the increased number of calculations needed to invert the larger system will tend to enhance computational round-off errors. Secondly, after a certain point a further increase in the number of discrete equations begins to become somewhat redundant. This results in a lower degree of linear independence of the individual equations in the matrix system.

The numerical solution errors induced by the WRM discretizement process can be expressed in terms of an "order" which is inversely related to some power of the number of basis functions, N employed in (23). Assuming that the mesh resolution is enhanced by using more nodes one would expect the error in the numerical solution to decrease, at least to some lower bound. More specifically, consider a second-order PDE system in M-dimensions, such as either the Helmholtz equation or the wave equation in the examples that were considered. Note that coupled first-order state-equation systems (such as Maxwell's curl equations) are usually also second-order decoupled systems. For a second-order system, if p-th order polynomial basis functions are used for $\overline{\overline{U}}_n(\overline{r})$, while q-th order polynomial weighting functions are used for $\overline{\overline{W}}_k(\overline{r})$, then it follows from results derived in [13] that the discretization error is of order:

$$\varepsilon'_{RMS} = O(N^{-\alpha}) \tag{48a}$$

where

$$\alpha = \text{Min}\{M(p+1), M(p+q)\} \tag{48b}$$

An obvious constraint for convergence to occur (namely, $\varepsilon'_{RMS} \to 0$ as $N \to \infty$) is that $\alpha \geq 1$. This requirement is satisfied for each of the three special cases of the WRM that we considered in subsection 1.2d. Recall, for instance, the 2-D example problems that we have previously encountered (with $M=2$). The FEM case used the *Galerkin* method with piecewise linear basis and weighting functions ($p=q=1$). This gives

$$\varepsilon'_{RMS} = O(N^{-4}) \qquad \text{Galerkin FEM Case} \qquad (49)$$

which indicates a strong tendency towards quick convergence, as N is increased. On the other hand, the finite-difference solutions (both time and frequency domain examples) employed *point collocation* using quadratic basis functions ($p=2$) and Dirac weighting functions ($q=-1$), resulting in weaker convergence:

$$\varepsilon'_{RMS} = O(N^{-2}) \qquad \text{Finite Difference Cases} \qquad (50)$$

A similar result to (50) is obtained for *subdomain collocation* using linear basis ($p=1$) and pulse weighting ($q=0$) functions.

It should be emphasized that the error in (48a) is *exclusive of* numeric round-off error and the associated condition number error amplification. This error is thus based on the assumption of an infinite wordlength computer. In reality, as N is increased the condition number also tends to increase, thus offsetting some of the reduction of error found by using more nodes. As N is increased further still, there comes a point where the growing round-off errors will overcome any further gains in accuracy, and the solution error will begin to creep upward with N. This behavior is illustrated in Fig. 10, where the effect of computer wordlength is depicted by different curves. In general, as the numeric wordlength is decreased the point of optimum accuracy occurs at lower N, beyond which the error increases. The effect of ill-conditioning in the physical system being discretized is to raise all of the $\varepsilon_{RMS}(N)$ curves.

In the time-domain case, poor stability of the system translates into more rapid divergence of the transient numerical solution than for a more stable system, all other parameters being equal. For the case of the wave equation, we have seen in subsection 1.2c that the Courant limit on space-time step size provides a well defined condition for stability – one which carries over into the temporal leapfrog solution of Maxwell's equations. There are similar, but not identical, stability conditions for *parabolic* PDE systems such as the diffusion equation. An excellent treatment of stability effects in time-domain integral equation solutions is given in [19] with much of this being valid for finite methods as well.

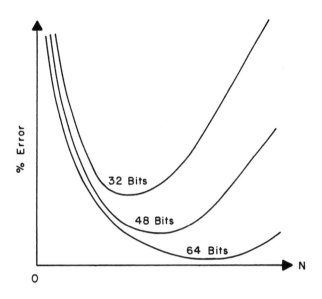

Figure 10 Solution convergence versus wordlength.

1.3   Mesh Termination

Having considered basic concepts related to discretizing frequency-domain (boundary-value) and time-domain (initial-value) electromagnetic problems in closed spatial regions, we will now turn our attention to some techniques for employing finite method solutions to field problems in open, unbounded regions.

a. *Unimoment Method*

The unimoment method, as developed by Mei [20], provides a self-consistent approach to coupling interior and exterior frequency-domain field problems across separable surface interfaces. This method was employed by Chang and Mei [21], Stovall and Mei [22] and Morgan and Mei [16] to open region scattering and antenna problems involving inhomogeneous 2-D and axisymmetric 3-D dielectrics. Further applications of the unimoment method, using finite elements, have been made to problems involving raindrop scattering [23], microwave energy deposition in the human head [24], scattering by multiple bodies [25] and even buried objects [26]. A recent unimoment application, considered by Fleming in Chapter 2 of this book, is scattering from composite axisymmetric objects having both metallic and penetrable parts.

As developed in the unimoment method, the exterior region fields are represented by a functional expansion in one of the separable coordinate systems for the vector Helmholtz equation [14: sect. 5.1]. The spatial interface for coupling the interior numerical solution to the unbounded exterior region is thus a constant coordinate surface of the separable system employed in the outside expansion. Spherical interfaces were utilized in [16] and [22–26] due to the relative ease of generation of exterior region spherical harmonic field expansions.

To understand the conceptual basis of the unimoment method, consider the solution of a scattering problem involving a 2-D cylindrical penetrable object of arbitrary cross section which is, perhaps, inhomogeneous. For either TE or TM (to $\hat{z}$) cases, having respectively $\overline{H} = f\hat{z}$ or $\overline{E} = f\hat{z}$, the undriven scalar Helmholtz equation in (29) is again applicable, but with a variable wavenumber, $\kappa = \sqrt{\epsilon(r,\theta)\mu(r,\theta)}$, within the scattering object

$$\{\nabla^2 + \kappa^2(r,\theta)\}\, f(r,\theta) = 0 \tag{51}$$

where we are using circular coordinates (r,θ).

The unimoment solution proceeds by enclosing the scatterer within a separable mathematical boundary, which we will choose to be circular in the 2-D (r,θ) cross section, as is illustrated in Fig. 11. Notice that there are two concentric circles, of radius r_1 and r_2, both of which enclose the scattering object. With specified Dirichlet BC's on the outer boundary, $f(r_1,\theta) = g(\theta)$, a finite method can be used to solve for nodal values of $f(r,\theta)$ for $r < r_1$. A necessary attribute of the interior mesh construction is that a set of the solution nodes lies on the inner circle, $r = r_2$. An example mesh, using linear triangular elements, is shown in Fig. 12.

Of course, in the scattering problem we do not know the total field, $f_1(\theta)$, on the r_1 boundary. With a knowledge of the incident field, we are to solve for the scattered field. To do this, we will first express the total field in the free space region (with wavenumber k_0) outside of the smallest circle centered at $r = 0$ which encloses the scatterer. The total field equals the sum of the known incident field and a truncated cylindrical harmonic expansion for the unknown scattered field

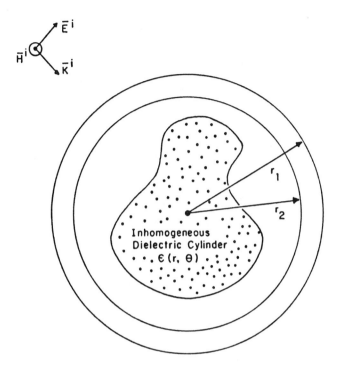

Figure 11 Unimoment matching contours for cylinder scattering problem.

$$f(r,\theta) = f^i(r,\theta) + a_0\, C_0(r) + \sum_{n=1}^{N} a_n\, C_n(r,\theta) + b_n\, S_n(r,\theta) \quad (52a)$$

where the cylindrical harmonics for the scattered field are

$$C_n(r,\theta) = H_n^{(2)}(k_0 r)\,\cos(n\theta) \quad (52b)$$

$$S_n(r,\theta) = H_n^{(2)}(k_0 r)\,\sin(n\theta) \quad (52c)$$

with $H_n^{(2)}$ equal to the Hankel function of the second kind. It is important to note that each cylindrical harmonic term satisfies the 2-D radiation conditions in the far-field of the scatterer, as $r \to \infty$:

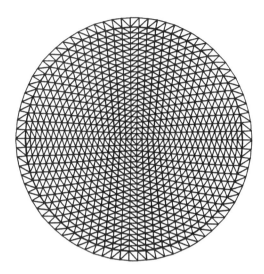

Figure 12   Cylindrical finite element mesh.

$$f(r,\theta) \to \chi(\theta) \frac{e^{-jk_0 r}}{\sqrt{k_0 r}} \tag{53a}$$

$$\frac{E_\theta}{H_z} \to \eta_0 \quad \text{(TE case)} \tag{53b}$$

$$-\frac{E_z}{H_\theta} \to \eta_0 \quad \text{(TM case)} \tag{53c}$$

where $\eta_0 = 120\pi\,\Omega$. Notice that the series representation in (52a) is only an approximation due to the truncation of the series at $N+1$ terms. In practice, this truncated series will converge rapidly to the exact scattered field for increasing N, when $N > k_0 r_2$.

To find the scattered field coefficients, a_n and b_n, we first solve the interior region problem for $2N+2$ separate BC's on $r = r_1$. These BC's are composed of the incident field, $f^i(r_1,\theta)$, and each of the scattered field modes: $C_n(r_1,\theta)$ for $n = 0,1,2,\cdots,N$ and $S_n(r_1,\theta)$ for $n = 1,2,\cdots,N$ (all evaluated on the outer boundary, r_1). The numerical solutions in the interior, $r < r_1$, which correspond to these applied BC's, are indicated by a tilde overbar. For example, the incident field BC, $f^i(r_1,\theta)$, produces an interior solution $\tilde{f}^i(r,\theta)$ for $r < r_1$ while a BC of $S_n(r_1,\theta)$ produces $\tilde{S}_n(r,\theta)$.

Using the principle of superposition, the numerical solution for the total field inside of the outer boundary will be given by

$$\tilde{f}(r,\theta) = \tilde{f}^i(r,\theta) + a_0\,\tilde{C}_0(r) + \sum_{n=1}^{N} a_n\,\tilde{C}_n(r,\theta) + b_n\,\tilde{S}_n(r,\theta) \quad (54)$$

To set up conditions obeyed by the the a_n and b_n coefficients, we simply equate the numerical solution in (54) to the analytical solution in (52) along the circular contour, $r = r_2$, resulting in

$$\sum_{n=1}^{N} a_n\,\{C_n(r_2,\theta) - \tilde{C}_n(r_2,\theta)\} + b_n\,\{S_n(r_2,\theta) - \tilde{S}_n(r_2,\theta)\}$$

$$+ a_0\,C_0(r_2) = \tilde{f}^i(r_2,\theta) - f^i(r_2,\theta) \quad (55)$$

The unknown scattered field coefficients may be approximated by using the weighted residual method (WRM) to generate a system of linear equations. To employ the WRM, we integrate (55) with respect to each of $2N + 1$ linearly independent weighting functions, $W_m(\theta)$ for $m = 0, 1, 2, \cdots, 2N$. In this case our inner product integrations will be defined by

$$\langle W_m(\theta), Z(\theta) \rangle = \int_0^{2\pi} W_m(\theta)\,Z(\theta)\,d\theta \quad (56)$$

Using this definition, and representing the difference terms in (55) by a Δ notation, the WRM equations become

$$\sum_{n=1}^{N} a_n\,\langle W_m(\theta), \Delta C_n(\theta) \rangle + b_n\,\langle W_m(\theta), \Delta S_n(\theta) \rangle$$

$$+ a_0\,\langle W_m(\theta), \Delta C_0(\theta) \rangle = \langle W_m(\theta), \Delta f^i(\theta) \rangle \quad (57)$$

enforced for $m = 0$ to $2N$.

By selecting Dirac function weights, $W_m(\theta) = \delta(\theta - \theta_m)$ with θ_m representing nodes along $r = r_2$, (57) will provide the point-matched form of the solution. A more accurate approach is to enforce (55) in the least-squares sense over the circle, including in-between the nodes. This is done by forming the least squares residual

$$\Omega_{\Delta f} = \int_0^{2\pi} |f(r_2, \theta) - \tilde{f}(r_2, \theta)|^2 \, d\theta \tag{58}$$

Upon substituting (57) and (58) into this equation, a quadratic form in the coefficients will result. The minimization of (58) is found by differentiating with respect to each of the unknown coefficients and nulling the result. In such a case, there results a system of linear equations for the coefficients having the form of (57), but with specified weighting functions which are proportional to the complex conjugates of the Δ-function differences

$$W_m(\theta) = \begin{cases} \Delta C_m^*(\theta) & \text{for } m = 0, 1, 2, \cdots, N \\ \\ \Delta S_m^*(\theta) & \text{for } m = N + 1, \cdots, 2N + 1 \end{cases} \tag{59}$$

The integrations to evaluate the matrix elements in (59) are performed either numerically, or semi-analytically by using the basis function expansions employed in the interior solution to represent both the difference functions and the weighting functions. In either case, the resultant $2N+1$ square matrix can be inverted to obtain the scattered field coefficients. The scattered field at any exterior point may then be obtained from its expansion in (52) and, if desired, the interior field can be found by using the weighted superposition of the stored interior field solutions. For $r \to \infty$, we have the well known asymptotic approximation [2–3]

$$H_n^{(2)}(k_0 r) \to \sqrt{\frac{2j}{\pi k_0 r}} \, j^n \, e^{-jk_0 r} \tag{60}$$

which can be used to obtain far-field expressions for the scattering pattern, as defined in (53a),

$$\chi(\theta) = \sqrt{\frac{2j}{\pi}} \left\{ a_0 + \sum_{n=1}^{N} j^n \left[a_n \cos(n\theta) + b_n \sin(n\theta) \right] \right\} \tag{61}$$

In the original unimoment method [20], the expansion coefficients were found by equating the analytical radial derivative of (52a) at r_2 to

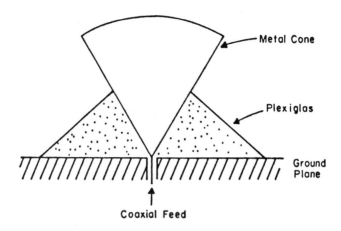

Figure 13   Experimental dielectrically loaded imaged conical antenna.

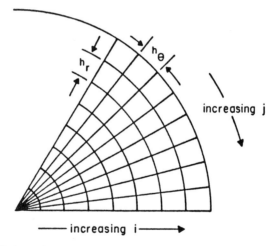

Figure 14   Finite difference mesh for the imaged conical antenna.

the finite difference approximation to the radial derivative found from use of the numerical solution in (54). The above procedure for matching fields, rather than derivatives, was adopted to both simplify the technique and to avoid extra error incurred by use of a finite difference derivative.

As mentioned earlier, the unimoment method has been employed in several computational efforts. One of the earliest of these involved

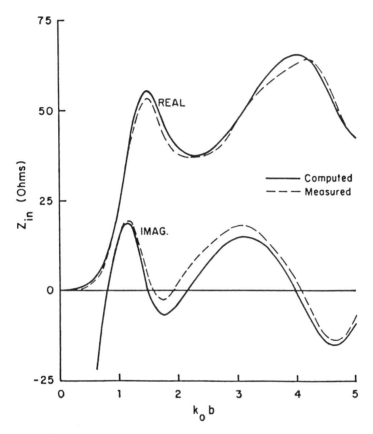

Figure 15 Comparison of measured and computed input impedance for loaded biconical antenna of half-height b.

the finite difference solution for radiation and input impedance of a finite length biconical antenna, loaded by various inhomogeneous dielectric configurations [22]. One such structure is depicted in Fig. 13. Since both the fields and material structure are axisymmetric (invariant to the ϕ-coordinate) the solution domain can be reduced to a single meridian plane, (r, θ) in spherical coordinates. A section of the the finite difference mesh is shown in Fig. 14. The interior region solution for this antenna problem was formulated using a special case of the "coupled azimuthal potential" (CAP) formulation, where the vector $\overline{E}$ and $\overline{H}$ fields are represented using two coupled scalar potential functions which are related to the azimuthal $(\widehat{\phi})$ field components. For the special case of axisymmetric fields in rotationally-symmetric material,

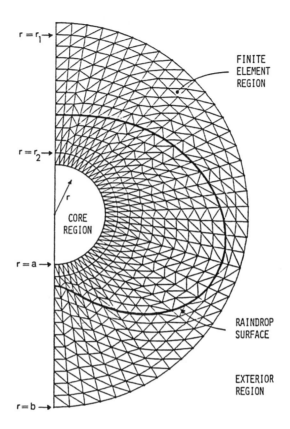

Figure 16 Semi-annular conformal finite element mesh.

as is found for the biconical antenna structure, only one azimuthal potential is needed. A sample result from [22] is shown in Fig. 15, which compares the computed and measured input impedance of a plexiglas loaded biconical antenna. The computation was performed at discrete frequencies over a 10:1 range, wherein the bicone height ranged from .16 λ_0 to 1.6 λ_0.

Details of the original CAP formulation for axisymmetric material are discussed in Chapter 2 of this book, as well as in [27]. A recent extension of the CAP formulation to arbitrary 3-D inhomogeneous isotropic media is the subject of Chapter 6.

A second application of the unimoment method is that of scattering by inhomogeneous bodies of revolution [16]. This effort employed a tri-regional finite element mesh in the (r, θ) meridional plane, as shown

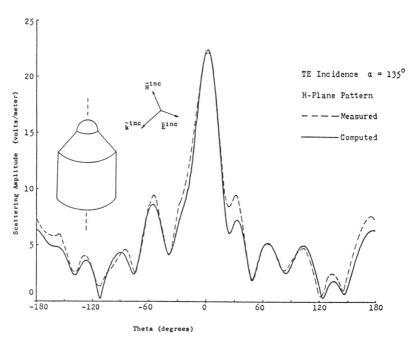

Figure 17 **Comparison of finite element computation for bistatic scattering to experimental results at 9.33 GHz.**

in Fig. 16. The CAP formulation was employed to represent the nonaxisymmetric fields using a Fourier series in the ϕ-coordinate. Spherical harmonic expansions were used to represent the scattered field outside of the mesh and the total fields within the spherical "core" region surrounded by the mesh. The sets of coefficients used in these field expansions were found by applying the various expansion modes for the potentials as BC's along the contours $r = a$ and $r = b$. In addition, the various incident fields being considered were applied along $r = b$. A finite element solution for each applied BC was then evaluated along the inner contours, $r = r_1$ and $r = r_2$. The total fields were assembled from these numerical solutions and equated in the least-squares sense to the original analytical expansions, resulting in a matrix equation for the coefficients. Such a procedure is a direct extension to that employed in our simple unimoment example which resulted in (59). Numerous comparisons to bistatic scattering measurements at 9.33 GHz were made for solid and hollow dielectric bodies of various shapes. A typical result is shown in Fig. 17, where the bistatic scattering is from a plexiglas body having cylindrical, conical and hemispherical portions.

Although the unimoment method offers a straightforward procedure for finite element or finite difference mesh termination in unbounded regions, the numerical solution within a 2-D circular or 3-D spherical interior region becomes inefficient for scatterer or radiator shapes that occupy only a small portion of the enclosed region. Examples of this are highly elongated or flattened structures such as thin cylinders and flat discs. Although it is possible to utilize a separable surface which is not circular or spherical to increase the numerical efficiency of the interior region solution, this will be offset by additional requirements in both generating the special functions that are needed in the exterior expansion and in computing the required moment integrations of these functions over the interface.

b. Boundary Integral Equation

Another approach to mesh termination is to replace the use of an exterior region modal expansion in the unimoment method with a surface integral equation system on the mesh boundary. After all, one purpose of the exterior field expansion was to ensure that the resultant numerical solution satisfied the radiation conditions in the far-field region of the scatterer or antenna. A properly formulated integral equation system will also ensure this, and will do so without any explicit restriction to use of a separable mesh boundary surface. Let us now look at this idea and the results of an early effort [28] in using it for scattering computations from 3-D axisymmetric objects.

A recent application to 2-D scattering by irregularly shaped and inhomogeneous objects is presented in detail in Chapter 3 of this book wherein the term "boundary element method" (BEM) is used. In the context of Chapter 3, BEM refers to the discretization procedure for solving surface (in 3-D) or contour (in 2-D) integral equations. The boundary element terminology is also used in Chapter 7, where it indicates special case finite elements being used at material interfaces to couple otherwise regular spatial finite difference lattices between homogeneous regions.

To consider the use of a boundary integral equation for mesh termination, let us return to our previous unimoment method example. This example considered 2-D scattering by an inhomogeneous dielectric object, as illustrated in Fig. 11. Rather than using a circular outer

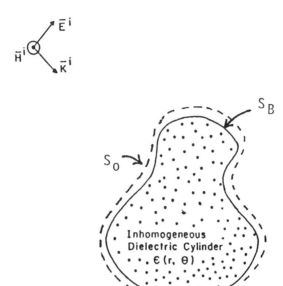

Figure 18 **Boundary integral equation contour enclosing inhomogeneous dielectric cylinder.**

mesh boundary, let us use a conformal boundary, S_0, as per Fig. 18. This boundary must enclose the scatterer and may, in fact, be congruent with the boundary surface of the object, to be denoted as S_B. Within the enclosed region, which contains inhomogeneous $\epsilon(\bar{r})$ and $\mu(\bar{r})$, we can use the finite element method to approximate the solution of the Helmholtz equation in (51) (but using x, y coordinates) for any specified Dirichlet BC on S_0. Let us define this BC using a basis function expansion (with unknown c_k coefficients) to represent the *total* field along the S_0 contour, having position variable s,

$$f(\bar{r})\bigg|_{S_0} = \sum_{k=1}^{N} c_k \, g_k(s) \qquad (62)$$

where g_k are the basis functions. These basis functions may have either full-range support (e.g. Fourier modes) or compact-support such as polynomial pulse functions. For the latter case, it may be expedient to use the unit amplitude finite element basis functions, u_k, associated with the S_0 nodes as the g_k's. With such a choice, the c_k's in (62) become the nodal values of the total field on S_0. The use of the finite element basis functions on the S_0 contour is adopted in Chapter 3. We will follow a more general route here in explaining the concept.

As in the unimoment example, let us use a tilde overbar to denote the finite element numerical solution which results from a given functional BC. For example, a BC of $g_k(s)$ on the boundary S_0 is said to produce a finite element solution within S_0 given by $\tilde{g}_k(\bar{r})$. Explicit enforcement of the radiation conditions in (52) will result by requiring the finite element solution to also satisfy a proper integral equation on the boundary, S_0. Such integral equations are readily found by using a principle-value limiting process, where an exterior field point is brought onto the S_0 surface [29]. For the special case of a smooth surface, one form of the integral equation is

$$\frac{1}{2} f(s) + \int_{S_{PV}} \left[G(s, s') \frac{\partial f(s')}{\partial n'} - f(s') \frac{\partial G(s, s')}{\partial n'} \right] ds' = f^i(s) \quad (63)$$

where s and s' are both points on S_0 and $\hat{n}'$ is the outward unit normal at s'. The free-space Green's function is given by

$$G(s, s') = -\frac{j}{4} H_0^{(2)}(k_0 |\bar{r} - \bar{r}'|) \quad (64)$$

with $|\bar{r} - \bar{r}'|$ equal to the distance between the s and s' contour points. The S_{PV} notation indicates Cauchy principle-value (PV) integration, where the point-wise singularity at $s = s'$ is removed. A similar integral equation is found for the TE case. Additional forms of 2-D integral equations are derived in Chapter 3.

To implement (64), using the BEM, the $\partial f / \partial n'$ integrand term needs to be approximated from the finite element solution. This approximation is obtained through numerically differentiating each $\tilde{g}_k(\bar{r})$ (due to the specified $g_k(s)$ BC). Using superposition, in terms of the still unknown c_k's, the integrand term becomes,

$$\left. \frac{\partial \tilde{f}}{\partial n'} \right|_{\bar{r}' \in S_0} = \sum_{k=1}^{N} c_k \frac{\partial \tilde{g}_k(s')}{\partial n'} \quad (65a)$$

where

$$\frac{\partial \tilde{g}_k(s')}{\partial n'} = \hat{n}' \cdot \nabla \tilde{g}_k(\bar{r}) \bigg|_{S_0} \quad (65b)$$

The BEM discretization is completed by substituting (62) and (65a) into (63), followed by rearrangement of terms to give

$$\sum_{k=1}^{N} c_k I_k(s) = f^i(s) \tag{66}$$

with

$$I_k(s) = \frac{1}{2} \tilde{g}_k(s) + \int_{S_{PV}} \left[G(s,s') \frac{\partial \tilde{g}_k(s')}{\partial n'} - \tilde{g}_k(s') \frac{\partial G(s,s')}{\partial n'} \right] ds' \tag{67}$$

A system of linear equations for the c_k's can be generated by weighted residual enforcement of (67)

$$\sum_{k=1}^{N} c_k \langle W_m(s), I_k(s) \rangle = \langle W_m(s), f^i(s) \rangle \quad \text{for } m = 1, 2, \cdots, N \tag{68}$$

where the weighting functions $W_m(s)$ can correspond, for instance, to any of those discussed in subsection 1.2d. Once the total field solution is found on S_0, the far-zone scattered field can be obtained by using a simplified Green's function integration. This integration formula is developed in the next subsection.

Note that (68) represents a full matrix system. When using the finite element basis functions for the g_k's, the order, N will equal the number of nodes on the S_0 contour. If the material inside of S_0 had been *homogeneous*, we could have formulated the problem using just an integral equation on S_0; there would have been no need to take on the extra effort required for the finite element solution. On the other hand, for the case of a general inhomogeneous material inside of S_0, an integral equation approach would incorporate all unknowns spanning the internal region. A *very large* full matrix could result. The hybrid approach just considered incorporates a sparse matrix solution for the interior region while needing a full matrix only on the enclosing boundary. For problems involving multi-wavelength sized inhomogeneous scatterers, the computational savings incurred can be very significant.

     An application of the boundary integral technique to scattering by axisymmetric 3-D objects was developed by Morgan, Chen, Hill and

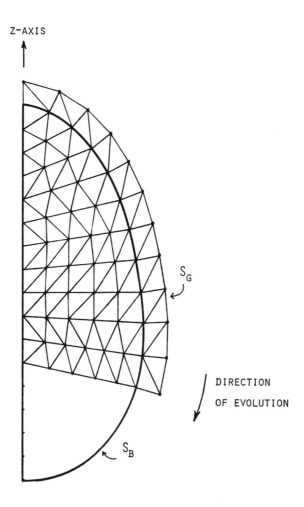

Figure 19 Surface conforming finite element mesh.

Barber [28]. This hybrid approach, named the "finite element boundary integral" (FEBI) method combines a finite element solution of the
interior region with the surface integral equations found in Waterman's
"extended boundary condition method" (EBCM) [30].

The FEBI procedure allows the use of a surface interface that
conforms to the outer boundary of the scattering object, as is shown
for the finite element mesh in Fig. 19. The finite element solution
proceeds in a similar manner to that of the unimoment method, with

incident field and scattered field spherical harmonic expansion modes being applied as BC's at the outer boundary, S_G. Numerical solutions are then found at the surface of the scattering body, S_B, for each of these applied BC's.

It should be noted, that for a specified origin, a truncated spherical harmonic scattered field expansion is uniformly convergent (with increasing truncation index) *outside* of the smallest geometrical sphere, centered about the origin, which encloses the scatterer. Since the boundaries at S_G and S_B do not usually conform to a spherical surface, the truncated spherical harmonic expansion for the scattered fields, as applied on S_B, may not be *complete* at all points on that surface. Such a phenomenon is related to the classical "Rayleigh hypothesis" [31]. As a result, we may not be able to obtain as a good match between the numerical solution at S_B and the original truncated analytical expansion, as we were able to do on the spherical surface for the unimoment method.

To evaluate the expansion coefficients for the boundary field in the FEBI, we can use a system of two combined field integral equations, as employed in the EBCM [30]. These integral equations are vector field 3-D versions of that in (63); they relate the tangential fields just inside of the boundary S_B to that just outside, without making use of a knowledge of the material structure inside of S_B.

The FEBI method has been shown to work well for scattering calculations involving moderately elongated lossy dielectric objects. An example computation, with comparison to that performed using the EBCM, is illustrated in Fig. 20. This approach tends to have convergence difficulties if the surface interface becomes extremely elongated or flattened (e.g. length to diameter ratios exceeding about 10). As just discussed, the culprit in this failure is the poorly convergent exterior region spherical harmonic expansion when used to represent the field over the surface of the scattering body.

The use of poorly convergent spherical harmonics as basis functions on radically non-spherical surfaces in the FEBI technique was a result of the attempt to combine the usual EBCM concept with finite elements. A better approach would be to have used the innate basis functions of the FEM on the surface. This has been done for 2-D cylinder scattering, as it appears in Chapter 3 and in a recent paper by Peterson [32].

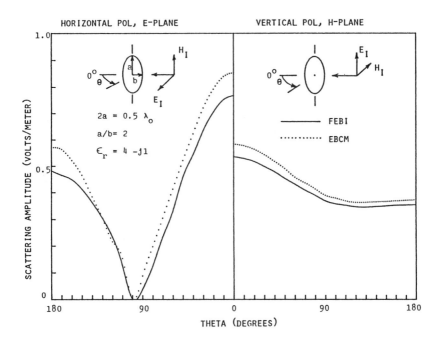

Figure 20 Scattering amplitude comparison for FEBI computation.

c. Field Feedback Formulation

The field feedback formulation (F^3) combines features from the unimoment method and the boundary integral equation technique to allow increased flexibility in coupling interior and exterior region time-harmonic field solutions [33]. As with these other two approaches, the interior boundary-value problem is initially decoupled from the outside region. The interior problem may then be formulated and computed using the most expedient approach that can accurately accommodate the level of material complexity that is present. Instead of using scattered field harmonic expansions (e.g. cylindrical in 2-D and spherical in 3-D), the exterior region scattered field is represented in terms of modes generated from Green's function surface integrations of equivalent currents which are obtained from the interior region solution. These modal scattered fields innately satisfy the radiation conditions but do not rely upon the use of separable coordinate surfaces for their completeness. A major advantage of the F^3 is its *modular* solution topology, where forward and feedback transfer matrices can be independently computed. These modules are connected for the complete scattering problem as a simple closed loop feedback network. This arrangement provides for either closed-form or iterative approaches as natural options in attaining the final scattering solution.

To explain the details of the F^3 approach via example, refer back to the problem of scattering by a dielectric cylinder, as depicted in Fig. 18. As shown there, the surface boundary contour of the object, S_B, is enclosed within a geometrical surface, S_0. Unlike the boundary integral equation method, where S_0 could have been equal to S_B, these two surfaces must now be distinct, with S_0 enclosing S_B. As before, the scattering problem is approached by first solving the Helmholtz equation inside of S_0 subject to the correct *total* field being applied as the boundary condition, as per (62). The $g_k(s)$ will now be denoted as $g_k(s_o)$ to emphasize that they are surface basis functions on S_0 and c_k are still to be determined.

Let us again assume that the finite element method is applied to the problem and that each of the $g_k(s_o)$ BC's on S_0 generates a numerical solution denoted by $\tilde{g}_k(\bar{r})$. We will further assume, although it is not necessary, that the g_k's are the unit-amplitude finite element basis functions evaluated on S_0, so that the c_k's become the corresponding nodal values of the total field on this surface. Next, we represent the numerical solution and its normal derivative ($D_n = \partial/\partial n$), evaluated on the object's surface S_B, as

$$\tilde{g}_k(s_b) = \sum_{m=1}^{M} a_{m,k}\, h_m(s_b) \tag{69a}$$

$$D_n\, \tilde{g}_k(s_b) = \sum_{m=1}^{M} a_{m,k}\, D_n\, h_m(s_b) \tag{69b}$$

where $h_m(s_b)$ is the m-th indexed unit-amplitude finite element basis function for nodes on S_B. The need for the normal derivative will be justified shortly. As an aside, the reader should note that we are assuming that there are N nodes on S_0 and M nodes on S_B.

Proceeding, we note that due to linearity a given c_k in (62) will produce a finite element solution and normal derivative along S_B given by $c_k\, \tilde{g}_k(s_b)$ and $c_k\, D_n\, \tilde{g}(s_b)$. Expanding on this idea, we can see that the total field on S_B is given in terms of its nodal values, d_m, as

$$\tilde{f}(s_b) = \sum_{m=1}^{M} d_m \, h_m(s_b) \tag{70a}$$

$$D_n \, \tilde{f}(s_b) = \sum_{m=1}^{M} d_m \, D_n \, h_m(s_b) \tag{70b}$$

with

$$d_m = \sum_{k=1}^{N} a_{m,k} \, c_k \tag{71}$$

As is apparent from (71), the finite element solution nodal values on S_B are given in terms of the nodal values of the BC on S_0 through the $M \times N$ array $\overline{\overline{A}}$, whose components are $a_{k,m}$. We will term this array as the "forward operator". By defining vectors of nodal values for the total fields on S_0 and S_B as

$$\overline{F}_0^{t} = [c_1, c_2, \cdots, c_N]^T \tag{72a}$$

$$\overline{F}_b^{t} = [d_1, d_2, \cdots, d_M]^T \tag{72b}$$

there results,

$$\overline{F}_b^{t} = \overline{\overline{A}} \cdot \overline{F}_0^{t} \tag{73}$$

Note that the c_k's in (72a) are the same total field coefficients as were defined in the basis function expansions of (62) and (65).

Our original assumption was that we had the total field available as a BC on S_0, via (62). Since only the incident field is known *a priori*, there remains the need to find the scattered field on S_0. On the other hand, if we know the total field and its normal derivative on S_B, we can evaluate the *scattered* field anywhere outside of S_B through a free-space Green's function convolution type integration, [14]. Applying this to find the scattered field on S_0 gives

$$f^s(s_o) = \int_{S_B} \left[G(s_o, s_b) \frac{\partial f(s_b)}{\partial n} - f(s_b) \frac{\partial G(s_o, s_b)}{\partial n} \right] ds_b \tag{74}$$

where $\hat{n}$ is the outward unit normal at s_b. The free-space Green's function is given by (64), with $\bar{r}$ positioned on S_0 and $\bar{r}'$ on S_B. It should be noted that by using the convolution operation in (74) we are implicitly enforcing the radiation conditions in (53) on the scattered field solution. This follows because the point source Green's function being used obeys these conditions. It was this property that guaranteed the proper far-field behavior of the scattered field produced by a surface integral equation solution.

As an aside, the total field and normal derivative within the Green's function integral in (74) can be replaced by the corresponding scattered field quantities on S_B. This is a well known result which follows from the equivalence theorem [2]. In essence, the Green's function integration of the incident field on S_B is zero for evaluation points outside of this contour, (e.g. the points s_o). Likewise, if s_o in (74) is changed to a point inside of S_B the result will be equal to the negative incident field, where the contribution of the scattered field component on S_B is zero.

Let us now return to the near field evaluation for points on S_0. Consider the scattered field on S_0 due to a single basis function, $h_m(s_b)$, existing on S_B,

$$\tilde{f}_m^s(s_o) = \sum_{k=1}^{N} b_{k,m}\, g_k(s_o) \tag{75}$$

$$= \int_{S_B} \left[G(s_o, s_b)\, D_n\, h_m(s_b) - h_m(s_b) \frac{\partial G(s_o, s_b)}{\partial n} \right] ds_b$$

Assuming for the moment that we have available the numerical solution on S_B, as indicated by (70), we can use superposition, along with (75), to obtain the corresponding scattered field on S_0,

$$\tilde{f}^s(s_o) = \sum_{k=1}^{N} e_k\, g_k(s_o) = \sum_{m=1}^{M} d_m\, f_m^s(s_o) \tag{76}$$

where the nodal values of the scattered field are given by

$$e_k = \sum_{m=1}^{M} b_{k,m}\, d_m \tag{77}$$

The role of the $N \times M$ array, $\overline{\overline{B}}$, whose elements are $b_{k,m}$, is to generate the *scattered* field on S_0 due to a specified *total* field on S_B. This array is termed the "feedback operator". Denoting the nodal total field vector on S_B using (72b) and the nodal scattered field vector on S_0 by

$$\overline{F}_0^s = [e_1, e_2, \cdots, e_N]^T \tag{78}$$

we obtain

$$\overline{F}_0^s = \overline{\overline{B}} \cdot \overline{F}_b^t \tag{79}$$

It may now be apparent what is going to happen next: we are going to "bootstrap" the solution by combining the scattered field in (76) with the known incident field, thus obtaining the total field on S_0. This, in turn, will allow us to find the total field on S_B, using (70), so we can then find the needed scattered field on S_0. Such a scheme describes a basic feedback system, as is illustrated in Fig. 21, where the *forward* and *feedback* operators represent the respective finite element solution and near-field Green's function integration. The $\overline{F}$-arrays represent the nodal values of the fields on the S_0 and S_B contours. On the outer geometric contour, S_0, the total field is the sum of the incident plus the scattered field: $\overline{F}_0^t = \overline{F}_0^i + \overline{F}_0^s$. Each of these nodal value arrays has N components. On the body contour, S_B, the total field nodal values are embodied in the M-element array, $\overline{F}_b^t$.

With the above ideas in mind, the matrix relationships in (73) and (79) provide the following geometric series representation for the total field on S_0

$$\overline{F}_0^t = [\overline{\overline{I}} + \overline{\overline{Q}} + \overline{\overline{Q}} \cdot \overline{\overline{Q}} + \overline{\overline{Q}} \cdot \overline{\overline{Q}} \cdot \overline{\overline{Q}} + \cdots] \cdot \overline{F}_0^i = \overline{\overline{T}} \cdot \overline{F}_0^i \tag{80}$$

where

$$\overline{\overline{Q}} = \overline{\overline{B}} \cdot \overline{\overline{A}} \tag{81}$$

is the "closed-loop gain" operator of the F^3 system.

In looking at Fig. 21, it should be apparent to the reader that the stability of the closed-loop system is an important issue. In particular, if the closed-loop gain operator has an array norm, $\|Q\| \geq 1$, then the series in (80) will not converge, indicating an unstable system. For a

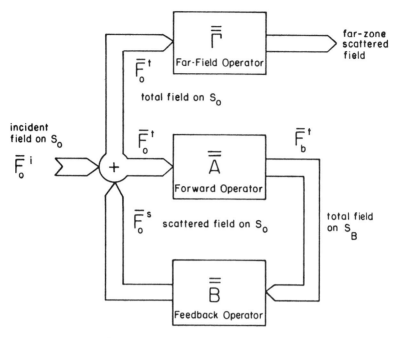

Figure 21 Field feedback system.

passive physical system, exhibiting either radiation damping and/or resistive dissipation, it can be argued that $||Q|| < 1$. On the other hand, real scattering structures exist, such as reentrant cavities, where, at selected resonant frequencies, large amounts of energy may be stored while relatively little power loss occurs due to radiation or dissipation per oscillation cycle. Such scatterers are said to be "high-Q" (borrowing the term *quality* factor from circuit theory). If the F^3 method is applied near the resonant frequencies of very high-Q structures, where $||Q|| \to 1$, then convergence of the iteration in (80) will be difficult to achieve numerically. This is not only a case of prohibitive computer time required to continue the iteration to large order in n; the major concern becomes the accumulation of roundoff error as this process proceeds. The difficulty in attaining accurate scattering solutions for ultra high-Q structures is not confined to the F^3 approach, but spans the whole gamut of numerical methods. An advantage of the F^3 is that the stability issue is obvious and well-defined.

Assuming that $||Q|| < 1$, where the concept of an *array norm* was defined in subsection 1.2f, the series in (80) can be summed to give the feedback system transfer matrix

$$\overline{\overline{T}} = [\overline{\overline{I}} - \overline{\overline{Q}}]^{-1} \tag{82}$$

This, of course, is analogous to the usual scalar transfer function formula for the total input to a feedback system. It may appear that we have overcome our convergence problem, due to roundoff, of numerically summing a truncated version of the series in (80). This is not the case; a marginally stable system having $\|Q\| \to 1$ will produce a poorly conditioned matrix, $\overline{\overline{I}} - \overline{\overline{Q}}$, which needs to be inverted in (82). Referring back to the discussion of matrix conditioning which resulted in (47), we can use the same approach as employed in [18] to show that the condition number is bounded by

$$C(I - A) \le \frac{1 + \|Q\|}{1 - \|Q\|} \tag{83}$$

It thus becomes obvious that as system stability is reduced, so is the conditioning of the direct matrix inversion in (82). It should be emphasized that in a recent study [34] no severe stability-conditioning problems were uncovered in computing the closed-loop gain, $\|Q\|$, for simple metallic and penetrable scatterers, including thin-wire structures. In the case of the highest Q scatterers, such as lossless cavities with small excitation ports at resonance, stability-conditioning problems should be expected in using the F^3, just as they should with other numerical methods.

An example 2-D finite element mesh for a semicircular dielectric cylindrical shell was shown in Fig. 12. Nodes are arranged to lie on both the body surface and the enclosing geometrical surface, as will usually be the case in implementing the F^3. Also, in this case, a single layer of triangular elements separates S_B from S_0 and $N = M$. The mesh could have been constructed with additional layers of elements between the two contours. The cost would have been additional unknowns to solve for in the finite element solution. If the extra element layer(s) had provided additional spatial separation between S_B and S_0 then the payoff would have been a less demanding accuracy in performing the near-field Green's function integration in (74) and (75).

After solving for $\overline{F}_0^t$ using either iteration, via (80), or closed form matrix inversion using (82), we may obtain the far-zone scattered fields by performing a simplified Green's function integration over S_0. Points on S_0 will be denoted by the vector $\overline{s}_o$. Starting with the integral form in (74), as applied to the S_0 contour rather than S_B, let us consider the case of the field point receding radially to infinity. We can then employ the asymptotic form for the Hankel function, as given in (60), to obtain a simplified integration for evaluating the complex scattering pattern, $\chi(\theta)$, using the definition in (53a). This results in

$$\chi(\theta) = \sqrt{\frac{\jmath}{8\pi}} \int_{S_0} \left\{ \jmath D_n f^t(s_o) + k_0(\hat{n} \cdot \hat{r}) f^t(s_o) \right\} e^{\jmath k_0 \bar{s}_o \cdot \hat{r}} \, ds_o \qquad (84)$$

Using the basis function expansions for the total field in (62) and (65), we can evaluate the scattering pattern as

$$\chi(\theta) = \sqrt{\frac{\jmath}{8\pi}} \sum_{k=1}^{N} c_k \int_{S_0} \left\{ \jmath D_n g_k(s_o) + k_0(\hat{n} \cdot \hat{r}) g_k(s_o) \right\} e^{\jmath k_0 \bar{s}_o \cdot \hat{r}} \, ds_o$$

$$= \sum_{k=1}^{N} c_k \, \gamma_k(\theta) = \overline{\Gamma}(\theta) \cdot \overline{F}_0^t \qquad (85)$$

where

$$\overline{\Gamma}(\theta) = [\gamma_1(\theta), \gamma_2(\theta), \cdots, \gamma_N(\theta)] \qquad (86)$$

with

$$\gamma(\theta) = \sqrt{\frac{\jmath}{8\pi}} \int_{S_0} \left\{ \jmath D_n g_k(s_o) + k_0(\hat{n} \cdot \hat{r}) g_k(s_o) \right\} e^{\jmath k_0 \bar{s}_o \cdot \hat{r}} \, ds_o \qquad (87)$$

The far-field Γ-operator is shown in Fig. 21 as a matrix. The j-th row of this matrix is formed from the elements of $\overline{\Gamma}(\theta_j)$, where the set of θ_j is the discrete scattering angles desired for evaluating the pattern in (85).

The bistatic radar cross section (RCS) can be easily obtained from a knowledge of the scattering pattern. Assuming a unit magnitude incident field, $|f^i(\bar{r})| = 1$, the result is

$$\sigma(\theta) = \lim_{r \to \infty} \frac{2\pi r \, |f^s(r, \theta)|^2}{|f^i|^2}$$

$$= \lambda_0 \, |\chi(\theta)|^2 \qquad (88)$$

For the case of 2-D scattering, this RCS represents the effective cross sectional *width*. If the incident field power density is multiplied by $\sigma(\theta_0)$ the resultant power is equal to that which would be radiated by an isotropic scattering pattern, $\chi_0 = \chi(\theta_0)$, which is constant in θ.

Let's pause now to summarize the steps in the F^3 solution for scattering. These steps are:

(1) Enclose the object within a geometrical boundary, S_0,

(2) Formulate the numerical solution of the interior problem using an appropriate finite method,

(3) Find the interior solution for each of the applied basis functions on S_0, saving the nodal values of the function and its normal derivative on the boundary of the object, S_B (these solutions form the columns of the forward operator, A-matrix),

(4) Perform near-field Green's function integrations on S_B to find the nodal fields on S_0 due to each basis function on S_B (these integrations form the columns of the feedback operator, B-matrix),

(5) Form the closed-loop operator, $\overline{\overline{Q}} = \overline{\overline{B}} \cdot \overline{\overline{A}}$, and evaluate the T-matrix, which relates the total field on S_0 to the known incident field, using either the closed form matrix inversion approach of (82) or the series iteration of (80),

(6) Finally, perform far-zone integrations over S_0, per (84), thus computing the radiation field and the RCS in (88), if desired.

The initial demonstration of the F^3 was for scattering by a finite-length metallic thin-wire, with associated finite element mesh shown in Fig. 22. This is obviously a case where the unimoment method would be quite inefficient, requiring a meridian spherical mesh to enclose the wire unless a spheroidal mesh was adopted, with the associated difficulties of generating the spheroidal harmonic functions. Using the F^3, the mesh has only a single column of triangular elements, which produces an interior solution matrix (whose inverse is $\overline{\overline{A}}$) having a nonzero bandwidth of only 3 matrix elements in this case. The Riccati transform allows ultra-fast inversion of this matrix. Comparisons of the magnitude and phase of current on an $L = 1\lambda_0$ thin-wire, as computed from the F^3 and Hallen's integral equation, is shown in Fig. 23. One source of error in the F^3 computation was the use of linear basis functions in the finite element calculation. These were used to represent the ϕ-component of the magnetic field. In the immediate vicinity of the thin-wire, H_ϕ is characterized by a rapidly decaying

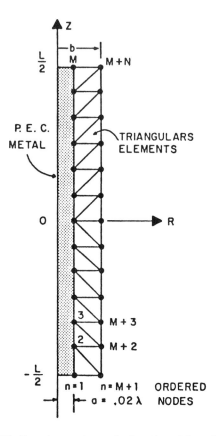

Figure 22 Finite element mesh for the thin-wire scatterer.

evanescence which is difficult to accurately interpolate using simple linear basis functions. More specialized basis functions would allow faster convergence of the solution for the thin-wire case. Much more rapid convergence was observed for thick cylinders.

A recent application of the F^3 has been made to scattering by 2-D dielectric cylinders, [35]. Uniformly excellent results in all validations were observed. An example is scattering by a dielectric semicircular shell of outer radius $0.3\lambda_0$, as originally computed by Richmond, using an E-field integral equation for the TM-case [36] while employing a cylindrical harmonic expansion approach for the TE-case [37]. The finite element mesh for the semicircular cylindrical shell is shown in Fig. 24, where the average element size is about $\lambda/20$ within the $\epsilon_r = 4$ dielectric material. A comparison of the computed normalized

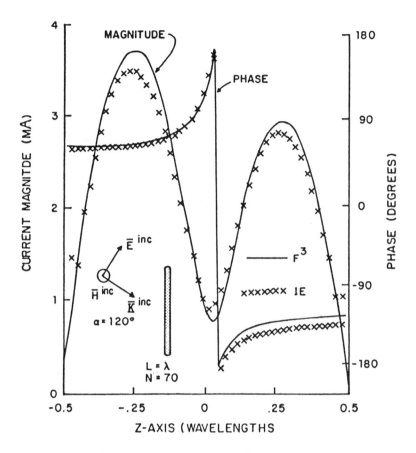

Figure 23 Comparisons of computed magnitudes and phases of complex current on a thin-wire scatterer.

bistatic RCS using the F^3 and Richmond's E-field integral equation is displayed for the TM-case in Fig. 25.

Efforts are underway to apply the F^3 to scattering by 3-D objects of general shape and composition using the generalized CAP formulation, as presented in Chapter 6, for computation of the forward A-operator. A major hurdle to overcome in applying the F^3 to scattering by *large* 3-D objects, having multiwavelength dimensions, is the tremendous CPU resources required to compute the near-field surface integrations in the feedback B-operator. The exact field at a point outside of the surface, S_B, depends upon the field (and normal derivative) over the entire S_B, as evidenced by the Green's function integral for-

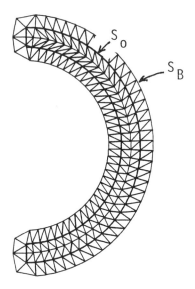

Figure 24 Conformal finite element mesh for a semicircular dielectric cylindrical shell.

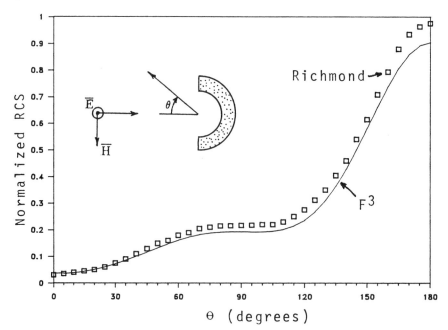

Figure 25 Comparisons of normalized RCS for a semicircular dielectric shell having $\epsilon_r=4$, inner radius=$0.25\lambda_0$ and outer radius=$0.30\lambda_0$.

mula in (74). In this integration, the effect on the field at $\bar{s}_o$ due to the
S_B field at $\bar{s}_o$ dies away with increasing distance when $|\bar{s}_o - \bar{s}_b| > \lambda_0$.
In 3-D, this decrease is even more rapid than in 2-D.

One approach to reducing the integration demands for large 3-D
problems is to adaptively neglect the integration contributions outside
of a local neighborhood of the field point. The cutoff would be dependent upon relative convergence of the integration. Along these same
lines is the idea of local radiation boundary conditions for terminating
the finite method mesh. Let us now briefly look at some of the basic
concepts behind this topic. Our elementary level considerations will
pave the way for the more advanced applications to be discussed in
Chapters 4, 5, 7 and 8.

d. Radiation Boundary Conditions

Additional methods exist for employing finite method solutions in
open region problems. One approach imposes a homogeneous Dirichlet
BC on the tangential field components at a sufficiently large distance
from the antenna or scatterer, [38]. For such an artificial assumption
to result in any degree of accuracy, the mesh termination boundary
must be far removed from the scatterer or antenna. This means that a
large finite method mesh is needed, with an accompanying large matrix
size in the frequency domain case. For time-domain calculations, the
null BC condition also results in an extended mesh, requiring much
computational effort in the causal updates of the many included nodes.

Another method employs "infinite elements", where unbounded
angular sections are used to surround the scatterer [5]. Within these
infinite elements, special basis functions are used which correspond to
assumed far-zone behavior of the scattered field. This requires that
the interface between the main mesh and the infinite elements lie in
the *quasi* far-field region of the scatterer. The result is again a large
mesh region, although not as big as that resulting from the zero BC
assumption.

We have seen one form of the far-zone conditions in (53), as applied
to 2-D scattering. For the 3-D case, the far-field behavior is embodied
in the Sommerfeld radiation condition [39]. For a scalar scattered
field, f^s, which satisfies the source-free Helmholtz equation in spherical
coordinates, (r, θ, ϕ), this far-field condition becomes

$$\lim_{r \to \infty} r \, \mathcal{L}(r) \, f^s(r, \theta, \phi) = 0 \qquad (89a)$$

where

$$\mathcal{L}(r) = \left[\frac{\partial}{\partial r} + jk_0 \right] \tag{89b}$$

By applying (89) to the $\hat{\theta}$ and $\hat{\phi}$ vector components of $\overline{E}^s$ and $\overline{H}^s$, followed by a substitution from Maxwell's curl equations, we will obtain the vector field form of Sommerfeld's conditions

$$\lim_{r \to \infty} r \left[\eta_0 \hat{r} \times \overline{H}^s + \overline{E}^s \right] = 0 \tag{90a}$$

$$\lim_{r \to \infty} r \left[\hat{r} \times \overline{E}^s - \eta_0 \overline{H}^s \right] = 0 \tag{90b}$$

Several efforts have used the Sommerfeld radiation condition, with applications in both the frequency and time-domains, as exemplified by [40–41].

To allow reduced mesh sizes, while retaining adequate accuracy of the enforced conditions on the outer mesh boundary, improved approaches have been developed in recent years involving radiation boundary operators. These operators come in two "flavors": extended annihilation [42–43], and one-way wave equations [44], both of which we will look at briefly. The equations that result from applying these operators at the mesh boundary are termed radiation boundary conditions (RBC's). A related RBC idea, as applied to time-harmonic surface integral equations, is the on-surface radiation condition (OSRC) [45]. The effect of the OSRC is to reduce the integral equation to either an ordinary differential equation on the surface, or a simple integration of *known* functions.

The annihilation operator approach can be considered as an extension to the far-field boundary conditions of Sommerfeld. As shown by Wilcox [46], outbound radiating fields which satisfy the Sommerfeld radiation condition in (89) can be represented by an inverse power series of the form

$$f^s(r, \theta, \phi) = e^{-jk_0 r} \sum_{n=1}^{\infty} \frac{\chi_n(\theta, \phi)}{r^n} \tag{91}$$

As r becomes larger, the series can be truncated at a decreasing index for a fixed level of accuracy. Ultimately, as $r \to \infty$, only the $n=1$ term is needed, producing a far-field condition which is the 3-D version of the 2-D result in (53). The $\mathcal{L}(r)$ operator in (89), when applied to (91), is seen to reduce the leading order term from r^{-1} to r^{-2}. Thus, for increasing r, $\mathcal{L} \cdot f^s$ decays to zero much faster than does f^s.

To extend this idea, consider the possibility of discovering enhanced annihilation operators, $\mathcal{B}_m$, which can cancel the first m terms of the series in (91) at *finite* values of r. The approximate boundary conditions, $\mathcal{B}_m f^s \approx 0$, for increasing m, should then be applicable to surfaces of decreasing distance from the scattering object. The construction of such operators was the approach taken by Bayliss and Turkel in [42]. As an example, consider

$$B_1(r) = \mathcal{L}(r) + \frac{1}{r} \tag{92}$$

which will annihilate the $n=1$ term in (91), while

$$B_2(r) = \left\{ \mathcal{L}(r) + \frac{3}{r} \right\} B_1(r) \tag{93}$$

cancels both the $n=1$ and $n=2$ terms. This procedure can be continued through the recurrence formula

$$B_{m+1}(r) = \left\{ \mathcal{L}(r) + \frac{2m+1}{r} \right\} B_m(r) \tag{94}$$

Since the RBC using (94) will have to be enforced using numerical differentiation in r, it becomes impractical to use large ordered $\mathcal{B}_m$'s; the m-th order operator contains $\partial/\partial r^m$ along with all lesser ordered derivatives. As it turns out, lower orders (e.g. $m=2$) are often sufficient to allow termination of the mesh close to the object's surface, at least for the class of 2-D convex homogeneous scatterers, as evidenced by results in Chapters 4, 5 and 8. For the 2-D case, slightly modified formulas are found for the $\mathcal{B}_m$'s since the Wilcox expansion in (91) must be changed to have the r^n term in the denominator replaced by $r^{n-1/2}$. Also, for the 2-D case, the 2nd-order radial derivatives in $\mathcal{B}_2$ can be replaced using a combination of a 2nd-order θ derivative with 1st-order radial derivative, using the Helmholtz equation. The annihilation operator RBC approach can be extended to the time-domain, as shown in [47] and Chapters 7 and 8.

Let us now investigate another method for generating the RBC. This is based upon the idea of a one-way wave equation, as developed by Engquist and Majda, [44]. As an example, let us reconsider the simple 2-D space-time wave equation that was covered in subsection 1.2c. In particular, assume we want to solve for the scattering due to an incident $+x$ directed pulse which impinges upon the Dirichlet BC, $u(a,t) = 0$, as illustrated in Fig. 26. A finite difference mesh as in Fig. 4 (or Fig. 5 for the leap-frog method) is overlaid on the *truncated* problem domain: $0 \leq x \leq a$ and $t \geq 0$. Since this is a scattering problem the actual spatial domain is unbounded, $-\infty < x \leq a$. The purpose of the RBC is to properly terminate the mesh at $x = 0$ so that the scattered wave is *absorbed* without reflection; hence, the term "absorbing boundary condition" is often used. Of course, this same terminology is equally applicable to the annihilation operator approach.

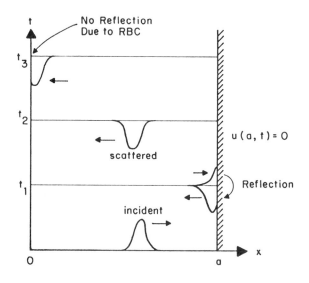

Figure 26 **RBC applied to simple space-time scattering problem.**

"Factoring" of the wave equation is a common technique for attaining one-way operators. Factoring of the (x,t) wave equation in (13) is particularly simple, resulting in the decomposition

$$\frac{\partial^2 u}{\partial x^2} - \frac{1}{c^2}\frac{\partial^2 u}{\partial t^2} = \left[\frac{\partial}{\partial x} - \frac{1}{c}\frac{\partial}{\partial t}\right]\left[\frac{\partial}{\partial x} + \frac{1}{c}\frac{\partial}{\partial t}\right] u(x,t)$$

$$= L^+(x,t)\,L^-(x,t)\,u(x,t) = 0 \qquad (95)$$

The L^+ operator cancels waves propagating in the $+x$ direction, such as the incident field in Fig. 26, while L^- cancels $-x$ traveling waves. Analytically applying L^- to the mesh termination boundary, at $x=0$, will provide an RBC to absorb the scattered wave without reflection

$$L^-(x,t)\,u(x,t)\bigg|_{x=0} = 0 \qquad (96)$$

For the grid in Fig. 4, with $u_{i,j} = u(x_i, t_j)$, the following finite difference approximation results by enforcing the RBC at $x = \Delta x/2$

$$u_{0,j+1} = u_{0,j-1} + 2\,\gamma\,(u_{1,j} - u_{0,j}) \qquad (97)$$

where γ is given in (16). This relationship would be used in lieu of that in (15) for the $i=0$ boundary nodes.

Formulation of one-way space-time operators for the cases of two and three spatial dimensions follows from the factoring concept in (95), but with some additional approximations required. For example, in (x, y, t) coordinates, the one-way operators can be written as

$$L^\pm(x, y, t) = \frac{\partial}{\partial x} \pm \mathcal{R} \qquad (98)$$

where $\mathcal{R}$ is a "pseudo-differential" operator which may be defined as

$$\mathcal{R} = \sqrt{\frac{1}{c^2}\frac{\partial^2}{\partial t^2} - \frac{\partial^2}{\partial y^2}} \qquad (99)$$

The implication of this symbolism is that a double application, $\mathcal{R} \cdot \mathcal{R}$, results in the operator within the radical in (99).

To be numerically usable, the radical in (99) may be interpreted as a convergent expansion of the derivatives contained within. An approximate RBC can then be generated by properly truncating the expansion and applying the resultant operator at the enclosing boundary. Such an approach was developed by Mur [48], who employed

a two-term Taylor series. Accuracy of the resultant RBC becomes
sensitive to the arrival angle of the scattered wave on the local boundary. Optimizations are possible using rational polynomial interpolates
(Padé, Chebyshev, etc.) for the one-way operator. The objective is to
improve the approximation of the operator and reduce the sensitivity
to arrival angle. Further details on the development and application
of one-way operators are given in Chapter 8. In addition, an excellent
review article on RBC's is also available [49].

1.4   Conclusion

The objective in this chapter has been twofold: (1) to provide a
tutorial overview of the concepts and terminology that are employed at
more advanced levels in later chapters; and (2) to consider some scattering applications which are not subsequently covered in this book,
such as those of the field feedback formulation (F^3). Our itinerary
in developing the principles was to first consider finite difference and
finite element methods (denoted as finite methods), as solved within
enclosed spatial regions. In the second part of the chapter we turned
our attention to various approaches for properly coupling closed region finite method solutions to the unbounded exterior domain of the
scattering problem.

Having a confining boundary is, in fact, the natural setting for
time-harmonic and time-domain PDE's, which form the basis for the
finite methods. Examples were developed in the first half of this chapter for discretizing differential equation formulated problems within
closed spatial regions. Finite difference grids were employed in the frequency and time-domains, and a basic finite element mesh was used
for a time-harmonic example. Pertinent equations were deduced for
solving each of the example problems and some specialized numerical
procedures were introduced for effecting these solutions.

Along the way, an attempt was made to unify the finite method
numerical procedures through introduction of the weighted residual
method (also known as the moment method in the realm of integral
operator equations). Within such a context, the finite difference technique can be seen as a special case of the finite element method –
one which employs Dirac weighting functions. It was demonstrated
that, when used with compact-support basis and weighting functions,
the finite methods yield only *local* interactions between discretized unknowns. This is a key advantage of the finite methods over integral

equation based techniques, where *global* type relationships usually exist among the unknowns. Local interactions, as produced by the finite methods, result in sparse matrix equations in the time-harmonic case and yield highly efficient causal updating algorithms in the time-domain. The topic of error analysis was also developed to give some basic insight into the numerical attributes of conditioning and stability, as associated respectively with frequency and time-domain solutions.

Since finite methods are innately posed as boundary- and initial-value problems, an *ad hoc* enforcement of the proper spatial "boundary conditions" at infinity (Sommerfeld radiation conditions) are required. Such an enforcement allows a finite-sized mesh to be used for the scattering problem in an unbounded domain. Different approaches are considered in section 1.3 for permitting mesh termination. Once again a sequence of examples was used as part of the tutorial to illustrate the basic ideas and methodology. Both time-harmonic and time-domain cases were considered, but with emphasis on the frequency domain.

One of the earliest of these techniques, the unimoment method, was presented here through a simple 2-D example. Some representative computational results were also given for 3-D axisymmetric scatterers and the unimoment method will be considered again in Chapter 2. For cases of highly elongated or flattened scattering structures, the unimoment method becomes somewhat inefficient. This is due to its fixed outer boundary shape which, for convenience, is usually circular in 2-D and spherical in 3-D. A large percentage of the enclosed mesh region becomes filled with a vacuum. In such cases, a more efficient approach is to use a mesh which is conformal to the scatterer.

The use of a boundary integral equation is one way to guarantee proper behavior of the scattered field. A simple 2-D example was presented to clarify the procedure. An early application to 3-D scattering was also considered using what was termed the finite-element boundary-integral method (FEBI). More will be said on the topic of boundary integral equations in Chapter 3, where a detailed application of this method is made to 2-D scattering from highly inhomogeneous structures.

The F^3 technique is similar in spirit to the boundary integral approach, but with increased flexibility. In fact, the boundary integral equation can be shown to be a special case of the F^3, when the two bounding surfaces become congruent and proper limiting conditions are applied. As with the boundary integral approach, the F^3 permits the use of a conformal mesh for field solutions within complicated scatterers composed of inhomogeneous and even anisotropic materials. As was shown, the F^3 casts the scattering problem into a vector-matrix equivalent of a simple feedback system, wherein the forward (interior problem) and feedback (radiated field) matrices may be computed *independently* and then combined to obtain a self-consistent scattering solution. Because of the F^3 system topology, either iterative or direct processing may be readily employed. The associated stability and condition number issues, and their relationship, were discussed. Results for scattering by 2-D penetrable objects and 3-D thin-wires were also presented. The future of the F^3 resides in extending the realm of practical electromagnetic calculations to electrically large, and quite complex, scattering configurations where volume integral equation techniques are numerically "bottlenecked" by their associated full matrices.

One of the most exciting (and controversial) recent developments in computational electromagnetics is in the area of radiation boundary conditions (RBC's). Such conditions are based upon numerical approximations to the behavior of outbound radiation fields. An RBC is applied at an enclosing boundary which does not need to be in the far-zone of the scatterer. In some cases, the boundary has been *very* close to the surface of the scattering object. RBC's have been developed through multiple approaches, two of which we briefly considered.

The computational power of RBC's stems from their potential for requiring only local interactions in the mesh termination equations. This is in contrast to the analytically exact boundary integral and F^3 approaches, where full global coupling at the mesh boundary is produced because of innate Green's function integrations. Within these boundary integrations, the scattered near-field at a given point is determined by the actual (or equivalent) source contributions over the entire integration surface. This dependence is stated as the classical Huygen's Principle [1]. However, the weighted effect of source contributions falls off with increasing distance from the field point. An important computational question concerns the possibility of ignoring the source contributions beyond some distance in exchange for a small increase in integration error. Although the RBC's do not explicitly perform the source integration, the implication of their success is that the scattered field at a near-field point is not strongly determined by other than the local behavior of equivalent sources in its immediate vicinity. This point is a major source of disagreement at the present time. Of particular concern are the cases of reentrant structures and highly resonant objects whose reactive fields are much stronger than their radiative fields over at least a portion of the equivalent source surface. In support of the RBC's is their record of success, as displayed by the results in Chapters 4, 5, 7 and 8. Very efficient computational algorithms result by combining the local mesh interactions in the finite methods with the local boundary interactions of an appropriate RBC. This global sparsity of interactions, if accurate, may ultimately drive virtually all large-scale electromagnetic computations (metallic as well as penetrable) into the use of finite methods.

References

[1] Stratton, J. A., *Electromagnetic Theory*, New York: McGraw-Hill, 1941.

[2] Harrington, R. F., *Field Computation by Moment Methods*, New York: Macmillan, 1968.

[3] Van Bladel, J., *Electromagnetic Fields*, New York: McGraw-Hill, 1964; (Reprinted) New York: Hemisphere, 1985.

[4] Kong, J. A., *Electromagnetic Wave Theory*, New York: Wiley, 1986.

[5] Bettess, P., "Infinite elements," *Int. J. Num. Meth. Eng.*, **11**, 53–64, 1977.

[6] Mei, K. K., M. A. Morgan, and S. K. Chang, "Finite methods in electromagnetic scattering," Chap. 10 in *Electromagnetic Scattering*, P. L. E. Ushlenghi, Ed., New York: Academic Press, 1978.

[7] Greenberg, M. D., *Foundations of Applied Mathematics*, Engelwood Cliffs: Prentice-Hall, 1978, 540–547.

[8] Stakgold, I., *Green's Functions and Boundary Value Problems*, New York: Wiley, 1979, Chap. 8.

[9] Courant, R., K. Friedrichs, and H. Lewy, "Über die partiellen differenzengleichungen der mathematischen physik," *Mathematische Annalen*, **100**, 32–74, 1928.

[10] Fox, P., "The solution of hyperbolic partial differential equations by difference methods," Chap. 16 in *Mathematical Methods for Digital Computers*, A. Ralston and H. S. Wolf, Eds. New York: Wiley, 1964.

[11] Lapidus, L., and G. F. Pinder, *Numerical Solution of Partial Differential Equations in Science and Engineering*, New York: Wiley, 1982.

[12] Yee, K. S., "Numerical solution of initial boundary value problems involving Maxwell's equations in isotropic media," *IEEE Trans. Antennas Propagat.*, **AP-14**, 302–307, 1966.

[13] Strang, G., and G. J. Fix, *An Analysis of the Finite Element Method*, Englewood Cliffs: Prentice-Hall, 1973.

[14] Morse, P. M., and H. Feshbach, *Methods of Theoretical Physics*, New York: McGraw-Hill, 1953.

[15] Tewarson, R. P., *Sparse Matrices*, New York: Academic, 1973.

[16] Morgan, M. A., and K. K. Mei, "Finite element computation of scattering by inhomogeneous penetrable bodies of revolution", *IEEE Trans. Antennas Propagat.*, **AP-27**, 202–214, 1979.

[17] Mittra, R., and C. A. Klein, "Stability and convergence of moment method solutions," Chap. 5 in *Numerical and Asymptotic Techniques in Electromagnetics*, R. Mittra, Ed., New York: Springer-Verlag, 1975.

[18] Isaacson E., and H. B. Keller, *Analysis of Numerical Methods*, New York: Wiley, 1966.

[19] Rynne, B. P., "Instabilities in time marching methods for scattering problems," *Electromagnetics*, **6**, 129–144, 1986.

[20] Mei, K. K., "Unimoment method of solving antenna and scattering problems," *IEEE Trans. Antennas Propagat.*, **AP-22**, 760–766, 1974.

[21] Chang, S. K., and K. K. Mei, "Application of the unimoment method to electromagnetic scattering of dielectric cylinders," *IEEE Trans. Antennas Propagat.*, **AP-24**, 35–42, 1976.

[22] Stovall, R. E., and K. K. Mei, "Application of a unimoment technique to a biconical antenna with inhomogeneous dielectric loading," *IEEE Trans. Antennas Propagat.*, **AP-23**, 335–341, 1975.

[23] Morgan, M. A., "Finite element computation of microwave scattering by raindrops," *Radio Science*, **15**, 1109–1119, 1980.

[24] Morgan, M. A., "Finite element calculation of microwave absorption by the cranial structure," *IEEE Trans. Biomed. Eng.*, **BME-28**, 687–695, 1981.

[25] Hunka, J. F., and K. K. Mei, "Electromagnetic scattering by two bodies of revolution, *Electromagnetics*, **1**, No. 3, 329–347, 1981.

[26] Chang, S. K., and K. K. Mei, "Multipole expansion technique for electromagnetic scattering by buried objects," *Electromagnetics*, **1**, No. 1, 73–89, 1981.

[27] Morgan, M. A., K. K. Mei, and S. K. Chang, "Coupled azimuthal potentials for electromagnetic field problems in inhomogeneous axially-symmetric media," *IEEE Trans. Antennas Propagat.*, **AP-25**, 413–417, 1977.

[28] Morgan, M. A., C. H. Chen, S. C. Hill, and P. W. Barber, "Finite element-boundary integral formulation for electromagnetic scattering," *J. Wave Motion*, **6**, 91–103, 1984.

[29] Poggio, A. J., and E. K. Miller, "Integral equation solutions of three-dimensional scattering problems," *Computer Techniques for Electromagnetics*, R. Mittra, Ed., New York: Pergamon Press, 1973.

[30] Waterman, P. C., "Scattering by dielectric obstacles," *Alta Frequenza*, **38**, (Speciale), 348–352, 1969.

[31] Miller, R. F., "Rayleigh hypothesis in scattering problems," *Electronics Letters*, **5**, No. 17, 416–418, 1969.

[32] Peterson, A. F., "A comparison of integral, differential and hybrid methods for TE-wave scattering from inhomogeneous dielectric cylinders," *J. Electromagnetic Waves Applicat.*, **3**, No. 2, 87–106, 1989.

[33] Morgan, M. A., and B. E. Welch, "The field feedback formulation for electromagnetic scattering problems," *IEEE Trans. Antennas Propagat.*, **AP-34**, 1377–1382, Dec. 1986.

[34] Morgan, M. A., "Stability considerations in the field feedback formulation," submitted to *IEEE Trans. Antennas Propagat.*, March 1989.

[35] Welch, T. B., *Electromagnetic Scattering from Two-Dimensional Objects Using the Field Feedback Formulation*, Engineer's Thesis, E.C.E. Dept., Naval Postgraduate School, Monterey, CA, March 1989.

[36] Richmond, J. H., "Scattering by a dielectric cylinder of arbitrary cross section shape," *IEEE Trans. Antennas Propagat.*, **AP-13**, 334–341, 1965.

[37] Richmond, J. H., "TE-wave scattering by a dielectric cylinder of arbitrary cross-section shape," *IEEE Trans. Antennas Propagat.*, **AP-14**, 460–464, 1966.

[38] Mabaya, N., P. E. Lagasse and P. Vandenbulcke, "Finite element analysis of optical waveguides," *IEEE Trans. Microwave Theory Tech.*, **MTT-29**, 600–605, 1981.

[39] Sommerfeld, A., *Partial Differential Equations in Physics*, New York: Academic, 1949.

[40] Merewether, D. E., "Transient currents induced on a metallic body of revolution by an electromagnetic pulse," *IEEE Trans. Electromagn. Compat.*, **EMC-13**, 41–44, 1971.

[41] Kriegsmann, G. A., and C. S. Morawetz, "Numerical solutions of exterior problems with the reduced wave equation," *J. Comp. Phys.*, **28**, 181–197, 1978.

[42] Bayliss, A., and E. Turkel, "Radiation boundary conditions for wave-like equations," *Commun. Pure Appl. Math.*, **23**, 707–725, 1980.

[43] Kriegsmann, G. A., and C. S. Morawetz, "Solving the Helmholtz equation for exterior problems with variable index of refraction: I," *SIAM J. Sci. Stat. Comput.*, **1**, 371–385, 1980.

[44] Engquist, B., and A. Majda, "Absorbing boundary conditions for the numerical simulation of waves," *Math. Comp.*, **31**, 629–651, 1977.

[45] Kriegsmann, G. A., A. Taflove, and K. R. Umashankar, "A new formulation of electromagnetic wave scattering using an on-surface radiation boundary condition," *IEEE Trans. Antennas Propagat.*, **35**, 153–161, 1987.

[46] Wilcox, C. H., "An expansion theorem for electromagnetic fields," *Commun. Pure Appl. Math.*, **9**, 115–132, 1956.

[47] Taflove, A., and K. R. Umashankar, "The finite-difference time-domain (FD-TD) method for electromagnetic scattering and interaction problems," *J. Electromag. Waves Applicat.*, **1**, 243–267, 1987.

[48] Mur, G., "Absorbing boundary conditions for the finite-difference approximation of time-domain electromagnetic field equations," *IEEE Trans. Electromag. Compat.*, **EMC-23**, 377–382, 1981.

[49] Moore, T. G., J. G. Blaschak, A. Taflove, and G. A. Kriegsmann, "Theory and application of radiation boundary operators," *IEEE Trans. Antennas Propagat.*, **36**, 1797–1812, 1988.

2

A FINITE ELEMENT METHOD
FOR COMPOSITE SCATTERERS

A. H. J. Fleming

2.1　Introduction

Due to the practical importance and difficulties associated with their closed form solutions, the experimental and computational study of conical antennas and scatterers, such as sphere-cones, round and flat-based and loaded bicones [1,2] has been closely connected with the evolution of numerical methods in electromagnetics. During the past two decades, the widespread use of such methods has allowed a broad range of important scattering problems involving non-standard shapes, boundary conditions and material composition to be solved. While computing speed and the availability of central memory remain a hurdle, interest in ever more complex processes provides a major driving force as instanced by recent studies involving composite objects [3–5].

The purpose of this chapter is to outline a differential method for the solution of composite scattering problems. In this section, we briefly survey some current problem types and solution methods. Section 2.2 discusses the unimoment technique [6] and the axisymmetric coupled azimuthal potentials (CAPs) [7]. Section 2.3 details the subsequent numerical procedure including the finite element method, the mesh and linear equation solver. The procedure is validated using standard Mei series calculations for spheres. In section 2.4, further tests of the method are performed using some standard shaped loaded and unloaded scatterers. Next, experimental results obtained from monostatic measurements are compared with computations for a series of loaded bicones. In Section 2.5, some conclusions are made about the procedure with particular regard for the method of incorporating conductors. Finally, some developments of the concepts of the CAP/unimoment method are discussed in Section 2.6.

Due to the computational economies afforded, bodies of revolution (BORs) or axisymmetric objects as illustrated in Fig. 1 have been the basis of many studies. The incident and impressed fields are not in general axisymmetric although they are azimuthally continuous and thus amenable to Fourier analysis. In order to get an approximate quantitative understanding of a complicated phenomenon such as microwave frequency hot spots in the human cranium, axisymmetry has been assumed [8]. Many problems remain however concerning essentially non-axisymmetric objects [9] while future composite studies such as therapeutic applicators promise to be most worthwhile [10].

Two major types of numerical method have been employed to date to solve scattering in the Rayleigh or resonance region via Maxwell's equations and associated boundary conditions, namely integral equation and differential equation methods. The two can be related by successively integrating by parts [11]. There are fundamental differences that make either method more appropriate for different applications. Integral equations distribute the sources over surfaces (2-D manifolds) so that the surface element intercoupling falls off relatively slowly with distance, generally resulting in dense matrices. However, since radiation conditions are incorporated as limits of integration, infinite regions are easily handled. On the other hand, differential methods give a description at each point in terms of the fields at the surrounding set

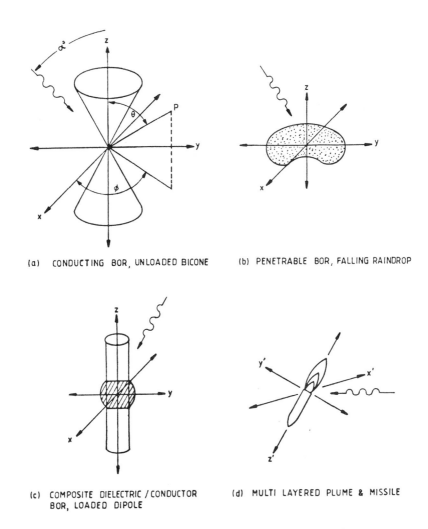

(a) CONDUCTING BOR, UNLOADED BICONE   (b) PENETRABLE BOR, FALLING RAINDROP

(c) COMPOSITE DIELECTRIC / CONDUCTOR   (d) MULTI LAYERED PLUME & MISSILE
     BOR, LOADED DIPOLE

Figure 1 Various axisymmetric scattering problems.

of nodes in a volume (3-D manifold). This provides a more localized effect, resulting in sparse matrices. Some means of coupling the differential method to the exterior infinite region is required however.

Integral equation methods which utilize the surface equivalence principle are most effective for applications involving piecewise homogeneous regions [12,13]. The missile plume problem (Fig. 1) was treated as a layered dielectric with a conducting inside surface [3]. Use of the moment method results in a block tridiagonal matrix consisting of dense submatrices. Recently, a comparison was made of different surface integral equation (SIE) formulations as applied to coated conductors [4]. At each surface, either electric or magnetic equivalent surface currents may be used, or both may be combined. The advantage of using single source formulations is the reduction in the required number of variables. Difficulties arise however depending upon whether or not associated over-constraints are satisfied. Thus at each single source layer surface, the solution can be affected by uniqueness problems at interior resonances when the permittivity of the coating is large.

Integral equation methods can be used for continuously inhomogeneous regions. A volume integral equation utilizing the polarization currents inside a volume and equivalent surface currents on an enclosing boundary surface can be formulated [14,15]. Three current components are required to be solved at each node in the volume. Thus the matrix, which is of order $3n^3$ where n is the number of nodes in the volume, becomes large for anything other than a coarse grid.

Where continuously varying inhomogeneities are present, such as biological systems, a differential method is appropriate. Furthermore, where inter-regional surfaces involve sharp reentrant angles, a numerical method based on differential equations accounts for the rapidly changing field solution near the cusp in a more direct manner; the mesh density is increased near the point. With the SIE approach, special care must be taken with the equations of continuity at such points.

Two differential methods, finite differences and finite elements have been used. With the finite difference method, approximate partial differences are applied directly to the field equations while the finite element method uses a weighting procedure to obtain a system of derived equations in which the errors are more evenly distributed throughout the problem domain.

While several techniques exist for coupling differential methods to the exterior region, such as infinite elements [16], *ballooning* [17] or the field feedback formulation [18], one effective means is the unimoment method [6]. Together with the unimoment method, the axisymmetric CAPs have been used to analyze structurally axisymmetric scattering, radiation, penetration and absorption problems. The CAP/unimoment formulation has proved over the past decade both powerful and flexible. Some applications have involved lossy dielectric objects [8,19,20]. Other extensions and hybrid techniques have been used [21,22]. Recently, the CAP equations were allied with the field feedback formulation to analyse thin dipoles [18].

Stovall and Mei [2] studied radiation from loaded bicones using the finite difference method allied with the unimoment method and a symmetric form of the CAPs which results in a single potential. No account as to the end shape of the bicone was taken. The present study was initiated in part to examine the effect of shifting the surface of the unimoment method outwards and thus allow the analysis of various composite antenna structures. It was considered that this shifting of the unimoment method surface might also avoid possible continuity complications at the cone-hemisphere junction.

A finite element method based on the theory of the axisymmetric CAPs was used together with a conductor surface skin model which was included in the finite element mesh. This part of the mesh which approximates the field distributions at an imperfect conductor surface was used instead of applying perfect conductor boundary conditions. The important parameters were found to be the conductivity of the skin region and the ratio of the internal nodal separation (the mesh density) to that used external to the conductor. Reducing the size of the mesh as it proceeds radially inside the conductor surface accounts for the large wave numbers inside the skin.

2.2   Formulation

The following formulation is specialized to bodies of revolution, but could be generalized to arbitrary 3-D inhomogeneous structures. The unimoment method is quite flexible and extensions of the CAP equations to piecewise axisymmetric, quasi-axisymmetric, and full 3-D have recently been suggested (see Chapter 6), [23].

We address a generic problem involving axisymmetric composite structures where the conducting region is assumed to enclose the origin of a normalized cylindrical coordinate system and the dielectric either totally or partially surrounds the internal metallic region. Biregional or triregional unimoment methods can be used to separate the inhomogeneity depending on the shape and nature of the conductor. In the inhomogeneous region, Maxwell's equations can be written as time-harmonic modal expansions (the axisymmetric CAP equations) appropriate for coupling to the free-space and core region spherical harmonics.

The inhomogeneities involve isotropic regions where the shape and the constitutive parameters are both assumed to be rotationally invariant: $\epsilon(r,\theta) = \epsilon_0 \epsilon_r(r,\theta); \mu(r,\theta) = \mu_0 \mu_r(r,\theta)$.

a. Unimoment Method

For the general case of an arbitrarily shaped scatterer, the unimoment method [6] uses a series of boundary trial functions in order to numerically enforce electromagnetic continuity at a surface surrounding the inhomogeneous region of the object under analysis. As illustrated in Fig. 2, this region can be surrounded both internally and externally by homogeneous core and free-space regions. Care needs to be taken in the selection of the boundary trial functions which should form a complete polynomial set.

Savings are possible by choice of canonical surfaces which allow the reuse of computed modal expansions. Using the appropriate modal series at nodes on the canonical surface, C, either for the scattered, incident or interior fields, continuity of the total electromagnetic fields and their normal derivatives is sought. Use of modal boundary conditions along C for the interior fields automatically ensures modal and total field continuity along C. What is needed then is to obtain the mix of modal coefficients which also ensures normal derivative continuity.

This can be done by obtaining the field values along a congruent curve C', enabling the normal derivative to be numerically estimated by using field differences between the two curves. This can be inaccurate depending on how the gradient estimates are derived. A simpler more accurate method of obtaining the desired continuity between regions is to ensure the total fields are also matched along C'.

For coupling with the CAP formulation the surfaces which separate these regions can be of any shape that permit the convenient orthogonal separation of the azimuthal coordinate, ϕ, into the spectral modes, $e^{\jmath m\phi}$. In the present application, spheres and spherical harmonics were used. Figure 3 shows in cross-section, a loaded dipole, the two spherical separable surfaces S_{HC} (homogeneous core) and S_F (free-space) and their congruents S_0 and S_1.

The modal azimuthal fields may be derived from

$$E_{\phi,m} = \frac{1}{\jmath\omega\epsilon r \sin\theta} \frac{\partial^2 A_{r,m}}{\partial r \partial\phi} + \frac{1}{r}\frac{\partial F_{r,m}}{\partial\theta} \tag{1a}$$

$$H_{\phi,m} = \frac{1}{\jmath\omega\mu r \sin\theta} \frac{\partial^2 F_{r,m}}{\partial r \partial\phi} - \frac{1}{r}\frac{\partial A_{r,m}}{\partial\theta} \tag{1b}$$

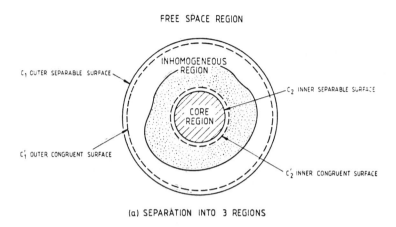

(a) SEPARATION INTO 3 REGIONS

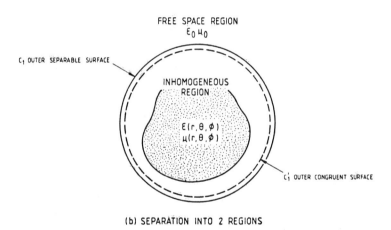

(b) SEPARATION INTO 2 REGIONS

Figure 2   Unimoment surfaces: (a) Triregional and (b) Biregional.

with the radial electric and magnetic vector potentials given by

$$F_{r,m} = \frac{\sqrt{\mu_r}}{k_0} \sum_{n=m}^{N_m} a_{m\,n} P_n^m(\cos\theta)\widehat{B}_n(kr)e^{jm\phi} \tag{1c}$$

$$A_{r,m} = \frac{\sqrt{\epsilon_r}}{\eta_0 k_0} \sum_{n=m}^{N_m} b_{m\,n} P_n^m(\cos\theta)\widehat{B}_n(kr)e^{jm\phi} \tag{1d}$$

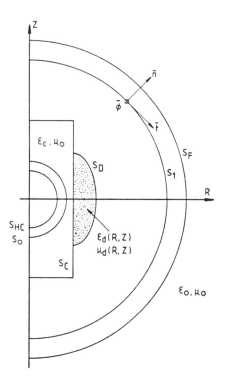

Figure 3   Semi-annular region for loaded dipole.

The complex propagation constant, in the assumed homogeneous material, is given by $k = \omega\sqrt{\mu\epsilon}$. Also, $\eta_0 = \sqrt{\mu_0/\epsilon_0} \approx 120\pi$ ohms, P_n^m are associated Legendre functions of the first kind, $\hat{B}_n$ are Riccati spherical Bessel functions, N_m is a truncation limit on the radial modal index, n, and m is the azimuthal modal index. The modal coefficients, a_{mn} and b_{mn}, are determined to numerically enforce continuity of the fields via the moment method.

While the above form of the unimoment method works well with nearly spherical objects, other three dimensional orthogonal systems may be used for other shapes, for instance thin wires, where spherical harmonics are inefficient and converge slowly. Similarly, objects such as the human body could be better modelled using spheroids and spheroidal harmonics.

b. Analytic CAP Formulation

The analytical derivation of the axisymmetric CAP formulation [24] begins by taking a Fourier series in the azimuthal coordinate ϕ, thus separating the azimuthal variable,

$$\overline{E}(R, Z, \phi) = \sum_{m=-\infty}^{\infty} \overline{e}_m(R, Z) e^{jm\phi} \tag{2a}$$

$$\eta_0 \overline{H}(R, Z, \phi) = \sum_{m=-\infty}^{\infty} \overline{h}_m(R, Z) e^{jm\phi} \tag{2b}$$

The magnetic field is scaled by the free-space impedance, η_0, which simplifies the resulting coupled set of partial differential equations. Use of a normalized cylindrical coordinate system ($R = k_0\rho$, $Z = k_0 z$) enables the application of cartesian finite elements in the cross-sectional plane (r, θ).

In the inhomogeneous isotropic region, Maxwell's curl equations for time-harmonic, source free regions where conductive media may be present, are rewritten using equations $(2a - b)$. The resulting set of equations may be written in partitioned matrix form

$$
\begin{bmatrix}
\dfrac{\epsilon_r}{R} & 0 & 0 & -j\dfrac{\partial}{\partial R} & 0 & j\dfrac{\partial}{\partial Z} \\[2mm]
0 & \dfrac{\mu_r}{R} & -j\dfrac{\partial}{\partial Z} & 0 & j\dfrac{\partial}{\partial R} & 0 \\[2mm]
0 & j\dfrac{\partial}{\partial Z} & -R\epsilon_r & m & 0 & 0 \\[2mm]
j\dfrac{\partial}{\partial R} & 0 & m & -R\mu_r & 0 & 0 \\[2mm]
0 & j\dfrac{\partial}{\partial R} & 0 & 0 & R\epsilon_r & m \\[2mm]
j\dfrac{\partial}{\partial Z} & 0 & 0 & 0 & m & R\mu_r
\end{bmatrix}
\begin{bmatrix}
\psi_{1,m} \\[2mm] \psi_{2,m} \\[2mm] e_{R,m} \\[2mm] h_{Z,m} \\[2mm] e_{Z,m} \\[2mm] h_{R,m}
\end{bmatrix}
=
\begin{bmatrix}
0 \\[2mm] 0 \\[2mm] 0 \\[2mm] 0 \\[2mm] 0 \\[2mm] 0
\end{bmatrix}
\tag{3}
$$

where $e^{jm\phi}$ terms have been omitted and the modal CAP variables $\psi_{1,m}$ and $\psi_{2,m}$ are defined in terms of the azimuthal modal field components, $e_{\phi,m}$ and $h_{\phi,m}$.

$$\psi_{1,m} = R\, e_{\phi,m} \qquad (4a)$$

$$\psi_{2,m} = R\, h_{\phi,m} \qquad (4b)$$

The 6×6 system of modal equations in (3) is seen to be block-reducible and any of the three pairings indicated can be used to convert these first order equations into an equivalent system involving only a collapsed 2×2 set of coupled second order partial differential equations.

For the axisymmetric structures involved, the CAP variables, $\psi_{1,m}$ and $\psi_{2,m}$, are continuous everywhere. This is so at all source-free cross-sectional junctions, even across conductor and dielectric interfaces. Naturally, field components in the cross-sectional plane normal to the CAPs may be discontinuous. Choosing the CAPs as problem variables results in the following 2×2 coupled system of partial differential equations:

$$\nabla \cdot \left[f_m(R\epsilon_r \nabla \psi_{1,m} + m\hat{\phi} \times \nabla \psi_{2,m}) \right] + \frac{\epsilon_r \psi_{1,m}}{R} = 0 \qquad (5a)$$

$$\nabla \cdot \left[f_m(R\mu_r \nabla \psi_{2,m} - m\hat{\phi} \times \nabla \psi_{1,m}) \right] + \frac{\mu_r \psi_{2,m}}{R} = 0 \qquad (5b)$$

where the cross sectional gradient operator is defined by

$$\nabla = \hat{R} \frac{\partial}{\partial R} + \hat{Z} \frac{\partial}{\partial Z} \qquad (6a)$$

and

$$f_m = \left[\epsilon_r(R, Z)\mu_r(R, Z)R^2 - m^2 \right]^{-1} \qquad (6b)$$

is the media variable which is a determinant of the disjoint first order system. It presents a complication in the form of a singularity at the cylindrical surface defined by

$$R_m(Z) = \frac{|m|}{\sqrt{\epsilon_r(R_m, Z)\mu_r(R_m, Z)}} \qquad (7)$$

for the lossless case when the relative parameters, ϵ_r and μ_r, are both real. Numerical errors are observed in the vicinity of these singularities. At points close to such surfaces, and there may be several when layered dielectrics are considered, these errors can be minimized by taking an

averaged value at the point from the CAPs at the surrounding nodes,
[25].

Using dyadic operator notation, the system in equation (5) can be
rewritten as

$$\overline{\overline{\mathcal{L}}} \cdot \overline{\Psi}(R, Z) = \overline{0} \qquad (8)$$

where the dyadic operator, $\overline{\overline{\mathcal{L}}}(R, Z)$, is given by

$$\overline{\overline{\mathcal{L}}} = \begin{bmatrix} \nabla \cdot (f_m R \epsilon_r \nabla) + \epsilon_r / R & m \nabla \cdot (f_m \hat{\phi} \times \nabla) \\ -m \nabla \cdot (f_m \hat{\phi} \times \nabla) & \nabla \cdot (f_m R \mu_r \nabla) + \mu_r / R \end{bmatrix} \qquad (9a)$$

and where the column vector is

$$\overline{\Psi}(R, Z) = \begin{bmatrix} \psi_{1,m} \\ \psi_{2,m} \end{bmatrix} \qquad (9b)$$

The operator in (9a) can be shown to be self-adjoint where the
boundary conditions along the unimoment perimeter are Dirichlet and
homogeneous Neumann along the Z-axis. If an appropriate numerical procedure is used, this self-adjointness results in symmetry of the
resulting system of linear equations.

2.3   Finite Element Method

The CAP equations require numerical solution within the inhomogeneous regions associated with the scattering problem. The choice
of finite elements leads to two equivalent numerical procedures in this
case, namely the variational method and the Galerkin method.

The variation statement of the problem is an energy density functional which again can be derived in two ways, one a heuristic method
using the system Euler Lagrange equations, the other from a generalized *stationary theorem*.

$$F = \int_S L(R, Z, \psi_1, \psi_2, \nabla \psi_1, \nabla \psi_2) \, dR \, dZ \qquad (10)$$

where the modal subscripts have been omitted for clarity and the La-
grangian is given by

$$L = f_m [\nabla \psi_1 \cdot (R \epsilon_r \nabla \psi_1 + m \hat{\phi} \times \nabla \psi_2) + \nabla \psi_2 \cdot (R \mu_r \nabla \psi_2$$
$$- m \hat{\phi} \times \nabla \psi_1)] - (\epsilon_r \psi_1^2 + \mu_r \psi_2^2) / R \tag{11}$$

The physical nature of this functional can be shown to be related to the difference between the time-varying and time-average radiated power densities via a *pseudo* (non-conjugate) Poynting vector [24]:

$$F = -J \oint_{\delta S} (\overline{e}_m \times \overline{h}_m) \cdot \hat{n} \, R \, |dc| \tag{12}$$

In (10), S is the finite element cross-sectional area and δS in (12) is the contour which bounds S while c is the length variable around this contour.

The variational method as applied to finite elements begins by using an approximate piecewise polynomial model of the true solution and then a representative approximation at each node of a mesh description of the problem. The problem variables now become the nodal approximates. Since the system is in dynamic equilibrium, the minimum energy condition can be used to derive the equivalent requirement on each nodal variable. Simply, equation (10) is differentiated with respect to these nodal variables and the result set to zero. The fact that the first variation gives a functional which is quadratic in form with respect to these nodal variables results in a system of linear equations. Using the interpolation base chosen, each finite element associated with each node contributes to the resulting linear system of equations.

Alternatively, the weighted residual Galerkin method can be applied to the CAP system of equations given by (8) and (9)

$$\langle W_i, \overline{\overline{\mathcal{L}}} \cdot \overline{\Psi}^*(R, Z) \rangle = \overline{0} \qquad \text{for } i = 1, n_I \tag{13}$$

where n_I is the total number of internal nodes within the finite element mesh, $W_i(R, Z)$ are weighting functions, $\overline{\Psi}^*(R, Z)$ are piecewise polynomial approximations to the exact CAP solution and the $\langle \cdot, \cdot \rangle$ represents an inner-product integration in (R, Z). The * superscript notation employed here and in the next section indicates the numerical approximation to the functional term and does *not* mean complex conjugation. In *Galerkin's* method, the weighting functions and the basis functions for $\overline{\Psi}^*$ are chosen to be equal.

Note that the variational method depends upon discovering the associated quadratic functional, which may or may not exist, whereas the Galerkin approach depends only upon the existence of a unique solution to the system of partial differential equations which depends partially upon the type of boundary conditions being applied. Once these uniqueness constraints are satisfied, Galerkin's method can be applied.

a. Modelling and Shape Functions

Central to the art of numerical modelling is the replacement of the exact solution at all points in the domain of interest with the nodal approximates using a piecewise polynomial representation. It is most essential that the choice of polynomial be representative of the true solution as far as possible given numerical convenience and error considerations. In seeking to obtain the solution of the CAP equations, it must be remembered that the true solution is azimuthally smooth due to the axisymmetry. Hence, the separation of the azimuthal coordinate by the spectral series eqns (2) should be a good approximation for the continuous azimuthal component of the solution. This is not so in all spherical directions, e.g. radial and elevational as inhomogeneities in these directions will cause discontinuities in the cross-sectional fields. For these directions, it is more accurate to use low order piecewise monomial functions $(1, x, x^2, \ldots)$.

In the present study, linear cross-sectional interpolation was employed. This was done in order to utilize the resulting discontinuous numerical solution across media interfaces. This models the exact solution at these boundaries, while also introducing small numerical errors at element interfaces everywhere else. It also allows the use of the Riccati transformation [2] to solve the resulting block-tridiagonal system of linear equations.

For the linear case, a triangular element e is considered. As per equation (9b), let

$$\overline{\Psi}_e^*(R, Z) = [\psi_1^*(R, Z), \psi_2^*(R, Z)]_e^T \qquad (14)$$

where T means transpose, represent the approximation to the exact CAP vector by using linear basis functions within the element. As previously mentioned, the * notation indicates numerical approximation and does not mean complex conjugation.

The linear interpolation model is chosen such that it forms a complete polynomial representation of order one within the triangular element.

$$\psi_1^*(R, Z) = a_1 R + a_2 Z + a_3 \tag{15a}$$

$$\psi_2^*(R, Z) = b_1 R + b_2 Z + b_3 \tag{15b}$$

It follows that,

$$\psi_1^*(R, Z) = \underline{P}(R, Z) \cdot \overline{a} \tag{16a}$$

$$\psi_2^*(R, Z) = \underline{P}(R, Z) \cdot \overline{b} \tag{16b}$$

where the row vector is given by $\underline{P}(R, Z) = [R, Z, 1]$ and

$$\overline{a} = \left\{ \begin{array}{c} a_1 \\ a_2 \\ a_3 \end{array} \right\} \qquad \overline{b} = \left\{ \begin{array}{c} b_1 \\ b_2 \\ b_3 \end{array} \right\}$$

By interpolation, $\overline{\Psi}_e^*(R, Z)$ can be derived in terms of the nodal values of the potentials. These nodal values are represented by the arrays

$$\overline{\psi}_k^e = \left[\begin{array}{c} \psi_k^*(R_1, Z_1) \\ \psi_k^*(R_2, Z_2) \\ \psi_k^*(R_3, Z_3) \end{array} \right] \tag{17}$$

where the ordered nodal coordinates of the triangle are (R_n, Z_n) for $n = 1, 2, 3$, with $k = 1, 2$ indicating the two CAP's.

Using the interpolation model at each node of the triangle leads to the fundamental finite element equations

$$\psi_k^*(R, Z) = \underline{N}_e(R, Z) \cdot \overline{\psi}_k^e \tag{18}$$

with $\underline{N}_e(R, Z) = \underline{P}(R, Z) \cdot \overline{\overline{G}}_e$. The transformation matrix is given in terms of the triangle node coordinates

$$\overline{\overline{G}}_e = \begin{bmatrix} R_1 & Z_1 & 1 \\ R_2 & Z_2 & 1 \\ R_3 & Z_3 & 1 \end{bmatrix}^{-1} \tag{19}$$

$$= \frac{1}{2A_e} \begin{bmatrix} (Z_2 - Z_3) & (Z_3 - Z_1) & (Z_1 - Z_2) \\ (R_3 - R_2) & (R_1 - R_3) & (R_2 - R_1) \\ (R_2 Z_3 - R_3 Z_2) & (R_3 Z_1 - R_1 Z_3) & (R_1 Z_2 - R_2 Z_1) \end{bmatrix}$$

where A_e is the area of the triangle.

The shape function vector, $\underline{N}_e(R, Z)$, is composed of three linear function components, $N_n(R, Z)$, each of which equates to unity at the n-th local node and zero at all other nodes in the element. The shape function equations in (18) effectively split the approximate solution into a geometric part and a nodal part. The geometric part is the shape function and depends only on (R, Z). On the other hand, the nodal variable approximates do not depend on the spatial variables directly but rather depend for accuracy on the numerical procedure used to model the underlying partial differential equations. The combined effect is a cross-sectional piecewise planar approximation to the exact wave solution.

The weighted residual Galerkin method can be applied using equations (13), where the weighting functions, W_i, become the components of the shape function vector in each element, resulting in

$$\sum_{e \in \{e(i)\}} \iint_{A_e} \overline{\overline{N}}_i \cdot \{\overline{\overline{\mathcal{L}}} \cdot \overline{\Psi}_e^*(R, Z)\} \, dA_e = \overline{0} \qquad \text{for } i = 1, n_I \tag{20a}$$

where

$$\overline{\overline{N}}_i(R, Z) = \begin{bmatrix} N_i(R, Z) & 0 \\ 0 & N_i(R, Z) \end{bmatrix} \tag{20b}$$

This sum is over the elements connected to the i-th internal mesh node, as is represented by the set $\{e(i)\}$. The dyadic operator, $\overline{\overline{\mathcal{L}}}(R, Z)$, is defined in (9).

Inserting the shape function equations from (18) yields at each node, $n = i, j, k$ within the element $e(i)$,

$$\sum_{e \in \{e(i)\}} \iint_{A_e} \overline{\overline{N}}_i \cdot \overline{\overline{\mathcal{L}}} \cdot \overline{\overline{N}}_n \cdot \begin{bmatrix} \psi_1^i \\ \psi_2^i \end{bmatrix} dA_e = \begin{bmatrix} 0 \\ 0 \end{bmatrix} \qquad (21)$$

The divergence theorem is used to reduce the admissibility constraints on the basis functions. This transfers a degree of this constraint to the weighting functions and produces the *weak* form often used in finite element applications [11]

$$\sum_{e \in \{e(i)\}} \iint_{A_e} \overline{\overline{\mathcal{L}}}_N(R, Z) \cdot \begin{bmatrix} \psi_1^i \\ \psi_2^i \end{bmatrix} dA_e = \begin{bmatrix} 0 \\ 0 \end{bmatrix} \qquad (22)$$

where $\overline{\overline{\mathcal{L}}}_N(R, Z)$ is given by

$$\begin{bmatrix} f_m \nabla N_i \cdot (R \epsilon_r \nabla N_n) - N_i N_n \epsilon_r / R & m \nabla N_i \cdot (f_m \hat{\phi} \times \nabla N_n) \\ -m \nabla N_i \cdot (f_m \hat{\phi} \times \nabla N_n) & f_m \nabla N_i \cdot (R \mu_r \nabla N_n) - N_i N_n \mu_r / R \end{bmatrix}$$

As stated, the variational method results in an equivalent system of equations to that generated by the coupled differential equations.

b. Conformal Mesh

The techniques used to define the placement of the finite elements throughout the domain of the inhomogeneous problem within the separable surfaces relate to both the linear equation solution method and the type of spatial problem being analyzed. As well, the degree of inhomogeneity and the presence of discontinuities of either media or geometry all affect the mesh generation process.

For near spherical geometries, the use of a double semi-circular boundary allows a constant radial width. Thus, a domain may be modelled by distorting what is essentially a regular polar coordinate mesh to conform to the dielectric-air interface (and additionally the conductor-dielectric interface for composite bodies).

The placement of nodes along each radial is performed in the manner discussed by Morgan [24] such that a regular polar mesh is minimally perturbed. The dielectric (and conductor) surface of revolution can be defined by an radius array $R_i = R(\theta_i)$, for $i = 1, I_{max}$. The

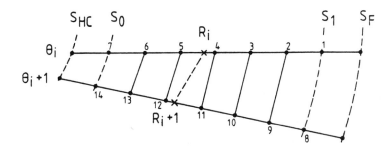

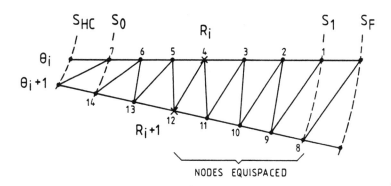

Figure 4 Conformal mesh generation for 3-node triangles.

object is to choose the node in the original undisturbed mesh that is closest to the surface R_i at each θ_i as shown in Fig. 4.

The same procedure can be generalized for multi-layered problems such as the tip effects of a multi-layered radome [22] and the analysis of *hot-spots* within the human cranium [8].

The convenience of the mesh is increased by keeping the number of nodes along each radial spoke constant. The topology is equivalent at each step starting from $\theta = 0°$ to $\theta = 180°$. Figure 5 illustrates the mesh for an off-set loaded conducting sphere where the global node numbering is shown for the first three radial steps. The grid can be adapted for regions of greater change, for example, the bicone shape near the half-angle.

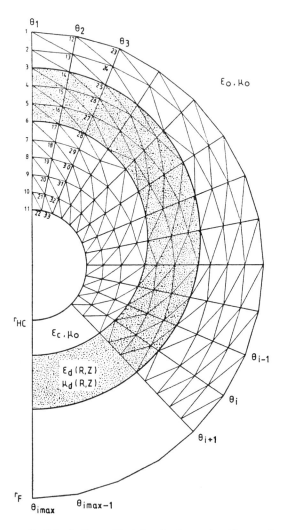

Figure 5 Mesh for offset loaded conducting sphere.

c. Riccati Transform

As was previously described, the system matrix is gradually loaded as the forward sweep continues until the last radial is reached. The resulting matrix is shown diagrammatically in Fig. 6. It can be seen that the structure is tridiagonal in sub-matrices formed by the partition into the nodal unknowns associated with each radial unknowns vector, $\overline{\Psi}_i$.

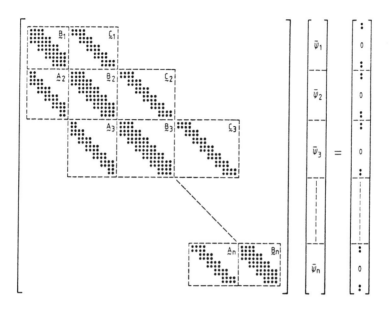

Figure 6 Single mode global system matrix.

The off-diagonal sub-matrices reflect the RH or LH nature of the local mesh distortions and are banded of half-width 3, whilst the main diagonal has a half-width of 4. Each submatrix can be stored in a banded profile fashion whereby only the band coefficients and the column number of the left-most entry of the band in each row is required.

The Riccati block-by-block elimination technique [2] can be used to solve the system of linear equations. The system matrix may be written in terms of a recursive sequence of submatrices.

$$\overline{\overline{A}}_i \cdot \overline{\Psi}_{i-1} + \overline{\overline{B}}_i \cdot \overline{\Psi}_i + \overline{\overline{C}}_i \cdot \overline{\Psi}_{i+1} = \overline{D}_i \qquad \text{for } i = 1, 2, \ldots I_{max} \quad (23)$$

where, by inspection, the initial and final submatrices

$$\overline{\overline{A}}_1 = \overline{\overline{C}}_1 = \overline{\overline{A}}_{I_{max}} = \overline{\overline{C}}_{I_{max}} = \overline{\overline{0}}$$

In all subsequent computations, the dimensions of the submatrices were kept constant because the nodal grid was so chosen. However, applications where this is not the case can be solved in the same fashion.

If the lengths of $\overline{\Psi}_{i-1}, \overline{\Psi}_i$, and $\overline{\Psi}_{i+1}$ are n_{i-1}, n_i, and n_{i+1}, respectively, then $\overline{\overline{A}}_i, \overline{\overline{B}}_i$ and $\overline{\overline{C}}_i$ have the dimensions $n_i \times n_{i-1}, n_i \times n_i$ and $n_i \times n_{i+1}$; the total dimension of the system matrix will be $\sum_{i=1}^{N} n_i$.

The Riccati matrix, $\overline{\overline{R}}_i$, and vector $\overline{S}_i$ are defined by the transformation

$$\overline{\Psi}_{i-1} = \overline{\overline{R}}_i \cdot \overline{\Psi}_i + \overline{S}_i \tag{24}$$

Substituting (24) into (23) and comparing with the form in (24) gives the following recursive relationships

$$\overline{\overline{R}}_{i+1} = -(\overline{\overline{B}}_i + \overline{\overline{A}}_i \cdot \overline{\overline{R}}_i)^{-1} \cdot \overline{\overline{C}}_i \tag{25a}$$

$$\overline{S}_{i+1} = -(\overline{\overline{B}}_i + \overline{\overline{A}}_i \cdot \overline{\overline{R}}_i) \cdot (\overline{D}_i - \overline{\overline{A}}_i \cdot \overline{S}_i) \tag{25b}$$

The boundary conditions yield the start and end matrix and vector at both ends

$$\overline{\overline{R}}_2 = \overline{\overline{B}}_1^{-1} \cdot \overline{\overline{C}}_1 \tag{26a}$$

$$\overline{S}_2 = \overline{\overline{B}}_1^{-1} \cdot \overline{D}_1 \tag{26b}$$

$$\overline{\overline{R}}_{(I_{max}+1)} = \overline{\overline{0}} \tag{26c}$$

$$\overline{S}_{(I_{max}+1)} = \overline{D}_{(I_{max})} \tag{26d}$$

It can be seen from Fig. 6 that $\overline{\Psi}_i$ has only two non-zero elements at θ_i (apart from the conditions on the z-axis at θ_0 and $\theta_{I_{max}}$). This allows a reduction in core storage requirements although a simple alternative technique is to use backing disk to store and retrieve $\overline{\overline{R}}_i$ and $\overline{S}_i$ as required.

Thus the, linear solution method starts by stepping forward a radial at a time beginning from $\theta = 0°$ to $\theta = 180°$ where at each step the recursive transform equations are used to successively eliminate the previous i-2th radial unknowns vector. The first and last radials lie on the Z-axis and, depending upon the mode being considered and on the CAP variables being used, these conditions are trivially loaded. Once the final radial at $\theta = 180°$ is reached, the forward evolution is complete and a back substitution stage is now commenced. The solution along each radial is obtained in turn as the backsweep proceeds. If necessary, these solutions can be found for all nodes in each vector; only the congruential nodes were required however for the present application.

d. Incorporation of Conductor Regions

Three methods may be used to incorporate the conducting region:

(a) Perfect conductor boundary conditions may be applied along the cross-sectional contour of the axisymmetric conductor/dielectric interface

$$\psi_{1,m} = 0 \tag{27a}$$

$$\frac{\partial \psi_{2,m}}{\partial n} = 0 \tag{27b}$$

(b) A complex permittivity may be used inside the conductor region where the conductivity of the medium is included; the finite element mesh finishes at an internal separable surface where internal core modes are applied within the unimoment method

$$\epsilon_r = \epsilon_r' - j\,\epsilon_r'' \tag{28a}$$

where

$$\epsilon_r'' = \sigma/\omega\epsilon_0 \tag{28b}$$

The use of a complex permittivity results from a reformulation of the underlying time-varying wave equations where a first order partial time derivative exists. This derivative can be incorporated within the same time-harmonic formulation as in equations (1) and (5) by redefining a complex propagation constant which can be related to the free-space wave number. Thus $k = k_r\,k_0$, where the normalization factor is $k_r = \sqrt{\epsilon_r' - j\sigma/\omega\epsilon}$, [26]. In general, the time-varying fields can be shown to be elliptic in direction at any point. The path of a free electron in such a field will also be elliptic; the concept of an eddy current is apparent.

Method (b) is illustrated by Fig. 5. An unreduced nodal separation or mesh step is shown in the conductor region (the mesh is stepped

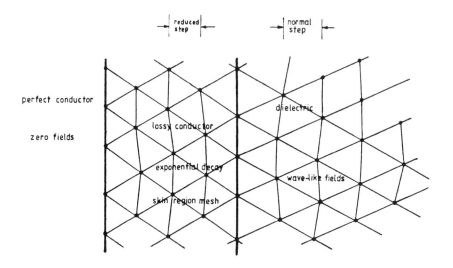

Figure 7 Conductor surface skin model.

inwards from the free-space separable surface at r_F, until the homogeneous core region separable surface at r_{HC} is reached). A range of *poor* conductors may be modelled in this fashion.

(c) An imperfect *skin* region can be modelled by utilizing the same complex permittivity concept as in (b) but terminating the mesh stepping at a boundary just inside the conductor surface; internal to this thin layer, the fields are presumed to have vanished but within the skin they are accounted for. In this case, the position of the internal boundary is varied depending upon precisely where the conductor surface is situated for a particular angle. It is not important precisely where the internal boundary is located, rather that the field gradients near the surface should be accounted for correctly and that the resulting submatrices be kept of nearly constant dimension. The unimoment method is simplified since no internal core modes are required. Within the skin, a reduced nodal separation can be used for modelling actual conductors such as aluminium. Figure 7 illustrates the concept of reducing the step at the surface.

Having previously tried methods (a) and (b), [27], (c) was chosen for numerical testing. The first objects selected for examination were spheres since the analytical Mie series solution was available for comparison for both unloaded and loaded spheres and for the additional case of an axial offset with respect to the Z-axis.

The initial problem was to determine what actual nodal step reductions should be used inside the conductor and with what range of ϵ_r''. Using two unloaded centred conducting sphere scatterers (radii $0.4\lambda_0$ and $0.8\lambda_0$), a broad range of step reductions and permittivities was tested to see what relationship would give valid results.

In both cases at each point, the problem parameters were varied such that two or so steps of an iterative multi-dimensional hill search were performed where at the top of the hill lay the optimized approximation to the exact solution. The parameters referred to are I_{max} the number of angular θ divisions, N_{max} the number of radial modes, DENS the nodal mesh density in nodes per wavelength and M_{max} the number of azimuthal modes (only the $m = 1$ mode is required for axial incidence).

Figures 8 and 9 show how ϵ_r'' relates to the step ratio and the forward scattering cross section solution for both sphere problems assuming axial incidence. It is seen in both that the simulation has a stable region between two unstable bounding regions which together demonstrate the quadratic nature of the conductor surface modelling error. The results indicate that there is a broad range of ϵ'' and step ratios within which the numerical errors due to the surface skin model are minimal. Further, as the spherical radius of any point increases, so does the stable region; unfortunately so do the computational requirements.

To further check the procedure, the complex scattering amplitudes for the $0.4\lambda_0$ unloaded sphere and an off-set loaded conducting sphere problem of radius $1.0\lambda_0$ were examined. These results afforded much insight into both amplitude and phase solutions for the finite element program, EMSCAT, which was based on that used by Morgan [24]. These results are shown in Figs. 10 and 11.

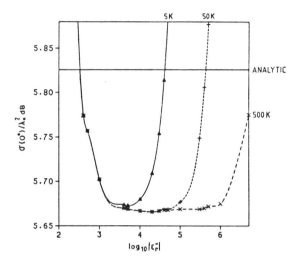

Figure 8   Forward scattering vs. ϵ_r'' within the skin of a $0.4\lambda_0$ radius conducting sphere for various mesh step reductions.

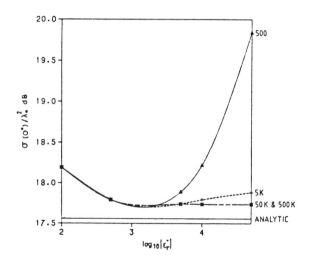

Figure 9   Forward scattering vs. ϵ_r'' within the skin of a $0.8\lambda_0$ radius conducting sphere for various mesh step reductions.

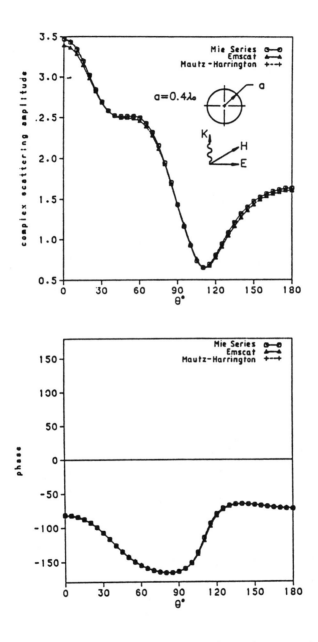

Figure 10 Complex scattering amplitude (magnitude and phase) for $0.4\lambda_0$ unloaded conducting sphere; E-plane pattern with TM incidence.

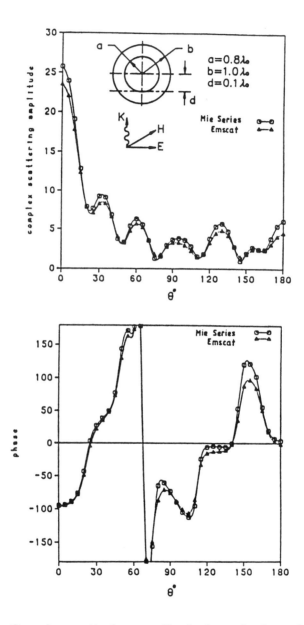

Figure 11   Complex scattering amplitude (magnitude and phase) for loaded offset conducting sphere: $a=0.8\lambda_0$, $b=1.0\lambda_0$, offset$=0.1\lambda_0$, $\epsilon_r=$ 2.60; E-plane pattern with TM incidence.

2.4   Numerical and Experimental Results

Having obtained a basic confidence in the procedure, a second phase of testing was carried out using more arbitrary shapes involving a wide range of radial distances and sharp corners which might better check the skin model. As a means of comparison, a moment method program based on the SIE approach was used [12]. Other results in the form of monostatic and bistatic radar cross sections were also available [1,4].

Figure 12 shows the bistatic results for a loaded ellipsoid, with $a_1 = 0.3\lambda_0, a_2 = 0.5\lambda_0, b_1 = 0.2\lambda_0, b_2 = 0.3\lambda_0$, and $\epsilon'_r = 4.0$. Figure 13 shows the back scattering cross section for an unloaded sphere-cone of base diameter $0.592\lambda_0$ and half angle $40°$. Again the results were reasonably good.

An empirical experiment was also conducted by constructing a range of loaded bicones and accurately measuring the far field scattering. The measurements were carried out at the antenna scattering range at the Defence Research Centre Salisbury (DRCS) in Adelaide, South Australia. Figure 14 shows the monocone pair (a) that screwed together with the various loadings (b)-(f). Monostatic radar cross sections were measured using two polarizations of plane wave (E and H vertical). The measurements were performed at two related frequencies, 9.33 GHz and 4.67 GHz.

Next, the biconical scatterers were numerically analyzed. Up to this point, the cross sectional shapes involved were relatively straight forward to program. With the necessity to model the constructed unloaded and loaded bicones, a more systematic approach was required. The solution was to incorporate a multi-layered capability together with a means of segmenting each contour into elemental shapes, such as sphere, bicone, cylinder etc., each of which was specified within an angular range. This facility, together with a method of varying the permittivity within each layer as the angular evolution is performed, enabled the structures to be modelled.

The back-scattering radar cross sections for the unloaded and loaded bicones, (a) through (f) of Fig. 14, are shown in Figs. 15 to 20. These results were obtained at a frequency of 9.33 GHz. The numerical parameters used were: for the unloaded bicone, $I_{max} = 151$, $N_{max} = 10, M_{max} = 7$ (m = 0,1,2...7), DENS = 31 and for the loaded bicones, $I_{max} = 131, N_{max} = 14, M_{max} = 7$, DENS = 31. Inside the skin region, in all cases, $\epsilon''_r = 500,000$ and the step reduction ratio was

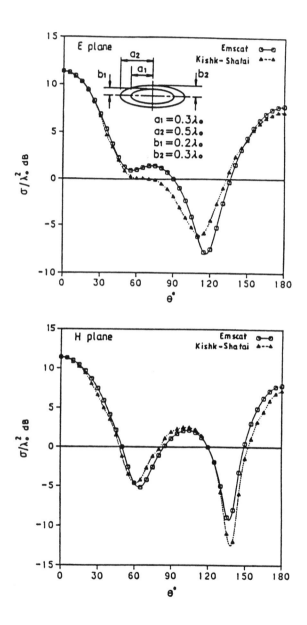

Figure 12 Bistatic radar cross section for a loaded ellipsoid: $a_1=0.3\lambda_0$, $a_2=0.5\lambda_0$, $b_1=0.2\lambda_0$, $b_2=0.3\lambda_0$, $\epsilon'_r = 4.0$; E- and H-plane patterns.

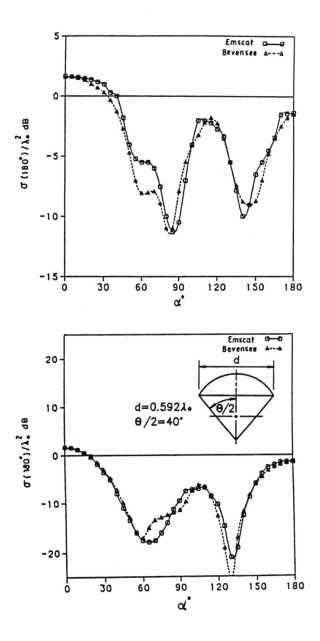

Figure 13 Back scattered radar cross section for an unloaded sphere-cone: base diameter=$0.592\lambda_0$, half-angle=$40°$; E- and H-plane patterns.

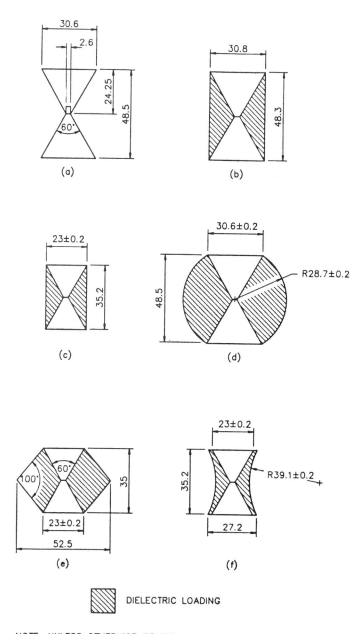

DIELECTRIC LOADING

NOTE: UNLESS OTHERWISE STATED, ALL DIMENSIONS ±0.1mm

Figure 14 Constructed bicone and loadings: (a) Unloaded bicone; (b) -
(f) Various dielectric loadings.

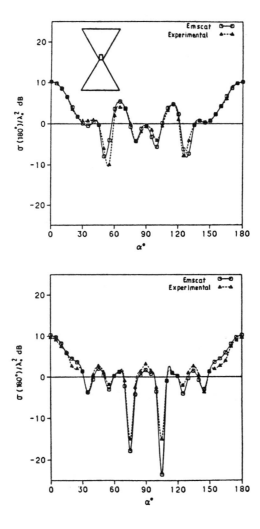

Figure 15   Back scattered radar cross section for the unloaded bicone in Fig. 14(a); (Upper) E**-plane and (Lower)** H**-plane.**

5000. The loading dielectric constant, ϵ_r' was measured to be 2.48. The cross section results for the range $0° - 180°$ were obtained by taking 37 individual problems, $\alpha = 0°, 5°, 10° \ldots 180°$, utilizing the economy of effort of the unimoment method. The errors for bicones (a),(b),(c) and (f) can be seen to be reasonable ($\pm 2dB$) where the experimental and

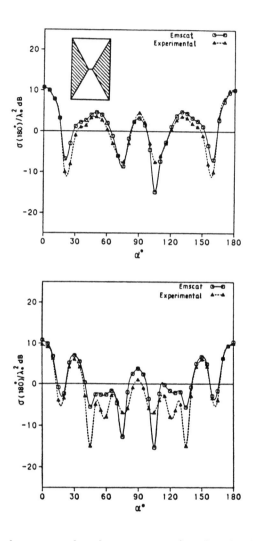

Figure 16 Back scattered radar cross section for the loaded bicone in Fig. 14(b); (Upper) E-plane and (Lower) H-plane.

numerical levels were above their respective noise floors. Loadings in bicones (d) and (e) protrude sufficiently to transverse the cylindrical singularity at $0.64\lambda_0$. The results for bicone (d) indicate the deterioration expected in the range $\theta = 46° - 134°$, while those for bicone (e) confirm that any effect is localized to a smaller range near broadside.

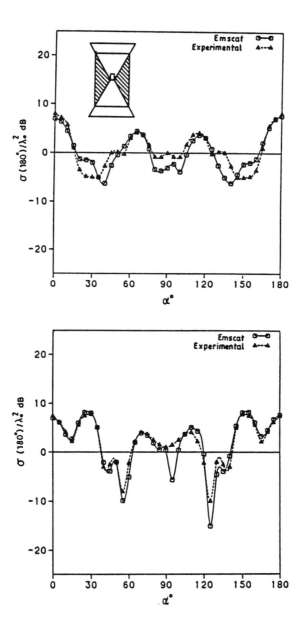

Figure 17 Back scattered radar cross section for the loaded bicone in Fig. 14(c); (Upper) *E*-plane and (Lower) *H*-plane.

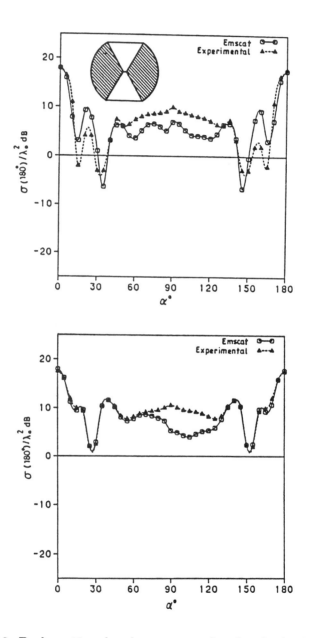

Figure 18   Back scattered radar cross section for the loaded bicone in Fig. 14(d); (Upper) *E*-plane and (Lower) *H*-plane.

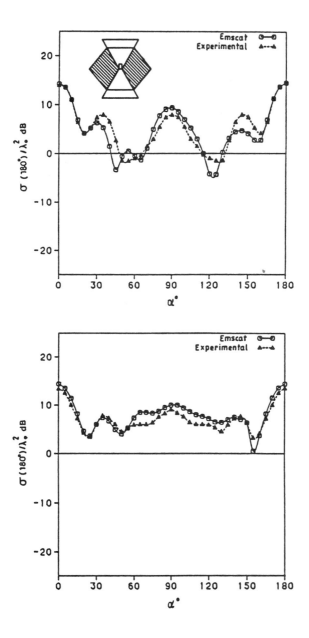

Figure 19 Back scattered radar cross section for the loaded bicone in Fig. 14(e); (Upper) *E*-plane and (Lower) *H*-plane.

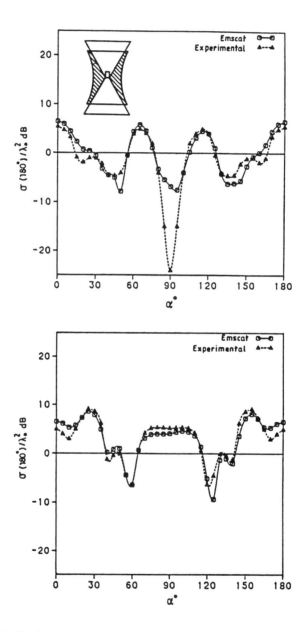

Figure 20   Back scattered radar cross section for the loaded bicone in Fig. 14(f); (Upper) E-plane and (Lower) H-plane.

2.5   Conclusions

The results of the experimental and numerical testing demonstrate inclusion of conductor surfaces within the CAP/unimoment algorithm. The method most successfully applied was the modelling of a thin surface skin region similar to the actual situation at a real conductor surface.

The selection of ϵ_r'' requires careful consideration. Those parts of the structure near the origin necessitate a higher skin permittivity to ensure accurate modelling which leads to extra computing resources such as dynamic range.

The model also requires the overheads associated with the extra nodes of the skin region. By using perfect boundary conditions, such overheads could be avoided at the cost of accuracy. Fortunately, these extra nodes are minimal since the solution form inside the skin is exponentially decaying and linear interpolation can accurately model the decay near the surface at relatively little cost. Throughout the computations, the core region unimoment method was not required which was achieved by setting the internal number of modes to zero. Thus, three extra nodes were included in the mesh beyond the conductor-dielectric interface. The test results of centred unloaded and loaded spheres indicate that accurate results can be obtained in this fashion.

The types of composite objects analyzed in Sections 2.3 and 2.4 were special cases in the sense that in each, the conductor formed the internal core region. Consider the case of a surgically implanted metallic plate which acts as a replacement for the bone covering the brain. In this case, the composite structure is not so straightforward and the conductor does not preclude the internal region if the origin is placed at the brain centre [8]. Structures such as this may be analyzed by inserting two skin regions on each side of the plate as the θ evolution proceeds. By once again ensuring that the number of nodes along each radial is kept fairly constant, the same solution procedure can be used.

2.6   Future Developments

All bodies of revolution may be called azimuthally homogeneous. Other more spatially arbitrary objects can be classified as:

- azimuthally piecewise homogeneous
- azimuthally continuously inhomogeneous with *slow* variations
- azimuthally continuously inhomogeneous with abrupt variations

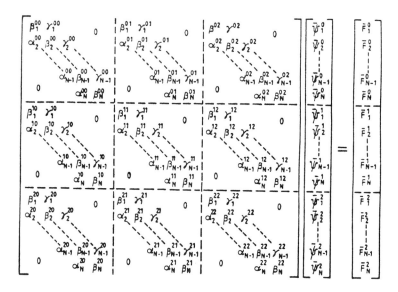

Figure 21   Global system matrix for quasi-axisymmetric case.

Thus, a range of geometries exist that lie between axisymmetric and arbitrarily 3-dimensional objects which can be called piecewise axisymmetric or quasi-axisymmetric.

Material objects whose constitutive properties vary around the azimuth form important modern problems. The human body might be approximated in a piecewise axisymmetric fashion. Nebular gases such as plume exhaust form an example of *slow* axial inhomogeneity. Likewise, there are structures that exhibit abrupt azimuthal discontinuities such as a half-sphere which is aligned with its equator along the Z-axis.

Many of the concepts behind the axisymmetric CAP/unimoment method are capable of being generalized to allow the solution of these more arbitrary electromagnetic problems (*Editor's Note:* See Chapter 6). Quasi-axisymmetric objects may be analyzed by using a fully coupled version of the CAP equations [23]. In addition to the spectral series for the fields, a second series for azimuthal variations in the constitutive parameters $\epsilon(\rho, \theta, \phi)$ and $\mu(\rho, \theta, \phi)$ can be used. Maxwell's equations no longer decouple or reduce at each mode and all 6 modal variables are required. However the resulting system, illustrated in Fig. 21 has a Toeplitz-like replication and importantly the unimoment

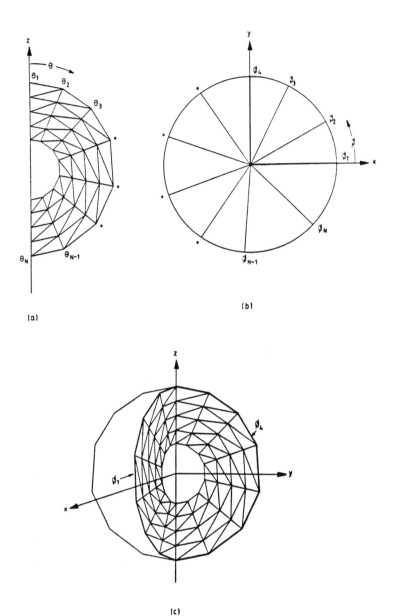

Figure 22 Azimuthally segmented mesh for the piecewise axisymmetric case: (a) Meridian section, (b) Azimuthal segments, (c) Open view of 3-D mesh structure.

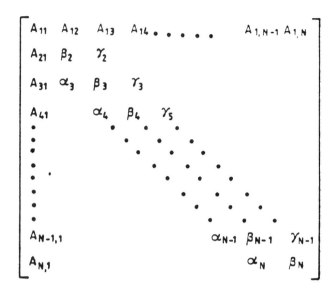

Figure 23   Global system matrix for piecewise axisymmetric case.

method can be applied to ensure continuity of the fields at the freespace separable contour. Although the submatrices are sparse, the overall matrix is dense and is now $3m$ times the size of the axisymmetric matrix, where m is the number of azimuthal modes required.

Continuous spectral functions are most appropriate in the axisymmetric and quasi-axisymmetric cases where the fields are azimuthally smooth. Other bases can be used for problems involving azimuthal discontinuities. Spectral functions, periodic in higher multiples of 2π such as 4π etc., or non-periodic bases including monomial functions may be used to account for jump discontinuities [28]. Piecewise spectral functions result in a piecewise axisymmetric formulation where the axisymmetric CAPs may be used within an azimuthal segment.

The axisymmetric conformal mesh generation procedure illustrated in Fig. 5 can be projected around the azimuth to sectionally conform to a three dimensional contour of arbitrary shape. As with the axisymmetric mesh, multi-layered objects or continuously inhomogeneous objects can be mapped. Figure 22 shows an azimuthally segmented mesh while the resulting submatrix structure is shown in Fig. 23. The topology is interesting in that a star connection forms along the Z-axis. A

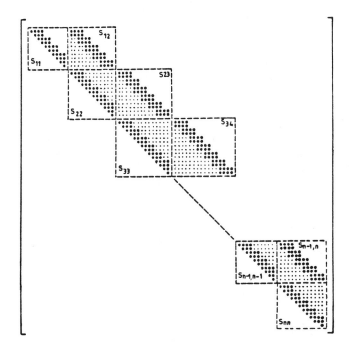

Figure 24   Sparse LU-decomposition of a block tridiagonal matrix.

simpler submatrix can be achieved where the region along the Z-axis is axisymmetric; here the unimoment method can be used to account for the possibly layered core regions.

Direct methods for solving large sparse systems of equations often suffer from complete fill-in of the submatrices. The Riccati transformation, as employed in Section 2.3 c., is one such method. Sparse factorization can avoid unnecessary computations resulting from fill-in. Recently, direct and iterative sparse factorization methods have been reported where the filled-in terms decay rapidly and may be ignored upon reaching some predetermined residual measure [29]. Such schemes would appear to be well suited to the present application and to the above suggestions for analyzing non-axisymmetric problems. Figure 24 illustrates Choleski LU factorization as applied to block-tridiagonal systems. The work factor using complete submatrix inversion is $O(n^3)$, where n is the dimension of a particular submatrix; it can be shown that this is reduced to order $O(r^2n)$ where r is a reduced bandwidth resulting from ignoring the residual fill-in terms.

Acknowledgements

The author would like to thank the management and staff of the Department of Defence, both at Victoria Barracks in Melbourne and at Salisbury in Adelaide, for their support and assistance. He also wishes to thank Prof. Michael Morgan (The Naval Postgraduate School, Monterey, CA) for his detailed communications. A debt of thanks is due to the author's supervisors, Dr. Don Sinnott (Defence Research Centre Salisbury, South Aust.) and Dr. Ken Mann (Chisholm Institute of Technology, Caulfield, Victoria). Dr. Stan Davies (Telecom Research Laboratories, Clayton) kindly assisted in the preparation of this document.

References

[1] Bevensee, R. M., *A Handbook of Conical Antennas and Scatterers*, Gordon and Breach Science Publishers, 1975.

[2] Stovall, R. E., and K. K. Mei, "Application of a unimoment technique to a biconical antenna with inhomogeneous loading", *IEEE Trans. Antennas Propagat.*, **AP-23**, 335–341, 1975.

[3] Govind, S., D. R. Wilton, and A. W. Glisson, "Scattering from inhomogeneous penetrable bodies of revolution," *IEEE Trans. on Antennas and Propagat.*, **AP-32**, 1163–1173, 1984.

[4] Kishk, A. A., and L. Shafai, "Numerical solution of scattering from coated bodies of revolution using different integral equation formulations", *IEE Proceedings*, **133**, Pt. H, No. 3, 1986.

[5] Joyner, A. H., B. Hocking, A. H. J. Fleming, and I. P. Macfarlane, "Metallic implants and exposure to RF radiation," *Radiation Protection Practice: Proc. IRPA 7th Int. Congress*, **1**, 477-484, 1988.

[6] Mei, K. K., "Unimoment method of solving antenna and scattering problems," *IEEE Trans. Antennas Propagat.*, **AP-22**, 760–766, 1974.

[7] Morgan, M. A., S. K. Chang, and K. K. Mei, "Coupled azimuthal potentials for electromagnetic field problems in axially symmetric media," *IEEE Trans. Antennas Propagat.*, **AP-25**, 413–417, 1977.

[8] Morgan, M. A., "Finite element computation of microwave absorption by the cranial structure," *IEEE Trans. Biomedical Eng.*, **BME-28**, 687–696, 1981.

[9] Durney, C. H., "EM dosimetry for models of humans and animals: a review of theoretical and numerical techniques," *Proc. IEEE*, **68**, 33–40, 1980.

[10] Moilel, R. A., S. K. Wolfson, Jr., R. G. Selker, and S. B. Weiner, "Materials for selective tissue heating in a radiofrequency EM field for the combined chemothermal treatment of brain tumors," *J. Biomed. Mater. Res.*, **10**, 327–334, 1976.

[11] Brebbia, C. A., "The boundary element method," Short Course Notes, Chisholm Institute of Technology, August 23–25, 1983.

[12] Mautz, J. R., and R. F. Harrington, "H-field, E-field and combined field solutions for conducting bodies of revolution," *AEU*, **32**, 157–164, 1978.

[13] Wu, T. K., and L. L. Tsai, "Scattering from arbitrarily-shaped lossy dielectric bodies of revolution," *Radio Science*, **12**, 709–718, 1977.

[14] Harrington, R. F., *Field Computation by Moment Methods*, New York: MacMillan, 1968.

[15] Hagmann, M. J., O. P. Gandhi, J. D'Andrea, and I. Chaterjee, "Head resonance: numerical solutions and experimental results," *IEEE Trans. Microwave Theory Tech.*, **MTT-27**, 809–813, 1979.

[16] Lynn, P. P., and H. A. Hadid, "Infinite elements with $1/r$ type decay," *Int. Journal for Numerical Methods in Engineering*, **17**, 347–355, 1981.

[17] Chiang, K. S., "Finite element method for cutoff frequencies of weakly guiding fibres of arbitrary cross-section," *Optical and Quantum Electronics*, **16**, 487–493, 1984.

[18] Morgan, M. A., and B. E. Welch, "The field feedback formulation for electromagnetic scattering computations," *IEEE Trans. on Antennas and Propagat.*, **AP-34**, 1377–1382, 1986.

[19] Morgan, M. A., and K. K. Mei, "Finite element computation of scattering by inhomogeneous bodies of revolution," *IEEE Trans. Antennas Propagat.*, **AP-27**, 203–214, 1979.

[20] Morgan, M. A., "Finite element computation of microwave scattering by raindrops," *Radio Science*, **15**, 1109–1119, 1980.

[21] Chang, H., and K. K. Mei, "Scattering of EM waves by buried or partly buried body of revolution," *IEEE Symposium on Antennas and Propagat.*, 653–656, 1981.

[22] Gupta, G. S., and A. Hizal, "Accounting for the tip scattering in radome analysis," *3rd Int. Conference on Antennas and Propagat., IEE*, 521–524, 1983.

[23] Fleming, A. H. J., *Numerical Analysis of Electromagnetic Scattering by Axisymmetric Inhomogeneous Composite Antenna Structures*, M. App. Sc. Thesis, Faculty of Technology, Chisholm Inst. of Tech., Caulfield, Australia, 1987.

[24] Morgan, M. A., *Numerical Computation of EM Scattering by Inhomogeneous Dielectric Bodies of Revolution*, Ph. D. Thesis, Dept. of Elec. Eng. and Comp. Sc., Univ. of California, Berkeley, Calif., 1976.

[25] Morgan, M. A., C. H. Chen, S. C. Hill, and P. W. Barber, "Finite element-boundary integral formulation for electromagnetic scattering," *Wave Motion*, North Holland, **6**, 91–103, 1984.

[26] King, R. W. P., and C. W. Harrison, Jr., *Antennas and Waves - A Modern Approach*, M.I.T. Press, Massachusetts, Chap. 4, 1969.

[27] Fleming, A. H. J., "Finite element solution to scattering from dielectrically loaded spheres," *Computational Techniques and Applications: CTAC-85*, Eds. J. Noye and C. Fletcher, North Holland, 763–774, 1986.

[28] Morgan, M. A., private communication, 1986.

[29] Lipitakis, E. A., "Generalized extended to the limit sparse factorization techniques for solving unsymmetric finite element systems," *Computing*, **32**, 255–270, 1984.

3

COUPLED FINITE ELEMENT AND BOUNDARY ELEMENT METHODS IN ELECTROMAGNETIC SCATTERING

K. L. Wu, G. Y. Delisle, D. G. Fang and M. Lecours

3.1   Introduction

The problem of electromagnetic scattering by various objects has always been a subject of interest for researchers in various disciplines. Many analytical and numerical methods have been proposed in order to handle the numerous electromagnetic scattering situations. For example, numerical techniques are available [1–3] to solve the integral equation which arises in the formulation of the induced or polarized current on or inside objects of various shapes. These techniques, however, lead to very tedious computations when a complicated structure is involved as well as to numerical evaluations that are most impractical when dealing with multi-media problems. The unimoment method calls for a finite element representation of the field inside the object while the scattered field is represented with an eigenfunction series expansion [4]. The boundary conditions, either physical or mathematical, are well-defined for a given boundary but only the circle appears to be a convenient computational choice in 2-D problems. Furthermore, in the original version of the unimoment method an inaccurate finite difference evaluation of the normal derivative of the numerical solution is used in the enforcement of continuity at the boundary with the normal derivative of the external cylindrical harmonic scattered field expansion.

More recently, the Boundary Element Method (BEM) [5] has been applied to electromagnetic scattering problems [6,7]. The main advantage of the BEM is the need to discretize only the boundary; in contrast, the Finite Element Method (FEM) considers the entire domain. Furthermore, it can easily take into account the radiation condition for unbounded situations such as scattering problems. A disadvantage of the BEM is that it leads to a fully populated system of equations, which is non-symmetric, in contrast with the sparsely populated and symmetric stiffness matrix obtained from the FEM. The BEM is usually restricted to homogeneous and isotropic problems because of the difficulty in seeking the needed fundamental solution for inhomogeneous and anisotropic problems. This weakness of the BEM does not encourage a search for the systematic solution to general problems with multi-media and anisotropic domains. The FEM is superior to the BEM in such cases, but it is difficult to introduce the radiation condition without increasing the requirements either in computer speed or storage capacity [9,10]. These facts suggest that a form of coupling between these two methods would be of great interest in many practical problems.

The main objective of this chapter is to present a combined FEM-BEM method that can be used to solve the scattering fields by an inhomogeneous arbitrary isotropic scatterer. This method can also be extended to handle the case of anisotropic materials with only slight modifications. In the proposed method, called coupled finite boundary element method (CFBM), an analytic relation between the field and its derivative on the boundary is used; no artificial boundary is needed. The importance of this feature is obvious when the scattering object is long and slender. Furthermore, the proposed method does not suffer from having non-unique solutions in the resonance case. We analyze several examples, and compare the results with those obtained by the BEM to validate our combined FEM-BEM method.

3.2   General Formulation

a. The Problem

To minimize the details, only the two-dimensional case is discussed. The domain of the problem is divided into two regions. One is the interior region R which includes the scatterer and is enclosed completely by the boundary, B, as shown in Fig. 1. B may be the physical boundary of the scatterer, but is not necessarily so. Another is the exterior region enclosed by B and the infinite boundary.

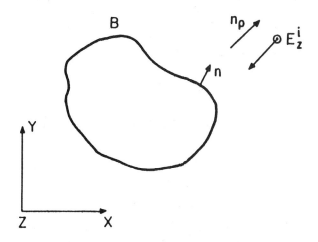

Figure 1   Two-dimensional dielectric scattering problem.

So the two-dimensional scattering problem can be treated mathematically as two separate problems. One can be considered as a closed boundary value problem which is described by the following differential equation (see Fig. 1)

$$(\nabla^2 + k^2)\, u' = 0 \ \text{ in } R \tag{1}$$

$$u' = \underline{u} \ \text{ on } B \tag{2}$$

$$q' = \underline{q} \ \text{ on } B \tag{3}$$

where q' is the outward normal derivative of u', $k = \sqrt{\epsilon_0 \epsilon_r \mu_0}$ and $\underline{u}, \underline{q}$ are known values.

The other can be regarded as an unbounded case and is expressed in integral equation form over the domain bounded by C, defined as the boundary B and the infinity as

$$u'(\bar{r}_f) = \int_C \left[\phi(\bar{r}_f | \bar{r}_o) \frac{\partial u(\bar{r}_o)}{\partial n'} - u(\bar{r}_o) \frac{\partial \phi(\bar{r}_f | \bar{r}_o)}{\partial n'} \right] d\Gamma + u^i(\bar{r}_f) \qquad (4)$$

where $u^i(\bar{r})$ and $u(\bar{r})$ are the incident and the scattered fields respectively, $u(\bar{r})$ satisfies the radiation condition, $\hat{n}'$ is an outward unit vector normal to the boundary C of outside region, $\bar{r}_f$ is an arbitrary field point and $\bar{r}_o$ is a point on the boundary.

In (4), the fundamental solution

$$\phi(\bar{r}_f | \bar{r}_o) = -\frac{j}{4} H_0^{(2)}(k | \bar{r}_f - \bar{r}_o|) \qquad (5)$$

is introduced, where $H_0^{(2)}(\cdot)$ is the Hankel function of the second kind and zero order.

b. Finite Element Method (FEM)

With the finite element approach, the primary dependent variables are replaced by a system of discretized variables over the domain under consideration. Therefore, the domain itself is discretized into finite elements which are connected at the nodals. The compatibility within the element and between element boundaries is ensured by the choice of the shape function. In the present analysis, the region R is discretized into a number of second order triangular elements as shown in Fig. 2.

Within an arbitrary shaped triangle, the field value u is written in terms of second-order complete polynomials as

$$u = \{N\}^T \{u\}_e \qquad (6)$$

where

$$\{N\} = [N_1, N_2, N_3, N_4, N_5, N_6]^T \qquad (7a)$$

and

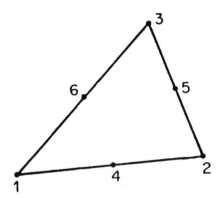

Figure 2   Second-order triangular element.

$${\{u_i\}}_e = [u_1, u_2, u_3, u_4, u_5, u_6]_e^T \tag{7b}$$

u_i being the field at the ith nodal point of the element. Column vectors are denoted by $\{\cdot\}$ while $\{\cdot\}^T$ represents a row vector where a T superscript denotes transpose. The shape functions N_1 through N_6 are given by

$$N_1 = L_1(2L_1 - 1) \tag{8a}$$

$$N_2 = L_2(2L_2 - 1) \tag{8b}$$

$$N_3 = L_3(2L_3 - 1) \tag{8c}$$

$$N_4 = 4L_1 L_2 \tag{8d}$$

$$N_5 = 4L_2 L_3 \tag{8e}$$

$$N_6 = 4L_1 L_3 \tag{8f}$$

where L_1, L_2 and L_3 are the area coordinates in the finite element approach. Substituting (6) into (1) and using a Galerkin procedure, after integrating by parts, results in

$$
\begin{bmatrix} [A_{RR}] & [A_{RB}] \\ [A_{BR}] & [A_{BB}] \end{bmatrix} \left\{ \begin{matrix} \{u'\}_R \\ \{u'\}_B \end{matrix} \right\} = \left\{ \begin{matrix} \{0\} \\ [B_B] \left\{ \dfrac{\partial u'}{\partial n} \right\}_B \end{matrix} \right\} \tag{9}
$$

where the matrix on the left hand side can be computed by using

$$
\begin{bmatrix} [A_{RR}] & [A_{RB}] \\ [A_{BR}] & [A_{BB}] \end{bmatrix} = \sum_e \iint \left[\frac{\partial \{N\}}{\partial x} \cdot \frac{\partial \{N\}^T}{\partial x} + \frac{\partial \{N\}}{\partial y} \cdot \frac{\partial \{N\}^T}{\partial y} \right.
$$

$$
\left. - \epsilon_r (1 - \jmath \tan \delta) k_0^2 \{N\}\{N\}^T \right] dx \, dy \tag{10}
$$

and

$$
[B_B] = \sum_e{}' \int_e \{N\}\{N\}^T \, d\Gamma \tag{11}
$$

In these equations, $k_0 = \omega^2 \epsilon_0 \mu_0$ and $\tan \delta$ is the loss tangent. The integral in (10) can be calculated analytically, and for a second order finite element, (11) can be expressed as

$$
[B_B] = \sum_e{}' \frac{l_e}{15} \begin{bmatrix} 2 & 1 & -0.5 \\ 1 & 8 & 1 \\ -0.5 & 1 & 2 \end{bmatrix} \tag{12}
$$

The components of $\{u'\}_R$ correspond to the nodal values in R and $\{u'\}_B$ on B, $\sum_e$ and $\sum_e'$ extend over all the different elements and elements related to boundary B respectively. The l_e is the length of e-th boundary element. Equation (9) is the FEM matrix equation.

c. Boundary Element Method (BEM)

The region under consideration for the exterior problem is enclosed by boundary B and a boundary at infinity. Because the radiation condition cannot be applied for the incident wave, the scattering wave should vanish at infinity. Equation (4) is then rewritten as

$$u(\bar{r}_f) = \int_B \left[\phi(\bar{r}_f|\bar{r}_o)\frac{\partial u(\bar{r}_o)}{\partial n'} - u(\bar{r}_o)\frac{\partial \phi(\bar{r}_f|\bar{r}_o)}{\partial n'} \right] d\Gamma \qquad (13)$$

$$u'(\bar{r}_f) = u(\bar{r}_f) + u^i(\bar{r}_f) \qquad (14)$$

If field point $\bar{r}_f$ is placed on the boundary B, a singularity will occur. To extract the contribution of the singularity, the integration path ΔB going around the point $\bar{r}_f$ is considered. Denoting $\partial u/\partial n'$ as q, (13) is rewritten as follows

$$u(\bar{r}_f) = \left[\lim_{\epsilon \to 0} \int_{B'} q\phi \, d\Gamma + \lim_{\epsilon \to 0} \int_{\Delta B} q\phi \, d\Gamma \right]$$

$$- \left[\lim_{\epsilon \to 0} \int_{B'} u\frac{\partial \phi}{\partial n'} \, d\Gamma + \lim_{\epsilon \to 0} \int_{\Delta B} u\frac{\partial \phi}{\partial n'} \, d\Gamma \right] \qquad (15)$$

The integrations over the boundary ΔB can be estimated by using the small argument asymptotic expression of the Hankel function

$$\lim_{\epsilon \to 0} \int_{\Delta B} u\frac{\partial \phi}{\partial n'} \, d\Gamma = \lim_{\epsilon \to 0} \int_{\Delta B} u\frac{1}{4}kH_1^{(2)}(k\epsilon) \, d\Gamma$$

$$= u\frac{1}{4}kH_1^{(2)}(k\epsilon)\epsilon\theta$$

$$= \frac{1}{4}k\theta u \lim_{\epsilon \to 0} \left[\epsilon \left\{ \frac{k\epsilon}{2} - j(\frac{2}{\pi}\frac{1}{k\epsilon}) \right\} \right]$$

$$= \frac{\theta}{2\pi}u(\bar{r}_f) \qquad (16)$$

$$\lim_{\epsilon \to 0} \int_{\Delta B} q\phi \, d\Gamma = \lim_{\epsilon \to 0} \int_{\Delta B} q\{\tfrac{\jmath}{4} H_0^{(2)}(k\epsilon)\} \, d\Gamma$$

$$= \lim_{\epsilon \to 0} \left[\frac{-\jmath}{4} q \left\{ 1 - \jmath \frac{2}{\pi} (ln(k\epsilon) + \gamma - ln2) \right\} \epsilon\theta \right]$$

$$= 0 \tag{17}$$

This then yields

$$(1 - \frac{\theta}{2\pi}) u_i(\overline{r}_f) + \int_B \frac{\partial \phi(\overline{r}_f | \overline{r}_0)}{\partial n'} u(\overline{r}_0) \, d\Gamma$$

$$= \int_B \phi(\overline{r}_f | \overline{r}_0) \frac{\partial u(\overline{r}_0)}{\partial n'} \, d\Gamma \tag{18}$$

with

$$\int_B = \lim_{\epsilon \to 0} \int_{B'}$$

where a Cauchy's principal value of integration is assumed in this case.

An approximate solution to (18) can be obtained by discretizing the boundary into the so-called boundary elements. These elements are similar to finite elements except that their dimensions are usually one less than the dimensions of the problem. For the present analysis, second-order boundary elements are used for the sake of compatibility with the second-order finite elements (Fig. 3).

Within each elements, u and q are defined respectively in terms of u_l and q_l at the three nodal points, $l = 1, 2, 3$, by using

$$u = \{M\}^T \{u\}_e \tag{19a}$$

$$q = \{M\}^T \{q\}_e \tag{19b}$$

where

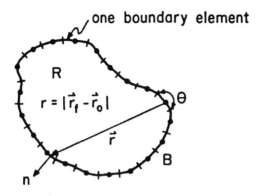

Figure 3   Integration on each boundary element.

$${u}_e = [u_1, u_2, u_3]^T \tag{20a}$$

$${q}_e = [q_1, q_2, q_3]^T \tag{20b}$$

$${M} = [M_1, M_2, M_3]^T \tag{20c}$$

The boundary element shape function, M_l, is given by

$$M_l = A_l \xi^2 + B_l \xi + C_l \tag{21}$$

where

$$A_1 = 1/2, \ A_2 = 1/2, \ A_3 = -1$$

$$B_1 = -1/2, \ B_2 = 1/2, \ B_3 = 0$$

and

$$C_1 = 0, \ C_2 = 0, \ C_3 = 1$$

When the normalized coordinate, ξ, is defined on the e-th boundary element, it can be easily checked that M_1, M_2, M_3 are equal to the finite element shape functions evaluated on the boundary. This characteristic aids in making the coupling of the FEM and the BEM accurate.

Substituting (9a),(9b) into (18), we obtain

$$\left[1 - \frac{\theta}{2\pi}\right] u_i + \sum_{e=1}^{N} [h_1, h_2, h_3]_e \left\{ \begin{array}{c} u_1 \\ u_2 \\ u_3 \end{array} \right\} = \sum_{e=1}^{N} [g_1, g_2, g_3]_e \left\{ \begin{array}{c} q_1 \\ q_2 \\ q_3 \end{array} \right\} \quad (22)$$

When the nodal point i does not belong to the e-th element, h_l and g_l can be calculated with Gaussian integration as

$$h_l = \frac{L}{2} \int_{-1}^{1} M_l \frac{\partial \phi(\overline{r}_f | \overline{r}_o)}{\partial n'} \, d\xi \quad (23)$$

$$g_l = \frac{l}{2} \int_{-1}^{1} M_l \phi(\overline{r}_f | \overline{r}_o) \, d\xi \quad (24)$$

where L is the length of the element. When the nodal point i belongs to the e-th element, considering the limit of $\epsilon \to 0$, we can get

$$h_l = 0 \quad (25)$$

and if the nodal point, i, coincides with the nodal point $l = 1, 2,$ or 3, g_l is given by [8]

$$g_l = (\frac{L}{2})[A_l I_2(2) - (2A_l - B_l)\{I_1(2) - 2/(\pi k^2 L^2)\}$$

$$+ (A_l - B_l + C_l) I_0(2)] \quad (26a)$$

$$g_l = (\frac{L}{2})[A_l I_2(2) - (2A_l + B_l)\{I_1(2) - 2/(\pi k^2 L^2)\}$$

$$+ (A_l + B_l + C_l) I_0(2)] \quad (26b)$$

$$g_l = L[A_l I_2(1) + C_l I_0(1)] \quad (26c)$$

respectively. Here I_0, I_1, and I_2 are calculated as follows:

$$I_0(\eta) = \int \frac{1}{4j} H_0^{(2)} \left[\frac{kL}{2}\eta\right] d\eta = -\frac{\eta}{4} \sum_{v=0}^{\infty} \frac{(-1)^v}{(2v+1)(v!)^2} \left[\frac{kL}{4}\eta\right]^{2v}$$

$$\cdot \left[\frac{2}{\pi}\left\{\gamma + \ln\left[\frac{kL}{4}\eta\right] - \frac{1}{2v+1} - \sum_{s=1}^{v}\frac{1}{s}\right\} + j\right] \tag{27a}$$

$$I_1(\eta) = \int \frac{\eta}{4j} H_0^{(2)} \left[\frac{kL}{2}\eta\right] d\eta = \frac{1}{4j}\frac{2\eta}{kL} H_1^{(2)} \left[\frac{kL}{2}\eta\right] \tag{27b}$$

$$I_2(\eta) = \int \frac{\eta^2}{4j} H_0^{(2)} \left[\frac{kL}{2}\eta\right] d\eta \tag{27c}$$

$$= \left[\frac{2}{kL}\right]^2 \left[\frac{kL}{2}\frac{\eta^2}{4j} H_1^{(2)} \left[\frac{kL}{2}\eta\right] + \frac{\eta}{4j} H_0^{(2)} \left[\frac{kL}{2}\eta\right] - I_0(\eta)\right]$$

where $\gamma = 0.57721...$ is Euler's constant. In matrix notation, (22) can be written as

$$\left[H_0\right]\left\{u\right\}_B = \left[G_0\right]\left\{q\right\}_B \tag{28}$$

This BEM matrix equation is to be used later on.

d. Combination of the FEM with BEM

Since the fundamental solution that is chosen for the BEM equation in the exterior region satisfies the radiation condition, it is not necessary to deal with the boundary at infinity. The FEM cannot, however, easily take into account this radiation condition. On the other hand, it is superior to the BEM in handling multi-media problems. In the proposed method, the BEM is therefore used for the region outside the boundary B, which may be the actual boundary of the obstacle, or any artificial geometrical boundary set up for the convenience of treating multi-media problems; fields inside of B are treated by the

FEM, with the interior and exterior problems being separately solved first and these solutions being subsequently coupled.

Figure 2 shows a second order finite element. Both boundary element and finite element are connected on the interface B. To ensure a correct coupling of boundary and finite elements at the interface, conditions of compatibility and equilibrium must be satisfied. The compatibility condition can be reached if both elements have common nodals at the interface and if the shape functions describing the field variation at the interface are identical for the BEM and the FEM. The equilibrium is satisfied when the field normal derivatives at the nodal point of the boundary element mesh are equal and opposite to that of the finite element mesh at the interface. So, on the boundary B, the following boundary conditions must be satisfied

$$\{u'\}_B = \{u\}_B + \{u^i\}_B \tag{29}$$

$$-V^I\left(\{\frac{\partial u'}{\partial n}\}_B\right) = V^{II}\left(\{\frac{\partial u}{\partial n'}\}_B + \{\frac{\partial u^i}{\partial n'}\}_B\right) \tag{30}$$

$$u = \begin{cases} E_z & \text{for TM case} \\ \\ H_z & \text{for TE case} \end{cases} \tag{31}$$

$$V^I = \begin{cases} 1.0 & \text{for TM case} \\ \\ \dfrac{1}{\epsilon_{r_I}} & \text{for TE case} \end{cases} \tag{32}$$

$$V^{II} = \begin{cases} 1.0 & \text{for TM case} \\ \\ \dfrac{1}{\epsilon_{r_{II}}} & \text{for TE case} \end{cases} \tag{33}$$

where ϵ_{r_I} and $\epsilon_{r_{II}}$ are the relative permittivities of the interior and the exterior, respectively. In addition, the incident wave is expressed as follows

$$u^i = u_0 \exp(jk|\bar{\rho}|) \tag{34}$$

The coordinate $\bar{\rho}$ is chosen in the direction of the incident wave and it is easy to obtain

$$q^i = \frac{\partial u^i}{\partial n} = -j k \hat{n} \cdot \hat{n}_\rho u^i \tag{35}$$

which can be expressed as

$$\{q^i\}_B = [D]\{u^i\}_B \tag{36}$$

where $[D]$ is a diagonal coefficient matrix.

Equations (29) and (30) form the bridge between the two different regions. This bridge connects FEM equation (9) with BEM equation (28). By substituting (29), (30), and (36) into (9) and merging (9) and (28) into one matrix relationship, the following is obtained for both interior and exterior regions

$$\begin{bmatrix} [A_{RR}] & [A_{RB}] & [0] \\ [A_{BR}] & [A_{BB}] & -[B_B] \\ [0] & [H_0] & [G_0] \end{bmatrix} \begin{Bmatrix} \{u\}_R \\ \{u^s\}_B \\ \{q^s\}_B \end{Bmatrix} = \begin{Bmatrix} -[A_{RB}]\{u^i\}_B \\ ([B_B][D] - [A_{BB}])\{u^i\}_B \\ \{0\} \end{Bmatrix} \tag{37}$$

With the help of (37), the scattered field and its normal derivative on the boundary B can be obtained provided that the incident wave is given. These quantities correspond to surface electric and magnetic sources. Generally we are interested in observable quantities in the far field, the solution of the final matrix equation (37) being merely an intermediate step. In the following, the results of the scattered fields are given. With the scattered fields, the radar cross section is easily obtained.

Using the asymptotic expression of the Hankel function, the far field pattern can be found by a modification of (16) as follows

$$E_z \Big|_{r \to \infty} = A \left[\sum_{e=1}^{N} [g_1', g_2', g_3']_e \begin{Bmatrix} q_1^s \\ q_2^s \\ q_3^s \end{Bmatrix}_e - \sum_{e=1}^{N} [h_1', h_2', h_3']_e \begin{Bmatrix} u_1^s \\ u_2^s \\ u_3^s \end{Bmatrix}_e \right] \tag{38}$$

with

$$h_1' = jk \int_{-1}^{1} (\frac{1}{2}\xi_2 - \frac{1}{2}\xi) \cos{(\bar{r}, \hat{n})} \, e^{-jk\Delta r} \, d\xi \qquad (39)$$

$$h_2' = jk \int_{-1}^{1} (\frac{1}{2}\xi_2 + \frac{1}{2}\xi) \cos{(\bar{r}, \hat{n})} \, e^{-jk\Delta r} \, d\xi \qquad (40)$$

$$h_3' = jk \int_{-1}^{1} (-\xi_2 + 1) \cos{(\bar{r}, \hat{n})} \, e^{-jk\Delta r} \, d\xi \qquad (41)$$

$$g_1' = \int_{-1}^{1} (\frac{1}{2}\xi_2 - \frac{1}{2}\xi) \, e^{-jk\Delta r} d\xi \qquad (42)$$

$$g_2' = \int_{-1}^{1} (\frac{1}{2}\xi_2 + \frac{1}{2}\xi) \, e^{-jk\Delta r} d\xi \qquad (43)$$

$$g_3' = - \int_{-1}^{1} (-\xi_2 + 1) \, e^{jk\Delta r} d\xi \qquad (44)$$

where Δr is the relative distance difference over the incoming wavefront and A is a constant amplitude.

Equation (38) is the expression sought-after for the scattered far field in terms of the surface electric and magnetic currents when the BEM is used for the outer region.

3.3   Implementation and Numerical Results

To show the validity and the implementation of the combined method, several examples are discussed. The procedure of solving a given problem using CFBM may be divided into three basic steps. First, it is necessary to choose a boundary B. The rule of thumb is to enclose the scatterer completely and let the interior domain be as small as possible in order to minimize the number of unknowns in the FEM mesh. If the near field distribution is required, the boundary B can be extended as far as needed, but at the expense of the computational effort. The second step in the solution development involves dividing the interior region into finite elements. Each element should be homogeneous; otherwise the inhomogeneous element technique must be used by slightly modifying equation (10). In fact, boundary elements are formed sequentially after finite element generation because boundary elements are just the finite elements on the boundary B. It should be noted that nodal numbering must be such that the boundary nodes of the interior region are identical to those of the exterior region. The final step in solving the problem is to fill in the matrix equation as described in section 2 and to solve it.

As a first example, a layered dielectric square cylinder is investigated ($\epsilon_1 = 2.89$, $\epsilon_2 = 1.0$, $\epsilon_3 = 2.89$) and the results are shown in Fig. 4 in dotted line. A dielectric hollow square cylinder is also analyzed with the same program and the results are plotted using a solid line on Fig. 4. It agrees well with the BEM solution of Yashiro and Ohkawa [7] which is superposed on our solution with triangular points for comparison purposes.

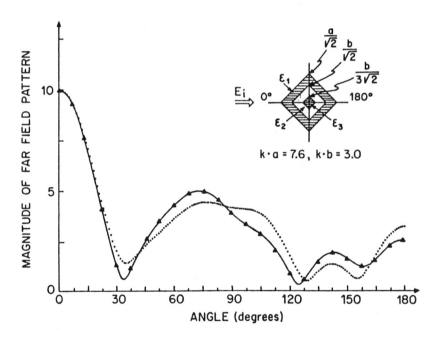

Figure 4 Far-field pattern for layered-square cylinders:
$\cdots$ **CFBM result for layered square cylinder ($\epsilon_1 = \epsilon_3 =2.89$, $\epsilon_2 =1.0$)**
— **CFBM result for hollow square cylinder**
▲▲ **BEM result for hollow square cylinder ($\epsilon_1 =2.89$, $\epsilon_2 = \epsilon_3 =1.0$).**

The second example is the scattering by the composite structure of a multi-dielectric cylinder ($\epsilon_1 = \epsilon_3 = 1.0$, $\epsilon_2 = 2.89$), as shown in

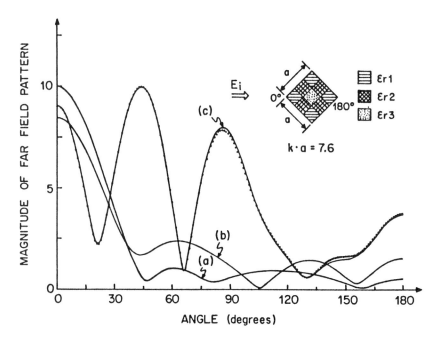

Figure 5 Far-field pattern for composite cylinders:
(a) — CFBM for composite cylinder ($\epsilon_1 = \epsilon_3 = 1.0$, $\epsilon_2 = 2.89$)
(b) — CFBM for cross dielectric cylinder ($\epsilon_1 = 1.0$, $\epsilon_2 = \epsilon_3 = 2.89$)
(c) — CFBM for dielectric square cylinder with $\epsilon_r = 2.89$
    $\cdots$ BEM solution for the dielectric square cylinder.

Fig. 5 (solid line (a)). Two special cases are also considered: one is the cross-dielectric cylinder ($\epsilon_1 = 1.0, \epsilon_2 = \epsilon_3 = 2.89$) (solid line (b)), the other is the dielectric square cylinder ($\epsilon_1 = \epsilon_2 = \epsilon_3 = 2.89$) (solid line (c)). The BEM result for the square cylinder case is also given (dotted line) for the purpose of checking the validity of our method.

Figure 6 shows the far field pattern corresponding to a perfectly conducting circular cylinder with dielectric periodic load. In this example, only the dielectric coated ring domain needs to be treated as the interior region. It should be noticed that the change of ϵ_r may cause large differences in the far field pattern. A comparison of the analytic solution and the CFBM solution at the resonant frequency [7] for the scattering of a perfectly conducting circular cylinder can be obtained by setting the ϵ_r of dielectric coating equal to 1.0 . There are excellent agreements between these two solutions, both for TM and TE cases. This demonstrates that the proposed method does not suffer from the

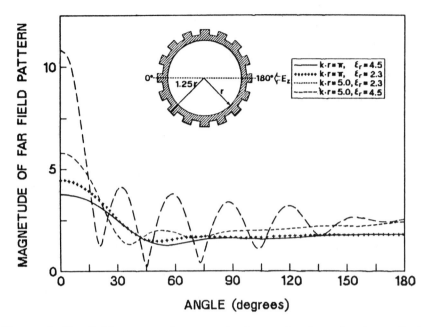

Figure 6 Far-field pattern for a perfectly conducting circular cylinder with dielectric periodic load.

non-uniqueness problem in the resonance case as the BEM does. The reason is that the BEM only involves an electric field integral equation which suffers from non-uniqueness. However, in the CFBM, the integral equation is complemented by a differential equation which is satisfied in the interior region.

The last numerical example is radio wave propagation in a building. To see the near field distribution around the building, the model of the structure is enclosed with an artificial boundary B as shown in Fig. 7. Because the thickness of the wall is much smaller than the dimension of the building, inhomogeneous finite elements are used where needed.

In all the cases considered above, the incident plane wave is TM polarized, although the mathematical treatment is generally applicable for both TE and TM cases. The method proposed here can be extended to cover some anisotropic cases. If the anisotropy involves coupling between x and y directions, the above treatment needs only slight modifications. In this chapter, only the case of an exterior source to

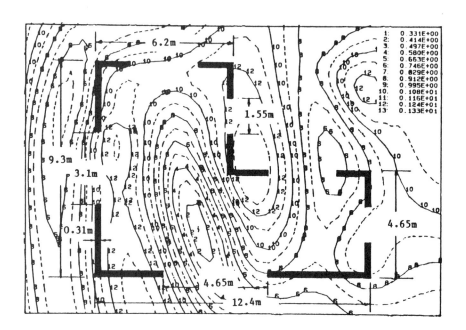

Figure 7 Equal level of normalized electric field distribution in a typical building. Dimensions of the building model are indicated in meters. The walls have assumed $\epsilon_r =5.0-j1.0$ and $k_0 =0.5$ radians/meter.

the cylinder has been considered. The internal source case can be developed using an analogous procedure.

3.4 Conclusion

It has been shown that the finite element and boundary element methods can be coupled together to study difficult electromagnetic scattering problems. This new procedure, known as the Coupled Finite-element Boundary-element Method (CFBM), is a unified numerical approach that can handle inhomogeneous arbitrary scatterers efficiently.

The method may be used in many situations where the evaluation of scattering by a complex dielectric object or the analysis of a coated structure is involved. But, for the case of homogeneous scatterers, the method loses its advantage and other numerical methods such as the moment method or BEM can be adopted.

In problems where the size of the resultant finite element matrix is much larger than that of the boundary element matrix, an appropriate treatment of the sparse matrix can save a great deal of computer time. This requires much less memory space to handle the full problem while still yielding a valid solution. The extension of the method to three dimensional scattering problems, including cases where the sources are internal to the scattering object is possible. This method may also be combined with the spectral domain technique to treat more complicated problems, for example, to solve the scattering problem of certain objects above or within a multi-layered medium by using the corresponding spatial Green's function which has been recently developed [11].

Acknowledgements

This research was financed by the Natural Sciences and Engineering Council, Ottawa, Canada, K1A 1H5.

References

[1] Harrington, R. F., *Field Computation by Moment Methods*, New York Macmillan, 1968.

[2] Okamoto, N., "Matrix formulation of scattering by a homogeneous gyrotropic cylinder," *IEEE Trans. Antennas Propagat.*, **AP-18**, 642–649, 1970.

[3] Richmond, J. H., "Scattering by dielectric cylinder of arbitrary cross section shape," *IEEE Trans. Antennas Propagat.*, **AP-13**, 334–341, 1965.

[4] Chang, S. K., and K. K. Mei, "Application of the unimoment method to electromagnetic scattering of dielectric cylinders," *IEEE Trans. Antennas Propagat.*, **AP-24**, 35–42, 1976.

[5] Brebbia, C. A., and S. Walker, *Boundary Element Techniques in Engineering*, Newnes-Butterworths, London, 1980.

[6] Kagami, S., and I. Fukou, "Application of boundary-element method to electromagnetic field problems," *IEEE Trans. Microwave Theory Tech.*, **MTT-32**, 455–461, 1984.

[7] Yaskiro, K. I., and S. Ohkawa, "Boundary element method for electromagnetic scattering from cylinders," *IEEE Trans. Antennas Propagat.*, **AP-23**, 383–389, April 1985.

[8] Koshiba, M., and M. Suzuki, "Application of the boundary-element method to waveguide discontinuities," *IEEE Trans. Microwave Theory Tech.*, **MTT-34**, 301–307, 1986.

[9] Silvester, P., and M. S. Hsich, "Finite-element solution of two-dimensional exterior field problems," *Proc. Inst. Elec. Eng.*, **118**, 1743–1747, 1971 .

[10] McDonald, B. H., and A. Wexler, "Finite-element solution of unbounded field problems," *IEEE Trans. Microwave Theory Tech.*, **MTT-20**, 841–847, 1972 .

[11] Fang, D. G., J. J. Yang, and G. Y. Delisle, "The discrete exact image theory for arbitrarily oriented dipoles in a multilayered medium," accepted for publication in *IEE Proc. Pt.H, Microwave, Antennas and Propagation.*

4

ABSORBING BOUNDARY CONDITIONS FOR THE DIRECT SOLUTION OF PARTIAL DIFFERENTIAL EQUATIONS ARISING IN ELECTROMAGNETIC SCATTERING PROBLEMS

R. Mittra and O. Ramahi

4.1 Introduction

In recent years, there has been an increasing interest [1–6] in the solution of electromagnetic scattering problems via a direct solution of Maxwell's equations using finite mathematics, e.g., the finite difference (FD) and finite element (FEM) techniques, because such a direct formulation of the scattering problem appears to be especially well-suited for scatterers of complex shape and with inhomogeneous coatings. Typically, an integral equation formulation, using the two-dimensional surface current distribution as the unknown and the method of moments (MOM) as the solution procedure, is more efficient than the partial differential equation schemes for perfectly conducting scatterers because the PDE formulation must work with the electric and magnetic field components at a large number of mesh points in the region surrounding the scatterer. However, this relative advantage of the integral equation schemes narrows for more complex, inhomogeneous scatterers where a three-dimensional, volume type of integral equation must be used. Furthermore, finite methods have an attractive feature–they generate highly sparse and banded matrices which can be efficiently handled using special algorithms. In contrast, the method of moment procedure yields a dense matrix equation that is typically solved using conventional schemes, e.g., the Gaussian elimination method, which is quite time-consuming for large matrices. Thus, PDE formulations have a potential advantage over the integral equation schemes for solving complex, large-body scattering problems.

When solving an open region scattering problem by using finite mathematics approaches, an artificial outer boundary is typically introduced in order to bound the region surrounding the scatterer that is subdivided into meshes for the purpose of discretization. This truncation of the open region enables one to limit the number of unknowns to a manageable size that can be fitted into the computer memory. However, such a truncation also introduces an error and, in order to model the physical problem as correctly as possible, an absorbing boundary condition (ABC) must be imposed on the outer boundary such that it appears as nearly transparent as possible to the waves impinging upon it from the interior. The functions of this absorbing boundary, of course, are to minimize the nonphysical reflections from this boundary and to simulate the condition in which the waves are entirely outgoing as closely as possible. Clearly, in the asymptotic limit where the outer boundary tends to infinity, the absorbing boundary condition should become identical to the Sommerfeld radiation condition. However, in practice, it is desirable to bring in the outer boundary as close to the scatterer as possible in order to reduce the number of mesh points and, hence, the size of the associated matrix. The important question is: How can this be done by enforcing a boundary condition on the outer boundary that suppresses the reflections from it and thus introduces little error in the solution due to truncation of the region external to the scatterer?

Several ABC's , typically in the form of boundary operators, have recently been reported in the literature. These can be broadly classified into two categories, viz., local and nonlocal. In principle, the nonlocal boundary conditions allow one to bring in the outer boundary as close to the scatterer as desired. However, they have the drawback that they destroy the highly sparse nature that is so characteristic, and distinctly advantageous feature for numerical solution, of the matrices generated via finite methods. These boundary conditions have been discussed by McDonald and Wexler [1] and by MacCamy and Marin [3] and the reader is referred to the above works for additional details.

In contrast, the local boundary conditions yield matrix operators that preserve, at least for the lower-order operators, the highly sparse and banded character of the resulting matrix equations and, hence, do not compromise the computational efficiency of the finite methods. However, not unexpectedly, the local operators are not exact in their modeling of the physical problem, since they are not totally absorbing in nature. As a result, using a local boundary condition introduces some error into the field solution, due primarily to reflections of the outgoing wave from the artificial outer boundary [2,4,5]. The local boundary condition is also inaccurate when traveling waves are excited on the scatterer and substantial global type of coupling exists between widely separated parts of the scatterer.

A number of authors have investigated local ABC's, notably Bayliss, Gunzburger, and Turkel [5], who have employed an asymptotic analysis to derive a series of local operators, referred to henceforth in this paper as the BGT operators. Using the pseudo-differential operator theory, Engquist and Majda [2] have generated a set of different operators which, although not as accurate as the BGT operators, are nonetheless designed to serve the same purpose, viz., a minimization of the reflections from the outer boundary by applying a local form of boundary condition on the fields at this boundary.

In the first part of this work, we begin by briefly reviewing the derivation of the Bayliss, Gunzburger, and Turkel (BGT) boundary operators. Next, we present an alternative approach to deriving the local form of boundary operators and compare the expression obtained from this approach to those based upon the BGT operator. Following this, we carry out a systematic study of the errors resulting from the application of the second and fourth order local operators on an arbitrary scattered field, which can in general be represented in terms of cylindrical harmonics. We do this by comparing the results obtained by using the approximate and the exact boundary conditions, the latter being readily derivable for these harmonics. We show that such an error analysis not only provides a great deal of physical insight into the mechanism by which the errors are introduced into the process of applying the local operators, but also suggests ways by which a systematic improvement of the ABC-based solution can be achieved. Next, we present the formulation of the ABC in the context of the finite element method (FEM) and provide illustrative numerical results for RCS computation from a number of different geometries.

The question of improvement of the ABC solution is an important one and, to the best of our knowledge, has not been addressed in the past. In this work we provide a systematic procedure based on a hybrid technique that combines the ABC approach with the Unimoment method [7] in a manner that realizes a considerable improvement over that achievable with either of these two individual approaches. A simple but illustrative example of such a procedure is included in the paper as are the results demonstrating the improvement.

The subject of three-dimensional ABC is discussed only briefly in this work, as it is intended to be covered more fully in a forthcoming paper [16]. However, the Appendix does include yet another approach for deriving the two-dimensional ABC based on the use of recursion relations for the expansion coefficients of the asymptotic representation for the field and generalizes it to the three-dimensional scalar and vector cases. Finally, the last section of the paper presents a direct approach for truncating the grid at the outer boundary and indicates how this approach can be conveniently applied to the 3-D vector case. This last approach is based on extrapolating the field using an asymptotic representation, introduced by Wilcox [11], in which the vector EM fields are expressed in terms of a series of inverse powers in r, the radial distance from the origin.

4.2   Derivation of the BGT Operators

In this section we briefly review the derivation of the BGT type of absorbing boundary condition by considering the example of a two-dimensional, perfectly-conducting scatterer. The conclusions, however, apply to general scatterers that may be combinations of p.e.c's (perfect electric conductors) and/or inhomogeneous dielectrics.

Consider a perfectly conducting cylindrical scatterer, shown in Fig. 1, whose cross-section is defined by the contour Γ_1. Let the exterior region of the scatterer be designated by the domain Ω. For a TM-polarized incident wave, the problem at hand is to solve the wave equation

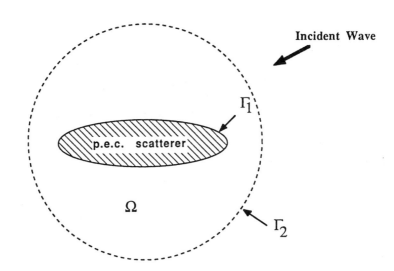

Figure 1 Geometry for the finite-mathematics approach to the scattering problem.

$$\nabla^2 u + k^2 u = 0 \qquad (1)$$

where the wave function u is proportional to the z-component of the scattered electric field. The wave function satisfies the boundary condition

$$u^i + u = 0 \text{ on } \Gamma_1 \qquad (2)$$

where u^i is the incident wave function .

Following Wilcox, an asymptotic expression for u can be written at large distances from the origin as follows:

$$u \approx \frac{e^{-\jmath k \rho}}{\sqrt{\rho}} \left[a_0(\phi) + \frac{a_1(\phi)}{\rho} + \frac{a_2(\phi)}{\rho^2} + \ldots \right] \qquad (3)$$

Defining u_ρ as the ρ derivative of u, we have, from (3),

$$u_\rho + \jmath k u = -\frac{e^{-\jmath k \rho}}{2\rho^{3/2}} \left[a_0(\phi) + 3\frac{a_1(\phi)}{\rho} + 5\frac{a_2(\phi)}{\rho^2} + \ldots \right] \qquad (4)$$

From (4), we obtain

$$(u_\rho + jku) = O\left[\frac{1}{\rho^{3/2}}\right] \tag{5}$$

From (5), we note that if we neglect terms on the order of $O(\rho^{-3/2})$ and smaller, we obtain $u_\rho + jku = 0$, which is precisely equivalent to the Sommerfeld radiation condition for u in two dimensions. Next, we show that we can obtain a higher-order boundary operator B_1, shown below, that yields terms on the order of $O(\rho^{-5/2})$ when applied to the wave function u. The operator B_1 is given by

$$B_1 = \frac{\partial}{\partial \rho} + jk + \frac{1}{2\rho} \tag{6}$$

and we readily find that, for a given ρ, B_1 introduces a higher-order (in ρ^{-1}) error than does the Sommerfeld radiation condition, since

$$B_1 u = u_\rho + jku + \frac{1}{2\rho}u = O\left[\frac{1}{\rho^{5/2}}\right] \tag{7}$$

Continuing along similar lines, the next higher-order operator B_2 can be derived by first defining $v = B_1 u$, and then showing that

$$\left(\frac{\partial}{\partial \rho} + jk + \frac{5}{2\rho}\right) v = O(\rho^{-9/2})$$

Thus, if we define

$$B_2 = \left(\frac{\partial}{\partial \rho} + jk + \frac{5}{2\rho}\right)\left(\frac{\partial}{\partial \rho} + jk + \frac{1}{2\rho}\right)$$

we see that

$$B_2 u = B_1 v = \left[\frac{\partial}{\partial \rho} + jk + \frac{5}{2\rho}\right]\left[\frac{\partial}{\partial \rho} + jk + \frac{1}{2\rho}\right] u = O\left[\frac{1}{\rho^{9/2}}\right] \tag{8}$$

Bayliss et al. have shown that a generalized operator B_m can be constructed by repeating the above procedure, where

$$B_m = \prod_{p=1}^{m}\left[\frac{\partial}{\partial \rho} + \frac{2\rho - 3/2}{\rho} + jk\right] \tag{9}$$

and

$$B_m u = O \left[\frac{1}{\rho^{2m+1/2}} \right] \tag{10}$$

Returning now to the PDE (1), we note that to solve it using the finite mathematics methods, the differential equation or its variational form must be discretized in a bounded region surrounding the scatterer. Let Γ_2 be the outer boundary where the ABC will be imposed using an m-th order boundary operator. Then for the case where u satisfies the boundary condition on the scatterer that the total $u = 0$, a complete statement of the approximated scattering problem in the bounded region reads

$$\nabla^2 u + k^2 u = 0 \quad \text{in } \Omega$$

$$u^i + u = 0 \quad \text{on } \Gamma_1$$

$$B_m u = 0 \quad \text{on } \Gamma_2 \tag{11}$$

Equation (11) can now be solved for u using the FD or FEM schemes and the field in region Ω as well as the scattered far field can be computed. If the solution obtained using a certain boundary operator B_n is not sufficiently accurate, then one has the option of either receding Γ_2 farther away from the scatterer, or employing higher-order boundary operators. However, the boundary operators with $n > 2$ are typically not recommended for numerical implementation because they spoil the sparsity of the matrix. It should also be noted that the boundary operators are asymptotic in nature and, consequently, using higher-order operators may not necessarily ensure a continued improvement of the solution when the outer boundary Γ_2 is close to the surface of the scatterer. Finally, even though according to (10) the estimate of the error in $B_n u$ is $O(1/\rho^{(2n+1/2)})$, the actual error in u may be substantially different from the estimated error in $B_n u$ given by (10). For instance, for the numerical example given in section 4 where B_2 is used to derive the solution to the problem of catering by a conducting cylinder of radius $ka = 50$, it is found that the maximum error in u on the boundary is approximately 20% of the incident field, i.e., about eight orders of magnitude greater than $(k\rho)^{-9/2}$ for $k\rho = 51$. Furthermore, it should be realized that the use of the n-th order ABC with a finite

n introduces reflections from the outer boundary and, hence, the solution generated using this boundary condition does not strictly satisfy the Wilcox-type representation (3) containing outgoing waves only.

4.3   Alternate Boundary Condition for 2-D Scattering

In this section, we present an alternate derivation of the boundary operators by postulating the higher-order radiation condition for u in the form of an asymptotic series in inverse powers of ρ with unknown coefficients, substituting this form into the differential equation, and systematically solving for the coefficients of the series representation for the extended radiation condition, or ABC. We begin with the following representation for u_ρ for large ρ, which contains higher order angular derivatives in ϕ, and not in ρ as in (8) or (10), and is found to be better-suited for numerical implementation

$$u_\rho \approx \alpha(\rho)u + \beta(\rho)\, u_{\phi\phi} \tag{12}$$

and write both α and β in the form of asymptotic series

$$\alpha(\rho) = \alpha_0 + \frac{\alpha_1}{\rho} + \frac{\alpha_2}{\rho^2} + \frac{\alpha_3}{\rho^3} \tag{13}$$

$$\beta(\rho) = \beta_0 + \frac{\beta_1}{\rho} + \frac{\beta_2}{\rho^2} + \frac{\beta_3}{\rho^3} \tag{14}$$

We now show that the unknown coefficients $\alpha(\rho)$ and $\beta(\rho)$, or more specifically α_n and β_n, can be systematically found via recursion relations. To this end, we substitute u_ρ, given in (12), into the wave equation (1). This yields

$$\left[\frac{\alpha}{\rho} + \alpha_\rho + \alpha^2 + k^2\right] u + \left[\frac{\beta}{\rho} + 2\alpha\beta + \beta_\rho + \frac{1}{\rho^2}\right] u_{\phi\phi} = 0 \tag{15}$$

where the fourth-order angular derivative $u_{\phi\phi\phi\phi}$ has been neglected for the purpose of deriving the second-order ABC operator. Since (15) is valid for an arbitrary ρ, the coefficients of u and $u_{\phi\phi}$ must be individually zero. Thus, we must have

$$\frac{\alpha}{\rho} + \alpha_\rho + \alpha^2 + k^2 = 0 \tag{16}$$

and

$$\frac{\beta}{\rho} + 2\alpha\beta + \beta_\rho + \frac{1}{\rho^2} = 0 \tag{17}$$

Substituting $\alpha(\rho)$ into (16), we obtain

$$(\alpha_0^2 + k^2) + (\alpha_0 + 2\alpha_0\alpha_1)\frac{1}{\rho} + (\alpha_1^2 + 2\alpha_0\alpha_2)\frac{1}{\rho^2}$$

$$+ (2\alpha_0\alpha_3 + 2\alpha_1\alpha_2 - \alpha_2)\frac{1}{\rho^3} + O\left[\frac{1}{\rho^4}\right] = 0 \tag{18}$$

Equating the coefficients of ρ^{-n} to 0, we have

$$\alpha_0^2 + k^2 = 0 \tag{19}$$

$$\alpha_0 + 2\alpha_0\alpha_1 = 0 \tag{20}$$

from which we can recursively derive

$$\alpha_0 = -\jmath k$$

$$\alpha_1 = -\frac{1}{2}$$

$$\alpha_2 = -\frac{\jmath}{8k}$$

$$\alpha_3 = \frac{1}{8k^2} \tag{21}$$

Thus, we can write

$$\alpha = \left[-\jmath k - \frac{1}{2\rho} - \frac{\jmath}{8k\rho^2} + \frac{1}{8k^2\rho^3}\right] \tag{22}$$

Substituting $\beta(\rho)$ into (17) and following the same procedure as outlined above, we obtain

$$\beta = \left[\frac{-\jmath}{2k\rho^2} + \frac{1}{2k^2\rho^3}\right] \tag{23}$$

Using the above expressions for α and β in (12), we obtain the second-order boundary operator $\mathcal{B}_2$

$$\mathcal{B}_2 u = u_\rho - \alpha(\rho)u - \beta(\rho)U_{\phi\phi} \qquad (24)$$

We can also rewrite the $\mathcal{B}_2$ operator, given in (8) as

$$\mathcal{B}_2 u = u_\rho - \left[\frac{1}{1 - \frac{J}{k\rho}}\right] \cdot \left\{\left[-Jk - \frac{3}{2\rho} + \frac{3J}{8k\rho^2}\right]u + \left[\frac{-J}{2k\rho^2}\right]u_{\phi\phi}\right\} \qquad (25)$$

where we have used (1) to trade the second order radial derivative with the second order angular derivative, the latter being better suited for numerical implementation. By expanding the coefficients of u and $u_{\phi\phi}$ in (25) and retaining terms up to order ρ^{-3}, we obtain

$$\mathcal{B}_2 u = u_\rho - \left[-Jk - \frac{1}{2\rho} - \frac{J}{8k\rho^2} + \frac{1}{8k^2\rho^3}\right]u + \left[\frac{-J}{2k\rho^2} + \frac{1}{2k^2\rho^3}\right]u_{\phi\phi}$$

$$(26)$$

We observe by comparison of (24) and (26), that the second order BGT operator is identical to $\mathcal{B}_2$, up to the order ρ^{-3} retained in $\alpha(\rho)$ and $\beta(\rho)$.

We can follow the procedure outlined above for the derivation of $\mathcal{B}_2$ to obtain higher order boundary operators that involve higher order angular derivatives. Following an analogous development, we represent higher order operators in the form

$$u_\rho = \alpha(\rho)u + \beta(\rho)u_{\phi\phi} + \gamma(\rho)u_{\phi\phi\phi} + \delta(\rho)u_{\phi\phi\phi\phi} + \dots \qquad (27)$$

where the radially dependent coefficients, α, β, γ and δ, can be found by following the same procedure used to derive the coefficients of the $\mathcal{B}_2$ operator. One finds that γ, the coefficient of $u_{\phi\phi\phi}$, must be zero in order for the above form in (27) to satisfy the Helmholtz equation in (1). Thus, the next higher order operator after $\mathcal{B}_2$ will have the fourth angular derivative in u instead of the third. Consequently, we designate this operator as $\mathcal{B}_4$ which is given by

$$\mathcal{B}_4 u = u_\rho - \alpha(\rho)u - \beta(\rho)u_{\phi\phi} - \delta(\rho)u_{\phi\phi\phi\phi} \qquad (28)$$

where $\alpha(\rho)$ and $\beta(\rho)$ are the same (within ρ^{-3}) as in (22) and (23) respectively, and $\delta(\rho)$ is given by

$$\delta(\rho) = \frac{\jmath}{8k^3\rho^4} \qquad (29)$$

In the next section we present comparative results for the two operators $\mathcal{B}_2$ and $\mathcal{B}_4$. Of course, it is evident that they both reduce to the Sommerfeld radiation condition when the outer boundary is placed sufficiently far away from the scatterer.

Before closing this section, we mention that an even more direct derivation of the $\mathcal{B}_2$ and $\mathcal{B}_4$ operators is possible by using the recursion relationship satisfied by coefficients $a_n(\phi)$ of ρ^{-n} appearing in the Wilcox-type expansion (3). This is shown in the Appendix, where the ABC's for three-dimensional scalar and vector wave functions, derived by using appropriate recursion relationships valid for the coefficients for the 3-D type of Wilcox's expansion, are also given for reference.

4.4   Performance of Boundary Operators

Typically, to assess the accuracy of the local boundary operators discussed above, one would apply these operators to the outer boundary, construct the field solution using one of the finite mathematics methods, and compare the results for the surface current, the far field, the radar cross section, etc., with those obtained using an alternate approach, e.g., the moment method or experimental measurements. However, in this paper we present a numerical comparison of the results of the application of the $\mathcal{B}_2$ and $\mathcal{B}_4$ operators on an arbitrary scattered field represented in terms of cylindrical harmonics, taking advantage of the fact that an exact boundary condition can be found for these harmonics. We show that such a comparison reveals a great deal of insight into the behavior of the local boundary operators, explains why they fail when they do, and provides a clue as to how the approximate numerical results obtained via the application of the second-order boundary operators can systematically be improved. It is well known that external to a cylindrical region circumscribing an arbitrary scatterer, the wave function u representing the scattered field can always be expressed as

$$u = \sum_{n=-N}^{N} a_n H_n^{(2)}(k\rho)e^{jn\phi} \tag{30}$$

Obviously, the representation above not only satisfies the radiation condition at infinity but is also outgoing for all values of ρ. To determine the sort of error that is introduced when we apply the second-order boundary operator (which we know satisfies the outgoing condition only approximately) to this representation, we substitute the representation for u in (30) into the boundary operator to obtain

$$u_\rho^{\text{exact}} = \sum_{n=-N}^{N} a_n \frac{\partial H_n^{(2)}(k\rho)}{\partial \rho} e^{jn\phi} \tag{31a}$$

From (27) we have

$$
\begin{aligned}
u_\rho^{\text{approx}} = \ &\alpha(\rho) \sum_{n=-N}^{N} a_n H_n^{(2)}(k\rho)e^{jn\phi} \\
&-\beta(\rho) \sum_{n=-N}^{N} a_n H_n^{(2)}(k\rho)n^2 e^{jn\phi} \\
&+\delta(\rho) \sum_{n=-N}^{N} a_n H_n^{(2)}(k\rho)n^4 e^{jn\phi}
\end{aligned}
\tag{31b}
$$

Using the separability in ϕ, we obtain the error, E_n, in the n-th harmonic content of u_ρ as

$$E_n = \frac{\partial H_n^{(2)}(k\rho)}{\partial \rho} - [\alpha(\rho) - n^2\beta(\rho) + n^4\delta(\rho)]H_n^{(2)}(k\rho) \tag{32}$$

where

$$
\begin{aligned}
\alpha(\rho) &= -jk - \frac{1}{2\rho} - \frac{j}{8k\rho^2} + \frac{1}{8k^2\rho^3} \\
\beta(\rho) &= -\frac{j}{2k\rho^2} + \frac{1}{2k^2\rho^3}
\end{aligned}
\tag{33}
$$

and

$$\delta(\rho) = \begin{cases} \dfrac{\jmath}{8k^3\rho^4} & \text{for} \quad \mathcal{B}_4 \\[2ex] 0 & \text{for} \quad \mathcal{B}_2 \end{cases} \tag{34}$$

A convenient way to estimate the error is to compare the two quantities $\gamma_n = H_n'/H_n = $ exact γ_n, with $\gamma_n^{(2)ap} = \alpha(\rho) - n^2\beta(\rho) = $ approximate $\gamma_n^{(2)}$, obtained from the second-order boundary operator, and $\gamma_n^{(4)ap} = \alpha(\rho) - n^2\beta(\rho) + n^4\delta(\rho)$. The quantity γ_n can be physically interpreted to be playing the role of the complex propagation constant for cylindrical fields, since it equals u_ρ/u. We also note that γ_n equals $-\jmath k$ in the far field where u satisfies the Sommerfeld radiation condition.

Figure 2 shows γ_n^{ap}'s calculated at $k\rho = 51$ using the $\mathcal{B}_2$ and $\mathcal{B}_4$ operators and compares them with the corresponding exact γ_n. From Fig. 2a, the imaginary part of γ_n computed by using the $\mathcal{B}_4$ operator is seen to be somewhat superior than the corresponding result derived from the $\mathcal{B}_2$ operator. However, the real part of γ_n^{ap}, which is shown in Fig. 2b, and which dominates when n is large, is seen to differ considerably from the exact γ_n for both. These figures clearly show that the error introduced by the boundary operators is not uniform for all harmonics. It is evident that the boundary operators work quite well for the lower-order harmonics, in that they yield results for γ_n^{ap} that compare very favorably with the exact $\gamma_n = u_\rho/u$ for the outgoing harmonics. The situation changes, however, for the higher-order harmonics, particularly for $n = 40$ on up, where they transition from being essentially propagating (γ_n essentially imaginary), into the evanescent region in which the exact γ_n acquires a significant real part. We note that the approximate γ_n's fail to predict this phenomenon correctly.

As a rule of thumb, to compute the scattered field at $\rho \geq ka$ for a scatterer of characteristic dimension ka, defined as the radius of the smallest circle that encloses the scatterer, the upper limit N for the series in (30) has to be set at least equal to M, where M is slightly larger than ka. Thus, suppose we have a scatterer whose characteristic dimension is given by $ka = 50$, and in an attempt to drastically reduce the number of mesh points, we impose the second-order boundary operator on a circle whose radius is either equal to or only slightly greater than 50. We should expect errors to be introduced into the satisfaction

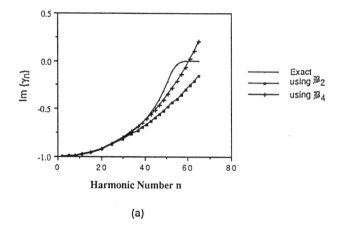

(a)

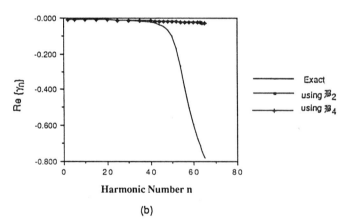

(b)

Figure 2 γ_n as calculated using the $\mathcal{B}_2$ and $\mathcal{B}_4$ operators, and the exact γ_n at $kb = 51$ (a) Imag(γ_n); (b) Real(γ_n).

of the outgoing type of boundary condition by the harmonic contents of the scattered field falling in the range $40 < n < 60$, that are essentially evanescent or in the transition region. This result provides us with the clue as to why the On-Surface Radiation Condition (OSRC) [12] is expected to work well only for a smooth, moderate-sized scatterer whose scattered field has a relatively low content of higher-order harmonics. It also predicts that when the ABC is applied on or close to the surface of a scatterer that generates a substantial amount of higher-order evanescent harmonics, e.g., a strip, it is likely to introduce significant

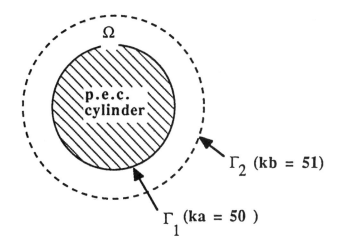

Figure 3 Geometry of p.e.c. cylinder of size $ka = 50$ and artificial boundary at $kb = 51$.

errors in the solution(see for instance [12]). Furthermore, an understanding of the physics of the behavior of higher-order harmonics is also helpful in developing methods by which the solution derived by applying the second-order boundary operator on a surface that is close to the scatterer can be significantly improved. In the following, we first illustrate the principles for implementing such improvement by considering the canonical problem of scattering by a circular cylinder. Next, we consider the case of a general scatterer and indicate how the same concept can be extended to this case.

Consider the problem of TM scattering ($\overline{E}$ parallel to the axis of the cylinder) from a perfectly conducting circular cylinder of radius $ka = 50$, as is illustrated in Fig. 3. We introduce an artificial outer boundary Γ_2 at $k\rho = 51$ and apply the second-order boundary operator $\mathcal{B}_2$ to the scattered field at this boundary. For this canonical problem, the resulting field problem can be solved analytically, and the solution for the scattered far field is shown in Fig. 4. Since we expect reflections from the outer boundary due to the application of the inexact boundary condition at Γ_2, we write the wave function u in the annular region Ω as a sum of outgoing and incoming harmonics, whose weight coefficients

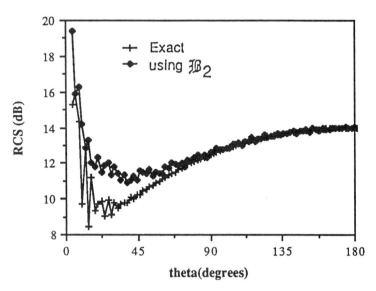

Figure 4 Comparison of exact bistatic RCS with that calculated using the ABC.

are given by a_n and b_n as follows

$$u = \sum_{n=-N}^{N} \left[a_n H_n^{(2)}(k\rho) + b_n H_n^{(1)}(k\rho) \right] e^{jn\phi} \tag{35}$$

Figures 5 and 6, which plot the incoming and outgoing coefficients, show that the higher-order harmonics generated by using the boundary operator are in error. Referring to Fig. 5, we see that the incoming harmonic coefficients b_n's, which should ideally be identically zero, are not negligibly small for $n > 45$. We also note that, for this example, they are slightly smaller for $\mathcal{B}_4$ than they are for $\mathcal{B}_2$. As for the outgoing harmonics a_n's, shown in Fig. 6, we note that the approximate solutions derived by using the ABC operators also deviate from the exact solution for the higher-order harmonics beyond $n > 45$.

The maximum error in the scattered field u computed by using the ABC is also a quantity of interest and, on the outer boundary located at $k\rho = 51$, this error is found to be 20.5 percent (normalized to the incident field) for $\mathcal{B}_2$ and 12.9 percent for $\mathcal{B}_4$. This is in spite of the fact that, according to (10), the error in the second order operator $\mathcal{B}_2$ was estimated to be on the order of 10^{-8}, and the estimate for the fourth order operator was considerably smaller than that. The reason

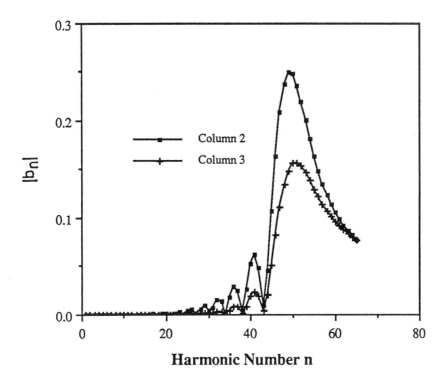

Figure 5   Magnitude of the coefficients of the incoming harmonics, $|b_n|$, **as generated by using the ABC.**

for this discrepancy can be readily explained if one recognizes that the error terms in the expression for $B_n u$ are dependent not only on the radius of the outer boundary, but also on the shape of the scatterer as well as the nature of the incident field. Specifically, the coefficient of the $\rho^{-9/2}$ term in the expression for $B_2 u$ may be quite large (on the order of 10^7 for the present problem) and, consequently, an error prediction based solely on the radius of the outer boundary where the ABC is applied may be substantially inaccurate.

Although, thus far we have only presented some representative results for the TM-case in this paper, we have also carried out similar calculations for the TE case and have found that, in general, the ABC approach works less well for this case than it does for the TM-polarized incident field. This will be evident from some of the results appearing in the next section where we discuss the implementation of the absorbing boundary condition in the context of the FEM formulation.

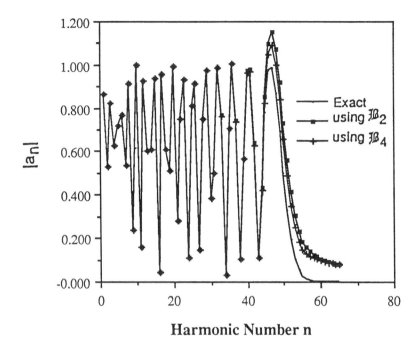

Figure 6 **Magnitude of the coefficients of the outgoing harmonics, $|a_n|$, generated by using the ABC and compared with the exact $|a_n|$.**

4.5 Absorbing Boundary Condition for the FEM

In this section, we describe the implementation of the ABC into the finite-element formulation, which is used very frequently in PDE approaches to solving scattering problems from complex targets. Detailed account of the finite-element method can be readily found in the existing literature (see for instance [13–15]) and, hence, only a brief summary of the governing equations are included here.

We return to (1), the wave equation satisfied by the scattered field and rewrite it below for convenience

$$\nabla^2 u + k^2 u = 0 \tag{36}$$

The first step in the FEM formulation is to multiply the above Helmholtz equation with a test function v, and integrate the product over the domain of the problem, viz., Ω (see Fig. 1). This gives

$$\int_{\Omega_1} (v\nabla^2 u + k^2 vu)\, ds = 0 \qquad (37)$$

The second step involves transferring the differentiation from the unknown function u to the testing function v via the Green's identity as follows

$$\int_\Omega v\nabla^2 u\, ds = -\int_\Omega \nabla u \cdot \nabla v\, ds + \int_{\Gamma_1+\Gamma_2} v\frac{\partial u}{\partial n}\, dl \qquad (38)$$

Substituting this identity into the variational from in (36), we arrive at the weak form of the Helmholtz equation

$$\int_\Omega (\nabla u \cdot \nabla v - k^2 vu)\, ds = \int_{\Gamma_1+\Gamma_2} v\frac{\partial u}{\partial n}\, dl \qquad (39)$$

where Γ_1 and Γ_2 describe the boundary of the solution region as shown in Fig. 1. Finally, the absorbing boundary condition is incorporated into the weak form by inserting the B_2 operator into the right hand side integral over Γ_2, which is the outer boundary contour. This gives

$$\int_\Omega (\nabla u \cdot \nabla v - k^2 vu)\, ds = \int_{\Gamma_1} v\frac{\partial u}{\partial n}\, dl + \int_{\Gamma_2} v(\alpha u + \beta u_{\phi\phi})\, dl \qquad (40)$$

Integrating the term in the integrand involving $u_{\phi\phi}$ by parts, and introducing a change of variables, we get

$$\int_\Omega (\nabla u \cdot \nabla v - k^2 vu)\, ds = \int_{\Gamma_1} v\frac{\partial u}{\partial n}\, dl + \int_{\Gamma_2} (\alpha vu - \beta \rho^2 v_l u_l)\, dl \qquad (41)$$

where v_l and u_l are the tangential derivatives along the outer contour Γ_2.

The form given in (41) is well-suited for numerical implementation, especially if first order finite elements are chosen to discretize the region Ω. Notice that if the ABC operator, e.g., B_4, were used in place of the B_2 operator employed above, second or higher-order angular derivatives would have appeared in the boundary integral. This would, in turn, have necessitated the use of second or higher order elements, and, consequently, would have resulted in decreased sparsity of the system matrix.

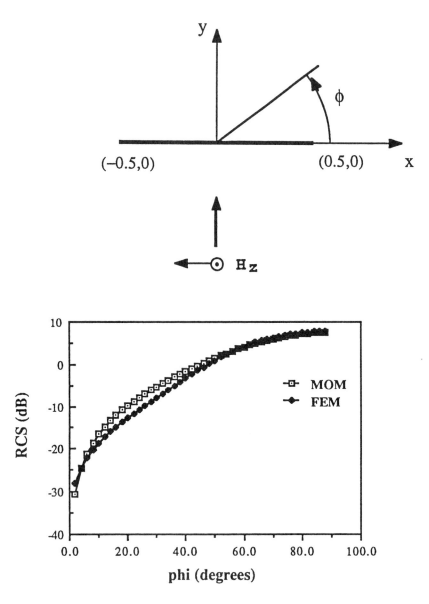

Figure 7 Bistatic radar cross section of a conducting strip, TE case, computed by using the ABC method with $\mathcal{B}_2$ operator applied at 1.1λ.

For the TM-polarization case, we have $u = E_z$, and since the field values are specified on the surface of the scatterer, there is no boundary-integral contribution from Γ_1 . For the TE-polarization,

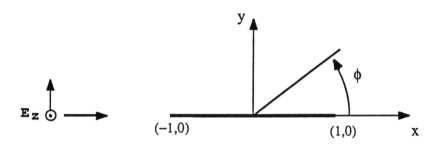

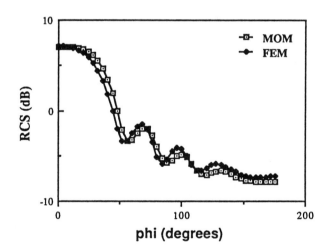

Figure 8 **Bistatic radar cross section of a conducting strip, TM case, computed by using the ABC method with** $\mathcal{B}_2$ **operator applied at 1.2λ.**

$u = H_z$, and the boundary condition on the p.e.c. cylinder is given by

$$\left[\frac{\partial u}{\partial n} + \frac{\partial u^{\text{inc}}}{\partial n} \right] = 0 \tag{42}$$

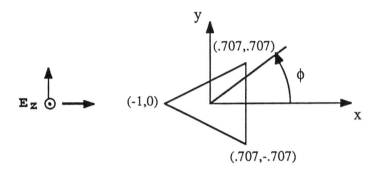

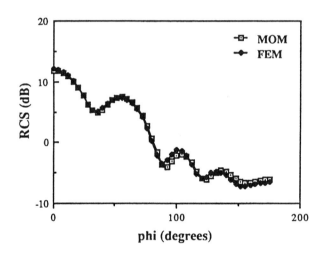

Figure 9 **Bistatic radar cross section of a conducting triangular cylinder, TM case, computed by using the ABC method with $\mathcal{B}_2$ operator applied at 1.3λ.**

This condition is substituted in the boundary integral over Γ_1 for the TE polarization. However, the condition on the outer boundary, viz., Γ_2, remains the same for both polarizations.

Numerical results for RCS computation from several representative structures will now be presented. The geometries considered are a 1λ strip, a triangular cylinder, and two circular cylinder geometries

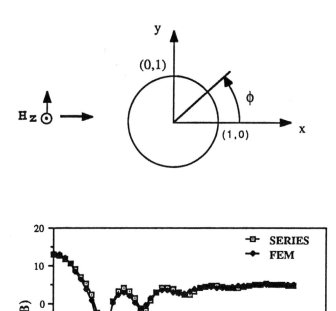

Figure 10 **Bistatic radar cross section of a conducting circular cylinder, TE case, computed by using the ABC method with B_2 operator applied at 1.1λ.**

of radii 1λ and 8λ, respectively. The bistatic radar cross sections of these scatterers are shown in Figs. 7 through 12, where they are also compared with the results derived from other available techniques e.g., the method of moments and the series solution for circular cylinders. It is evident from these results that for small scatterers the ABC approach yields results that are in excellent agreement with the method

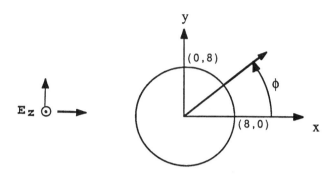

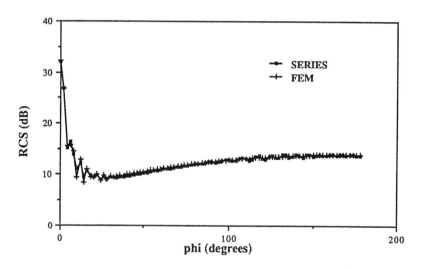

Figure 11 Bistatic radar cross section of a conducting circular cylinder of radius 8λ, TM case, computed by using the ABC method with B_2 operator applied at 8.2λ.

of moments, regardless of the polarization of the incident field. For larger scatterers, it is found that the ABC approach continues to work reasonably well for the TM polarization, as is evident from the example of Fig. 11 for a cylinder of radius 8λ. For TE polarization the ABC deteriorates more rapidly and the errors in the solution show up sooner than they do for the TM case, i.e., for smaller body sizes in terms of

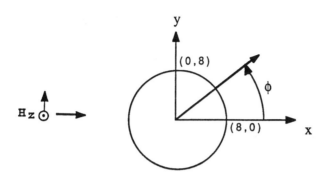

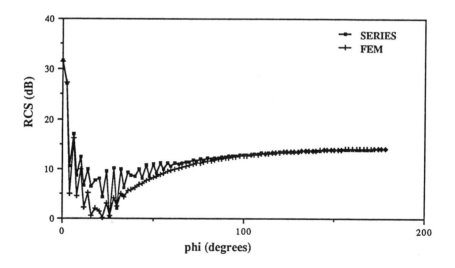

Figure 12 Bistatic radar cross section of a conducting circular cylinder of radius 8λ, TE case, computed by using the ABC method with B_2 operator applied at 8.2λ.

ka. We see, for instance, from Figs. 11 and 12, that the results for the 8λ cylinder are less accurate for the TE case than they are for the comparable TM case.

4.6   Improvement in the ABC-Based Solution

As a first step toward improving the ABC-based solution, we might attempt to purify the approximate solution by filtering out all of the incoming harmonic contributions and using only the outgoing harmonics to compute the far scattered fields. This can always be done, in general, even for an arbitrary scatterer, by starting with the computed values of u and u_ρ on the outer boundary $\rho = b$, Fourier analyzing these values to determine the coefficients of the incoming and outgoing harmonics and, deleting the incoming harmonics while retaining the outgoing ones with their coefficients intact. While this procedure is simple, and would in general yield a better solution for the far field, it can be further refined by recognizing that that the coefficients of the outgoing harmonics are still in error and should be corrected for improved accuracy.

To achieve improvement in the result beyond that obtainable via the simple deletion of the incoming harmonics, we must attempt to annihilate, or at least minimize, the coefficients of the higher-order incoming harmonics that are significant while *simultaneously* adjusting the outgoing harmonic coefficients associated with the same harmonics. The procedure followed for this test problem is explicitly outlined below.

By enforcing the boundary condition on the perfect electric conductor at ka and applying the boundary operator at kb, we obtain the matrix equation

$$\begin{bmatrix} H_n^{(1)}(ka) & H_n^{(2)}(ka) \\ H_n^{(1)}(kb) & H_n^{(2)}(kb) \end{bmatrix} \begin{bmatrix} b_n \\ a_n \end{bmatrix} = \begin{bmatrix} -\jmath^{-n} J_n(ka) \\ (a_n + \eta_n) H_n^{(2)}(kb) \end{bmatrix} \quad (43)$$

where η_n's are the corrections in the coefficients of the outgoing harmonics a_n, and are to be determined by imposing the condition that $b_n = 0$. Letting $b_n = 0$, we get

$$(a_n + \eta_n) = \frac{-\jmath^{-n} J_n(ka)}{H_n^{(2)}(ka)} \quad (44)$$

$$\eta_n = \left[\frac{-\jmath^{-n} J_n(ka)}{H_n^{(2)}(ka)} - a_n \right] \quad (45)$$

In Fig. 4, we presented the exact as well as the approximate bistatic RCS, the latter having been calculated using the second-order

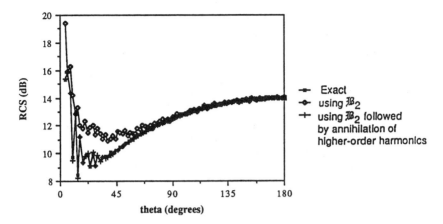

Figure 13 **Effect of annihilating the harmonics** $n=40$ **through 60 in the ABC solution on the scattered field.**

boundary operator $\mathcal{B}_2$, by filtering out the incoming harmonics and retaining only the outgoing ones. We note, first of all, that the RCS results are quite accurate in the forward scatter and backscatter directions, and in the vicinity of these angles, but they do deviate from the true results at other angles. Figure 13 shows the effect of annihilating the higher-order incoming harmonics ranging from $n = 40$ to 60, while simultaneously adjusting the coefficients of the corresponding outgoing harmonics. It is evident that a significant improvement is obtained at the angles where the far field, computed by using the the original $\mathcal{B}_2$ solution and retaining only the outgoing waves without further modification, was in error.

For the canonical problem of a circular cylinder, it was possible for us to systematically improve, by analytical means, the approximate results for the scattered field obtained via the application of the second-order ABC. Obviously, we would expect to have to resort to numerical means when the scatterer is of arbitrary shape. In the following, we indicate how an approach that embodies the concepts of the Unimoment method developed by Mei and his co-workers [7–9], can be employed to improve the ABC-based solution for an arbitrary scatterer in a numerically efficient manner.

The first step in the application of the Unimoment method is to enclose the scatterer with an artificial boundary which is separable in nature, e.g., a circular boundary for the two-dimensional scattering problem. This step not only allows one to conveniently express the solution for the scattered field in the external region in terms of cylindrical wave functions, but it also decouples the exterior problem from the interior one except, of course, via the continuity conditions on the tangential fields to be imposed at the common boundary. Next, one solves the interior problem N times, where N is the number of cylindrical harmonics needed to adequately represent the total field on the outer boundary. The boundary condition imposed on the wave function in the process of deriving these interior solutions, via the FD/FEM method, is that the total field u equals $e^{jn\phi}, n = 0, 1, 2, \ldots N$. The interior solution can be represented on the outer boundary as a weighted sum of the boundary functions $e^{jn\phi}$ with the weight coefficients yet to be determined.

To this end, we represent the scattered field in the exterior region in terms of a finite series of outgoing cylindrical wave functions. Finally, the continuity conditions on the field and its derivative are enforced at the artificial boundary, resulting in a matrix equation of the order $4N \times 4N$ whose solution leads to the determination of the weight coefficients.

As mentioned earlier, for a scatterer of characteristic dimension ka, on the order of N harmonics are needed for the solution to be accurately represented, implying that N boundary functions should be employed at the artificial boundary in the Unimoment method. Suppose, however, that we generate an initial solution by applying the second-order $\mathcal{B}_2$ operator at Γ_2, where Γ_2 barely encloses the scatterer. Then, from the behavior of γ_n's investigated above, we know that the lower-order harmonic contents of this solution will be accurate and only the higher-order harmonics will require correction. This suggests that we can improve the ABC solution by following a Unimoment type of procedure, but by applying it to only a small fraction of the total number of harmonics needed to represent the scattered field at the outer boundary. This not only reduces the time it takes to generate the matrices representing the continuity equations applied at Γ_2, because of the reduction in the size of this matrix to a fraction of that in the Unimoment method, but it also reduces the matrix storage and solution time. Both of these are important factors in determining the feasibility of solving large-body scattering problems.

Strictly speaking, the procedure outlined above is based on the premise that there exists little or no coupling between the higher-order harmonics that are being modified and the lower-order harmonics that are being left intact once they have been generated via the application of the ABC. We recall that for the canonical problem of the cylinder there was absolutely no coupling between the various harmonics. However, for a general scatterer, the harmonics do couple to each other, in the sense that a single harmonic in the incident field can produce all the harmonics in the scattered field. Fortunately, numerical experiments performed on different scatterer geometries have shown that this coupling between the harmonics, introduced by the arbitrary shape of the scatterer, is confined only to the adjacent harmonics, i.e., it is very much of the near-neighbor type. Furthermore, the coupling is even weaker between the propagating and the evanescent harmonics. As a result, to improve the ABC solution it is usually adequate to consider only a few, say about 10 harmonics for a body with a ka size of 50, with some of the harmonics falling in the transition region and the rest being evanescent. One suppresses the incoming portions of the scattered field for these harmonics while simultaneously adjusting their outgoing parts, by solving a 40×40 matrix equation (the size of the matrix is 4 times the number of harmonics), which neglects their coupling to the lower-order harmonics that have presumably been calculated sufficiently accurately using the second-order boundary operator. The realization of time saving in this approach, vis-a-vis the conventional Unimoment method, results from two factors. First, the number of times the interior problem needs to be solved is only a fraction of that in the Unimoment method; and, second, the matrix equation that corresponds to the continuity condition is also smaller by the same reduction ratio. It is also important to recognize that if one attempted to derive the solution strictly using the ABC, the outer boundary would have to be moved outward to a radius of about 2 to 3 ka, or even higher, and consequently, the number of mesh points would increase substantially, as would the computation time and the storage requirement. Figure 14 shows the effect of correcting for the harmonics $n = 40$ to 60 in the scattered field for the TE scattering from the 8λ cylinder. The corrected solution is seen to agree very well with the exact solution.

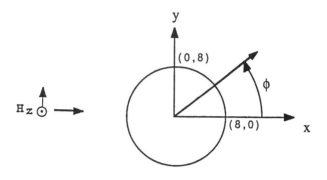

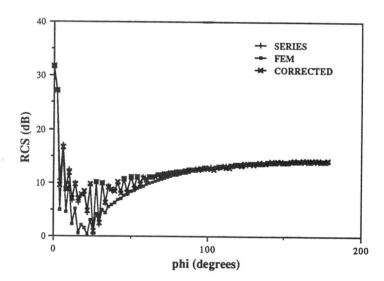

Figure 14   Effect of correcting for the harmonics $n=40$ through 60 in the Finite Element ABC solution for a conducting cylinder of radius 8λ, TE case, with $\mathcal{B}_2$ applied at 8.2λ.

4.7   ABC for 3-D Scalar and Vector Fields

As shown in the Appendix, the 3-D counterpart of the scalar and vector absorbing boundary conditions can be derived by using recursion relations for the coefficients of the inverse powers of r in the asymptotic representation given by Wilcox. One could either choose to use these

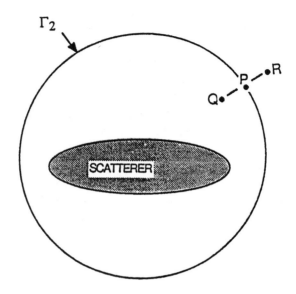

Figure 15 Geometry Pertaining to 3-D ABC.

boundary conditions to truncate the mesh at the outer boundary and use the 3-D version of the weak form given in (41) in the context of FEM, or employ a direct procedure outlined below that serves the same purpose.

Consider the point P on the outer boundary Γ_2, and the points R and Q lying just outside and inside the boundary, respectively, on the same radial line as shown in Fig. 15. In the Finite Difference method, we can truncate the mesh at Γ_2 provided we can write the field value at the point R by first expressing it in terms of the radial derivative of the field at P and then trading this derivative for the angular derivatives at P by using, say, a vector form of ABC. Alternatively, we can achieve the same goal by expressing the field value at R in terms of the values at P and Q, lying on the same radial line, via extrapolation as follows. We first use the two-term Wilcox representation

$$E(r) = \frac{e^{-jkr}}{r} \left[E_0(\theta, \phi) + E_1(\theta, \phi) \frac{1}{r} \right] \qquad (46)$$

and solve for the two coefficients E_0 and E_1 appearing inside the brackets of the above equation, in terms of the field values of E at Q and P. This allows us to express the field value at R using (46) and enables us to truncate the mesh at Γ_2. Note that no explicit angular derivatives are needed in this procedure, although they do get implicitly involved through the radial derivatives via the wave equation satisfied by the fields.

The procedure described above can be generalized to the case where the points P, Q, R do not all lie on a radial line. However, the angular derivatives are explicitly needed in this situation.

Numerical study of this approach for truncating the FD mesh in a region surrounding a scatterer for a 3-D vector scattering problem has been carried out successfully [16] in connection with the body of revolution (BOR) problem. Taking advantage of the azimuthal symmetry of this geometry, a modified form of the coupled azimuthal potentials (CAP's) introduced by Morgan, Chang, and Mei [10] can be used to solve the vector BOR problem. Specifically, the potentials are $u_m(r,\theta)$ and $v_m(r,\theta)$, where

$$E_\phi(r,\theta,\phi) = \sum_{m=-\infty}^{\infty} u_m(r,\theta)e^{Jm\phi} \qquad (47)$$

$$\eta_0 H_\phi(r,\theta,\phi) = \sum_{m=-\infty}^{\infty} v_m(r,\theta)e^{Jm\phi} \qquad (48)$$

Note that these potentials have the advantage of being continuous across dielectric interfaces, whereas the Debye potentials, typically used to solve the sphere problem, do not enjoy the same feature. It can be shown (for details see Chapters 2 and 6) that u_m and v_m satisfy the following coupled differential equations

$$
\begin{aligned}
A_1 u_m + B_1 \frac{\partial u_m}{\partial r} + C_1 \frac{\partial u_m}{\partial \theta} + D_1 \frac{\partial^2 u_m}{\partial r^2} + E_1 \frac{\partial^2 u_m}{\partial \theta^2} \\
+ F_1 v_m + G_1 \frac{\partial v_m}{\partial r} + H_1 \frac{\partial v_m}{\partial \theta} = 0
\end{aligned}
\qquad (49)
$$

$$
\begin{aligned}
A_2 v_m + B_2 \frac{\partial v_m}{\partial r} + C_2 \frac{\partial v_m}{\partial \theta} + D_2 \frac{\partial^2 v_m}{\partial r^2} + E_2 \frac{\partial^2 v_m}{\partial \theta^2} \\
+ F_2 u_m + G_2 \frac{\partial u_m}{\partial r} + H_2 \frac{\partial u_m}{\partial \theta} = 0
\end{aligned}
\qquad (50)
$$

where $A_1, \ldots H_1, A_2, \ldots, H_2$ are known functions of $m, r, \theta, \epsilon_r(r,\theta)$, and $\mu_r(r,\theta)$.

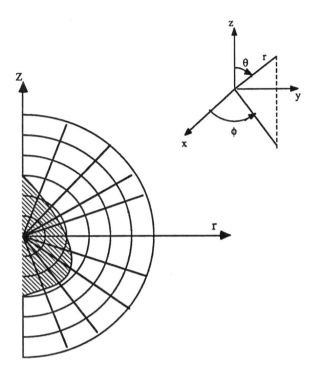

Figure 16 Geometry of the body of revolution problem showing the finite difference grid.

Next, consider a finite difference formulation in which a mesh consisting of nodes distributed along lines of constant r and constant θ is used (see Fig. 16.)

The above two equations are enforced at each interior point of the mesh. For those nodes on the outer boundary, the usual finite difference approximation to $\partial/\partial r$ and $\partial^2/\partial r^2$ cannot be used because of truncation. However, from the Wilcox expansion for the scattered fields, we see that u_m and v_m satisfy the following

$$u_m(r,\theta) = \frac{e^{-\jmath kr}}{r}\left[A_{0m}(\theta) + \frac{A_{1m}(\theta)}{r} + \frac{A_{2m}(\theta)}{r^2} + \ldots\right] \quad (51)$$

$$v_m(r,\theta) = \frac{e^{-\jmath kr}}{r}\left[B_{0m}(\theta) + \frac{B_{1m}(\theta)}{r} + \frac{B_{2m}(\theta)}{r^2} + \ldots\right] \quad (52)$$

If the outer boundary is sufficiently far from the scatterer, the terms of order $(1/r)^2$ and higher make a negligible contribution. Thus, under this approximation, we have:

$$u_m(r,\theta) = \frac{e^{-jkr}}{r} \left[A_{0m}(\theta) + \frac{A_{1m}(\theta)}{r} \right] \tag{53}$$

$$v_m(r,\theta) = \frac{e^{-jkr}}{r} \left[B_{0m}(\theta) + \frac{B_{1m}(\theta)}{r} \right] \tag{54}$$

We can now solve A_{0m}, A_{1m}, B_{0m}, and B_{1m} along a radial line, i.e., say $\theta = \theta_p$, in terms of the nodal values of u_m and v_m at P and Q (see Fig. 15). Once we have done this, we can substitute back into the two-term expansions to find the values of u_m and v_m at $\theta = \theta_p$ for any $r > r_p$. Thus, we can now find the needed expressions for $\partial u_m/\partial r, \partial^2 u_m/\partial r^2, \partial v_m/\partial r$, and $\partial^2 v_m/\partial r^2$ at node P in order to enforce the two coupled partial differential equations at this boundary node. It is worthwhile noting that no explicit absorbing boundary conditions in terms of the normal and angular derivatives are needed in this procedure, as they are in the approaches discussed earlier.

The above procedure has been used to investigate the problem of scattering by different shape BOR's including p.e.c. spheres of various sizes [16]. Good results have been obtained using meshes with outer boundary as close to the scatterer as $r = 1.4a$, or even less, where a is the radius of the sphere.

Next, we present some representative numerical results for the sphere, together with comparisons with the exact series solutions. The numerical values have been obtained using an outer radius which is 1.4 times the radius of the spheres. Figures 17 through 19 exhibit the results for a p.e.c. sphere of radius a where $ka=16.0$. The incident field is z-polarized and traveling in the negative x-direction. Figure 17 is a plot of both the calculated and the analytical values for the magnitude of J_θ, the transverse component of the current induced on the surface of the sphere in the plane $\phi = 0°$. The two results are seen to compare quite favorably with each other. In Figs. 18 and 19 we present the plots of the magnitude and phase , respectively, of the radial variation of the scattered H_ϕ as a function of the normalized distance from the surface of the sphere in the plane $\phi = 0°$ and in the direction $\theta = 90°$. This plot illustrates the fact that the scattered field does indeed begin to exhibit an outward traveling wave behavior

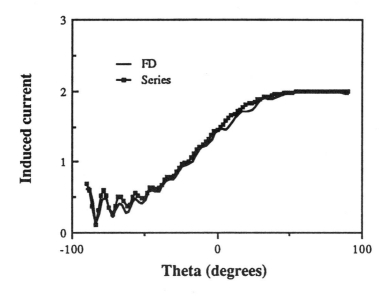

Figure 17 Transverse component of the induced current J_θ on a sphere vs. θ, in the plane $\phi = 0°$.

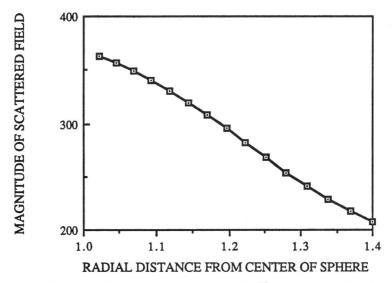

Figure 18 Magnitude of the scattered field, H_ϕ, vs. normalized radial distance in the plane, $\phi = 0°$, at $\theta = 90°$.

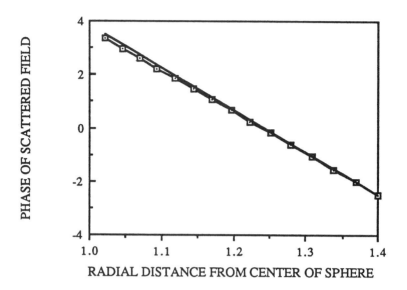

Figure 19 **Phase of the scattered field, H_ϕ, vs. normalized radial distance in the plane, $\phi = 0°$, at $\theta = 90°$ (-□-), and the phase of a traveling wave field with $\exp(-jkr)$ variation (—).**

of the type $(e^{-jkr})/r$, assumed in the asymptotic representation, even at distances not far from the surface of the sphere. In Fig. 19, the top plot is that of the phase of the function e^{-jkr} and it is evident that the the phase variation of the calculated value of the scattered H field indeed exhibits a similar behavior.

Appendix:

Derivation of ABC's Using Recursion Relations

a. 2-D Absorbing Boundary Condition

In this appendix, we present an alternative derivation of the absorbing boundary condition, based on the use of recursion relationships satisfied by the coefficients $a_n(\phi)$ in the Wilcox expansion, which is repeated below for convenience

$$u(\rho, \phi) = \frac{e^{-jk\rho}}{\rho^{1/2}} \sum_{n=0}^{\infty} \frac{a_n(\phi)}{\rho^n} \tag{A1}$$

Imposing the requirement that $u(\rho, \phi)$ satisfy the wave equation $\nabla^2 u + k^2 u = 0$, one can readily derive the recursion relationship

$$-2jk(n+1)a_{n+1} = \left(n + \tfrac{1}{2}\right)^2 a_n + D a_n \tag{A2}$$

where $D = \partial^2/\partial\phi^2$.

Next, we use (A1) to express the radial derivative uf u, i.e. u_ρ, as

$$u_\rho = -jk\, u - \frac{e^{-jk\rho}}{\rho^{3/2}} \sum_{n=0}^{\infty} \frac{\left(n + \tfrac{1}{2}\right) a_n}{\rho^n}$$

$$\tag{A3}$$

$$= \left(-jk - \frac{1}{2\rho}\right) u - \frac{e^{-jk\rho}}{\rho^{5/2}} \sum_{n=1}^{\infty} \frac{n a_n}{\rho^{n-1}}$$

Replacing $n a_n$ in the summation in A3 using A2, we get

$$u_\rho = \left(-jk - \frac{1}{2\rho} + \frac{1}{8jk\rho^2}\right) u$$

$$\tag{A4}$$

$$+ \frac{1}{2jk\rho^2} D u + \frac{e^{-jk\rho}}{jk\rho^{7/2}} \sum_{n=1}^{\infty} \frac{n a_n}{\rho^{n-1}} + O\left(\frac{1}{\rho^{9/2}}\right)$$

Once again, replacing $n a_n$ in (A4) and using the recursion relation, we get

$$u_\rho = \left(-jk - \frac{1}{2\rho} + \frac{1}{8jk\rho^2} + \frac{1}{8k^2\rho^3}\right) u$$

$$+ \left(\frac{1}{2jk\rho^2} + \frac{1}{2k^2\rho^3}\right) D u + O\left(\frac{1}{\rho^{9/2}}\right) \tag{A5}$$

$$= \alpha(\rho)\, u + \beta(\rho)\, u_{\phi\phi}$$

Equation (A5) is seen to be identical to (12) with $\alpha(\rho)$ and $\beta(\rho)$ given by (22) and (23).

b. 3-D Scalar Absorbing Boundary Condition

We present below, for reference, the outline of the derivation of the three-dimensional scalar boundary conditions. For details the reader is referred to [10].

Let $u(r, \theta, \phi)$ satisfy the scalar wave equation

$$\nabla^2 u + k^2 u = 0 \qquad (A6)$$

and be expressed asymptotically as

$$u = \frac{e^{-jkr}}{r} \sum_{n=0}^{\infty} \frac{a_n(\theta, \phi)}{r^n} \qquad (A7)$$

Then it can be shown that the a_n satisfy the recursion relationship

$$-2jk\, n a_n = n(n-1)\, a_{n-1} + D a_{n-1} \qquad (A8)$$

Using (A7) to write u_r, and incorporating the recursion relationship repeatedly in the resulting expression, yields the following compact form for u_r, after a slight rearrangement

$$u_r = -jk\{\alpha(r)\, u + \beta(r)\, Du\} \qquad (A9)$$

where D = Beltrami's operator and Df is given by

$$Df = \frac{1}{\sin\theta} \frac{\partial}{\partial\theta}\left(\sin\theta \frac{\partial f}{\partial\theta}\right) + \frac{1}{\sin^2\theta} \frac{\partial^2 f}{\partial\phi^2} \qquad (A10a)$$

and

$$\alpha(r) = \left(1 + \frac{1}{jkr}\right); \quad \beta(r) = \frac{1}{2(kr)^2 \alpha(r)} \qquad (A10b)$$

up to and including terms of order r^{-4}.

Equation (A9) is the desired representation for the 3-D ABC for a scalar u.

c. 3-D Vector Boundary Condition

For a 3-D vector field $\overline{E}$ (or $\overline{H}$) one can follow exactly the same procedure as in the previous section of this appendix, to express $\hat{r} \times \nabla \times \overline{E}$ in terms of E and its angular derivatives. Only a thumbnail sketch of the derivation is presented here and the reader is referred to [16] for further details.

The first step is to use the Wilcox representation

$$\overline{E} = \frac{e^{-jkr}}{r} \sum_{n=0}^{\infty} \frac{\overline{A}_n(\theta, \phi)}{r^n} \tag{A11}$$

From (A11), we can get

$$\nabla \times \overline{E} = \left\{ -jk\,\hat{r} \times - \frac{(1+D_1)}{r} \right\} \overline{E} - \frac{e^{-jkr}}{r^2} \sum_{n=1}^{\infty} \frac{n\overline{A}_{nt}}{r^n} \tag{A12}$$

where $\overline{A}_{nt} = \hat{r} \times \overline{A}_n$, is the transverse component of $\overline{A}_n$ and, for the vector $\overline{F}$, $D_1\overline{F}$ is given by

$$D_1\overline{F} = \frac{1}{\sin\theta} \left[\frac{\partial}{\partial\theta}(\sin\theta F^\phi) - \frac{\partial F^\theta}{\partial\theta} \right] \hat{r}$$

$$+ \frac{1}{\sin\theta} \left[\frac{\partial F^r}{\partial\theta} - \sin\theta\, F^\phi \right] \hat{\theta} + \left[F^\theta - \frac{\partial F^r}{\partial\theta} \right] \hat{\phi}$$

Using the recursion relation

$$-2jk\,n\overline{A}_{nt} = n(n-1)(\overline{A}_{n-1})_t + D_4\,\overline{A}_{n-1} \tag{A13}$$

where

$$D_4\,\overline{A}_n = (DA_n^\theta + D_\theta\,\overline{A}_n)\hat{\theta} + (DA_n^\phi + D_\phi\,\overline{A}_n)\hat{\theta}$$

$$D_\theta\,\overline{A}_n = 2\frac{\partial A_n^r}{\partial\theta} - \frac{1}{\sin^2\theta} A_n^\theta - \frac{2\cos\theta}{\sin^2\theta}\frac{\partial A_n^\phi}{\partial\phi} \tag{A14}$$

$$D_\phi\,\overline{A}_n = \frac{2}{\sin\theta}\frac{\partial A_n^r}{\partial\phi} + \frac{2\cos\theta}{\sin^2\theta}\frac{\partial A_n^\theta}{\partial\phi} - \frac{1}{\sin^2\theta} A_n^\phi$$

and D is Beltrami's operator, we can once again derive the representation, correct to r^{-4}.

$$\nabla \times \overline{E} = \overline{\alpha}(r)\,\overline{E} + \beta(r)\,D_4\,\overline{E} \qquad \text{(A15)}$$

where

$$\overline{\alpha}(r) = -jk\left(\hat{r} \times \left(1 + \frac{1}{jkr}\right) - \frac{D_1}{jkr}\right) \qquad \text{(A16)}$$

and

$$\beta(r) = \frac{1}{2jkr^2}\frac{1}{(1 + 1/jkr)} \qquad \text{(A17)}$$

Equation (A15) is the desired relationship for the vector ABC.

Acknowledgements

The authors are pleased to acknowledge many helpful discussions with Prof. A. F. Peterson, and Messrs. Rick Gordon, Ahmed Khebir, and Ammar Kouki of the Electromagnetic Communication Laboratory at the University of Illinois. We are especially thankful to Rick Gordon for his contributions to section 4.7 and to the material presented in the Appendix.

This work was supported in part by the Joint Services Electronics Program under Grant #N00014-84-C-0149.

References

[1] McDonald, B. H., and A. Wexler, "Finite element solution of unbounded field problems," *IEEE Trans. Microwave Theory Tech.*, **MTT-20**, 841–847, 1972.

[2] Engquist, B., and A. Majda, "Radiation boundary conditions for the numerical simulation of waves," *Math. Comp.*, **31**, 629–651, 1977.

[3] MacCamy, R., and S. Marin, "A finite element method for exterior interface problems," *Int. J. Math. & Math. Sci.*, **3**, 311–350, 1980.

[4] Kriegsmann, G. A., and C. S. Morawetz, "Solving the Helmholtz equation for exterior problems with variable index of refraction: I," *SIAM J. Sci. Stat.*, **1**, 371–385, 1980.

[5] Bayliss, A., M. Gunzburger, and E. Turkel, "Boundary conditions for the numerical solution of elliptic equations in exterior regions," *SIAM J. Appl. Math.*, **42**, 430–451, 1982.

[6] Meltz, G., B. J. McCartin, and L. J. Bahrmasel, "Application of the control region approximation to electromagnetic scattering," *URSI Radio Science Meeting Program and Abstracts*, p. 185, Blacksburg, Virginia, June 1987. Also, see Chapter 5 of this book.

[7] Mei, K. K., "Unimoment method of solving antenna and scattering problem," *IEEE Trans. Antennas Propagat.*, **AP-22**, 760–766, 1974.

[8] Chang, S. K., and K. K. Mei, "Application of the unimoment method to electromagnetic scattering of dielectric cylinders," *IEEE Trans. Antennas Propagat.*, **AP-24**, 34–42, 1976.

[9] Morgan, M. A., and K. K. Mei, "Finite-element computation of scattering by inhomogeneous penetrable bodies of revolution," *IEEE Trans. Antennas Propagat.*, **AP-27**, 202–214, 1979.

[10] Morgan, M. A., S. K. Chang, and K. K. Mei, "Coupled azimuthal potentials for electromagnetic field problems in inhomogeneous axially symmetric media," *IEEE Trans. Antennas Propagat*, **AP-25**, 413–417, 1977

[11] Wilcox, C. H., "An expansion theorem for electromagnetic fields," *Comm. Pure & Appl. Math.*, **9**, 115–134, 1956.

[12] Kriegsmann, G. A., A. Taflove, and K. R. Umashankar, "A new formulation of electromagnetic wave scattering using an on-surface radiation boundary condition approach," *IEEE Trans. Antennas Propagat.*, **AP-35**, 153–161, 1987. Also, see Chapter 8.

[13] Silvester, P., and R. L. Ferrari, *Finite Elements for Electrical Engineers.* Cambridge, U.K. : Cambridge University Press, 1983

[14] Strang, G. and G. J. Fix, *An Analysis of the Finite Element Method.* Englewood Cliffs, N.J. : Prentice-Hall, Inc., 1973.

[15] Reddy, J. N., *An Introduction to the Finite-Element Method.* New York, N.Y. : McGraw-Hill, 1984.

[16] Mittra, R., and R. Gordon, "Radar scattering from bodies of revolution using an efficient partial differential equation algorithm," Submitted to *IEEE Trans. Antennas Propagat.*

5

APPLICATION OF THE
CONTROL REGION APPROXIMATION
TO TWO-DIMENSIONAL
ELECTROMAGNETIC SCATTERING

B. J. McCartin, L. J. Bahrmasel and G. Meltz

5.1   Introduction

The scattering of electromagnetic waves by geometrically complex objects is a very interesting theoretical problem that has important implications for many applications. This problem has traditionally been treated either by approximate methods such as the geometric theory of diffraction [1] or by "exact" methods such as integral equation formulations [2]. The approximate methods have the advantage that they are very efficient yet they ignore some basic scattering mechanisms such as travelling waves. The integral equation methods such as the moment method incorporate such contributors but at the price of being very computationally intensive for large, complicated scatterers. In this paper, we propose a numerical method of solution which incorporates a complete physical model yet ultimately is capable of efficiently treating large, complex three dimensional targets. Herein, we present the two dimensional algorithm.

The basic idea is to bring to bear numerical methods that have proved powerful in such areas as fluid dynamics and solid mechanics. Thus, two dimensional scattering is first formulated as an exterior boundary value problem, which in both the transverse magnetic and transverse electric cases involves a generalized Helmholtz equation. This formulation easily permits complex scatterers composed of lossy dielectric and magnetic materials. Also, thin coatings are readily treated by a surface impedance boundary condition.

Asymptotic boundary conditions are applied [3,4], thus allowing a truncation of the computational domain at a finite distance. Two of the more popular candidates are compared on a model problem. The prospect of using higher order boundary conditions is assessed with the negative conclusion that this is not practicable. An a posteriori method to assess the accuracy of these approximate boundary conditions is suggested.

With these formulational issues aside, attention is next focused on discretizing the boundary value problem. The Control Region Approximation, originally developed for compressible aerodynamic [5] calculations and subsequently extended for semiconductor device simulation [6], is suitably modified for and applied to our scattering problem [7]. In this method, an arbitrary set of discrete points, at which the field will be approximated, is chosen. Each such point is then surrounded by a control region (Dirichlet region). The conservation form of the Helmholtz equation is then enforced on each control region. This involves the numerical approximation of field flux through the control region boundary. The approximation is very easily achieved by utilizing an orthogonality property (duality) of the Dirichlet and Delaunay tessellations [8].

The assembly of the discrete equations, one for each mesh point, results in a coefficient matrix of extremely sparse structure. Thus, the highly developed sparse direct methods [9] may be applied allowing the efficient calculation of monostatic cross sections. In addition to the geometric flexibility offered by the arbitrariness of mesh point locations, a number of other significant benefits are accrued from this method. Because the continuous equation is expressed in conservation form prior to discretization, there is a corresponding discrete conservation law which avoids the local sources and sinks which can appear in finite element discretizations [10]. This conservation form also guarantees enforcement of appropriate interface conditions between layers. The flux balance nature of this discretization naturally accommodates both the impedance boundary condition along the scatterer and the asymptotic radiation condition along the outer computational boundary. The scheme is second order accurate in smooth regions. Second order accuracy is preserved at corners by appropriate treatment of the singularities present. The accuracy is further enhanced by replacing the traditional polynomial basis functions by alternative trigonometric basis functions.

The solution of the discrete equations is accomplished using the Yale Sparse Matrix Package (YSMP) [11] and relevant features of this package are summarized. Also included are details of the postprocessing calculation of the scattering cross section since in many contexts this is the parameter of primary interest. Finally, a collection of test cases for canonical geometries is presented which illustrate the capabilities of this method. The numerical results are concluded by the comparison of our calculated results with actual test data on a very complex configuration. These results clearly indicate the worth of two dimensional simulation for this problem. The necessary extensions of this technique required to provide fully three dimensional simulation are considered.

5.2   Problem Formulation

Consider the scattering of a two-dimensional electromagnetic wave by a cylindrical obstacle of arbitrary cross-section (Fig. 1). The general solution of such a problem can be obtained by the superposition of Transverse Magnetic (TM) and Transverse Electric (TE) components [12] where

$$\overline{E} = \begin{bmatrix} 0 \\ 0 \\ E_z(x,y) \end{bmatrix} ; \quad \overline{H} = \begin{bmatrix} H_x(x,y) \\ H_y(x,y) \\ 0 \end{bmatrix} \quad \text{(TM Case)} \qquad (1a)$$

$$\overline{E} = \begin{bmatrix} E_x(x,y) \\ E_y(x,y) \\ 0 \end{bmatrix} ; \quad \overline{H} = \begin{bmatrix} 0 \\ 0 \\ H_z(x,y) \end{bmatrix} \quad \text{(TE Case)} \qquad (1b)$$

In the above, we have assumed a harmonic time dependence

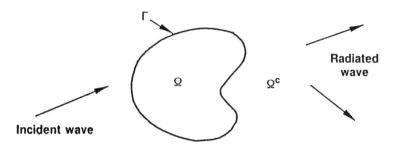

Figure 1 Problem formulation.

$$\tilde{E}(\overline{r},t) = Re\{e^{\jmath\omega t}\overline{E}(\overline{r})\}$$

$$\tilde{H}(\overline{r},t) = Re\{e^{\jmath\omega t}\overline{H}(\overline{r})\} \tag{2}$$

where $(\tilde{E},\tilde{H})$ is the physical field and $(\overline{E},\overline{H})$ is the phasor field.

Upon substitution into Maxwell's equations we obtain the generalized Helmholtz equation

$$\nabla_t \cdot (a\nabla_t u) + bu = 0 \tag{3}$$

where ∇_t is the transverse gradient and

$$u = E_z, \ a = 1/\mu, \ b = \omega^2\epsilon \quad \text{(TM Case)} \tag{4a}$$

$$u = H_z, \ a = 1/\epsilon, \ b = \omega^2\mu \quad \text{(TE Case)} \tag{4b}$$

and ϵ and μ are the complex permittivity and permeability, respectively, each of which may be arbitrary functions of position. Thus, the problem has been reduced to the solution of scalar Helmholtz equations.

These equations must be supplemented by appropriate boundary conditions at the surface of any conductors. In particular, we wish to incorporate the impedance boundary condition [13]

$$\overline{E} - (\overline{E}\cdot\hat{n})\hat{n} = \eta_S\hat{n} \times \overline{H} \tag{5}$$

where η_S is the surface impedance. This condition reduces to

$$\frac{\partial u}{\partial n} + \gamma u = 0 \tag{6}$$

where

$$\gamma = \begin{cases} -\jmath\dfrac{\omega\mu}{\eta_S} & \text{(TM Case)} \\[2ex] +\jmath\omega\epsilon\eta_S & \text{(TE Case)} \end{cases} \tag{7}$$

and $\hat{n}$ is the unit normal to the cross-section. Note that $\eta_S = 0$ (perfect conductor) reduces to

$$u = 0 \quad \text{(TM Case)} \tag{8a}$$

$$u_n = 0 \quad \text{(TE Case)} \tag{8b}$$

As it stands, this formulation is not sufficient to guarantee a unique solution. An additional condition is needed to insure that the scattered field is composed of outgoing waves only. Incoming scattered waves are excluded by the Sommerfeld radiation condition

$$\frac{\partial u_S}{\partial r} + \jmath\kappa u_S = O(r^{-1/2}); \quad \kappa^2 = \omega^2\mu\epsilon \tag{9}$$

where the total field has been decomposed into the sum of an incident, u_I, and a scattered, u_S, field

$$u = u_I + u_S \tag{10}$$

Thus, the formulation reduces to the following exterior boundary value problem for the scattered field

$$\nabla \cdot (a\nabla u_S) + bu_S = F = -[\nabla \cdot (a\nabla u_I) + bu_I] \text{ in } \Omega \tag{11a}$$

$$\nabla u_S \cdot \hat{n} + \gamma u_S = -[\nabla u_I \cdot \hat{n} + \gamma u_I] \text{ on } \partial\Omega \tag{11b}$$

$$\frac{\partial u_S}{\partial r} + \jmath\kappa u_S = O(r^{-1/2}) \tag{11c}$$

where we have dropped the subscript on the gradient operator. Note that no restrictions are placed upon the form of u_I, e.g. it need not be a plane wave. Moreover, the sources generating the incident field may be located at infinity or at a finite distance.

5.3   Asymptotic Boundary Conditions

The radiation boundary condition

$$\frac{\partial u_S}{\partial r} + \jmath \kappa u_S = O(r^{-1/2}) \tag{12}$$

is a condition which seemingly must be applied infinitely far from the scatterer. Since we are constrained to solve our boundary value problem in a finite domain, we must replace this far-field condition by a near-field equivalent. This near-field expression is in the form of an integral equation along the outer boundary [14]. Discretization of this equation leads to corresponding full matrix rows thus destroying the sparsity crucial to the efficiency of our approach. Thus, we seek a local differential radiation condition approximating the nonlocal integral condition. Such conditions have received considerable attention in the computational acoustics literature [3,4]. We consider two of these approaches in what follows.

The first asymptotic boundary condition we treat is due to Engquist and Majda [3]; a more elementary presentation is given in [15]. The basic idea is to eliminate reflected waves in the frequency domain. However, this results in a non-rational dispersion relation which yields a pseudodifferential operator rather than a differential operator. Thus, a totally non-reflecting differential boundary condition is not achievable. Instead, Engquist and Majda employ Padé approximants to the dispersion relation and use the corresponding differential operator as an approximation to the Sommerfeld operator. The particular boundary condition of interest is

$$(E-M)_2 : \frac{\partial u_S}{\partial r} = \left(-\jmath \kappa - \frac{1}{2r}\right) u_S + \frac{1}{2\kappa^2 r^2}\left(-\jmath \kappa + \frac{1}{r}\right)\frac{\partial^2 u_S}{\partial \theta^2} \tag{13}$$

The second asymptotic boundary condition we consider is due to Bayliss and Turkel [4]; a more elementary presentation is available in [16]. In this method, the scattered field is expanded in an asymptotic series of outgoing waves. The coefficients in the local boundary operator are then obtained by annihilating successive terms in this expansion. The particular boundary condition of interest is

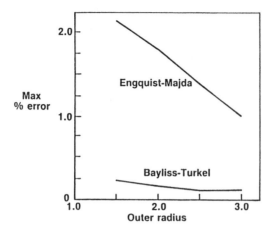

Figure 2   Comparison of boundary conditions.

$(B - T)_2$:

$$\frac{\partial u_S}{\partial r} = \frac{1}{1 - \jmath/\kappa r} \cdot \left[\left(-\jmath\kappa - \frac{3}{2r} + \frac{3\jmath}{8\kappa r^2}\right) u_S - \frac{\jmath}{2\kappa r^2} \frac{\partial^2 u_S}{\partial \theta^2}\right] \quad (14)$$

Note that both of these boundary conditions asymptotically yield the Sommerfeld condition

$$\frac{\partial u_S}{\partial r} = -\jmath\kappa u_S \text{ as } r \to \infty \quad (15)$$

It should also be pointed out that each boundary condition is one member of a whole family of boundary conditions. The particular representative has been selected on the basis of compatibility with the interior Helmholtz equation. The prospects for using higher order boundary conditions will be discussed below.

Let us compare $(E - M)_2$ with $(B - T)_2$ on a model problem. In particular, consider the scattering of a TM wave by a perfectly conducting cylinder of size $\kappa a = 1$. The mesh density is selected so that discretization error is negligble so that any error is primarily due to the approximate nature of the outer boundary condition which is enforced on a circumscribing circle. The maximum percentage field errors are then calculated and compared for various locations of the outer boundary. The result, which is displayed in Fig. 2, indicates a clear advantage for $(B - T)_2$ in this problem. Clearly, the smaller the computational domain the more efficient the overall computation.

The question naturally arises as to whether we can improve the accuracy by increasing the order of the Bayliss-Turkel operator. Let us address this question in some generality. In general,

$$u_S = \sum_n a_n H_n(\kappa r) e^{\jmath n\theta} \tag{16a}$$

$$\frac{\partial u_S}{\partial r} = \sum_n a_n \kappa H_n'(\kappa r) e^{\jmath n\theta} \tag{16b}$$

so that the impedance of the n-th Fourier mode is $\kappa H_n'(\kappa r)/H_n(\kappa r)$.

At a fixed outer radius, R, we consider rational approximation in the frequency domain

$$\frac{H_n'(\kappa r)}{H_n(\kappa r)} \approx \frac{\alpha_0 + \alpha_1 n + - - - \alpha_i n^i}{\beta_0 + \beta_1 n + - - - - + \beta_\jmath n^\jmath} \tag{17}$$

which corresponds in the spatial domain to

$$\beta_0 \frac{\partial}{\partial r} u_S + \beta_1 \frac{\partial^2}{\partial r \partial \theta} u_S + - - - - + \beta_\jmath \frac{\partial^{\jmath+1}}{\partial r \partial \theta^\jmath} u_S$$
$$= \kappa \, \alpha_0 u_S + \alpha_1 \frac{\partial}{\partial \theta} u_S + - - - - + \alpha_i \frac{\partial^i}{\partial \theta^i} u_S \tag{18}$$

If the original rational approximation is good then this boundary condition will provide a good impedance match for the Fourier modes and thus reflections from the outer boundary will be negligible.

The efficiency of higher order boundary conditions is now seen to be governed by how well we can approximate H_n'/H_n by rational functions in the frequency domain. Figures 3a and 3b show the real and imaginary parts, respectively of $H_n'(50)/H_n(50)$ together with u_r/u for $(B - T)_2$. We see that $(B - T)_2$ provides a good match for the real part of the impedance for the first 40 modes while the match for the imaginary part is good only for 20 modes. Suppose that we have a scatterer that has excited 60 modes [17]. Can we construct a rational function providing good impedance matches over the entire spectrum present?

To answer this question we have utilized the IMSL routine IRATCU [18] which constructs the rational weighted Chebyshev approximation of specified degree. By exhaustive search we determined

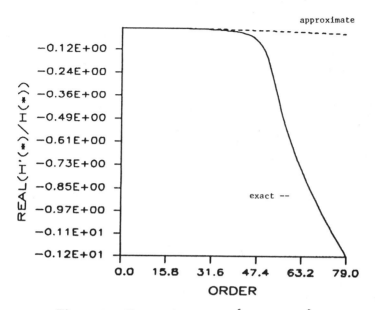

Figure 3a Comparison of Re{Impedence}.

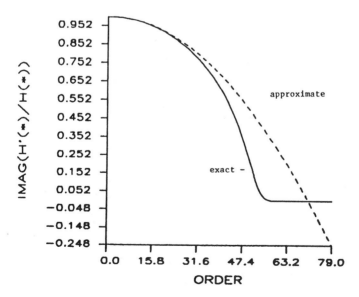

Figure 3b Comparison of Im{Impedence}.

that i = 9, j = 8 for the real part and i = 8, j = 9 for the imaginary part are required to produce good impedance matches for all 60 modes. These approximations are shown in Figs. 4a and 4b.

The high degree of these rational functions in the frequency domain implies a corresponding high degree of the differential operators in the spatial domain. As such, these boundary conditions destroy the very sparsity that they are intended to preserve. This negative result places $(B-T)_2$ in a rather special position; i.e., it is a low order boundary operator that provides good impedance matches for many problems. Yet, to significantly improve upon it requires a vast increase in the order of the boundary condition.

Note that the effectiveness of the asymptotic boundary condition can be assessed *a posteriori* [17] by expanding u_S along Γ in the form

$$u_S \approx \sum_n [a_n H_n^{(1)}(\kappa R) + b_n H_n^{(2)}(\kappa R)]e^{\jmath n\theta} \tag{19}$$

using the calculated values of u_S and $\partial u_S/\partial r$ where

$$\frac{\partial u_S}{\partial R} \approx \sum_n \kappa[a_n H_n^{(1)'}(\kappa R) + b_n H_n^{(2)'}(\kappa R)]e^{\jmath n\theta} \tag{20}$$

Thus, we first employ an FFT to produce

$$u_S = \sum_n A_n e^{\jmath n\theta}, \frac{\partial u_S}{\partial R} = \sum_n B_n e^{\jmath n\theta} \tag{21}$$

and then solve for a_n, b_n as

$$a_n = \frac{\kappa H_n^{(2)'}(\kappa R)A_n - H_n^{(2)}(\kappa R)B_n}{\kappa[H_n^{(1)}(\kappa R)H_n^{(2)'}(\kappa R) - H_n^{(2)}(\kappa R)H_n^{(1)'}(\kappa R)]} \tag{22a}$$

$$b_n = \frac{-\kappa H_n^{(1)'}(\kappa R)A_n + H_n^{(1)}(\kappa R)B_n}{\kappa[H_n^{(1)}(\kappa R)H_n^{(2)'}(\kappa R) - H_n^{(2)}(\kappa R)H_n^{(1)'}(\kappa R)]} \tag{22b}$$

Any nonzero a_n corresponds to a reflected wave from the computational boundary.

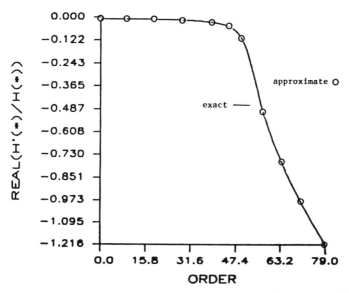

Figure 4a Best rational approximation to Re{Impedence}.

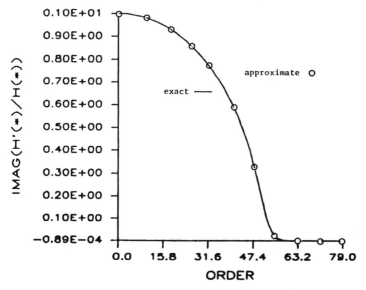

Figure 4b Best rational approximation to Im{Impedence}.

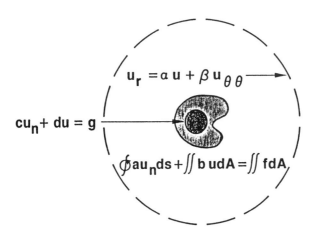

Figure 5 Boundary value problem.

5.4   Discretization

The previous sections have reduced our problem to the solution of the following boundary value problem (Fig. 5)

$$\nabla \cdot (a\nabla u_S) + bu_S = -[\nabla \cdot (a\nabla u_I) + bu_I] \text{ in } \Omega \qquad (23a)$$

$$\nabla u_S \cdot \widehat{n} + \gamma u_S = -[\nabla u_I \cdot \widehat{n} + \gamma u_I] \text{ on } C_i \qquad (23b)$$

$$\frac{\partial u_S}{\partial r} + \alpha u_S + \beta \frac{\partial^2 u_S}{\partial \theta^2} = 0 \text{ on } C_0 \qquad (23c)$$

In the above, a, b, and γ are (possibly discontinuous) spatially varying complex functions while α and β are complex constants. This continuous formulation must be suitably discretized for computer simulation. Moreover, this discretization must be achieved for arbitrarily shaped scatterers. We effect this discretization via the Control Region Approximation which we now describe.

We first reformulate our problem in integral (conservation) form by integrating over a two-dimensional domain, D, and applying the divergence theorem resulting in

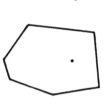

Figure 6a   Mesh points.

$$\int_{\partial D} a\, \frac{\partial u_S}{\partial \nu}\, d\sigma + \iint_D b\, u_S\, dA = -\int_{\partial D} a\, \frac{\partial u_I}{\partial \nu}\, d\sigma - \iint_D b\, u_I\, dA \quad (24)$$

The distinct advantage of this reformulation is that it still applies when the coefficients are discontinuous as they typically are in applications involving layered media.

We next select a discrete set of points (grid points, nodal points, etc.,) at which we will approximate the scattered field (Fig. 6a). The rational selection of this point set is, in general, nontrivial and is beyond the purview of this paper. Assuming these points given, we next associate a control region with each point. The control region associated with point P is defined to be the set of all points in the plane closer to P than to any of its neighbors and is known as the Dirichlet region [19] (Fig. 6b) (a.k.a Voronoi region, Thiessen region, Wigner-Seitz cell). The Dirichlet regions are convex polygons whose union is a tessellation of the solution domain known as the Dirichlet tessellation.

The line segments connecting grid points which share an edge of a Dirichlet polygon form a triangulation known as the Delaunay triangulation [20] (Fig. 6c). This triangulation possesses a number of desirable properties relative to finite element discretizations. The Delaunay triangulation is, however, of secondary importance in the present

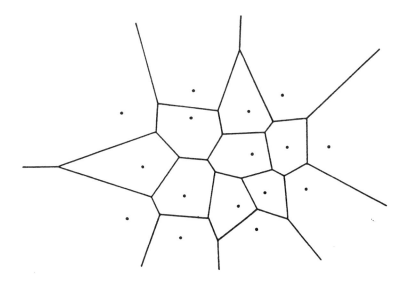

Figure 6b   Dirichlet tessellation.

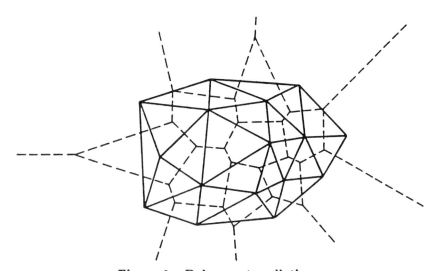

Figure 6c   Delaunay tessellation.

method where the Dirichlet tessellation is the fundamental construct. It is important to observe that a Delaunay edge is orthogonal to the corresponding Dirichlet edge. We shall refer to this property as duality. The Delaunay triangles are also used in Watson's method for the construction of the Dirichlet regions [21].

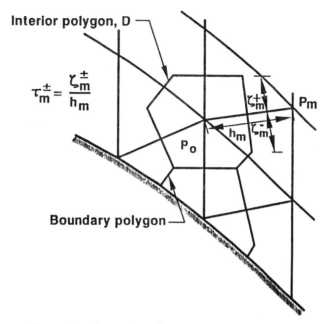

Interior polygon, D

$$\tau_m^{\pm} = \frac{\zeta_m^{\pm}}{h_m}$$

ζ_m^+ P_m

P_0

h_m ζ_m^-

Boundary polygon

Figure 7 Control region approximation.

We now enforce the conservation form equation upon each control region. After performing the numerical integrations, we arrive at the following discrete equation at point P_0

$$\sum_m (\tau_m^- a_m^- + \tau_m^+ a_m^+)(u_m - u_0) + \sum_m b_{m,0} \, A_{m,0} \, u_0$$
$$= \sum_m F_{m,0} \, A_{m,0} \tag{25}$$

where m indexes the polygon sides in Fig. 7. In the above, F represents the source terms due to the incident field and must include appropriate δ-functions along the triangle edges due to discontinuities in a. Note that we have taken advantage of the Dirichlet-Delaunay duality in approximating the normal derivative (flux) terms. It is important to observe that each discrete equation contributes a matrix row which is extremely sparse so that the resulting system can thus be solved very efficiently.

The above difference equation is based upon representing the unknown fields locally by polynomials. However, it is clear that the

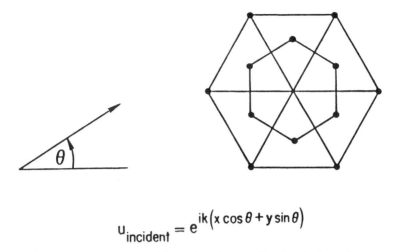

$$u_{\text{incident}} = e^{ik\left(x\cos\theta + y\sin\theta\right)}$$

Figure 8a Model problem for alternative basis functions.

solutions we seek are oscillatory and hence are well approximated by polynomials only on fine meshes. This suggests the use of alternative, in this instance trigonometric, basis functions for the local field representation. The use of one-dimensional Green's functions along the triangle edges [22] yields the flux approximation

$$\frac{\partial u_S}{\partial \nu} \approx \frac{\kappa \cos(\kappa \Delta \nu)}{\sin(\kappa \Delta \nu)}(u_m - u_0) \longrightarrow \frac{u_m - u_0}{\Delta \nu} \text{ as } \kappa \Delta \nu \to 0 \qquad (26)$$

In order to compare this approximation to the traditional central difference formula we utilize a model problem. Consider an incident uniform plane wave (Fig. 8a)

$$u_i = e^{j\kappa(x \cos \theta + y \sin \theta)} \qquad (27)$$

impinging upon a regular hexagonal lattice. Placing Dirichlet conditions on the boundary, we then solve for the field at the central point. This provides a measure of the accuracy of the difference approximation versus κh where κ is the wave number and h is the mesh parameter. Figure 8b displays the performance of both the old and new difference schemes. It is readily apparent that applying the alternative basis function representation reduces the error, or what is the same thing, allows the use of a coarser mesh to achieve a fixed level of

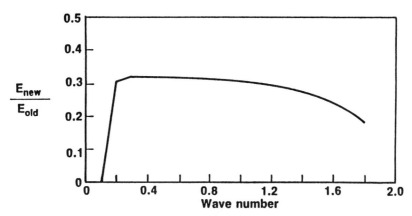

Figure 8b Comparison of absolute error of difference schemes.

resolution. This in turn allows simulation for larger objects with fixed computation time.

The discrete formulation described above must be modified when the scatterer possesses sharp protruding corners. This is due to the singular nature of the derivatives of the field in the neighborhood of such a point [23]. Consider a reentrant corner of exterior measure $\gamma\pi$ (Fig. 9). Locally, the field behaves like

$$u \sim a + b(\theta)r^{1/\alpha} \tag{28}$$

Fitting this form to the unknown fields at the end points of a triangle edge yields

$$u(r, \theta) \sim u_0 + (\bar{u} - u_0)\left(\frac{r}{\bar{r}}\right)^{1/\alpha} \tag{29}$$

and hence

$$u_r\left(\frac{\bar{r}}{2}, \bar{\theta}\right) \sim \frac{\bar{u} - u_0}{\alpha\bar{r}} \tag{30}$$

Some additional observations on the above discretization procedure are in order. The shape of the scatterer is completely arbitrary since the mesh point distribution is essentially unconstrained. Moreover, the material properties may vary continuously, i.e. may be inhomogeneous, or may change abruptly, i.e. may be heterogeneous. Since the governing equation has been written in conservation form, the correct weak solution will be captured in the heterogeneous case without the explicit imposition of jump conditions. Also, the conservation law

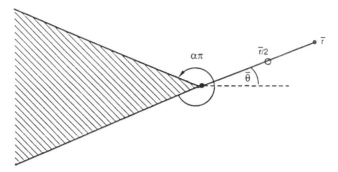

Figure 9   Corner singularity.

itself is preserved in its discrete counterpart, thus avoiding the spurious sources and sinks which can appear in finite element methods. Both the impedance boundary condition and the asymptotic radiation condition involve specification of boundary fluxes and are hence easily incorporated. The scheme as proposed possesses formal second order accuracy which has been preserved by the singularity treatment and enhanced by the inclusion of alternative basis functions. Finally, all the basic ingredients of this technique are extendable to three spatial dimensions as well as to time dependent phenomena.

5.5   Solution of Discrete Equations

The previously described discretization procedure applied to each grid point results in a linear system of equations

$$Au = F \qquad (31)$$

where each element of this matrix-vector equation corresponds to a particular point. What is significant here is that the coefficient matrix A is extremely sparse with an average of seven nonzeroes per row (2D) regardless of how many unknowns. This allows the use of the highly developed sparse direct methods which provide efficient solution (both in terms of storage and operation count) of such systems thus allowing simulation of larger objects.

In this work, the Yale Sparse Matrix Package (YSMP) is employed. An LU decomposition is first performed on A, viz.

$$A = LU \tag{32}$$

where L and U are lower and upper triangular, respectively. Then

$$Lv = F \tag{33}$$

is solved by forward substitution followed by solving

$$Uu = v \tag{34}$$

by backward substitution. YSMP provides for automatic reordering of the equations to minimize fill-in during the factorization phase resulting in savings during the subsequent forward and backward substitutions as well as further economizing on storage. An option is also provided for a symbolic LU factorization to precede the numerical LU factorization which reduces execution time if many systems with the same sparsity pattern must be solved. This occurs, for example, when nonlinear materials are treated.

The significance of organizing the computation in this fashion lies in the fact that the LU factorization phase is more costly than the forward/backward substitution phase. If we have many systems with the same coefficient matrix but different righthand sides, we need only do a single factorization thus accruing great savings in computation time. This is precisely the case when we wish to construct the monostatic cross-section since the incident fields appear only in the source terms of the differential equation and boundary conditions. In practice, it has been found that YSMP can handle scatterers up to length 20λ of arbitrary shape and material properties in an engineering workstation computing environment.

5.6 Cross Section Calculation

In many instances, it is a functional of the field, the scattering cross section, rather than the field itself which is of primary interest. Although rightfully a post-processing operation, the scattering cross section is of such importance that we include a discussion of its computation here.

The scattering cross section, $\chi(\theta)$, is defined as the scattered power per unit length in a fixed direction normalized by that of the incident field, i.e.

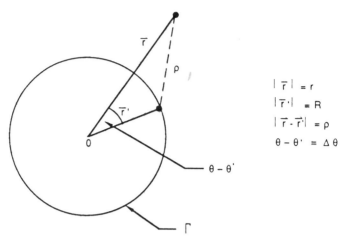

Figure 10 Scattering cross section calculation.

$$\chi(\theta) = \lim_{r\to\infty} 2\pi r \frac{|\overline{E}_S|^2}{|\overline{E}_i|^2} = \lim_{r\to\infty} 2\pi r \frac{|\overline{H}_S|^2}{|\overline{H}_i|^2} \tag{35}$$

which for either TM or TE waves can be written as

$$\chi(\theta) = \lim_{r\to\infty} 2\pi r |u_S|^2 \tag{36}$$

where we have assumed that $|u_i| = 1$ as it is, for example, in the case of a uniform plane wave.

Given u_S along the contour (see Fig. 10), we can calculate u_S at any exterior point from [14]

$$u_S(\overline{r}) = \int_\Gamma \left[G(\overline{r},\overline{r}') \frac{\partial u_S(\overline{r}')}{\partial n'} - \frac{\partial G(\overline{r},\overline{r}')}{\partial n'} u_S(\overline{r}') \right] dl' \tag{37}$$

where $G(\overline{r},\overline{r}') = \frac{1}{4j} H_0^{(2)}(\kappa\rho); \rho = |\overline{r} - \overline{r}'|$ is the outgoing free-space Green's function for the Helmholtz equation and $\partial/\partial n' = \partial/\partial R$. For large enough values of r the asymptotic form for the Hankel function gives the approximation

$$H_0^{(2)}(\kappa\rho) \sim \sqrt{\frac{2j}{\pi\kappa\rho}} e^{-j\kappa\rho} \sim \sqrt{\frac{2j}{\pi\kappa r}} e^{-j\kappa(r - R\cos\Delta\theta)} \tag{38}$$

where $\Delta\theta = \theta - \theta'$. Thus, for large r,

$$u_S(\bar{r}) \sim \frac{R_J}{4}\sqrt{\frac{2J}{\pi\kappa r}}e^{-J\kappa r}\int_0^{2\pi} F[u_S(\bar{r}')]e^{+J\kappa R\ \cos\ \Delta\theta}\,d\theta' \qquad (39a)$$

with

$$F[u_S(\bar{r}')] = \left[\frac{\partial u_S(\bar{r}')}{\partial R} - (J\kappa\cos\Delta\theta)u_S(\bar{r}')\right] \qquad (39b)$$

which leads to

$$\chi(\theta) = \frac{R^2}{4\kappa}\left|\int_0^{2\pi} F[u_S(\bar{r}')]e^{+J\kappa R\cos\Delta\theta}\,d\theta'\right|^2 \qquad (39c)$$

Care must be exercised in performing the numerical integration since the integrand is highly oscillatory [24]. In the present work, we make the approximation

$$\int_0^{2\pi}\left[\frac{\partial u_S(\bar{r}')}{\partial R} - (J\kappa\cos\Delta\theta)u_S(\bar{r}')\right]e^{J\kappa R\cos\Delta\theta}\,d\theta' \approx$$

$$\sum_i\left\{\frac{\overline{\partial u_S^i}}{\partial R}\int_{\theta_i'}^{\theta_{i+1}'}\Psi(R,\Delta\theta)\,d\theta' - J\kappa\overline{u_S^i}\int_{\theta_i'}^{\theta_{i+1}'}\cos\Delta\theta\,\Psi(R,\Delta\theta)\,d\theta'\right\}$$

$$\qquad (40a)$$

with

$$\Psi(R,\Delta\theta) = e^{J\kappa R\cos\Delta\theta} \qquad (40b)$$

where $\overline{u_S^i}$ is the average value of u_S over the i-th panel. Accurate values of $\partial u_S/\partial R$ can be obtained from flux balances along the outer contour. A linear approximation is then made to $\cos\Delta\theta$ on each panel. The remaining integrals are then analytically evaluated. The resulting approximate expression for $\chi(\theta)$ takes the form of a discrete convolution and hence can be rapidly evaluated using FFT techniques.

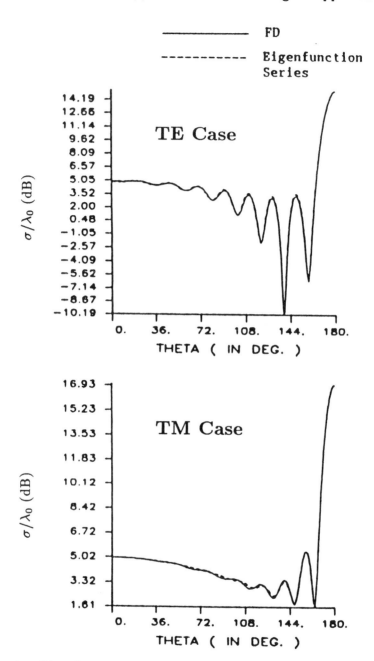

Figure 11   Bistatic patterns for a PEC circular cylinder ($k_0 a = 10$).
Outer computational boundary at $1.5a$.

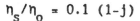

$$\eta_s/\eta_0 = 0.1 \ (1-j)$$

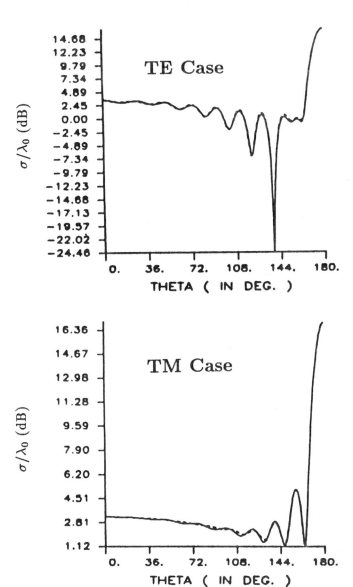

Figure 12 Bistatic patterns for an impedence sheet circular cylinder ($k_0a = 10$). (a) TE. (b) TM.

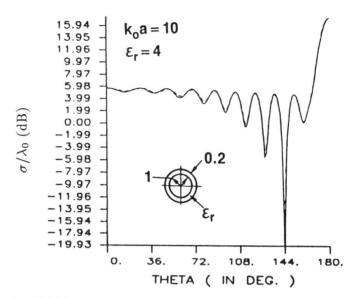

Figure 13 TE bistatic pattern for a dielectric clad PEC circular cylinder
($k_0a = 10$). Outer computational boundary at $1.5a$. ($a =$ radius of inner
conductor).

5.7   Numerical Results

The generality and accuracy of using an asymptotic outer
boundary condition with the control region finite difference formulation to solve two- dimensional scattering problems are illustrated
in this section. The method is applied to a wide variety of targets,
including smooth, perfectly electrically conducting (PEC) scatterers,
objects with edges, coatings, thin films and cavities. The validity of the
technique is examined by comparing the monostatic or bistatic cross
sections, or the surface currents, with known solutions and measurements.

Highly accurate results were obtained for small and large PEC
circular cylinders with dielectric coatings, impedance sheet claddings
and axial slots. Figure 11 shows a comparison of the finite difference
bistatic RCS results with the eigenfunction series expansion solutions
for both TE and TM scattering. The radius, a, of the cylinder is
$(10/2\pi)\lambda$ and the outer boundary condition is applied at 1.5 a, well
within the Fresnel near zone of the scatterer. A polar mesh containing
about 10,000 nodes was used in these examples. Excellent results were
also obtained for a lossy impedance sheet cladding, Fig. 12, and a fairly

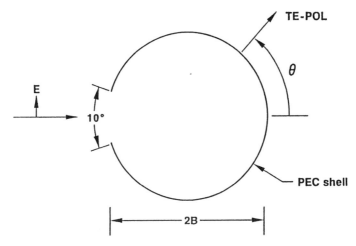

Figure 14 TE scattering from an axially slotted circular cylinder.

thick lossless dielectric layer, Fig. 13. The former case illustrates the use of the control region method to solve the wave equation with mixed interior boundary conditions. Dielectric coatings with large jumps in properties are also treated accurately as shown by the latter example.

An interesting use of the technique is to investigate the coupling between the scattered fields in a cavity-backed aperture (Fig. 14) and the currents on the exterior of the surrounding enclosure. If the Q of the cavity is large, that is if the coupling aperture is narrow, then the scattered fields will be extremely wavelength sensitive. In Fig. 15, we compare our results with the generalized dual series solutions obtained by Ziolkowski and Grant [25]. The solutions are in close agreement at both resonances and antiresonances which are extremely narrow. Finite difference and eigenfunction series solutions for the closed cylinder are also plotted for comparison.

The complete details of the near field are obtained without additional computation in our method. A contour plot of the scattered axial magnetic field (Fig. 16) at $k_0 B = \pi$ reveals the nature of the resonance in the monostatic cross section. The field pattern within the cavity is, apart from the values near the slot on the left-hand side of the figure, very nearly the same as the TE_{21} circular waveguide mode. It is clear that the effect of various types of wall loadings, posts and other obstacles within the cavity could be examined using the control region finite difference solution. Any shape of slot-coupled cylindrical cavity can be studied with this method.

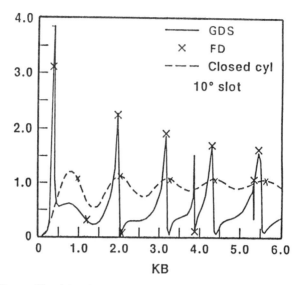

Figure 15 Normalized backscatter cross section $(\pi \cdot B)$ of a cavity-backed axial slot in a cylinder [24].

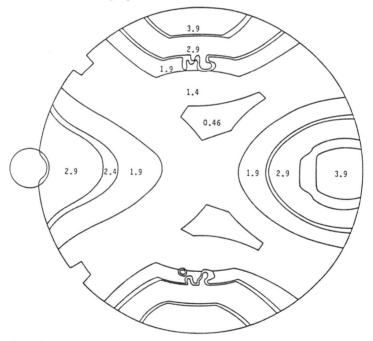

Figure 16 Scattered axial magnetic field strength contours for $10°$ slotted PEC cylinder $(k_0 B = \pi)$. The slot is illuminated by a TE plane wave from $180°$.

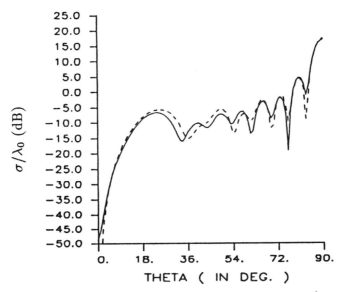

Figure 17 TE backscatter pattern from a PEC flat plate ($k_0W = 26.6$) computed using control region FD technique (———) and the approximate (– – –) Sommerfield-MacDonald expression [27].

The interaction between travelling waves and edges or joins, that have discontinuities in curvature, is another problem which can be investigated using the control region method. Here the capability of inspecting the near fields under conditions where travelling wave components are dominant can provide important insight as to the effect of lossy layers, variation in curvature, or surface impedance changes. TE scattering from a flat strip of width $(26.6/2\pi)\lambda$ (Fig. 17) shows a travelling wave lobe at 24°. A near field contour plot of the scattered $|H_z|$ field (Fig. 18) shows the buildup of the end-fire radiation and the standing wave formed by the incident and reflected components of the travelling wave excited by the 24° plane wave illumination. A lossy fairly thick (0.2λ) dielectric layer (Fig. 19) suppresses the travelling wave lobe, but increases the edge scattering. The outer computational boundary had a radius of 1.5ℓ where ℓ = half-length of strip and 10,000 mesh points were employed for these calculations.

Similar travelling wave interactions are also apparent in the illuminated side currents of a PEC square cylinder (Fig. 20). Note the excellent agreement between finite difference and method-of-moment results [26].

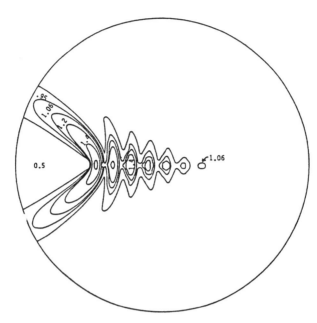

Figure 18 Contour plots of the scattered axial magnetic field strength for TE illumination of a PEC flat plate at $\theta = 24°$. Note the traveling wave interference pattern and the strong end-fire radiation.

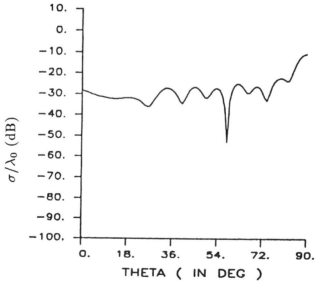

Figure 19 TE backscatter pattern for a lossy dielectric clad $t = 0.1a$ PEC plate ($k_0 a = 13.3$, $\epsilon_r = 2 + j$).

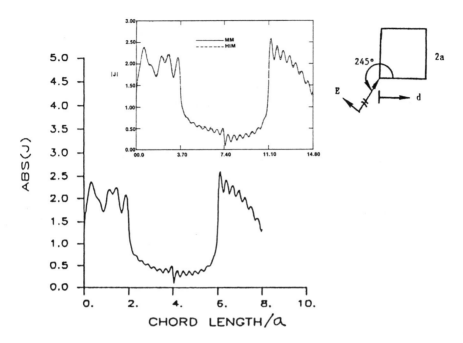

Figure 20 Magnitude of current on a square PEC cylinder illuminated by a TE plane wave at 245° ($k_0 a = 3.7\pi$). The graph in the insert is from Murthy, Hill, and Thiele [25].

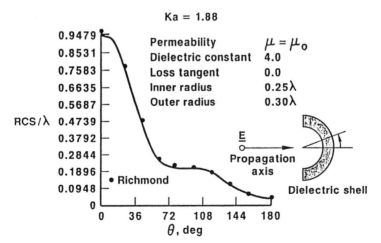

Figure 21 TM bistatic scattering pattern for a thin dielectric half-shell ($k_0 a = 1.88$) moment method results are from [26].

Scattering from curved dielectric shells and spar-shell airfoil shapes were also computed by the control region technique. Reentrant structures, similar to the dielectric shell, particularly those exhibiting strong multiple bounce returns are difficult to analyze by approximate methods. Results for the concave dielectric strip (Fig. 21) are in good agreement with the moment method solution obtained by Richmond [27].

Scattering from airfoil-section cylinders both PEC and dielectric layered were also investigated with our method. The airfoil contour (Fig. 22) is similar to the NACA series 65A shape (with $C_L = 0.532$). The TM bistatic patterns with incidence-illumination normal to the face, camber and edges of the airfoil are shown in Fig. 23. Good agreement (Table 1) is obtained with moment method results and measured values.

Table 1. Comparison of Measured and Computed RCS

Aspect	Airfoil RCS in DBSM		
	FD	MoM	Measured
TE	-13.2	-10.4	-7.6
Camber	9.9	12.3	11.8
LE	-11.8	-9.2	-7.0
Face	13.3	15.6	15.0

$R_0 =$ **FD outer boundary=1.6a**, $k_0 a = 11.34$, $a_0 =$ **half-chord of airfoil.**

TM scattering cross sections for a spar-shell airfoil (Fig. 23) are compared with measured values in Fig. 24. The outer radius of the boundary is at $1.5a$, where a is the semi-chord width. The outer shell has an $\epsilon = 4.2\epsilon_0$ and its thickness is 0.02λ. The spar is metal and the dielectric fill is lossless with $\epsilon = 1.28\epsilon_0$. The computed scattering widths were used to estimate the RCS of the 19 in. long experimental model by neglecting the scattering from the end caps. The cross section of the finite cylinder is approximated by

$$\sigma_{3D} \cong 8(h^2/\lambda) \cdot \sigma_{2D} \qquad (41)$$

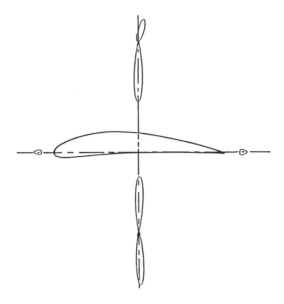

Figure 22 Bistatic cross section patterns for a PEC airfoil contour cylinder ($k_0 W = 22.68$).

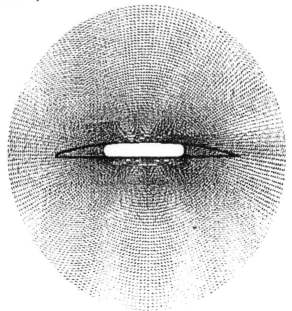

Figure 23 Spar-shell airfoil cylinder configuration.

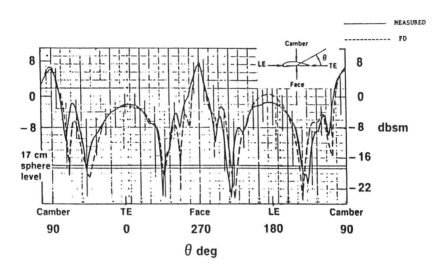

Figure 24   TM monostatic pattern of a spar-shell airfoil cylinder ($k_0 W$ = 22.68).

where $2h$ = cylinder length [28]. Results are shown for an airfoil with 3.5λ chord width. The differences between the computed and measured returns is probably ascribable to leading and trailing edge details of the airfoil which were not modeled in the analysis. Most of the features of the scattering pattern are quite accurately reproduced by the finite difference result. The overall agreement is seen to be quite good and reflects the useful engineering data obtainable from such a 2D finite differences analysis.

5.8   Conclusion

The preceding sections have shown by theoretical consideration and numerical examples that the Control Region Approximation combined with an outer asymptotic boundary condition provides a very powerful general tool for the analysis of electromagnetic scattering by complex targets. Accurate and efficient calculations of both near field quantities, such as surface currents, travelling waves, and cavity resonances, and far field quantities, such as monostatic and bistatic cross sections, are provided. We conclude with a consideration of improvements to the two dimensional algorithm, extension to a three dimensional algorithm, and use of similar techniques for time-dependent scattering problems.

The two dimensional algorithm could be enhanced in a number of directions. Higher order discretizations are achievable by allowing the flux to vary along a Dirichlet edge. This would allow a reduction in mesh density. The outer boundary is presently circular. The use of more general outer contours, e.g. ellipses for long slender bodies, would permit a smaller computational domain and hence fewer mesh points. Finally, and perhaps most importantly, iteration of the right hand side of the outer asymptotic boundary condition may offer one possible way to sidestep our negative result pertaining to the use of higher order boundary conditions. Each iteration would be relatively inexpensive since only the source terms would change.

Extension of the algorithm to three dimensions (3D) is a complex multi-faceted problem. There are a number of choices for a suitable formulation of the governing equations and the asymptotic boundary condition. Recent results [17,29] for specialized bodies of revolution, using a pair of scalar potentials to represent the field [30], appear promising. Asymptotic boundary conditions, analogous to Bayliss-Turkel, can also be derived for the 3D vector problem [31]. Algorithms to provide Dirichlet/Delaunay tessellations in three dimensions must be constructed. Furthermore, since the 3D formulation may not lead only to divergence operators, shear terms as well as the usual flux terms must be dealt with on the boundaries of the Dirichlet boxes. Finally, the sheer number of equations resulting from discretizing a region of space as well as from treating a vector problem will likely make the computational needs of present sparse matrix solvers very intensive. Utilization of parallel algorithms and architectures will almost certainly be necessary for large targets.

The use of time-marching algorithms for electromagnetics problems has heretofore been rather limited. Most previous work has been restricted to Cartesian grids with their attendant limitations. However, in areas such as computational fluid dynamics, time marching is standard fare in both 2D and 3D. The Dirichlet/Delaunay duality can be utilized to make the spatial discretization provided by the Control Region Approximation compatible with many of the standard time-marching schemes such as the Lax-Wendroff method.

In summary, the Control Region Approximation provides a new and powerful approach to solving for electromagnetic scattering from complex inhomogeneous targets. The method is completely general in that it can accommodate scatterers of arbitrary shape and composition while incorporating a physical model which includes all scattering mechanisms. The sparse structure of the discrete model allows economical use of computer resources.

Acknowledgements

The authors would like to acknowledge several illuminating discussions with Prof. Raj Mittra of the University of Illinois at Urbana-Champaign. The cooperation of Prof. Andrew Peterson, also of the University of Illinois, in providing moment method computations for the PEC airfoil is greatly appreciated. They would also like to express their gratitude for the support and encouragement of the Sikorsky Aircraft and Advanced Systems Divisions of United Technologies. The extensive editorial comments of Dr. Joseph R. Caspar of UTRC are felt to have greatly improved the quality of presentation in this paper.

References

[1] Keller, J. B., "Geometrical theory of diffraction," *J. Opt. Soc. Am.*, **52**, 116–130, 1962.

[2] Harrington, R. F., *Field Computation by Moment Methods*, Krieger, 1985.

[3] Engquist, B., and A. Majda, "Absorbing boundary conditions for the numerical simulation of waves," *Math. Comp.*, **31**, 629–651, 1977.

[4] Bayliss, A., and E. Turkel, "Radiation boundary conditions for wave-like equations," *Comm. Pure and Appl. Math.*, **33**, 707–725, 1980.

[5] Caspar, J. R., D. E. Hobbs, and R. L. Davis, "Calculation of two-dimensional potential cascade flow using finite area methods," *AIAA J.*, **18**, 103–109, 1980.

[6] McCartin, B. J., J. R. Caspar, R. E. LaBarre, G. A. Peterson, and R. H. Hobbs, "Steady state numerical analysis of single carrier two-dimensional semiconductor devices using the control area ap-

proximation," *NASECODE III Proceedings*, J. J. H. Miller (Ed.), Boole Press, 185–190, 1983.

[7] McCartin, B. J., "Solution of complex Helmholtz equations in arbitrary geometries," *SIAM Nat. Mtg.*, Boston, MA, July 24, 1986.

[8] McCartin, B. J., "Discretization of the semiconductor device equations," *New Problems and New Solutions for Device and Process Modelling*, Boole Press, 72–80, 1985.

[9] Eisenstat, S. C., M. C. Gursky, M. H. Schultz, and A. H. Sherman, Yale Sparse Matrix Package I. The Symmetric Codes, Yale U. Dept. of Comp. Sci. RR#112.

[10] Zienkiewicz, O. C., and Y. K. Cheung, "Finite elements in the solution of field problems," *The Engineer*, 507–510, 1985.

[11] Eisenstat, S. C., M. C. Gursky, M. H. Schultz, and A. H. Sherman, Yale Sparse Matrix Package II. The Nonsymmetric Codes, Yale U. Dept. of Comp. Sci. RR#114.

[12] Kong, J. A., *Electromagnetic Wave Theory*, Wiley, 1986.

[13] Wang, D. S., "Limits and validity of the impedance boundary condition on penetrable surfaces," *IEEE Trans. Antennas Propagat.*, **AP-35**, 453–457, 1987.

[14] Baker, B.B., and E.T. Copson, *The Mathematical Theory of Huyghen's Principle*, Chelsea, 1987.

[15] Trefethen, L. N., "Well-posedness of one-way wave equations and absorbing boundary conditions," *ICASE* Report No. 85–30, 1985.

[16] Hariharan, S. I., "Absorbing boundary conditions for exterior boundary value problems," *ICASE* Report No. 85–33, 1985.

[17] Mittra, R., O. Ramahi, G. Meltz, and B. J. McCartin, "A new look at the asymptotic boundary conditions for differential equation approaches to solving open region scattering problems," *Proc. 1987 URSI Radio Sci. Mtg.*, p. 251.

[18] IMSL Library Reference Manual, Edition 9, Volume 2, Chapter I, IRATCU 1–4, Houston, TX, 1983.

[19] Dirichlet, G. L., "Über die reduction der positiven quadratischen formen mit drei unbestimmten ganzen zahlen," *Z. Reine Angew. Math.*, **40**, 209–227, 1850.

[20] Delaunay, B., "Sur la sphere vide," Bull. Sci. USSR (VII), *Classe Sci., Mat. Nat.*, 793–800, 1934.

[21] Watson, D. F., "Computing the N-dimensional Delaunay tessellation with applications to Voronoi polytopes," *Comp. J.*, **24**, 167–172, 1981.

[22] McCartin, B. J., "Alternative basis functions using Green's functions," in preparation – contact authors for updated citation.

[23] Birkhoff, G., and R. E. Lynch, *Numerical Solution of Elliptic Problems,* SIAM, 1984.

[24] Davis, P. J., and P. Rabinowitz, *Methods of Numerical Integration,* Academic Press, 1975.

[25] Ziolkowski, R. W., and J. B. Grant, "Scattering from cavity-backed apertures: The generalized dual series solution of the concentrically loaded E-pol slit cylinder problem," *IEEE Trans. Antennas Propagat.,* **AP-35**, 504–528, 1987.

[26] Murthy, P. K., K. C. Hill, and G. A. Thiele, "A hybrid-iterative method for scattering problems," *IEEE Trans. Antennas Propagat.,* **AP-34**, 1986.

[27] Richmond, J. H., "Scattering by a dielectric cylinder of arbitrary cross section shape," *IEEE Trans. Antennas Propagat.,* **AP-13**, 1965.

[28] Ruck, G. T., *Radar Cross Section Handbook,* **2**, 499–504, Plenum Press, New York, 1970.

[29] Mittra, R., and O. Ramahi, "Absorbing boundary conditions for the direct solution of partial differential equations arising in electromagnetic scattering problems," this text, Chapter 4.

[30] Morgan, M. A., and K. K. Mei, "Finite element computation of scattering by inhomogeneous penetrable bodies of revolution," *IEEE Trans. Antennas Propagat.,* **AP-27**, 202–214, 1979.

[31] Wilcox, C. H. "An expansion theorem for electromagnetic fields," *Comm. Pure and Appl. Math.,* **IX**, 115–134, 1956.

6

COUPLED POTENTIALS FOR ELECTROMAGNETIC FIELDS IN INHOMOGENEOUS MEDIA

M. A. Morgan

6.1   Introduction

Electromagnetic interaction with complex inhomogeneous structures has become a topic of expanded interest within the computational fields community in recent years. This has resulted, at least in part, from advances in the incorporation of materials in the engineering design of modern electronics such as antennas, scatterers, lenses, waveguiding and coupling structures, active devices and multi-layer high-speed integrated circuits. Even with the processing power of large mainframes there exists limits on the levels of material complexity and physical wavelength dimensions that can be practically accommodated due to computation time and memory constraints.

The analytical and numerical formulations which are employed in the solution of a given field problem play key roles in the requisite computational requirements. This influence is reflected in *both* the number of discrete unknowns generated and in the density of explicit interactions between these unknowns. Classical TE and TM potential formulations, as generalized by Bromwich in 1919 [1], may be used to represent the six vector components of the electromagnetic field using two uncoupled scalar potentials in selected separable coordinate systems. Such TE and TM potential representations are restricted to uniform media and some special cases of one-dimensional inhomogeneity such as spherical stratification.

In the mid-1970's, the use of dual scalar potentials was extended to rotationally symmetric materials, having arbitrary inhomogeneity in the other two dimensions, through the development of the coupled azimuthal potential (CAP) formulation by Morgan, Chang and Mei [2–4]. The CAP representation utilizes two continuous potentials to generate the Fourier azimuthal modes of the time-harmonic vector field. It has since been used as the basis for finite element solutions of radiation, scattering and penetration problems, [5–11].

A two-fold generalization of the CAP formulation is presented here, one which removes both the restriction to axisymmetry of the inhomogeneous media and extends the development to general orthogonal curvilinear coordinates. This new coupled potential (CP) formulation retains two attributes of the original CAP representation: (1) the 6 field unknowns in Maxwell's time-harmonic equations are generated by two scalar potential functions; and (2) partial differential equations are used, resulting in sparse global system matrices. These two properties reduce both the number of discrete unknowns and the density of coupling between the unknowns. The solution of open region radiation and scattering problems can be approached by use of one of the exterior region coupling schemes such as the unimoment method [12], the field feedback formulation [13], or a near-field radiation boundary condition [14].

The analytics of the generalized CP formulation will be presented in the following section, with developments first made in curvilinear orthogonal coordinates and then specifically applied in the circular cylindrical system. The generating equations for the vector fields will initially be considered followed by variational and weighted residual solution approaches for the potentials. Efficient numerical methods for solving these equations will be developed in section 6.3. This will be followed, in section 6.4, by validations of the accuracy and convergence of the resultant algorithms. Included are tests of the vector field generation, using *natural* basis functions, as well as a solution demonstration of the Galerkin equations for a simple 3-D boundary value problem, using a sparse matrix block decomposition technique.

In the final section of this chapter, some future enhancements of the CP formulation and its pending application to scattering by complex material structures will be discussed.

6.2 Coupled Potential Formulation

a. Fields in Orthogonal Coordinates

In developing the CP formulation, we will use an impedance normalized phasor magnetic field: $\overline{H} = -\jmath\eta_0\,\mathcal{H}$, where $\mathcal{H}$ is the usual magnetic field, having SI units of A/m, and η_0 is the free-space wave impedance of $120\pi\ \Omega$. The normalized $\overline{H}$ thus has the same V/m units as the usual electric field, $\overline{E}$. A simplified set of Maxwell's source-free curl equations results, being written here using coordinate-free notation,

$$\nabla \times \overline{E}(\overline{r}) = k_0\,\mu_r(\overline{r})\,\overline{H}(\overline{r}) \tag{1a}$$

$$\nabla \times \overline{H}(\overline{r}) = k_0\,\epsilon_r(\overline{r})\,\overline{E}(\overline{r}) \tag{1b}$$

where $k_0 = 2\pi/\lambda_0$ is the wavenumber, while $\epsilon_r(\overline{r})$ and $\mu_r(\overline{r})$ are the relative dielectric and magnetic parameters in the inhomogeneous media. The constitutive parameters, $\epsilon_r(\overline{r})$ and $\mu_r(\overline{r})$, may be either piecewise constant or continuously variable spatial functions. For regions containing lossy material one or both of these functions will be complex.

We will initially develop two versions of the generating equations which provide the vector fields in terms of two scalar coupled potentials. One of these forms will use dual first order partial differential equation (PDE) systems, each having the form of a transport equation. The other development will take the form of second-order PDE systems which will be used later to construct the natural basis functions for the numerical application in circular cylindrical coordinates.

To begin the CP derivation, we will employ a generic right-hand system of curvilinear orthogonal coordinates, to be denoted by (u_1, u_2, u_3) where each u_i is some specified function in the cartesian space (x, y, z). At each spatial point, local unit vectors are defined by

$$\widehat{u}_i = \frac{\nabla u_i}{|\nabla u_i|} \quad \text{for } i = 1, 3 \tag{2}$$

The field vectors are then expressible in component form using the unit vector basis at each point. For example,

$$\overline{E}(\overline{r}) = E_1(\overline{r})\,\widehat{u}_1 + E_2(\overline{r})\,\widehat{u}_2 + E_3(\overline{r})\,\widehat{u}_3 \tag{3}$$

The local unit vectors at each point form an *orthonormal* basis, as illustrated in Fig. 1. An additional constraint will be imposed on the coordinate system to be used in the current application, as will be addressed shortly. There will, however, be *no need* for separable coordinates with the differential operators to be employed. As a result, a virtual infinity of custom coordinate systems can be designed for applications of this formulation. Such coordinates may, for instance, be made conformal to the external surface of some complicated metallic object.

We next need to define scale factors, h_i, to transform differential coordinate variations, du_i to the corresponding metrical changes in arc length, $ds_i = h_i\, du_i$ for $i = 1, 3$. For example, in the spherical coordinate system, with $(u_1, u_2, u_3) = (r, \theta, \phi)$, we have $h_1 = 1$, $h_2 = r$ and $h_3 = r \sin \theta$. Using subscript notation for partial derivatives, (e.g. $D_1 = \partial/\partial u_1$), the curl equations in (1) become

$$D_2(h_3\, E_3) - D_3(h_2\, E_2) = \mu_r \alpha_1 (h_1\, H_1) \tag{4a}$$

$$D_3(h_1\, E_1) - D_1(h_3\, E_3) = \mu_r \alpha_2 (h_2\, H_2) \tag{4b}$$

$$D_1(h_2\, E_2) - D_2(h_1\, E_1) = \mu_r \alpha_3 (h_3\, H_3) \tag{4c}$$

$$D_2(h_3\, H_3) - D_3(h_2\, H_2) = \epsilon_r \alpha_1 (h_1\, E_1) \tag{4d}$$

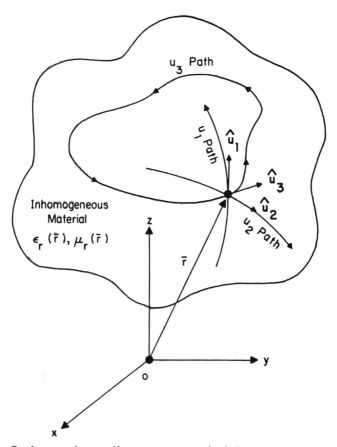

Figure 1 Orthogonal coordinate contours in inhomogeneous material.

$$D_3(h_1 H_1) - D_1(h_3 H_3) = \epsilon_r \alpha_2(h_2 E_2) \tag{4e}$$

$$D_1(h_2 H_2) - D_2(h_1 H_1) = \epsilon_r \alpha_3(h_3 E_3) \tag{4f}$$

where $\alpha_i(\bar{r})$ are wavenumber normalized scale factor ratios

$$\alpha_1(\bar{r}) = k_0 \frac{h_2 h_3}{h_1} \tag{5a}$$

$$\alpha_2(\bar{r}) = k_0 \frac{h_1 h_3}{h_2} \tag{5b}$$

$$\alpha_3(\overline{r}) = k_0 \frac{h_1 h_2}{h_3} \tag{5c}$$

b. Transverse Field Generation

Using (4a), (4b), (4d) and (4e), we can define CP's in terms of E_3 and H_3 to drive dual systems of first-order differential equations (DE's) for the remaining four vector field components. These coupled systems are written in matrix form as

$$D_3 \overline{V}_p + \overline{\overline{M}}_p \cdot \overline{V}_p = \overline{U}_p \quad \text{for } p = 1, 2 \tag{6}$$

The cross-coupling arrays in (6) are given by

$$\overline{\overline{M}}_1(\overline{r}) = \begin{bmatrix} 0 & \mu_r \alpha_2 \\ -\epsilon_r \alpha_1 & 0 \end{bmatrix} \tag{7a}$$

$$\overline{\overline{M}}_2(\overline{r}) = \begin{bmatrix} 0 & \mu_r \alpha_1 \\ -\epsilon_r \alpha_2 & 0 \end{bmatrix} \tag{7b}$$

while the transverse (to $\hat{u}_3$) field arrays are defined by

$$\overline{V}_1(\overline{r}) = \begin{bmatrix} h_1 E_1 \\ -h_2 H_2 \end{bmatrix} \tag{8a}$$

$$\overline{V}_2(\overline{r}) = \begin{bmatrix} h_2 E_2 \\ h_1 H_1 \end{bmatrix} \tag{8b}$$

The CP's, which are defined by

$$\psi_1(\overline{r}) = h_3(\overline{r}) E_3(\overline{r}) \tag{9a}$$

$$\psi_2(\overline{r}) = h_3(\overline{r}) H_3(\overline{r}) \tag{9b}$$

are differentiated to form the driving arrays in (6)

$$\overline{U}_1(\overline{r}) = \begin{bmatrix} D_1 \psi_1 \\ -D_2 \psi_2 \end{bmatrix} \tag{10a}$$

$$\overline{U}_2(\overline{r}) = \begin{bmatrix} D_2 \psi_1 \\ D_1 \psi_2 \end{bmatrix} \tag{10b}$$

The generating equations in (6) may, in principle, be solved for the transverse fields in terms of the CP derivative driving arrays. A unique solution, however, is predicated upon specified boundary conditions (BC's) on the unknown vectors, $\overline{V}_p$. In the computational portion of this work, to be described in section 6.3, cyclic BC's are used with (6). To this end, the $u_3(x, y, z)$ coordinate is assumed to be periodic, thus forming closed contours in space, as is illustrated in Fig. 1. Some example coordinate systems that fit this description are elliptic cylindrical, spheroidal, paraboloidal as well as the more standard circular cylindrical and spherical systems, [15]. Although a cyclic u_3-coordinate is defined in this application, it is conceivable that the CP formulation can be employed without such a restriction.

An alternate, second-order set of generating equations for the non-$\hat{u}_3$ field components results from a judicious substitution within the first-order systems in (6)

$$\overline{\overline{L}}_e \cdot \overline{E}_t = D_3 \left\{ \frac{1}{\mu_r} \overline{\overline{\alpha}}_1 \cdot \nabla_t \psi_1 \right\} - \hat{u}_3 \times \nabla_t \psi_2 \tag{11a}$$

$$\overline{\overline{L}}_h \cdot \overline{H}_t = D_3 \left\{ \frac{1}{\epsilon_r} \overline{\overline{\alpha}}_1 \cdot \nabla_t \psi_2 \right\} - \hat{u}_3 \times \nabla_t \psi_1 \tag{11b}$$

In these equations we are employing vector-dyadic notation, where

$$\overline{E}_t = (h_1 E_1) \hat{u}_1 + (h_2 E_2) \hat{u}_2 \tag{12a}$$

$$\overline{H}_t = (h_1 H_1) \hat{u}_2 + (h_2 H_2) \hat{u}_2 \tag{12b}$$

are the scaled transverse field vectors, while

$$\nabla_t = \hat{u}_1 D_1 + \hat{u}_2 D_2 \tag{13}$$

is a "gradient" operator in transverse (to $\hat{u}_3$) coordinates (u_1, u_2). The linear dyadic operators appearing on the left-hand side of (11) are given by

$$\overline{\overline{L}}_e = D_3 \left\{ \frac{1}{\mu_r} \overline{\overline{\alpha}}_1 D_3 \right\} + \epsilon_r \overline{\overline{\alpha}}_2 \tag{14a}$$

$$\overline{\overline{L}}_h = D_3 \left\{ \frac{1}{\epsilon_r} \overline{\overline{\alpha}}_1 D_3 \right\} + \mu_r \overline{\overline{\alpha}}_2 \tag{14b}$$

where the $\overline{\overline{\alpha}}_i$-dyadics in (11) and (14) are defined as

$$\overline{\overline{\alpha}}_1(\overline{r}) = \alpha_2^{-1}(\overline{r}) \hat{u}_1 \hat{u}_1 + \alpha_1^{-1}(\overline{r}) \hat{u}_2 \hat{u}_2 \tag{15a}$$

$$\overline{\overline{\alpha}}_2(\overline{r}) = \alpha_1(\overline{r}) \hat{u}_1 \hat{u}_1 + \alpha_2(\overline{r}) \hat{u}_2 \hat{u}_2 \tag{15b}$$

In *local* spatial domains, where μ_r and ϵ_r are functions of (u_1, u_2), but not of u_3, (we will employ this approximation in the numerical work that follows) the second-order DE's in (11) simplify to

$$\overline{\overline{L}} \cdot \overline{E}_t = D_3 \{ \overline{\overline{\alpha}}_1 \cdot \nabla_t \psi_1 \} - \mu_r \hat{u}_3 \times \nabla_t \psi_2 \tag{16a}$$

$$\overline{\overline{L}} \cdot \overline{H}_t = D_3 \{ \overline{\overline{\alpha}}_1 \cdot \nabla_t \psi_2 \} - \epsilon_r \hat{u}_3 \times \nabla_t \psi_1 \tag{16b}$$

with the single dyadic operator given by

$$\overline{\overline{L}}(\overline{r}) = D_3 \{ \overline{\overline{\alpha}}_1 D_3 \} + \mu_r \epsilon_r \overline{\overline{\alpha}}_2 \tag{17}$$

Now that the transverse field generating equations have been developed, it may be worth comparing them to the classical formulation for TE and TM modes in straight waveguide sections. In particular, if we set $u_3 = z$ and assume homogeneous constitutive parameters, we can partially separate variables in (16), using an $\exp(-\gamma z)$ propagation factor. The result will be explicit functional relationships yielding the transverse (to z) fields $\overline{E}_t$ and $\overline{H}_t$ in terms of transverse derivatives of $\psi_1 = E_z$ and $\psi_2 = H_z$, where we note that the h_3 scale factor in (9) is unity. These are the standard waveguide field generating equations shown, for instance, by Silver in [16].

The CP formulation is thus an extension to these earlier waveguide field ideas, with *spatial curvature* being introduced here in the u_3

direction of propagation. This curvature prohibits (except for $\gamma = 0$) the separation of the fields into the usual TE and TM (to u_3) sub-fields, as is permitted when using a linear coordinate (e.g. $u_3 = z$). The TE and TM field partitioning results by the optional decoupling of the CP's, each of which is found to solve the usual Helmholtz operator eigenvalue problem in the transverse cross section of the waveguiding structure. For the general case of curvilinear coordinates, the CP's remain coupled, satisfying a more complex relationship, as we will now investigate.

c. Coupled Potential Interactions

The solution of either the first-order (6) or second-order (11) forms of the transverse field generating equations offers the means to evaluate E_1, E_2, H_1 and H_2 through an assumed knowledge of the potentials $\psi_1 = h_3 E_3$ and $\psi_2 = h_3 H_3$. To complete the analytical development of the CP formulation we need to consider the necessary equations from which to obtain the potentials. A direct approach is to utilize the remaining Maxwell's equations in (4) that were not used for transverse field generation. These two equations, namely (4c) and (4f), can be expressed as

$$\epsilon_r \, \alpha_3 \, \psi_1 - \widehat{u}_3 \cdot \nabla_t \times \overline{H}_t = 0 \tag{18a}$$

$$\mu_r \, \alpha_3 \, \psi_2 - \widehat{u}_3 \cdot \nabla_t \times \overline{E}_t = 0 \tag{18b}$$

The use of (18) for computing the CP's requires the explicit sub-stitution of $\overline{E}_t$ and $\overline{H}_t$ obtained from solutions of either (6) or (11). At this stage in the development, we can express these solutions in the sense of *formal* inverses to $\overline{\overline{L}}_e$ and $\overline{\overline{L}}_h$. These dyadic operators, as defined in (14), can be "inverted" by approximate numerical methods. The simplifying idea is to consider the operators as ordinary DE's in the u_3-coordinate, with (u_1, u_2) held constant. An example of this type of process will be considered in section 6.3.

After numerically eliminating $\overline{E}_t$ and $\overline{H}_t$ from (18), there remains the problem of solving for the CP's. Enforcement of the DE's in (18) can be performed by the well-known method of weighted residuals [17] (known as the moment method when applied to integral equations in electromagnetics). It is this approach that will be developed later in this chapter. The result will be a set of *Galerkin* equations for the potentials where the basis (expansion) and weighting (testing) functions will come from the same set.

An alternate procedure for the solution of the potentials is to employ a generalized variational principle for isotropic media, based upon self-reaction [18]. The interior region solution of Maxwell's equations, for specified Dirichlet boundary conditions of the CP's on an enclosing surface, S, will yield the stationary point of the following complex energy-power functional

$$F = \jmath k_0 \iiint_V \epsilon_r \overline{E} \cdot \overline{E} - \mu_r \overline{H} \cdot \overline{H} \, dv - \iint_S \overline{E} \times \overline{H} \cdot \hat{n} \, dS \qquad (19)$$

To make this a functional solely of the potentials, one can substitute $\psi_1 = h_3 E_3$ and $\psi_2 = h_3 H_3$ and replace $\overline{E}_t$ and $\overline{H}_t$ by their formal inverse relationships to the CP's. As for the case of the Galerkin approach, the transverse fields are obtained numerically in terms of discrete spatial point values of the potentials. We will consider, by example, how this is done in section 6.3.

Before proceeding, it is worthwhile at this stage to summarize the key steps that have been described:

(1) Using generalized orthogonal coordinates, Maxwell's curl equations were rewritten to yield coupled first-order PDE's in (6) for the scaled transverse (to $\hat{u}_3$) field components in terms of the transverse derivatives of the scaled longitudinal field components, which are defined to be the coupled potentials: $\psi_1 = h_3 E_3$ and $\psi_2 = h_3 H_3$. These "state-equations" are implicitly of second-order in u_3.

(2) By cross-substituting between these equations, the second-order set of PDE's is found (11) for generating the transverse field components in terms of the derivatives of the CP's.

(3) The goal of the derivation is to recast the vector field problem in the inhomogeneous media into one of dealing only with the two scalar CP's. Through employing a numerical inverse to either the first- or second-order generating equations, the desired reduction to a solution for the CP's can be attained. One way is to substitute the transverse field solutions into the remaining Maxwell's equations in (18). The other is to use the complex energy-power

functional in (19). Our numerical example in section 6.3 will illustrate this final elimination step via (18).

d. Circular Cylindrical Case

At this juncture we will take a brief diversion to reexpress the CP formulation in circular cylindrical coordinates. This will serve as an example of applying the generic curvilinear expressions to a commonly used coordinate system. In addition, these specialized expressions will be employed in the computational validations that will be considered in the next two sections.

Using circular cylindrical coordinates $(u_1, u_2, u_3) = (z, \rho, \phi)$, the scale factors are given by $h_1 = h_2 = 1$ and $h_3 = \rho$. Note that we have not followed the standard (ρ, ϕ, z) ordering. The reason for this is to identify the ϕ coordinate as u_3, which is assumed to be periodic, while retaining a "right-hand" system. Continuing, the wavenumber multiplied scale factor ratios in (5) become $\alpha_1 = \alpha_2 = k_0 \rho$ while $\alpha_3 = k_0 / \rho$.

Noting that $D_1 = D_z$, $D_2 = D_\rho$, while $D_3 = D_\phi$, the dual first-order systems in (6) can be combined into a single equation

$$D_\phi \overline{\overline{V}}(\overline{r}) + \overline{\overline{M}}(\overline{r}) \cdot \overline{\overline{V}}(\overline{r}) = \overline{\overline{U}}(\overline{r}) \tag{20}$$

Since $\overline{\overline{M}}_1 = \overline{\overline{M}}_2$, only one cross-coupling array,

$$\overline{\overline{M}}(\overline{r}) = k_0 \, \rho \begin{bmatrix} 0 & \mu_r(\overline{r}) \\ -\epsilon_r(\overline{r}) & 0 \end{bmatrix} \tag{21}$$

needs to be used for the case of circular cylindrical coordinates. In addition, the $\overline{V}_p$ vectors in (8) and the $\overline{U}_p$ vectors in (10) have each been respectively combined to form the columns of individual 2×2 arrays,

$$\overline{\overline{V}}(\overline{r}) = \begin{bmatrix} E_z & E_\rho \\ -H_\rho & H_z \end{bmatrix} \tag{22}$$

and

$$\overline{\overline{U}}(\bar{r}) = \begin{bmatrix} D_z\,\psi_1 & D_\rho\,\psi_1 \\ -D_\rho\,\psi_2 & D_z\,\psi_2 \end{bmatrix} \tag{23}$$

The CP's in (23) are found from (9), via $\psi_1 = \rho\,E_\phi$ and $\psi_2 = \rho\,H_\phi$.

Since $\alpha_1 = \alpha_2$ in (15), the two dyad components of $\overline{\overline{\alpha}}_1$ are equal, as are the two components of $\overline{\overline{\alpha}}_2$. The second-order PDE systems in (14) can thus be simplified, resulting in non-dyadic forms

$$\mathcal{L}_e\,\overline{E}_t = D_\phi\,\{\frac{1}{\mu_r}\nabla_t\,\psi_1\} - k_0\,\rho\,\hat{\phi}\times\nabla_t\,\psi_2 \tag{24a}$$

$$\mathcal{L}_h\,\overline{H}_t = D_\phi\,\{\frac{1}{\epsilon_r}\nabla_t\,\psi_2\} - k_0\,\rho\,\hat{\phi}\times\nabla_t\,\psi_1 \tag{24b}$$

In these equations, the transverse fields (with $h_1 = h_2 = 1$) are

$$\overline{E}_t = E_\rho\,\hat{\rho} + E_z\,\hat{z} \tag{25a}$$

$$\overline{H}_t = H_\rho\,\hat{\rho} + H_z\,\hat{z} \tag{25b}$$

while

$$\nabla_t = \hat{\rho}\,D_\rho + \hat{z}\,D_z \tag{26}$$

is the transverse (to $\hat{\phi}$) gradient operator. The linear operators appearing on the left-hand side of (24) are given by

$$\mathcal{L}_e = D_\phi\{\frac{1}{\mu_r}\,D_\phi\} + \epsilon_r\,(k_0\,\rho)^2 \tag{27a}$$

$$\mathcal{L}_h = D_\phi\{\frac{1}{\epsilon_r}\,D_\phi\} + \mu_r\,(k_0\,\rho)^2 \tag{27b}$$

e. Axisymmetric Specialization

Before proceeding to the numerical implementation of the CP formulation, let us briefly consider the special case of rotationally symmetric material. This will illustrate the connection to the original coupled azimuthal potential (CAP) equations, as developed in [2–4] and Chapter 2. The CAP equations result as a special case of the CP formulation.

For the case of local spatial domains where μ_r and ϵ_r are functions of $(u_1, u_2) = (z, \rho)$, but not of $u_3 = \phi$, as considered in deriving (16) and (17), the PDE's in (24) simplify to

$$\mathcal{L}\,\overline{E}_t = D_\phi \nabla_t \psi_1 - \mu_r \, k_0 \, \rho \, \widehat{\phi} \times \nabla_t \psi_2 \tag{28a}$$

$$\mathcal{L}\,\overline{H}_t = D_\phi \nabla_t \psi_2 - \epsilon_r \, k_0 \, \rho \, \widehat{\phi} \times \nabla_t \psi_1 \tag{28b}$$

where

$$\mathcal{L} = D_\phi^2 + \mu_r \, \epsilon_r \, (k_0 \, \rho)^2 \tag{29}$$

We now expand the field vectors in a Fourier series in the ϕ-coordinate

$$\overline{E}(\overline{r}) = \overline{E}_t(\overline{r}) + E_\phi(\overline{r})\,\widehat{\phi} = \sum_{m=-\infty}^{\infty} \overline{e}_m\,(\rho, z)\,\exp(\jmath m \phi) \tag{30a}$$

$$\overline{H}(\overline{r}) = \overline{H}_t(\overline{r}) + H_\phi(\overline{r})\,\widehat{\phi} = \sum_{m=-\infty}^{\infty} \overline{h}_m\,(\rho, z)\,\exp(\jmath m \phi) \tag{30b}$$

When these expansions are substituted into (28), it is found that the operation of $\mathcal{L}$ on the m-th modal transverse field reduces to a multiplication by

$$f_m(\rho, z) = \mu_r(\rho, z)\,\epsilon_r(\rho, z)\,(k_0 \, \rho)^2 - m^2 \tag{31}$$

The modal transverse field vectors are then obtained by using

$$\overline{e}_{t,m}\,(\rho, z) = f_m^{-1}\,[\jmath m \,\nabla_t \psi_{1,m} - \mu_r \, k_0 \, \rho \, \widehat{\phi} \times \nabla_t \psi_{2,m}] \tag{32a}$$

$$\overline{h}_{t,m}\,(\rho, z) = f_m^{-1}\,[\jmath m \,\nabla_t \psi_{2,m} - \epsilon_r \, k_0 \, \rho \, \widehat{\phi} \times \nabla_t \psi_{1,m}] \tag{32b}$$

where the m-th order modes of the CAP's are

$$\psi_{1,m}(\rho, z) = \rho\, e_{\phi,m}(\rho, z) \tag{32c}$$

$$\psi_{2,m}(\rho, z) = \rho\, h_{\phi,m}(\rho, z) \tag{32d}$$

as was found in the original axisymmetric CAP formulation [2–4].

Thus, by employing a Fourier series field expansion within axisymmetric material, we can obtain an exact analytical inverse to the transverse field generating equations on a mode-by-mode basis. A pathological case exists, however. When dealing with lossless material, where μ_r and ϵ_r are both *real* spatial functions, the $f_m(\rho, z)$ denominator in the transverse field equations above will be zero on spatial surfaces where

$$k_0\,\rho = \frac{|m|}{\sqrt{\mu_r(\rho, z)\,\epsilon_r(\rho, z)}} \tag{33}$$

On these surfaces, the generating equations in (32) become indeterminate and the operator in (29) will have complementary (undriven) solutions which satisfy the requisite periodicity. These resonant solutions are similar in nature to modes in microstrip ring-resonators or quantum states of atoms. A practical concern, to be considered in section 6.4, is that numerical difficulties may arise close to these radii.

If the Fourier series in (30) are used in the general inhomogeneous case, as is embodied in (24), the individual m-th order modes will not decouple from one another. Furthermore, if either μ_r or ϵ_r have azimuthal discontinuities then the resultant ϕ-coordinate step functions in the respective H_ϕ or E_ϕ will produce pointwise convergence difficulties in the Fourier series, *a la* the Gibbs phenomenon [19].

For the case of material that has a slowly varying inhomogeneity in ϕ, a possible approach is to employ the Fourier expansions in (30), as well as azimuthal Fourier series for both μ_r and ϵ_r. This concept is considered by Fleming in Chapter 2 of this text and in [11]. The resultant convolutions of the field modes and the material modes can be truncated to provide approximate generating equations for the transverse fields in the form of algebraic linear systems. By assuming a quasi-axisymmetric case, where only a few terms are needed in the Fourier series for the media, this approach may be a viable alternative to that which is considered here.

The CAP formulation is completed by developing the equations from which to obtain the potentials, ψ_1 and ψ_2. One approach is to substitute the transverse field expressions in (32) into the two Maxwell's equations in (18), rewritten in circular cylindrical coordinates as

$$k_0\, \epsilon_r\, E_\phi - \hat{\phi} \cdot \nabla_t \times \overline{H}_t = 0 \qquad (34\text{a})$$

$$k_0\, \mu_r\, H_\phi - \hat{\phi} \cdot \nabla_t \times \overline{E}_t = 0 \qquad (34\text{b})$$

The substitution of $\overline{E}_t$ and $\overline{H}_t$, as found from (32), into (34) will yield a pair of 2nd-order coupled PDE's for the modal potentials. This was the procedure that was used in deriving the original CAP equations. The coupled PDE's for $\psi_{1,m}$ and $\psi_{2,m}$ appear in equations (5a) and (5b) of Chapter 2.

The complex functional in (19) was mentioned as an alternative to the weighted residual enforcement of (18). This type of variational approach was used in developing most of the finite element algorithms for scattering involving rotationally symmetric objects. The complex functional for the CAP's was found by using either of two equivalent general principles relating differential and variational formulations: the *Euler-Lagrange* equations [20] and the *stationary* theorem [21]. These approaches lead to a functional which is similar to the general form in (19) for this special case. The details of the derivation are in [3] while the results are discussed by Fleming in section 2.3.

6.3 Numerical Algorithm

a. Finite Element Mesh

We will employ a finite element method (FEM) using the special $u_3 = \phi$ form of circular cylindrical coordinates, as was considered in subsection 6.2d: namely, (z, ρ, ϕ). The building block for the FEM in static and time-harmonic problems is the spatial element, of which there are numerous standard forms [17]. In this case, we will span the desired region of 3-D space using multi-element rings and disks, as is depicted in Fig. 2. Disks are rings of elements having zero inner radius; they are connected to the z-axis. The rings are each composed of N pentahedral elements while the disks are constructed from N quadrahedral elements.

Within each element, the basis functions for E_ϕ and H_ϕ will have quadratic variation in the transverse (z, ρ) coordinates while being con-

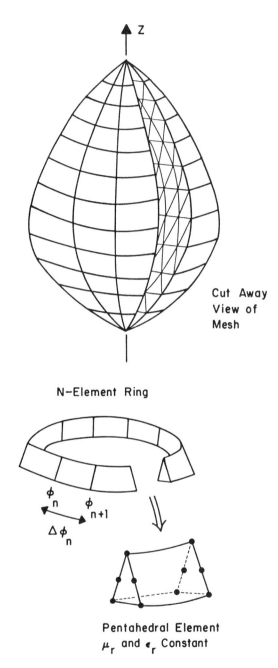

Figure 2 Finite element mesh and N-element ring.

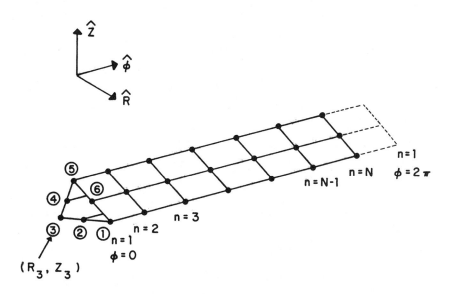

Figure 3 Nodal topology of unwrapped N-element ring.

stant in ϕ. The transverse fields, $\overline{E}_t$ and $\overline{H}_t$, will also have a quadratic approximation in the transverse coordinates, while having *natural* basis function ϕ-variations which conform analytically to the assumed basis function behavior of ψ_1 and ψ_2.

Within each element, the generally complex-valued material parameters, ϵ_r and μ_r, are assumed to be spatially constant. These elements will, by necessity, have dimensions which are much smaller than the wavelength. At the same time, the elements will be small enough to accurately resolve the spatial material variation of the structure being modeled.

b. Discrete Transport Equation

Let us now consider the numerical solution, within each ring or disk, for the transverse fields in terms of ψ_1 and ψ_2. Referring to Fig. 3, which is an opened out version on one of the element "rings" in Fig. 2, we will seek a discrete form of (20) that relates the transverse field arrays at the triangular end-segments (in ϕ) of the n-th element. Such a transport equation will take the form

$$\overline{\overline{V}}_{n+1} = \overline{\overline{A}}_n \cdot \overline{\overline{V}}_n + \overline{\overline{B}}_n \tag{35}$$

where $\overline{\overline{V}}_n$ is a shorthand notation for $\overline{\overline{V}}(z,\rho,\phi_n)$. The subscript is used here to denote the array values at the n-th ϕ-step and should not be confused with the p-subscript used in (6) to indicate two types of $\overline{V}$-vectors. Respective transition and driving matrices, $\overline{\overline{A}}_n$ and $\overline{\overline{B}}_n$, will depend in part upon the ϕ-coordinate variations of the basis functions which are selected for the individual field components within the element.

A straightforward approach to discretizing (20) is to use central differences. This is based upon an assumed piecewise linear interpolate to the ϕ-variation of the various field components. To provide acceptable accuracy, this method was found to require very fine segmentation in ϕ, thus increasing the number of discrete unknowns in the solution.

c. Natural Basis Functions

A dramatic reduction in the required ϕ-resolution results from the use of "natural" basis functions for $\overline{\overline{V}}$ within each element. These bases are exact analytical solutions within the element for the assumed functional form of ψ_1 and ψ_2. The initial approach used to obtain the natural basis functions was to solve the first-order system in (20), using the variation of parameters method [22]. This first required finding the complementary solutions of (20), when $\overline{\overline{U}} = \overline{\overline{0}}$, and is lengthy to describe. A more concise technique, which yields the same result, solves the second-order system in (28). As an example, by defining the driving vector on the right-hand side of (28a) as

$$\overline{P} = D_\phi \nabla_t \psi_1 - \mu_r k_0 \rho \hat{\phi} \times \nabla_t \psi_2 \tag{36}$$

and noting that μ_r and ϵ_r are assumed constant *in the element*, we obtain the general solution [22]

$$\overline{E}_t(z,\rho,\phi) = C_1(z,\rho)\sin(\beta\phi) + C_2(z,\rho)\cos(\beta\phi)$$

$$+ \beta^{-1}\int_0^\phi \overline{P}(z,\rho,\phi')\sin\beta(\phi-\phi')\,d\phi' \tag{37}$$

with

$$\beta = k_0\,\rho\,\sqrt{\epsilon_r\,\mu_r} \tag{38}$$

The vector functions $\overline{C}_1$ and $\overline{C}_2$ will depend upon the functional form of $\overline{P}$, as well as the boundary conditions on $\overline{E}_t$ at both ϕ_n and ϕ_{n+1}. A solution of (28b), for $\overline{H}_t$, will have a form that is similar to (37), but with different $\overline{C}$'s and a modified integrand, replacing $\overline{P}$.

We will employ pulse basis functions in the ϕ-coordinate for ψ_1 and ψ_2, thus giving a piecewise constant "staircase" interpolation around each multi-element ring or disk. This eliminates the D_ϕ-term in (36), giving a ϕ-constant $\overline{P}$-vector within the element,

$$\overline{P}(z,\rho) = -\mu_r k_0 \rho \,\hat{\phi} \times \nabla_t \psi_2 \tag{39}$$

A simplified form for (37) results, with the lower limit of the evaluated integration being added to the $\overline{C}_2$ term,

$$\overline{E}_t = \overline{C}_1(z,\rho)\sin(\beta\phi) + \overline{C}_2(z,\rho)\cos(\beta\phi) - \beta^{-2}\overline{P}(z,\rho) \tag{40a}$$

A similar result is obtained for the transverse magnetic field

$$\overline{H}_t = \overline{C}_3(z,\rho)\sin(\beta\phi) + \overline{C}_4(z,\rho)\cos(\beta\phi) - \beta^{-2}\overline{Q}(z,\rho) \tag{40b}$$

where

$$\overline{Q}(z,\rho) = -\epsilon_r k_0 \rho \,\hat{\phi} \times \nabla_t \psi_1 \tag{41}$$

The $\overline{C}_p$'s in (40) are *not* independent since the transverse fields in (28) must also satisfy (20). Upon substituting the vector components from (40) into (20), followed by some judicious algebraic manipulation to eliminate the vector function, $\overline{C}_p$'s within the element, the matrix components of the transport equation in (35) can be obtained

$$\overline{\overline{A}}_n = \begin{bmatrix} \cos(\beta\Delta\phi_n) & -\sqrt{\frac{\mu_r}{\epsilon_r}}\sin(\beta\Delta\phi_n) \\[2mm] \sqrt{\frac{\mu_r}{\epsilon_r}}\sin(\beta\Delta\phi_n) & \cos(\beta\Delta\phi_n) \end{bmatrix} \tag{42}$$

$$\overline{\overline{B}}_n = \begin{bmatrix} \beta^{-1}\sin(\beta\Delta\phi_n) & -\frac{1}{k_0\rho\epsilon_r}\{1 - \cos(\beta\Delta\phi_n)\} \\[2mm] \frac{1}{k_0\rho\mu_r}\{1 - \cos(\beta\Delta\phi_n)\} & \beta^{-1}\sin(\beta\Delta\phi_n) \end{bmatrix} \cdot \overline{\overline{U}}_n \tag{43}$$

where $\overline{\overline{U}}_n$, as defined by (23), does not vary with ϕ within the n-th element and $\Delta\phi_n = \phi_{n+1} - \phi_n$.

The numerical solution of the transport equation in (35) proceeds by defining a Riccati transform relationship [7]

$$\overline{\overline{V}}_{n+1} = \overline{\overline{R}}_n \cdot \overline{\overline{V}}_1 + \overline{\overline{S}}_n \qquad (44)$$

Substitution into (35) gives the recurrence formulas

$$\overline{\overline{R}}_n = \overline{\overline{A}}_n \cdot \overline{\overline{R}}_{n-1} \qquad (45)$$

$$\overline{\overline{S}}_n = \overline{\overline{A}}_n \cdot \overline{\overline{S}}_{n-1} + \overline{\overline{B}}_n \qquad (46)$$

with initial conditions $\overline{\overline{R}}_1 = \overline{\overline{A}}_1$ and $\overline{\overline{S}}_1 = \overline{\overline{B}}_1$. These formulas are used to generate and store the $\overline{\overline{R}}_n$'s and $\overline{\overline{S}}_n$'s for $n=1$ to N, where N is the number of ϕ-segments. Enforcing the periodicity of the solution, using $\overline{\overline{V}}_{N+1} = \overline{\overline{V}}_1$, gives the initial condition to be used in (25)

$$\overline{\overline{V}}_1 = [\overline{\overline{I}} - \overline{\overline{R}}_N]^{-1} \cdot \overline{\overline{S}}_N \qquad (47)$$

where $\overline{\overline{I}}$ is the 2×2 identity matrix.

d. Galerkin Method

Let us now consider additional details of the particular numerical approach that has been developed. Referring to the unwrapped element ring in Fig. 3, the potentials are represented within a multi-element ring or disk by basis function expansions having the form

$$\psi_1(z,\rho,\phi) = k_0\,\rho \sum_{m=1}^{N} \sum_{k=1}^{6} e_\phi(m,k)32\,q_k(z,\rho)\,p_m(\phi) \qquad (48a)$$

$$\psi_2(z,\rho,\phi) = k_0\,\rho \sum_{m=1}^{N} \sum_{k=1}^{6} h_\phi(m,k)\,q_k(z,\rho)\,p_m(\phi) \qquad (48b)$$

where the pulse functions are given by

$$p_m(\phi) = \begin{cases} 1 & \phi_m < \phi < \phi_{m+1} \\ 0 & \text{otherwise} \end{cases} \tag{49}$$

The quadratic basis function, q_k, has unit value at the k-th node within the triangular cross section of the element ring or disk, while being zero at each of the other 5 nodes. Explicit formulae are available for the q_k's [17]. The unknowns in (48) are the discrete field values, $e_\phi(m,k)$ and $h_\phi(m,k)$, which are defined, respectively, as E_ϕ and H_ϕ at the centers of the azimuthal arc-segments $(z,\rho) = (z_k, \rho_k)$, connecting each of the k-th nodes in the m-th element, again referring to Fig. 3.

The next step is to relate the transverse fields, using the natural basis functions, to the arc-segment values of E_ϕ and H_ϕ in (48). This is done by defining a numerical Green's dyadic, $\overline{\overline{G}}$, for the transverse field solution of the first-order transport equation in (20). The domain of the solution is the circular ϕ-contour composed of the j-th arc-segments within the multi-element ring or disk. The Green's dyadic that we seek will solve (20) with a diagonal $\overline{\overline{U}} = p_m(\phi)\overline{\overline{I}}$. More specifically,

$$D_\phi \overline{\overline{G}}(j,m,\phi) + \overline{\overline{M}}(z_j,\rho_j,\phi) \cdot \overline{\overline{G}}(j,m,\phi) = \begin{bmatrix} p_m(\phi) & 0 \\ 0 & p_m(\phi) \end{bmatrix} \tag{50}$$

The numerical solution to (50) is found by using the method embodied in (42) to (47), where the $\overline{\overline{U}}_n$ to be employed in (43) is the driving array defined above. Comparing (50) to (20), and using superposition in conjunction with (28), the transverse field array can be numerically evaluated along the (z_j,ρ_j) circular ϕ-contour by using

$$\overline{\overline{V}}(z_j,\rho_j,\phi) = \sum_{m=1}^{N} \sum_{k=1}^{6} \overline{\overline{G}}(j,m,\phi) \cdot \begin{bmatrix} e_\phi(m,k) & 0 \\ 0 & h_\phi(m,k) \end{bmatrix} \cdot \overline{\overline{DQ}}(j,k) \tag{51}$$

The DQ-array is given by

$$\overline{\overline{DQ}}(j,k) = \begin{bmatrix} D_z\{\rho\, q_k(z,\rho)\} & D_\rho\{\rho\, q_k(z,\rho)\} \\ -D_\rho\{\rho\, q_k(z,\rho)\} & D_z\{\rho\, q_k(z,\rho)\} \end{bmatrix} \tag{52}$$

which is evaluated at $(z, \rho) = (z_j, \rho_j)$. The transverse field array can now be expanded in the element cross section by use of quadratic basis functions in (z, ρ), giving

$$\overline{\overline{V}}(z, \rho, \phi) = \sum_{j=1}^{6} \overline{\overline{V}}(z_j, \rho_j, \phi) \, q_j(z, \rho) \tag{53}$$

The Galerkin equations are formed by weighted residual enforcement of (34), using the quadratic-pulse functions which first appeared in (48), $q_i(z, \rho) \, p_n(\phi)$, as weights. For each pair of unknown $e_\phi(n, i)$ and $h_\phi(n, i)$, we obtain the two weighted residual equations

$$\iiint q_i(z, \rho) \, p_n(\phi) \{k_0 \, \epsilon_r \, E_\phi + D_\rho H_z - D_z H_\rho\} \, d\rho \, dz \, d\phi = 0 \tag{54a}$$

$$\iiint q_i(z, \rho) \, p_n(\phi) \{k_0 \, \mu_r \, H_\phi + D_\rho E_z - D_z E_\rho\} \, d\rho \, dz \, d\phi = 0 \tag{54b}$$

These 3-D integrations are over all elements which share the (z_i, ρ_i) arc-segment in the support interval $\phi_n < \phi < \phi_{n+1}$. By substituting field components from (53) into (54) and performing the indicated array multiplications, we obtain the discretized versions of (54)

$$k_0 \sum_{k=1}^{6} e_\phi(n, k) \, \epsilon_r(n) \, W_1(i, k)$$

$$+ \sum_{m=1}^{N} \sum_{k=1}^{6} e_\phi(m, k) \left\{ \sum_{j=1}^{6} T_{21}(j, m, n) \, W_2(i, j, k) \right\} \tag{55a}$$

$$+ \sum_{m=1}^{N} \sum_{k=1}^{6} h_\phi(m, k) \left\{ \sum_{j=1}^{6} T_{22}(j, m, n) \, W_3(i, j, k) \right\} = 0$$

and

$$k_0 \sum_{k=1}^{6} h_\phi(n,k)\,\mu_r(n)\,W_1(i,k)$$

$$-\sum_{m=1}^{N}\sum_{k=1}^{6} h_\phi(m,k)\left\{\sum_{j=1}^{6} T_{21}(j,m,n)\,W_2(i,j,k)\right\} \tag{55b}$$

$$+\sum_{m=1}^{N}\sum_{k=1}^{6} e_\phi(m,k)\left\{\sum_{j=1}^{6} T_{11}(j,m,n)\,W_3(i,j,k)\right\} = 0$$

where

$$T_{uv}(j,m,n) = \frac{1}{\Delta\phi_n} \int_{\phi_n}^{\phi_{n+1}} G_{uv}(j,m,\phi)\,d\phi \tag{56}$$

are the integrated elements of the Green's dyadic in (50), while

$$W_1(i,k) = \iint q_i(z,\rho)\,q_k(z,\rho)\,d\rho\,dz \tag{57a}$$

$$W_2(i,j,k) = DQ_{12}(j,k) \iint q_i \cdot (D_\rho\,q_j)\,d\rho\,dz \tag{57b}$$

$$+ DQ_{11}(j,k) \iint q_i \cdot (D_z\,q_j)\,d\rho\,dz$$

$$W_3(i,j,k) = DQ_{22}(j,k) \iint q_i \cdot (D_\rho\,q_j)\,d\rho\,dz \tag{57c}$$

$$+ DQ_{21}(j,k) \iint q_i \cdot (D_z\,q_j)\,d\rho\,dz$$

are products of elements of the DQ-array in (52) and moment integrals. These integrations can be evaluated analytically by using available formulae for polynomial integrands [17]. The relative complex material constants within the n-th element in the N-element ring or disk being considered are defined by $\epsilon_r(n)$ and $\mu_r(n)$. To complete the evaluation of the Galerkin equations in (54), one must add together the contributions of (55) from each ring or disk which is associated with the unknown $e_\phi(n,i)$ and $h_\phi(n,i)$. The result will be a sparse linear system, which can be made to have a banded block structure by proper ordering of the azimuthal field unknowns. Driving the sparse linear system will be the contributions from (55) which entail "known" boundary values of $e_\phi(m,k)$ and $h_\phi(m,k)$ at the exterior surface surrounding the finite element mesh.

6.4   Computer Validations

a. Transverse Fields

The numerical algorithm for generating the transverse fields from the potentials was extensively tested before being used to implement the Galerkin equations. One set of tests imposed azimuthal field boundary conditions, using an obliquely incident, TM-polarized, plane wave having magnitude $E^i = 10V/m$, at the $6N$ arc-segments of an isolated N-element ring or disk, as is illustrated in Fig. 4. Transverse fields were then computed at the $6N$ point-nodes and compared to the known field components for cases of lossy and lossless media. These are *not* scattering solutions since the boundary values are known. All computations described in this chapter were performed with single precision (32 bit) arithmetic using compiled FORTRAN 77 source code on an 80386 based personal computer using an 80387 math coprocessor.

Example calculations appear in Figs. 5 and 6, where the magnitudes and phases of E_ρ are compared to the exact field of a $\theta^i = 45°$ canted incidence plane wave at the point-nodes on the circular contour, (z_1, ρ_1, ϕ_n) for $n = 1$ to N. In the free space case of Fig. 5, the contour radius is $\rho = 1.0\lambda_0$, while the radius is $\lambda_0/2$ in the $\epsilon_r = 4 - j1$ case of Fig. 6. The right-angle sides in the triangular element cross section are $\lambda_0/15$ in length for the free-space case and are $\lambda_0/30$ in length for the lossy material case. Convergence data are summarized for the free space case in Table 1, which lists the RMS percentage errors of the computed transverse field components versus the number of ϕ-segments in the ring, N, and the size of the right-angle sides of the triangular elements. An obvious implication of this data is that

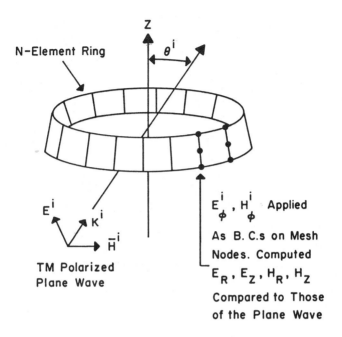

Figure 4   Element ring transverse field testing.

convergence to a lower error level requires both increases in N and reductions in the meridian element dimensions.

Table 1. Percentage Errors in Transverse Fields

	$L = \lambda_0/10$			$L = \lambda_0/15$			$L = \lambda_0/20$		
N	E_ρ	E_z	H_ρ	E_ρ	E_z	H_ρ	E_ρ	E_z	H_ρ
16	15	23	19	12	23	19	12	23	19
32	7	5	5	4	5	4	2	5	4
64	6	4	5	3	2	2	2	1	1

Computed fields are evaluated on an N-element ring of radius $1\lambda_0$ for a triangular element with right-angle sides of length L.

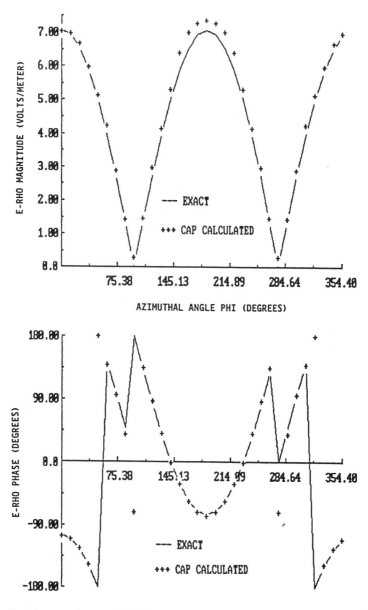

Figure 5 Comparison of CAP calculated and exact E_ρ at $\rho=1.0\lambda_0$ for plane wave in free space having $E^i=10$ V/m, with $L=\lambda_0/15$ and $N=32$. (a) Magnitude comparison. (b) Phase comparison.

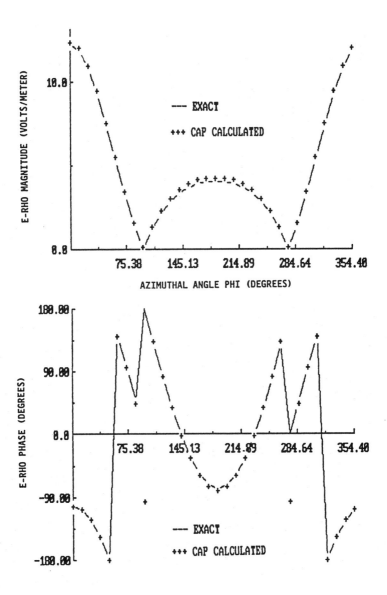

Figure 6 Comparison of CAP calculated and exact E_ρ at $\rho=\lambda_0/2$ for a plane wave in $\epsilon_r = 4 - j$ with $L=\lambda_0/30$ and $N=32$. (a) Magnitude comparison. (b) Phase comparison.

The convergence tests were repeated for a wide variety of radii, materials and element sizes. In addition, known field configurations involving spherical and cylindrical harmonics were used. These various tests established the need for quadratic elements in the q_k's of (48), vice linear elements which were first used. Also, the development of the natural basis functions was motivated by the slow convergence of early tests which used central differences in ϕ to discretize equation (20).

The effect of resonant solutions on the transverse field equations was also studied. As was noted in section 6.2, $\overline{E}_t$ and $\overline{H}_t$ (or $\overline{\overline{V}}$) can have non-zero periodic solutions over contours with radius defined in (33), *without* being driven by the CP's. These resonant solutions will thus tend to induce ill-conditioning of the numerical solution near these radii, in a similar manner to that observed for surface integral equations at frequencies near that of the cavity resonances of the enclosed volume. An important question that was initially addressed is: what is the spatial sensitivity about the resonant radius in the presence of low material losses? The transverse field generating program was used to test plane wave solutions for the N-element ring, as the radius of the $k = 1$ node contour was stepped through a neighborhood of the resonance. The pointwise percentage errors in computing E_ρ at an element node in the proximity of the smallest resonant radius is shown in Fig. 7 for the case of a $\theta^i = 45°$ incident TM plane wave. The E_z and H_ρ had similar error profiles. Extensive tests revealed that for the lossless case, significant errors were induced at the nodes that came closer than about $\lambda_0/20$ to the resonant radius for the case of triangular element right angle sides having a length of $\lambda_0/10$.

For smaller element sizes, yielding enhanced accuracy of the gradient approximations used to drive the system in (20), this proximity effect became less severe, with closer approaches being tolerated. On the other hand, as N was increased beyond that needed to reduce the arc-segment size to about $\lambda/8$, no further error reduction was noted. This is to be expected since the natural basis functions are exact solutions to (20) for the pulse basis expansions in ϕ of the potentials. However, the gradients that drive (20) are being applied to the quadratic expansions for the potentials in (z, ρ) at the nodes of the triangles. This is akin to a "backward difference" formula and is well known to require small segmentation to converge well. The effect of a close-by resonant radius is to enhance the effects of *any* errors in the driver of

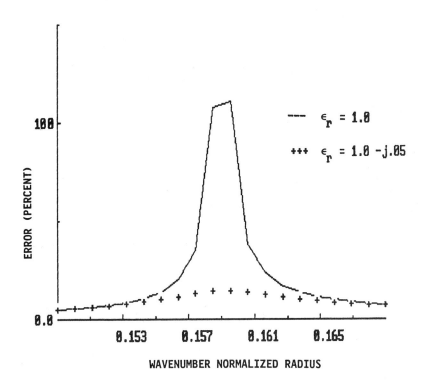

Figure 7 Percentage error in E_ρ calculation at element node near $2\pi\rho=1$ resonant radius for lossless and low-loss cases. Element right-angle sides are $\lambda/15$.

(20).

The resonance error problem was greatly alleviated by the introduction of even a slight loss in the material. This can be seen for the lossy case in Fig. 7, where the loss tangent is only 5%. Some possible numerical "fixes" for the resonant errors are to: (1) perturb the finite element mesh to put the singular radius at the midpoint between nodes; (2) introduce small losses in otherwise lossless material and; (3) seek out improved approximations for the potential gradients by employing better (z, ρ) basis expansions. Finally, it should be pointed out that the weighting integrals contained in the Galerkin equations in (54) tend to average these point-wise errors thus reducing the effects of the resonance instability.

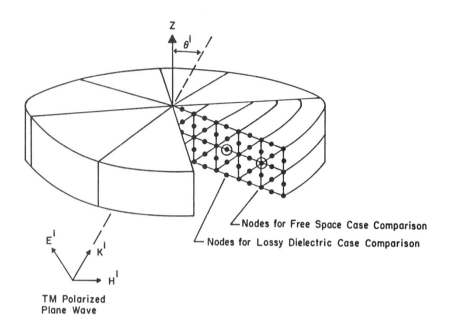

Figure 8 Cylindrical mesh used to test Galerkin solution for interior E_ρ and H_ϕ fields using plane wave boundary values on exterior surface.

b. Coupled Potentials

The discretized Galerkin equations in (55) were tested on a limited basis by computing the interior arc-segment values of E_ϕ and H_ϕ in the cylindrical finite element mesh which is displayed in Fig. 8. For the two examples to be considered, there were 8 azimuthal segments in the mesh, with 5 radial and 2 vertical increments, as is shown. This required the solution for a total of 480 complex unknowns which were generated by specified boundary values on the exterior surface of the cylinder. By forming vertical arrays, $\overline{X}_i$, composed of the 48 unknown E_ϕ and H_ϕ complex values in each of the 10 vertical mesh segments (3 nodes high and 8 segments around), the Galerkin equations produce a global linear system having the form

$$
\begin{bmatrix}
\overline{\overline{C}}_1 & \overline{\overline{D}}_1 & \overline{\overline{E}}_1 & & & & & \\
\overline{\overline{B}}_2 & \overline{\overline{C}}_2 & \overline{\overline{D}}_2 & & & & & \\
\overline{\overline{A}}_3 & \overline{\overline{B}}_3 & \overline{\overline{C}}_3 & \overline{\overline{D}}_3 & \overline{\overline{E}}_3 & & 0 & \\
& & \overline{\overline{B}}_4 & \overline{\overline{C}}_4 & \overline{\overline{D}}_4 & & & \\
& & & & \cdot & & & \\
& 0 & & & & \cdot & & \\
& & & & \overline{\overline{A}}_9 & \overline{\overline{B}}_9 & \overline{\overline{C}}_9 & \overline{\overline{D}}_9 \\
& & & & & & \overline{\overline{B}}_{10} & \overline{\overline{C}}_{10}
\end{bmatrix}
\begin{bmatrix}
\overline{X}_1 \\ \overline{X}_2 \\ \overline{X}_3 \\ \overline{X}_4 \\ \cdot \\ \cdot \\ \overline{X}_9 \\ \overline{X}_{10}
\end{bmatrix}
=
\begin{bmatrix}
\overline{Y}_1 \\ \overline{Y}_2 \\ \overline{Y}_3 \\ \overline{Y}_4 \\ \cdot \\ \cdot \\ \overline{Y}_9 \\ \overline{Y}_{10}
\end{bmatrix}
$$

$$(58)$$

where the 48×48 complex sub-arrays, $\overline{\overline{A}}_i, \overline{\overline{B}}_i$, etc., are themselves sparse matrices. The $\overline{Y}_i$'s are formed from the boundary node contributions to (55).

There exist several methods for solving sparse blocked linear systems such as this [23]. A particularly simple approach was developed here, which implements the standard Gaussian elimination algorithm [24], but on a block-by-block basis. In such a scheme, the block submatrices and driving vectors are written to disk in sequence as they are generated. The system inversion is then performed by reading only the needed groups of these arrays into random access memory (RAM) at any one time. Such a procedure allows very large systems to be solved by using a minimum of RAM.

Magnitude and phase comparisons are shown for respective lossless and lossy cases in Figs. 9 and 10 for a $\theta^i = 45°$ TM-polarized incident plane wave. It should again be noted that this is not a scattering solution test: the incident field is applied only as a boundary condition for the potentials on the exterior surface. The Galerkin generated interior fields are then compared to the original plane wave along constant (z, ρ) circular contours inside of the mesh. The triangular element right-angle sides were $\lambda_0/15$ in the free space case and $\lambda_0/30$ in

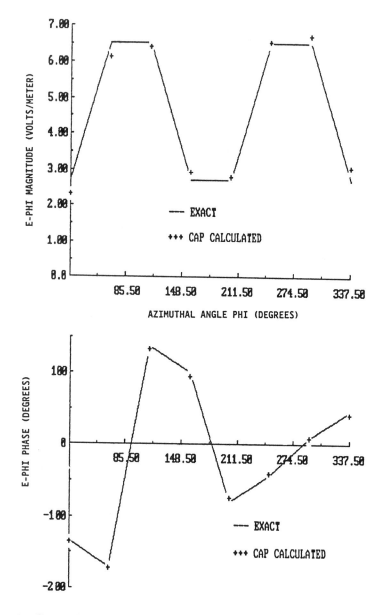

Figure 9   Comparison of CAP calculated and exact E_ϕ at $R=0.267\lambda_0$ for plane wave in free space with $L=\lambda_0/15$ and $N=8$. (a) Magnitude comparison. (b) Phase comparison.

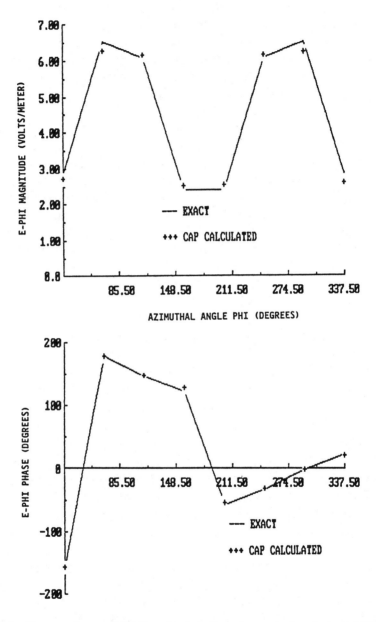

Figure 10 Comparison of CAP calculated and exact E_ϕ at $R=0.083\lambda_0$ for plane wave in $\epsilon_r=4$ - j with $L=\lambda/30$ and $N=8$. (a) Magnitude comparison. (b) Phase comparison.

the $\epsilon_r = 4 - j1$ case. In both instances, the outside circumference of the cylinder is over 2λ in the medium. The use of natural basis functions for the transverse fields yielded acceptable accuracy when using only $N = 8$ azimuthal segments over this outside circumference. Also, there are two resonant radii within the mesh for the lossless case. No increased errors in the Galerkin solution were observed for nodes that were close to these radii.

6.5 Discussion

The analytics and example numerics of a generalized coupled potential (CP) formulation have been described here along with the results of initial validations. These preliminary tests accompanied the development of basis functions for the potentials and the transverse field vectors. The sensitivity of the solutions to the instability of the generating equations near the singular radii in the lossless case was considered. This was followed by an example solution for the potentials within a cylindrical mesh subject to applied boundary values on the surface. A special block elimination method was used to solve the Galerkin equation sparse matrix system using a micro computer. Excellent accuracy was obtained in all such tests, having anywhere from a few hundred to well over a thousand complex unknowns. By employing faster Cray-class computers, this technique can readily handle hundreds of thousands of unknowns with computation times measured in minutes, not hours.

Future enhancements of the formulation are pending, in conjunction with numerous possible applications. For example, the use of circular rings will not be optimal for modeling some structures, such as aircraft, in that many extra elements may be required in the empty space surrounding the object. Circular rings were used in this initial implementation of the formulation, thus permitting convenient testing of its numerical performance for the special case of local circular cylindrical coordinates. By using more general orthogonal coordinate systems, as was initially considered in section 6.2, it should be possible to develop efficient numerical algorithms based on the CP formulation which can be applied to realistic 3-D material structures. Another option is to use non-circular rings and disks generated from elements having stepwise variable radii of curvature along each coordinate contour. In such a case, the sectionally curved elements become geometric building blocks for complex structures. The continuing development of this formulation will employ these and other enhancements to minimize the number of unknowns while increasing their solution accuracy.

The long-term goal is to employ this formulation for the computation of scattering by highly irregular and inhomogeneous material structures. This can be accomplished through the use of the *field feedback formulation* (F^3) [13], where the boundary value problem in the spatial region containing the scattering structure will be solved by using the coupled azimuthal potentials. This is conceptually related to the *boundary element method* (see Chapter 3) for coupling interior and exterior regions in a scattering problem. The boundary value solution will provide the "forward matrix operator" in the F^3. Used in conjunction with surface integrations to form the "feedback operator", the recursive linear system that results can be solved either directly or via iteration to obtain the scattered fields. A second possible option for scattering solution implementation is through a near field *radiation boundary condition*, examples of which are considered in Chapters 4, 5 and 8, as well as [14].

Acknowledgements

This research was sponsored by the Navy Direct Funding Program at the Naval Postgraduate School, Monterey, California.

References

[1] Bromwich, T. J. I'a., "Electromagnetic waves," *Phil. Mag.*, S.6. **38**, No. 223, 143–164, 1919.

[2] Morgan, M. A., and K. K. Mei, "Numerical computation of E.M. scattering by inhomogeneous bodies of revolution," *Abstracts for the 1974 URSI Symposium on E.M. Wave Theory*, London, England, July, 1974.

[3] Morgan, M. A., S. K. Chang, and K. K. Mei, "Coupled potential formulation for 3-D E.M. boundary value problems in inhomogeneous axially symmetric media," *Abstracts for the 1975 IEEE/AP-S Symposium*, Urbana, IL, June 1975.

[4] Morgan, M. A., K. K. Mei, and S. K. Chang, "Coupled azimuthal

potentials for electromagnetic field problems in inhomogeneous axially-symmetric media," *IEEE Trans. Antennas Propagat.*, **AP-25**, 413–417, 1977.

[5] Stovall, R. E., and K. K. Mei, "Application of a unimoment technique to a biconical antenna with inhomogeneous dielectric loading," *IEEE Trans. Antennas Propagat.*, **AP-23**, 335–341, 1975.

[6] Mei, K. K., M. A. Morgan, and S. K. Chang, "Finite methods in electromagnetic scattering," Chap. 10 in *Electromagnetic Scattering*, P. L. E. Ushlenghi, Ed., New York: Academic Press, 1978.

[7] Morgan, M. A., and K. K. Mei, "Finite element computation of scattering by inhomogeneous penetrable bodies of revolution," *IEEE Trans. Antennas Propagat.*, **AP-27**, 202–214, 1979.

[8] Morgan, M. A., "Finite element computation of microwave scattering by raindrops," *Radio Science*, **15**, 1109–1119, 1980.

[9] Morgan, M. A., "Finite element calculation of microwave absorption by the cranial structure," *IEEE Trans. Biomed. Eng.*, **BME-28**, 687–695, 1981.

[10] Morgan, M. A., C. H. Chen, S. C. Hill, and P. W. Barber, "Finite element - boundary integral formulation for electromagnetic scattering," *J. Wave Motion*, **6**, 91–103, 1984.

[11] Fleming, A. H. J., *Numerical Analysis of Electromagnetic Scattering by Axisymmetric Composite Antenna Structures*, M.S. Thesis, Faculty of Technology, Chisholm, Inst. of Tech., Caulfield, Australia, March 1987.

[12] Mei, K. K., "Unimoment method of solving antenna and scattering problems," *IEEE Trans. Antennas Propagat.*, **AP-22**, 760–766, 1974.

[13] Morgan, M. A., and B. E. Welch, "The field feedback formulation for electromagnetic scattering problems," *IEEE Trans. Antennas Propagat.*, **AP-34**, 1377–1382, 1986.

[14] Kriegsmann, G. A., A. Taflove, and K. R. Umashankar, "A new formulation of electromagnetic wave scattering using an on-surface radiation boundary condition," *IEEE Trans. Antennas Propagat.*, **AP-35**, 153–161, 1987.

[15] Stratton, J. A., *Electromagnetic Theory*, New York: McGraw-Hill, 1941, Chap. 2.

[16] Silver, S., "Microwave Transmission Lines," Chap. 7 in *Microwave Antenna Theory and Design*, S. Silver, Ed., New York: McGraw-Hill, M.I.T. Rad. Lab. Series Vol. 12, 1949; (Reprinted) New York: Dover, 1965 and; London: Peregrinus, 1984.

[17] Lapidus, L., and G. F. Pinder, *Numerical Solution of Partial Differential Equations in Science and Engineering*, New York: Wiley Interscience, 1982, Chaps. 2 and 3.

[18] Jeng, S. K., and C. H. Chen, "On variational electromagnetics: theory and application," *IEEE Trans. Antennas Propagat.*, **AP-32**, 902–907, 1985.

[19] Oppenheim, A. V., and R. W. Schafer, *Digital Signal Processing*, Englewood Cliffs: Prentice-Hall, 1975, 238–241.

[20] Morse, P. M., and H. Feshbach, *Methods of Theoretical Physics*, New York: McGraw-Hill, 1953, 275-280.

[21] Stakgold, I., *Green's Functions and Boundary Value Problems*, New York: Wiley Interscience, 1979, 520–557.

[22] Greenberg, M. D., *Foundations of Applied Mathematics*, Englewood Cliffs: Prentice-Hall, 1978, 417–421.

[23] Tewarson, R. P., *Sparse Matrices*, New York: Academic Press, 1973.

[24] Golub, G. H., and C. F. Van Loan, *Matrix Computations*, Baltimore: John Hopkins Univ. Press, 1984, Chap. 4.

7

THE METHOD OF CONFORMING BOUNDARY ELEMENTS FOR TRANSIENT ELECTROMAGNETICS

A. C. Cangellaris and K. K. Mei

7.1   Introduction

Traditionally, electromagnetic wave scattering computations are done in the frequency domain. Recently, however, there has been an increasing interest in the solution of transient electromagnetic scattering, which is prompted by a number of reasons. Current development in wideband radar design for higher resolution has created interest in the investigation of the impulse response of conducting bodies for target identification purposes. The electromagnetic pulse (EMP) problem is another area of great interest which is, essentially, a transient problem. Nonlinear scattering and radiation problems, which have become of great interest in recent years, are, in general, more easily addressed by obtaining the transient solution directly. The ability to compute accurately the transient electromagnetic fields in the presence of dispersive media is of great importance in remote sensing methods for determining the electromagnetic parameters of inaccessible regions. The simplicity with which the time-dependent form of Maxwell's equations can be integrated in the presence of composite structures with different electric and magnetic properties suggests the possibility for a transient analysis of integrated dielectric waveguides and other components for microwave and millimeter-wave integrated circuits.

The time-dependent integral equation formulation, first reported by Bennett and Weeks [1], has dominated the numerical solution of transient electromagnetic scattering over the past years [2–4]. More recently, iterative methods have been introduced in the solution of the above integral equations [5,6], as an alternative to the marching-on-in-time procedure which was found to lead to rapid growth of spurious oscillations [7] due to the accumulation of numerical error. The new generation of computers, with the vast memory capacities and the parallel processing architecture that favors simple sequential operations, has opened new possibilities for the direct time-domain solution of electromagnetic problems. A very interesting finite-difference scheme was first presented by Yee [8] . Its simplicity and efficiency attracted many investigators and the method found many applications [9–14] (also see Chapter 8 of this book). A severe limitation of this formulation was the use of square or cubic cells to approximate the geometry of the scatterer. These cells introduce important boundary distortion in the problem which affects the satisfaction of the related electromagnetic boundary conditions on conducting surfaces and/or dielectric interfaces. The hope for a more flexible method led to the use of the conformal finite-differences [15] and later on to the point-matched finite-elements, the conforming boundary elements, as well as other finite-elements formulations of the problem [16]. The point-matched finite elements were used to study transient electromagnetic scattering from buried objects [17], while an introduction to the method of conforming boundary elements was presented in a recent paper by Cangellaris, et al. [18]. Two additional modified time-domain finite-difference schemes for use with nonrectangular structures have been reported recently [19,20].

In this paper, the method of conforming boundary elements is reviewed and extended to geometries with corners and wedges. Furthermore, the various errors introduced by the numerical discretization are examined in detail. The importance of the artificial boundary that truncates the computational domain, as well as its impact on the numerical solution is also discussed. Numerical examples in two and three dimensions are presented, along with comparisons with available experimental results. These examples demonstrate the efficiency of the method and its versatility in dealing with large, composite structures of arbitrary shape.

7.2 Initial Boundary Value Problem

The general problem this paper is dealing with is the interaction of an electromagnetic wave with perfectly conducting and/or dielectric obstacles in free space. No restriction is imposed on the dielectric permittivity of the structure, which can have any desired spatial variation $\epsilon(\overline{r})$. We must mention that losses in the dielectrics can be accounted for by introducing a finite conductivity $\sigma(\overline{r})$. Since linearity is assumed, one can decompose the total field into incident and scattered fields. The incident field $\overline{E}^{in}$ is defined to be the field that would exist in the absence of the scatterers. If $\overline{E}^{tot}$ denotes the total field, then the scattered field is defined as

$$\overline{E}^{sc} = \overline{E}^{tot} - \overline{E}^{in} \tag{1}$$

In a source-free region the macroscopic electromagnetic phenomena are governed by Maxwell's equations

$$\nabla \times \overline{E}^{tot}(\overline{r}, t) = -\mu_0 \frac{\partial \overline{H}^{tot}}{\partial t} \tag{2a}$$

$$\nabla \times \overline{H}^{tot}(\overline{r}, t) = \epsilon(\overline{r}) \frac{\partial \overline{E}^{tot}}{\partial t} + \sigma(\overline{r}) \overline{E}^{tot} \tag{2b}$$

For a well-posed initial boundary value problem, the uniqueness theorem for Maxwell's equations [21] requires that

(a) $\overline{E}(\overline{r}, t = 0)$ and $\overline{H}(\overline{r}, t = 0)$ must be known everywhere inside the domain of interest. Notice that if the *known* incident field is not allowed to reach the scatterer before $t = 0$, then the initial condition for the unknown scattered fields is

$$\overline{E}^{sc}(\overline{r}, t = 0) = \overline{H}^{sc}(\overline{r}, t = 0) = 0 \tag{3}$$

(b) The tangential component of $\overline{E}^{tot}$ or $\overline{H}^{tot}$ on the boundaries of the domain of interest must be known for all $t \geq 0$.

For the case of a perfect conductor, its surface is part of the boundary, and on it

$$\hat{n} \times \overline{E}^{tot}(t) = 0 \qquad (4)$$

where $\hat{n}$ is the unit normal vector on the surface. For the boundary at infinity, Sommerfeld's radiation condition [22] must hold; that is, the *scattered* fields must be of an outward travelling wave type. Since the numerical technique under consideration can treat only a finite computational domain, an artificial boundary is introduced and an equivalent radiation condition is imposed on this truncation boundary. The validity of such an approximation is of great importance and is discussed in section 7.3. Finally, we must mention that for the boundary between two regions (i) and (j) with different dielectric and conducting characteristics, the following conditions must be satisfied for all t

$$\hat{n} \times \overline{E}_{(i)}^{tot} = \hat{n} \times \overline{E}_{(j)}^{tot} \qquad (5a)$$

$$\hat{n} \cdot \left(\epsilon_{(i)} \frac{\partial \overline{E}_{(i)}^{tot}}{\partial t} + \sigma_{(i)} \overline{E}_{(i)}^{tot} \right) = \hat{n} \cdot \left(\epsilon_{(j)} \frac{\partial \overline{E}_{(j)}^{tot}}{\partial t} + \sigma_{(j)} \overline{E}_{(j)}^{tot} \right) \qquad (5b)$$

where $\hat{n}$ is the unit normal vector on the interface. In what follows, we restrict ourselves to lossless media and we drop the conduction current term in (2b) and (5b). The details for the treatment of lossy media can be found in [17].

7.3 Method of Conforming Boundary Elements

A detailed, tutorial presentation of the point-matched time-domain finite-element method and its special case of the conforming boundary elements can be found in [18]. Here we shall present a summary of the method and its advantages, accompanied by a more detailed discussion of some of the discretization issues that were considered rather briefly in [18].

The computational domain which is truncated by means of an artificial radiation boundary is discretized as shown in Fig. 1. This layout results into two complementary meshes, one for the electric and one for the magnetic field, positioned in such a way that an element of each of the meshes encloses a node of the other. We assume that $\overline{E}$ and $\overline{H}$ can be written in the general functional forms

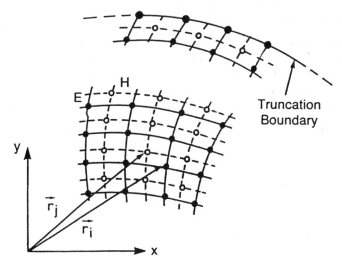

Figure 1 Finite-element discretization of computational domain.

$$\overline{E}(\overline{r},t) \approx \sum_{i=1}^{M} \phi_i(\overline{r})\overline{E}_i(t) \tag{6a}$$

$$\overline{H}(\overline{r},t) \approx \sum_{j=1}^{M} \psi_j(\overline{r})\overline{H}_j(t) \tag{6b}$$

where $\overline{E}_i$'s and $\overline{H}_j$'s are the nodal values of the electric and magnetic fields, respectively, and ϕ_i's and ψ_j's are known basis functions which allow us to describe any desirable variation of the fields within the elements. By an appropriate definition of these functions we can make the field within an element be dependent only on its values at the nodes of the element [18]. Then one can show that a point-matching (collocation) procedure reduces $(2a, 2b)$ to the following system of state equations

$$\frac{d\overline{H}_j}{dt} = -\frac{1}{\mu_0} \sum_{l=1}^{L} (\nabla \phi_l(\overline{r}))_{\overline{r}=\overline{r}_j} \times \overline{E}_l(t), \qquad j = 1,2,\ldots,N \tag{7a}$$

$$\frac{d\overline{E}_i}{dt} = \frac{1}{\epsilon(\overline{r}_i)} \sum_{l=1}^{L} (\nabla \psi_l(\overline{r}))_{\overline{r}=\overline{r}_i} \times \overline{H}_l(t), \qquad i = 1,2,\ldots,M \tag{7b}$$

where, N is the number of magnetic nodes, M is the number of electric nodes, and L is the number of nodes of a single element. For the two-dimensional quadrilateral $L = 4$, while for the three-dimensional hexahedron $L = 8$. The above system of state equations must now be integrated in time. For this purpose, the "leap-frog" method is used [23] (a basic discussion appears in Chapter 1). According to this method, the electric and magnetic fields are discretized in time with time step (δt), with the temporal nodes of $\overline{H}$ between those of $\overline{E}$. Using the simplified notation

$$\overline{E}^n = \overline{E}[t = n(\delta t)] \tag{8a}$$

$$\overline{H}^{n+\frac{1}{2}} = \overline{H}[t = (n + \frac{1}{2})(\delta t)], \qquad n = 0, 1, \ldots \tag{8b}$$

we approximate the time derivatives in (7) by the central difference formulas

$$\left(\frac{d\overline{H}_j}{dt}\right)_{n(\delta t)} \approx \frac{\overline{H}_j^{n+\frac{1}{2}} - \overline{H}_j^{n-\frac{1}{2}}}{\delta t} \tag{9a}$$

$$\left(\frac{d\overline{E}_i}{dt}\right)_{(n+\frac{1}{2})(\delta t)} \approx \frac{\overline{E}_i^{n+1} - \overline{E}_i^n}{\delta t} \tag{9b}$$

Substituting (9a,b) in (7a,b) and rearranging we obtain the following explicit recurrence formulas

$$\overline{H}_j^{n+\frac{1}{2}} = \overline{H}_j^{n-\frac{1}{2}} - \frac{(\delta t)}{\mu_0} \sum_{l=1}^{L} (\nabla \phi_l(\overline{r}))_{\overline{r}=\overline{r}_j} \times \overline{E}_l^n, \qquad j = 1, 2, \ldots, N \tag{10a}$$

$$\overline{E}_i^{n+1} = \overline{E}_i^n + \frac{(\delta t)}{\epsilon(\overline{r}_i)} \sum_{l=1}^{L} (\nabla \psi_l(\overline{r}))_{\overline{r}=\overline{r}_i} \times \overline{H}_l^{n+\frac{1}{2}}, \qquad i = 1, 2, \ldots, M \tag{10b}$$

Once the initial conditions at $t = 0$ are known, (10a,b) can be used alternatively to update $\overline{H}_j$'s and $\overline{E}_i$'s at $n = 1, 2, \ldots$.

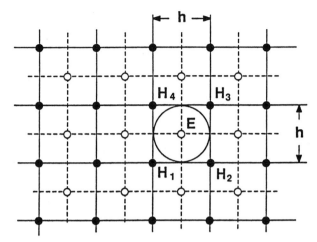

Figure 2   Characteristic circle for the leap-frog scheme.

The method of conforming boundary elements is a special case of the previously discussed point-matched finite-element method. The basic idea behind it is to relax the memory requirements for the storage of coordinates of all the nodes of the finite element mesh by limiting the irregularly shaped elements to the boundary of the scatterer only. In this aspect, this method can be considered as a technique which puts together the advantages of both the finite-element and the finite-difference methods. That is, the few irregularly shaped boundary elements conform the geometry of interest, while the regularity of the rest of the grid is conserved to take advantage of the attractive feature of the finite-difference method where the index numbers of each node contain the nodal coordinates. It is also known that the leap-frog integration of (10a,b) is stable under the condition [23]

$$c(\delta t) \leq h \qquad (11)$$

where c is the velocity of propagation in the medium. Notice that with this scheme the Courant limit can be reached in all cases regardless of the number of dimensions of the problem. This can be demonstrated easily by viewing the leap-frog scheme proposed above as a two-step integration of the time-dependent wave equation. Then, the theory of characteristics states that the numerical scheme is stable, if, and only if, the domain of dependence for the discrete equation includes that for the differential equation. For the two-dimensional case considering the electric node E in Fig. 2, the domain of dependence for the discrete equation that updates the value of this node by half a time step is the square $H_1 H_2 H_3 H_4$. On the other hand, the characteristics for the wave equation in two dimensions are the conical surfaces

$$(x - x_0)^2 + (y - y_0)^2 = (ct)^2 \tag{12}$$

with apex at the node under consideration. If we take as the time origin the plane (ct_0) on which the magnetic nodes H_1, H_2, H_3, H_4 have been updated, then the characteristic through E cuts on this plane the circle

$$(x - x_0)^2 + (y - y_0)^2 = \left(c\frac{\delta t}{2}\right)^2 \tag{13}$$

as the domain of dependence for the wave equation. Then, it is easily seen that for stability (11) must hold. The above reasoning can be extended to the study of the stability condition on irregular grids. However, one needs to check, one by one, all the irregular elements in order to derive the stability condition that must be satisfied over the entire mesh. Equation (11) suggests that h should be kept uniform throughout the finite-element mesh in order to avoid limiting the time step to unrealistically small values. Obviously, the method of conforming boundary elements has control of the size of the smallest element while the various automatic mesh generation techniques leave that to chance or, at least, must introduce additional sophisticated restrictions in order to redistribute the nodes for better uniformity [24]. As far as the interpolation functions are concerned, notice that the ∇ operation in $(10a, b)$ restricts us to choose element functions with continuous first derivatives inside the elements. For our purposes the isoparametric quadrilateral elements with the associated bilinear interpolation functions are chosen for 2-D geometries [25], while hexahedron isoparametric elements constitute a natural extension to three dimensions [26]. One can easily check [27] that with this type of elements the numerical scheme of $(10a, b)$ is consistent, and also that positioning of the nodes at the center of gravity of the element ensures the second order accuracy of the numerical approximation. This, in turn, brings us to some necessary discussion related to the conforming elements themselves. In order to keep (11) valid all over the computational domain, we try to use conforming boundary elements that are large enough to *contain* a regular element. However, the selection of these elements should be such that very large elements will also be excluded. As an example for the selection procedure, consider the element $(B_3 E_5 E_9 B_4)$

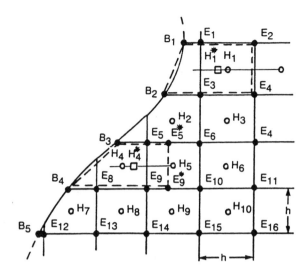

Figure 3 Conforming boundary elements.

of Fig. 3. Obviously, it is not large enough for our purposes, while at the same time the element $(B_3 E_6 E_{10} B_4)$ is too large. An additional element is then introduced, identified with the dashed line in Fig. 3, where the points E_5^* and E_9^* are such that the length of the segment $(B_3 E_5^*)$ equals h. Of course, the electric field at the new nodes E_5^* and E_9^* is determined by interpolation. Since the original node H_4 no longer coincides with the center of gravity of the electric element, an additional magnetic node H_4^* is positioned at the center of gravity of the new element and the value of the original magnetic node (if needed) is computed by extrapolation as in the element under consideration, or by interpolation as in the element $(B_1 E_2 E_4 B_2)$ of the same figure. For smooth, well-resolved geometries, one rarely encounters elements where such an extrapolation procedure is needed. Hence, the departure from the second-order accuracy of the solution due to the first-order accurate extrapolation is very localized and does not affect the overall accuracy and the stability of the numerical integration. There are also some electric nodes that are computed by interpolation, for example, E_{12}, E_8, E_5, E_3, E_1 in Fig. 3.

Finally, we must mention that the boundary condition (4) defines only the tangential component of the electric field for those electric nodes that lie on the conducting surface. Therefore, the continuity equation on the conducting surface

$$\nabla \cdot \overline{J} + \frac{\partial \rho}{\partial t} = 0 \qquad (14)$$

is implemented for the computation of the normal component of the electric field. Using the relations

$$\overline{J} = \hat{n} \times \overline{H}^{tot} \qquad (15a)$$

$$\rho = \hat{n} \cdot \overline{D}^{tot} \qquad (15b)$$

in (14), we get

$$\nabla_0 \cdot (\hat{n} \times \overline{H}^{tot}) = -\hat{n} \cdot \frac{\partial \overline{D}^{tot}}{\partial t} \qquad (16)$$

where $\nabla_0 \cdot$ is the surface divergence, involving derivatives along the surface of the body only, and $\hat{n}$ is the unit normal on the surface. The details about the numerical implementation of (16) for the case of conforming boundary elements can be found in [18]. In the same paper, a simple technique for treating interfaces between two media with different dielectric constants was introduced. It is well-known that at such dielectric interfaces the field components or their derivatives are discontinuous. Therefore the interpolation functions over elements that include the interface must be modified to include the appropriate discontinuity. Instead of constructing the appropriate interpolation function (a process that is rather complicated in 2-D and 3-D), fictitious nodes are introduced on either side of the interface which allow us to compute the correct spatial derivatives of the fields using central differences. The values of these fictitious nodes are found rigorously by using the boundary conditions at the interface. For more details on the method, the reader is referred to [18].

Before leaving this section, we would like to point out that *noise* is introduced by the numerical processing. This numerical noise affects the high frequency information. This noise is due to the dispersion introduced by the numerical discretization of the hyperbolic system of Maxwell's curl equations. This dispersion effect results in a *phase error*, the magnitude of which increases with frequency [28, 29] and results in a loss of accuracy. In other words, an initial signal that is not monochromatic will change form as it propagates. Spurious oscillations contaminate the results, particularly when the initial data is in

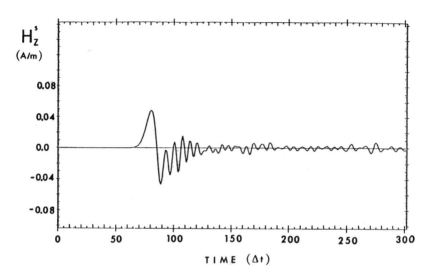

Figure 4 Spurious oscillations due to discontinuity in the initial data.

the form of a sharp signal. These oscillations are demonstrated in Fig.
4 where the back-scattered field from an infinite conducting circular
cylinder is presented under the excitation of one half of a Gaussian
pulse, that is, a pulse terminated abruptly at its peak value. Another
type of numerical error that occurs in the discretization of hyperbolic
equations on two- and three-dimensional grids is due to the numerical
anisotropy of the velocity of propagation [29]. That is, the velocity
of propagation of numerical sinusoidal solutions, in addition to being
dependent upon frequency, is also dependent upon direction of propagation. This numerical anisotropy depends on the scheme used for the
space discretization. The expression for the numerical phase velocity in
terms of the size of the mesh, the frequency of interest, and the direction of propagation can be found by considering the sinusoidal numerical solution to the discretized hyperbolic system. One can show [27]
that for the leap-frog scheme of (10a,b) on a regular two-dimensional
square grid of size h the numerical phase velocity for a sinusoidal wave
of angular frequency ω and with its propagation vector at an angle α
with respect to the x-axis is

$$c^\star = c \left\{ \left[\cos\alpha \frac{\sin(0.5\,\omega h \cos\alpha)}{0.5\,\omega h \cos\alpha} \cos(0.5\,\omega h \sin\alpha) \right]^2 \right.$$

$$\left. + \left[\sin\alpha \frac{\sin(0.5\,\omega h \sin\alpha)}{0.5\,\omega h \sin\alpha} \cos(0.5\,\omega h \cos\alpha) \right]^2 \right\}^{\frac{1}{2}} \tag{17}$$

where c is the velocity of propagation in the medium. Notice that for a well-resolved wave $\omega h \to 0$ and $c^\star \to c$. From (17), one can easily check that the numerical anisotropy is less than 4% for wavelengths longer than $8h$. This sets an upper limit on the highest frequency in the spectrum of the propagating pulses or, translated into the time domain, sets a lower limit on the rise and fall times of the pulses.

Another issue of importance in the numerical discretization is the ratio of the size of the scatterer to the effective width of the exciting pulse. It is well-known that the scattering parameters of a structure can be described in terms of its poles in the complex frequency domain. The number of the poles is determined by the effective maximum frequency of the exciting pulse, which in turn is determined by the spatial width of the pulse. Therefore, for accurate information on the nature of the target, one should decrease the pulse width. This, of course, results in larger number of spatial and temporal samples and consequently, larger storage requirements and longer computational time. There is, therefore, a tradeoff between accurate high-frequency information and cost of computation.

Finally, another source of error in the numerical solution is the numerical condition used at the artificial boundary that truncates the computational domain, and is discussed in the next section.

7.4   Radiation Boundary Condition

The general problem of transient electromagnetic scattering or radiation requires the solution of Maxwell's partial differential equations on an infinite domain. However, for computational expediency, one has to operate within a bounded domain. An artificial boundary is then constructed and appropriate conditions are sought on this boundary in order to simulate an infinite domain. It is desirable that no *reflections* occur from this artificial boundary back into the domain of interest.

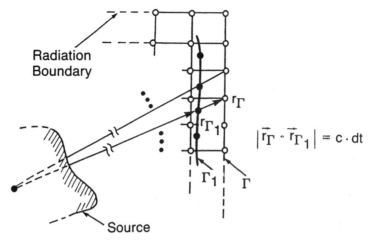

Figure 5 **Computation of the scattered field on the radiation boundary.**

This is not possible in general, and special restrictions are imposed in order to minimize these reflections. There is a large amount of literature devoted to this subject [30–33]. An exact termination method implements Huygen's principle but is expensive both in storage and computation [33]. From a computational point of view an attractive absorbing boundary condition is one that involves only local spatial and time derivative operations consistent with the simple algorithm of the finite difference or finite element method.

As shown in Fig. 5, a numerical surface Γ is introduced in order to truncate the computational domain. The scheme adopted here for the numerical computation of the fields on Γ is based on the fact that, outside a surface enclosing all the sources of radiation, one can always represent the solution of the scalar wave equation in the following form [34]

$$u(t, r, \theta, \phi) = \sum_{i=1}^{\infty} \frac{f_i\left(t - \frac{r}{c}, \theta, \phi\right)}{r^i} \tag{18}$$

where r, θ, ϕ are spherical coordinates and c is the velocity of propagation. Moreover, f_i's can be uniquely determined if the radiation field f_1 at infinity is known. The result in (18) is for the scalar wave equation in three dimensions. For the two-dimensional case, one finds [17] an equivalent expansion

$$u(t,\rho,\phi) = \sum_{i=0}^{\infty} \frac{f_i \left(t - \frac{\rho}{c}, \phi\right)}{\rho^{i+\frac{1}{2}}} \tag{19}$$

where ρ, ϕ are polar coordinates. Bayliss and Turkel [40] proposed a family of differential operators B_m constructed in such a way that the mth operator will annihilate the first m terms in the above expansions. In other words, application of the differential operator of order m is equivalent to enforcing the field continuity of the inner solution with the m leading terms of the above expansions on the surface Γ. The higher the order of the operator the more terms are included, and the truncation boundary can be brought closer to the scatterer. As a matter of fact, the use of a second-order radiation boundary condition for Maxwell's equations proposed by Mur [32] has permitted time-domain finite-difference studies of very large targets implementing grids that are truncated within only one or two wavelengths from the target [14] (also see Chapter 8 in this book). Here, we summarize the results for a simple first-order radiation boundary condition that was found to be very efficient from a computational point of view, and we discuss its limitations and the numerical errors associated with it.

If we assume that the surface Γ is far away from the scatterer so that the radiation field will dominate, it is expected that the use of the first term in the above expansions (18,19) will be sufficient to express the behavior of the radiation field there. Hence, we can approximately write

$$u(t,r,\theta,\phi) \approx \frac{1}{r} f_1 \left(t - \frac{r}{c}, \theta, \phi\right) \tag{20}$$

$$u(t,\rho,\phi) \approx \frac{1}{\sqrt{\rho}} f_0 \left(t - \frac{\rho}{c}, \phi\right) \tag{21}$$

and the value of the field on Γ can be extrapolated from the knowledge of the field at a point on Γ_1 (Fig. 5)

$$u(t,r_\Gamma,\theta,\phi) \approx \frac{r_{\Gamma_1}}{r_\Gamma} u \left(t - \frac{r_\Gamma - r_{\Gamma_1}}{c}, \theta, \phi\right) \tag{22}$$

$$u(t,\rho_\Gamma,\phi) \approx \left(\frac{\rho_{\Gamma_1}}{\rho_\Gamma}\right)^{\frac{1}{2}} u \left(t - \frac{\rho_\Gamma - \rho_{\Gamma_1}}{c}, \phi\right) \tag{23}$$

In order to simplify further the numerical implementation of the radiation condition, a convenient choice for the interior point ρ_{r_1} would be

$$\rho_r = \rho_{r_1} + c(\delta t) \qquad (24)$$

where δt is the time step in the numerical integration. The boundary value at ρ_r can then be updated directly from the value of the field at ρ_{r_1} at the previous time step.

The above analysis can be applied directly to those field components that satisfy the scalar wave equation, i.e., those components that behave like potentials. For two-dimensional problems, this is the case for the E_z component in the TM-case and the H_z component in the TE-case. As far as the three-dimensional case is concerned, one can easily show that the quantity (rE_r) satisfies the scalar wave equation in spherical coordinates [35]. Then according to (20), on the radiation boundary we have

$$E_r(t,r,\theta,\phi) \approx \frac{1}{r^2} f_r\left(t - \frac{r}{c}, \theta, \phi\right) \qquad (25)$$

On the other hand, E_θ and E_ϕ do not satisfy the wave equation in spherical coordinates and a radiation condition for them is not that obvious. However, starting with Maxwell's curl equations in spherical coordinates and assuming that the r^{-2} dependence of E_r and H_r makes them negligible compared to (rE_ϕ), (rE_θ) and (rH_ϕ), (rH_θ) in the far-field region, one can show [27] that (rE_ϕ) and (rE_θ) satisfy approximately the one-dimensional wave equation. Therefore, we can write

$$rE_\phi \approx f_\phi\left(t - \frac{r}{c}, \theta, \phi\right) \qquad (26)$$

$$rE_\theta \approx f_\theta\left(t - \frac{r}{c}, \theta, \phi\right) \qquad (27)$$

Equations (25), (26), and (27) constitute a set of first-order radiation conditions for the artificial boundary in three dimensions.

From the previous discussion, it becomes apparent that the radiation boundary condition imposed on the truncating boundary is an approximate one. Actually, in order to make the numerical implementation of the radiation condition as simple as possible, we assumed the far-field behavior of the solution in the vicinity of the absorbing boundary. We expect then our solution to be reasonably accurate only if the radiation boundary is indeed in the far-field region for our specific problem. As stated earlier, a choice of a second-order radiation condition would allow us to position the truncation boundary closer to the scatterer; however, its numerical implementation on the finite-element grid was found to be rather involved compared to the adopted first-order scheme. In frequency domain, the far-field region (defined by $r > r_{far}$) for a scatterer with maximum linear dimension d_{max}, is given by Fraunhofer's estimate [36]

$$r_{far} \geq 2\frac{d_{max}^2}{\lambda} \qquad (28)$$

where λ is the wavelength of the excitation. This is a frequency dependent relation which states that the radiation boundary must be positioned further and further away from the scatterer as the frequency increases. In other words, for a non-monochromatic signal, as is the case of a general time-varying excitation, a fixed radiation boundary will behave differently for the different frequencies of its spectrum. More specifically, the reflection will be stronger for the higher frequencies. It seems, therefore, that for best results condition (28) must be applied for the smallest wavelength in the pulse spectrum. As we discussed earlier, the minimum effective wavelength on a specific grid with space increment h is $\lambda_{min} \approx 8h$. Therefore, for pulse excitation (28) should be used with $\lambda = 8h$, unless it is known that the power spectrum of the incident pulse is negligible above some frequency f_b such that $\lambda_b = c/f_b > \lambda_{min}$. In that case, (28) should be used with $\lambda = \lambda_b$.

It is interesting to observe that since the numerical phase velocity $c^\star$ is dependent on frequency and direction of propagation, it would be more accurate to use $c^\star$ instead of c in the radiation condition. Actually, the error we make by assuming that the numerical velocity of propagation is c instead of $c^\star$, could be expressed by using the concept of a *reflection coefficient* $\rho(\alpha, \omega)$

$$\rho(\alpha, \omega) = \frac{c - c^\star}{c + c^\star} \qquad (29)$$

From (17) and (29), we see that such a reflection coefficient is dependent on both frequency and direction of propagation. Furthermore,

(29) makes apparent the fact that significant reflection occurs for wavelengths less than $8h$. Notice that this is a direct consequence of the numerical discretization of the hyperbolic system and reflections at such wavelengths will be present regardless of how far away from the structure we position the artificial boundary.

Another important aspect is the effect of the radiation boundary condition on the overall stability of the numerical computation. A vast amount of theoretical work has been dedicated to the stability of the numerical approximation of hyperbolic equations coupled with boundary conditions on single or multiple artificial boundaries [37–39]. Usually, the instabilities that are due to the presence of the artificial boundary appear as oscillating modes that support the propagation of the *reflected* waves from the artificial boundary back to the computational domain. A study of such modes can be done by examining the numerical group velocity of the solution of Maxwell's equations. Using the numerical phase velocity c^*, as expressed by (17), the group velocity can be found from the relation

$$v_g = \frac{d(\omega c^*(\omega))}{d\omega} \qquad (30)$$

One can then show [27] that the numerical group velocity becomes negative for wavelengths shorter than $4h$. This tells us that reflections from the artificial boundary will propagate back to the computational domain as high frequency noise. Unfortunately, these spurious oscillations cannot always be suppressed. Nevertheless, they have been found not to cause any instability in agreement with theoretical predictions based on energy methods [40].

7.5   Field Singularities at Wedges and Corners

When Maxwell's equations are solved in the vicinity of a conducting wedge, singularities in some of the field components or in their spatial derivatives will be present. Then, it is very important to know the manner in which these singular components become infinite for the numerical evaluation of the fields. This knowledge allows us to incorporate the singularity in the numerical algorithm in order to increase its speed of convergence. In our study of the singular field behavior, it is sufficient to consider only distances which are small with respect to the wavelength of interest. As discussed in section 7.2, the effective wavelengths on the grid are limited to $\lambda_{min} \simeq 8h$, hence, it is

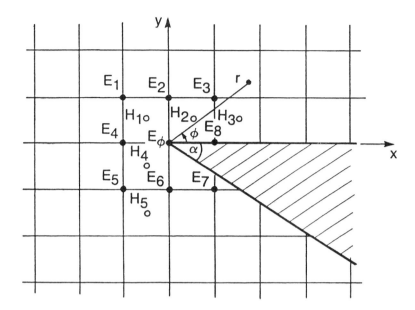

Figure 6   The grid around a conducting wedge.

reasonable to restrict the distances to be no longer than $2h$.

It is well-known that Meixner's condition must be used in the vicinity of a conducting wedge in order to have a unique solution for the specific boundary value problem [35]. Meixner's condition states that the electromagnetic energy density must be integrable over any finite domain even if the domain contains singularities of the fields. We must mention here that according to our definition for the scattered fields, the singularities which do occur are in the scattered field components and not in the incident field.

Let us consider first the TM-case, where the electric field has only one component along the direction of the axis of the wedge (see Fig. 6). One can show [35] that the behavior of the fields at the tip is

$$E_z(r, \phi, t) = A(t) r^\nu \sin \nu\phi \tag{31}$$

$$H_x(r, \phi, t) = B(t) r^{\nu-1} \cos(1 - \nu)\phi \tag{32}$$

$$H_y(r, \phi, t) = C(t) r^{\nu-1} \sin(1 - \nu)\phi \tag{33}$$

where (r, ϕ) are the polar coordinates with origin at the tip of the wedge, α is the angle of the wedge, and

$$\nu = \frac{\pi}{2\pi - \alpha} \tag{34}$$

Notice that H_x and H_y are singular for $\alpha < \pi$. This singular behavior makes questionable the use of smooth interpolation functions over magnetic elements that are close to the edge for the computation of E_z at the electric nodes inside these elements. (See, for example, nodes E_1 and E_2 in Fig. 6.) In order to check this, three different approaches were taken. In the first approach, the isoparametric interpolation functions were used for the computation of the spatial derivatives of the magnetic fields, neglecting their singular behavior. The second approach was based on (31). For example, the value of the electric field at node E_3 was used in order to update the field at node E_2 through the formula

$$E_2 = E_3 \left(\frac{r_3}{r_2} \right)^\nu \frac{\sin \nu \phi_3}{\sin \nu \phi_2} \tag{35}$$

The value at node E_3 was found normally from the finite-element algorithm, since the magnetic element that contains the node is away from the edge and no singularities are present. The third and last approach was to use the exact results by Keller and Blank [41] for the electromagnetic scattering of pulses by perfectly conducting wedges.

The above approaches were used to solve the problem of scattering by a perfectly conducting semi-infinite plane. The geometry is shown in the insert of Fig. 7a. The incident pulse is a Gaussian with effective spatial width $15h$ and of amplitude $1V/m$. The early-time electric field for points A and B is shown in Fig. 7a and Fig. 7b, respectively. We notice that away from the wedge all three approaches give essentially the same result. On the other hand, for the point close to the tip of the wedge, the incorporation of the singularity increased the speed of convergence giving a better early time result.

The TE-case is considered next. Note that the magnetic field has only one component polarized along the axis of the wedge, while the electric field has both E_x and E_y components. The behavior of the field components at the vicinity of the edge is [35]

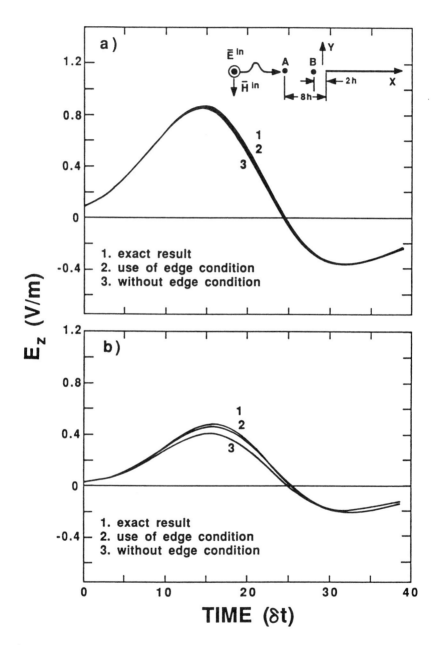

Figure 7 TM-scattering by a perfectly conducting semi-infinite plane.

$$H_z(r, \phi, t) = A_1(t) + A_2(t)r^\nu \cos \nu\phi \tag{36}$$

$$E_x(r, \phi, t) = B(t)r^{\nu-1} \sin(1-\nu)\phi \tag{37}$$

$$E_y(r, \phi, t) = C(t)r^{\nu-1} \cos(1-\nu)\phi \tag{38}$$

where ν is given by (34). Notice that for $\alpha < \pi$ both E_x and E_y become infinite at the edge. Two different approaches were used for the numerical simulation of the problem and were compared with the exact result of [41]. In the first approach, the singular behavior of the electric field was neglected and the leap-frog scheme was used. Only a slight modification was introduced for the computation of the electric field at the node that lies on the edge. In order to understand the motivation for this modification, let us examine (37) and (38) more carefully. First of all, it is obvious that by trying to calculate *some* value for the electric field at the tip we consciously introduce some error, since from (37) and (38) E_x and E_y are infinite there. However, we already decided that we shall neglect this singularity at the moment and we shall assume that E_x and E_y have some specific value. From (37), it is also obvious that as $r \to 0$, $E_x = 0$ on the plane $\phi = 0$, and $E_x = B(t)r^{\nu-1} \sin(\pi - \alpha) \neq 0$ on the plane $\phi = 2\pi - \alpha$. That is, even if we assume that E_x never becomes infinite, we must account for its discontinuity as $r \to 0$, since it may affect the stability of the numerical scheme [42]. An ingenious way to take care of such discontinuities in the solution of hyperbolic systems was introduced by Lax [43]. His scheme replaces the explicit approximation of the time derivative of the field at node i

$$\frac{\partial E}{\partial t} \approx \frac{E_i^{n+1} - E_i^n}{\delta t}$$

by

$$\frac{\partial E}{\partial t} \approx \frac{1}{\delta t}\left[E_i^{n+1} - \frac{1}{2}\left(E_{i+1}^n + E_{i-1}^n\right)\right] \tag{39}$$

One can easily show that the last approximation introduces an *artificial diffusion* term into the discretized equation which helps the stability of the numerical scheme. Using this technique, the following discrete equations are used for the computation of the electric field at the node at the tip (see Fig. 6)

$$\frac{1}{\delta t} \left[E_{0x}^{n+1} - \frac{1}{2} \left(E_{4x}^n + E_{8x}^n \right) \right] = \frac{1}{\epsilon_0} \frac{H_1^{n+\frac{1}{2}} - H_4^{n+\frac{1}{2}}}{h} \tag{40}$$

$$\frac{1}{\delta t} \left[E_{0y}^{n+1} - \frac{1}{2} \left(E_{2y}^n + E_{6y}^n \right) \right] = -\frac{1}{\epsilon_0} \frac{H_2^{n+\frac{1}{2}} - H_1^{n+\frac{1}{2}}}{h} \tag{41}$$

The second approach avoids the computation of the electric field at the node at the tip, and makes use of the known behavior of the magnetic field in order to compute the values of the magnetic nodes around the edge. More specifically, for the geometry shown in Fig. 6, the magnetic field at nodes H_1, H_2, and H_4 cannot be found using the numerical algorithm since the electric field at E_0 is not known. Using the known values of the magnetic field at nodes H_3 and H_5, the coefficients A_1 and A_2 in (36) can be specified. Equation (36) is then used to compute H_z at H_1, H_2, and H_4.

The above schemes were tested and compared with the exact solution for the problem of TE-scattering by a square wedge. The geometry configuration is shown in the insert of Fig. 8a. The results for the magnetic field at points A and B are shown in Figs. 8a and 8b, respectively. We notice that for the point B close to the edge, the incorporation of the known behavior of the field gives a better result for the early-time response. The same is true for the early-time response at point A, but we notice that for later times both numerical schemes give essentially the same result as the exact solution. It is interesting to notice the effect of the artificial diffusion term which was used for the computation of curve 3. Its use gives an $\approx 8\%$ error at the peak value of the field. Experimenting with three-dimensional geometries that feature sharp corners or conical tips, we found that the use of the artificial diffusion term results in incorrect values for the fields at the vicinity of the corner. To cure this, a simple algorithm was introduced [44] which accounts for the singular behavior of the fields. The results in [44] demonstrate that in the scattering problem the differences between the use of the diffusion term and the incorporation of the singularity of the fields are limited to the region very close to the corner. The reason the error does not propagate is that the corner field, despite its singularity, only contains small part of the incident power, and eventually is covered up by fields scattered from other parts of the body.

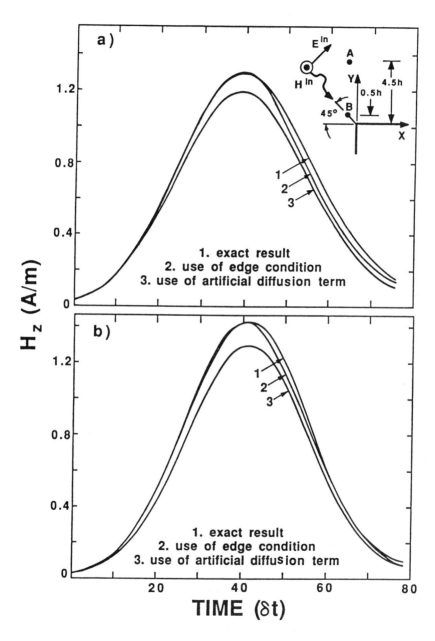

Figure 8   TE-scattering by a perfectly conducting square wedge.

This suggests that in the computation of the far-field the simple diffusion algorithm is quite adequate, assuming that no interfering obstacles (such as slots) exist in the vicinity of a corner or a wedge.

7.6 Numerical Results

The simplicity and the flexibility of the method of the conforming boundary elements allows us to study the scattering characteristics of a wide variety of scatterers. The solution of the finite-element problem gives the electric and magnetic fields everywhere on the computational grid. Probably the most useful result for the problem of scattering by perfect conductors is the induced current on their surface. Once this is found as a function of time well-known formulas can be used for the far-field computation [1]. Nevertheless, near-field information is also useful in many cases, especially in problems involving electromagnetic coupling effects, antennas on conducting structures, design of lenses, etc. One can also argue that under the assumption that the truncation boundary is set far away from the scatterer, the shape of the scattered pulse there resembles quite accurately the far-field. Our numerical simulation results showed that this was indeed the case. We actually found that the limit for r_{far} set by (28) was rather conservative. Using the fact that the lower bound for the wavelengths of the propagating waves on the grid is approximately $\lambda_{min} = 8h$ as discussed in section 7.2, (28) gives for a scatterer of $d_{max} = 20h$, $r_{far} \geq 100h$. Our results for a circular cylinder of diameter $20h$ showed that the scattered pulse had reached its far-field state at distances of about $40h$. Experimenting with different geometries and different polarizations of the incident field, we found that computed scattered fields can be assumed to have reached their far-field state for distances r such that

$$2d_{max} < r_{far} < \frac{d_{max}^2}{\lambda_{min}} \qquad (42)$$

where it is assumed that $d_{max} > 2\lambda_{min}$. The lower limit $2d_{max}$ was found appropriate for two-dimensional geometries, while three-dimensional geometries seem to push r_{far} to the upper limit of (42), possibly due to the resonances associated with the finite dimensions of the scatterer.

In [18] the simple case of a circular cylinder illuminated by a plane wave pulse for both TE- and TM-polarizations was considered in order to compare the performance of the method with the one of the time-domain integral equation [45]. A very good agreement was found for both polarizations with 3%-5% differences in the peak values. Here, the scattering from geometries with wedges and corners, as well as the propagation through lens-like media is investigated. For such problems, the solution through a time-domain integral equation formulation becomes rather involved [47].

First, the TM-scattering by a perfectly conducting cylinder with attached fins is computed. The incident pulse is a Gaussian,

$$g(t) = \exp(-\frac{(t - t_0)^2}{T^2}) \qquad (43)$$

with the parameters t_0, T chosen in such a way that its spatial width is approximately equal to the diameter of the scatterer. The discretization parameters were, $h = 0.1$ m and $\delta t = 0.7 h/c$. The response for broadside incidence (wave vector along $\phi = 0°$) is shown in Fig. 9 for a distance $r_{far} = 2 d_{max}$. Looking at the response in the backscatter direction, we see two positive peaks, the first due to specular reflection from the front side of the cylinder, and the second due to reflection from the fins. There is also a negative swing. As a matter of fact, this negative swing is predicted by the physical optics approximation [45], even (erroneously) for a cylinder without fins. Since the physical optics approximation becomes better as the relative size of the scatterer's flat region increases, it is quite reasonable that its results for the cylinder with attached fins are more accurate than those for a plain cylinder. In Fig. 10 the TM-scattering for end-on incidence (wave vector along $\phi = 90°$) is shown. Notice the shorting effect of the fin in the backscattered field. By the time-domain reciprocity theorem [46], the scattered field should be the same if the direction of the incident and scattered fields are interchanged. Indeed, the field scattered in the direction of the plane of the fin for broadside incidence in Fig. 9 is the same with the field scattered off the circular side with end-on incidence in Fig. 10. Results for a variety of two-dimensional structures can be found in [27].

As far as three-dimensional geometries are concerned, one can, in principle, apply the method of conforming boundary elements in a very straightforward manner once the numerical mesh has been generated. Even though the automated generation of conforming three-dimensional boundary elements can be quite complicated, there are two large classes of three-dimensional scatterers that can be solved in a very simple manner. The first class includes bodies of revolution un-

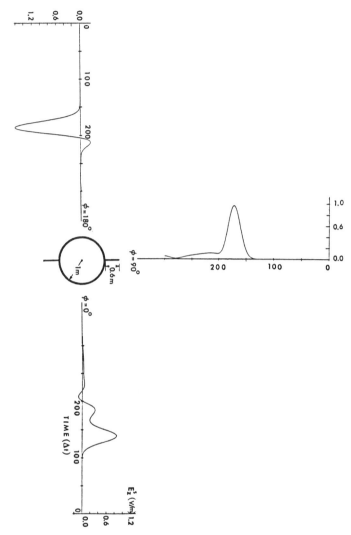

Figure 9 TM-scattering by a perfectly conducting cylinder with attached fins (broadside incidence).

der the assumption of azimuthal excitation. Such a problem is readily solved as a two-dimensional one. The second class consists of bodies generated by finite portions of infinite cylindrical structures of arbitrary cross-sections. The finite-element mesh for such structures can be generated by stacking two-dimensional grids along the axis of the

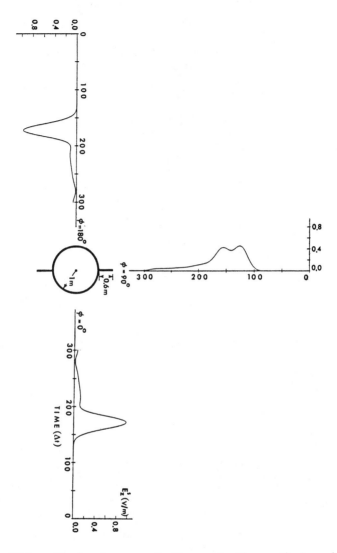

Figure 10 TM-scattering by a perfectly conducting cylinder with attached fins (end-on incidence).

structure. Such scatterers can become more complex by attaching fins to them.

Here, we present results for scattering by a cross formed by an electrically thick cylinder and a flat plate. The geometry is shown in Fig. 11. Experimental results for the induced electric charge and cur-

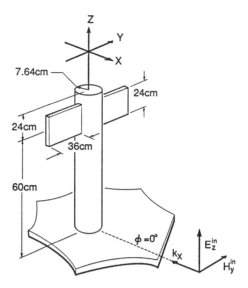

Figure 11   Conducting cylinder with attached fins.

rent densities for the geometry under consideration were available [48] and allowed us to evaluate our numerical computations. The incident field was a plane-wave sinusoidal with $\lambda = 48$ cm. For this excitation, the cylinder of Fig. 11 is a wavelength in circumference and 1.75λ high above the ground plane. Each of the arms of the flat plate is 0.75λ long, 0.2125λ wide and 0.0255λ thick. The plate is centered at a height of 1.25λ from the ground plane. The source used for the experiment was a dipole inside a corner reflector at a distance 7.5λ from the axis of the cylinder. Hence, the incident wave in the measurements was a spherical wave instead of plane one as it was assumed in the numerical simulation. The grid size h was chosen to be half the radius of the cylinder and the flat plates were assumed to have zero thickness. The computational mesh used was $(60h) \times (30h) \times (50h)$. Figure 12 illustrates the magnitude and the relative phase of the induced current density J_z along the flat plate at about 2 cm off the lower edge. The solid lines are the experimental results while the dots show the computed ones. We notice a very good agreement. An extensive presentation of the results and the comparison between theory and experiment is being prepared for publication [49].

   The next example considers radiation from a slot on an infinite perfectly conducting plane. The infinite conducting plane coincides

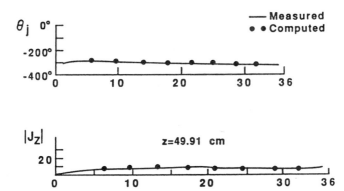

Figure 12 Induced current density J_z (amplitude and phase) along the fin.

with the xy-plane of the coordinate system and the slot is along the x-axis with its center coinciding with the origin. The length of the slot is 0.25 m and it is fed at its center by a voltage source. The excitation is a step voltage which is not abrupt, but it rises to its final constant value in the sense of a gaussian curve terminated at its peak, and from then on maintaining its peak value. The time step used in the computation was $\delta t = 0.79$ ps and the effective rise time of the step was $21(\delta t) = 16.59$ ps. The radiated electric field on the xz-plane for different angles and at a distance of 0.5 m from the origin is shown in Fig. 13. By Fourier transforming the transient response, we can compare our results with the exact frequency-domain results for radiation from a half-wavelength slot [50]. The specific slot is half-wavelength long at $f=600$ MHz. The comparison between our numerical solution and theory is shown in Fig. 14. It is worth mentioning that the theoretical result is for the far-field normalized to the computed value at 90°, while our numerical result is for a distance of one wavelength away from the origin. Therefore, we expect that the effect of the near-field will be present in our result and this should justify the little discrepancy from the theoretical solution. The next step was to position a hemispherical Maxwell's fish-eye lens [35] in front of the slot. The center of the hemispherical lens is on the z-axis, 0.75 m away from the origin, and its radius is $a = 0.75$ m. The relative dielectric permittivity of the lens

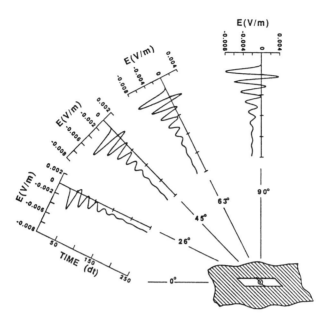

Figure 13 Transient radiation from a slot on an infinite ground plane.

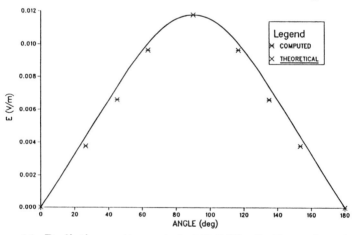

Figure 14 Radiation pattern at $f=600$ MHz (half-wavelength slot).

$$\epsilon_r = \frac{4}{\left[1 + \left(\frac{r}{a}\right)^2\right]^2}$$

varies nonlinearly with radius from four at the center of the hemisphere to one at $r = a$, and helps the focusing of the energy radiated by a

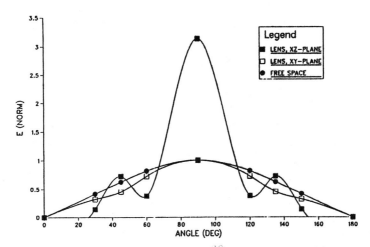

Figure 15 Radiation patterns (xz-plane, xy-plane) at f=600 MHz in the presence of a fish-eye lens.

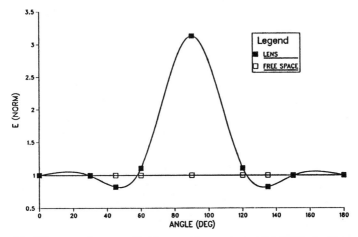

Figure 16 The yz-plane radiation pattern at f=600 MHz in the presence of a fish-eye lens.

point source at the focus. Figure 15 demonstrates this focusing effect comparing the radiation patterns for f=600 MHz. Notice that the peak of the beam at 90° on the xz-plane is about 9.9 dB above the one that occurs when the slot radiates in free-space. Finally, Fig. 16 demonstrates the fact that the radiation pattern on the yz-plane is not isotropic anymore. In conclusion, Figs. 15 and 16 make clear that the presence of the lens improved significantly the directivity of the slot in the direction of the z-axis.

7.7 Discussion

One of the special features in the method of conforming boundary elements is that instead of generating the appropriate finite-element mesh, boundary elements are introduced close to the surface of the scatterer by combining the elements of a uniform rectangular grid with line segments that approximate the geometry of interest. Therefore, only the coordinates of these boundary elements need to be stored at the expense of a more sophisticated software for the construction of these elements. This, of course, results in big savings in computer memory, hence making possible the solution of complex problems which cannot be handled efficiently by the traditional frequency-domain techniques or the time-dependent integral equation approaches. The direct results of the numerical solution are the electric and magnetic field everywhere on the mesh at discrete time instants.

The numerical integration implements a simple explicit scheme, hence avoiding any matrix inversion. Various types of numerical errors associated with the discretization of Maxwell's equations have been discussed. The need for additional numerical conditions for the computation of the scattered fields on the truncation boundary was demonstrated and an approximate first-order radiation condition was discussed. Relations between the size of the scatterer, the characteristics of the exciting pulse, and the distance of the radiation boundary from the scatterer were given for minimizing the unphysical reflections from the artificial boundary. While second-order radiation boundary conditions are available that allow the truncation boundary to be brought closer to the scatterer, their implementation in the conforming boundary element algorithm is not as straightforward as in the time domain finite difference algorithm. In general, the choice of the order of the radiation condition to be used will depend on the available computer memory resources. The numerical simulation of the field singularities at the vicinity of conducting edges and corners was also examined. Finally, several applications of the proposed method to two- and three-dimensional problems in radiation and scattering were presented.

From the point of view of the computer simulation technology, the method was found to be a very powerful and programmer-friendly tool. Its efficiency is remarkable. A typical three-dimensional problem with

750,000 unknowns takes four minutes CPU time on a Cray-1 for 300 time steps. The modeling capability is excellent for two-dimensional geometries as well as three-dimensional ones that can be decomposed into cylindrical subregions of constant cross-section.

Acknowledgements

This work was sponsored by the Office of Naval Research under Contract N0014-86-K-042.

References

[1] Bennett, C. L., and W. L. Weeks, "Electromagnetic pulse response of cylindrical scatterers," *1968 International Antennas and Propagation Symposium*, Boston, Mass., September 1968.

[2] Liu, T. K., and K. K. Mei, "A time-domain integral equation solution for linear antennas and scatterers," *Radio Science*, 8, 797–804, 1973.

[3] Miller, E. K., "Some computational aspects of transient electromagnetics," *EMP Interaction Notes*, Note 143, 1972.

[4] Miller, E. K., and J. A. Landt, "Direct time domain techniques for transient radiation and scattering from wires," *Proc. IEEE*, 68, 1397–1423, 1980.

[5] Sarkar, T. K., "The application of the conjugate gradient method for the solution of transient scattering," *International URSI Symposium*, Santiago, Spain, 1983.

[6] Huiser, A. J. M., A. Quatropani, and H. P. Baltes, "Numerical solution of electromagnetic scattering problems. Case of perfectly conducting cylinders," *Optics*, Comm. 37, 307–310, 1981.

[7] Tijhuis, A. G.,"Towards a stable marching-on-in-time method for two dimensional transient electromagnetic scattering problems," *International URSI Symposium*, Santiago, Spain, 1983.

[8] Yee, K. S.,"Numerical solution of initial boundary value problems involving Maxwell equations in isotropic media," *IEEE Trans. Antennas Propagat.*, **AP-14**, 302–307, 1966.

[9] Taylor, C. D., D. Lam, and T. H. Shumpert, "Electromagnetic

pulse scattering in time-varying inhomogeneous media," *IEEE Trans. Antennas Propagat.*, **AP-17**, 585–589, 1969.

[10] Merewether, D. E., "Transient currents induced on a metallic body of revolution by an electromagnetic pulse," *IEEE Trans. Elec. Comp.*, **EMC-13**, 41–44, 1971.

[11] Holland, R., L. Simpson, and K. S. Kunz, "Finite-difference analysis of EMP coupling to lossy dielectric structures," *IEEE Trans. Elec. Comp.*, **EMC-22**, 203–209, 1980.

[12] Taflove, A., and K. R. Umashankar, "A hybrid moment method/finite-difference time-domain approach to electromagnetic coupling and aperture penetration into complex geometries," *IEEE Trans. Antennas Propagat.*, **AP-30**, 617–627, 1982.

[13] Borup, D. T., D. M. Sullivan, and O. P. Gandhi, "Comparison of the FFT conjugate gradient method and the finite-difference time-domain method for the 2-D absorption problem," *IEEE Trans. Microwave Theory Tech.*, **MTT-35**, 383–395, 1987.

[14] Taflove, A., and K. Umashankar, "The finite-difference time-domain (FD-TD) method for electromagnetic scattering and interaction problems," *Journal of Electromagnetic Waves and Applications*, **1**, 243–267, 1987.

[15] Mei, K. K., A. Cangellaris, and D. J. Angelakos, "Conformal time-domain finite-difference method," *International URSI Symposium*, Santiago, Spain, 1983.

[16] Ray, S. L., and N. K. Madsen, "Finite element analysis of electromagnetic aperture coupling problems," *North American Radio Science Meeting*, Vancouver Canada, 1985.

[17] Lin, C. C., *Numerical Modeling of Two-Dimensional Time-Domain Electromagnetic Scattering by Underground Inhomogeneities*, Ph. D. Dissertation, Dept. EECS, University of California, Berkeley, 1985.

[18] Cangellaris, A. C., C. C. Lin, and K. K. Mei, "Point-matched time-domain finite element methods for electromagnetic radiation and scattering," *IEEE Trans. Antennas Propagat.*, **AP-35**, 1160–1173, October 1987.

[19] Ziolkowski, R. W., and N. K. Madsen, "Discretized exterior differential form approach to the numerical solution of Maxwell's equations," *APS-URSI Meeting*, Blacksburg, Virginia, 1987.

[20] Jurgens, T. G., A. Taflove, and K. R. Umashankar," Conformal FD-TD modeling of objects with smooth curved surfaces," *APS-URSI Meeting*, Blacksburg, Virginia, 1987.

[21] Stratton, J. A., *Electromagnetic Theory*, McGraw Hill, New York, 1941.

[22] Sommerfeld, A., *Partial Differential Equations in Physics*, Academic Press, New York, 1949.

[23] Abarbanel, S., and D. Gottlieb, "A note on the leap-frog scheme in two and three dimensions," *J. Comp. Phys.*, **21**, 351–355, 1976.

[24] Thompson, J. F., *Numerical Grid Generation*, Elsevier Science Pub., New York, 1982.

[25] Ergatudis, I., B. M. Irons, and O. C. Zienkiewicz, "Curved isoparametric quadrilateral elements for finite element analysis," *Int. J. Solids Struct.*, **4**, 31–42, 1968.

[26] Huebner, K. H., *The Finite Element Method for Engineers*, John Wiley and Sons, New York, 1975.

[27] Cangellaris, A. C., *Time-Domain Computation of Electromagnetic Wave Scattering by the Method of Conforming Boundary Elements*, Ph. D. Dissertation, EECS Department, University of California, Berkeley, 1985.

[28] Richtmyer, R. D., and K. W. Morton, *Difference Methods for Initial Value Problems*, John Wiley and Sons, New York, 1967.

[29] Vichnevetsky, R., and J. Bowles, *Fourier Analysis of Numerical Approximations of Hyperbolic Equations*, SIAM, Philadelphia, 1982.

[30] Majda, A., and B. Engquist, "Radiation boundary conditions for acoustic and elastic wave calculations," *Comm. Pure Appl. Math.*, **32**, 313–357, 1979.

[31] Gottlieb, D., and E. Turkel, "Boundary conditions for multistep finite difference methods for time dependent equations," *J. Comp. Phys.*, **26**, 181–196, 1978.

[32] Mur, G., "Absorbing boundary conditions for finite-difference approximation of the time-domain electromagnetic field equations," *IEEE Trans. Elec. Comp.*, **EMC-23**, 1073–1077, 1981.

[33] Ziolkowski, R. W., N. K. Madsen, and R. C. Carpenter, "Three-dimensional computer modeling of electromagnetic fields: A global lookback lattice transaction scheme," *J. Comp. Phys.*, **50**, 360–408, 1983.

[34] Friedlander, F. G., "On the radiation field of pulse solutions of the wave equation," *Proc. Royal Soc. of London*, **269**, 53–65, 1962.

[35] Van Bladel, J. A., *Electromagnetic Fields*, McGraw-Hill, New York, 1964.

[36] Collin, R. E., and F. J. Zucker, (eds.), *Antenna Theory, Part I*, McGraw-Hill, New York, 1969.

[37] Gustafsson, B., H.-O. Kreiss, and A. Sundström, "Stability theory of difference approximations for mixed initial boundary value problems II," *Math. of Comp.*, **26**, 649–686, 1975.

[38] Gustafsson, B., and H.-O. Kreiss, "Boundary conditions for time dependent problems with an artificial boundary," *J. Comp. Phys.*, **30**, 333–351, 1979.

[39] Trefethen, L. N., "Group velocity interpretation of the stability theory of Gustafsson, Kreiss and Sundström," *J. Comp. Phys.*, **49**, 199–217, 1983.

[40] Bayliss, A., and E. Turkel, "Radiation boundary conditions for wave-like equations," *Comm. Pure Appl. Math.*, **33**, 707–725, 1980.

[41] Keller, J. B., and A. Blank, "Diffraction and reflection of pulses by wedges and corners," *Comm. Pure Appl. Math.*, **4**, 75–94, 1951.

[42] Smith, G. D., *Numerical Solution of Partial Differential Equations: Finite Difference Methods*, 2nd ed., Oxford Univ. Press, 1978.

[43] Lax, P. D., "Weak solutions of non-linear hyperbolic equations and their numerical computations," *Comm. Pure Appl. Math.*, **7**, 157–193, 1954.

[44] Mei, K. K., and A. C. Cangellaris, "Applications of field singularities at wedges and corners to time domain finite difference or finite element methods of field computations," *Radio Science*, **22**, 1239–1246, 1987.

[45] Bennett, C. L., *A Technique for Computing the Approximate Electromagnetic Impulse Response of Conducting Bodies*, Ph. D. Dissertation, School of Electrical Engineering, Purdue University, 1968.

[46] Cheo, B. R., "A reciprocity theorem for electromagnetic fields with general time dependence," *IEEE Trans. Antennas Propagat.*, **AP-13**, 278–284, 1965.

[47] Bennett, C. L., A. M. Auckenthaler, and J. D. DeLorenzo, "Transient scattering by three-dimensional conducting surfaces with wires," *International APS Symposium*, Los Angeles, California, 1971.

[48] King, R. W. P., and D. J. Blejer, "Surface currents and charges on a cross formed by an electrically thick cylinder and a flat plate in a normally incident plane-wave field," *Radio Science*, **14**, 753–763, 1979.

[49] Cangellaris, A. C., K. K. Mei, and D. Giri, "Time-domain finite element computation and experimental verification of electromagnetic wave scattering by complex conducting structures," in preparation – contact authors for updated citation.

[50] Elliott, R. S., *Antenna Theory and Design*, Prentice-Hall, Inc., Englewood Cliffs, N.J., 1981.

8

THE FINITE-DIFFERENCE TIME-DOMAIN METHOD FOR NUMERICAL MODELING OF ELECTROMAGNETIC WAVE INTERACTIONS WITH ARBITRARY STRUCTURES

A. Taflove and K. R. Umashankar

8.1   Introduction

Accurate numerical modeling of full-vector electromagnetic wave interactions with arbitrary structures is difficult. Typical structures of engineering interest have shapes, apertures, cavities, and material compositions or surface loadings which produce near fields that cannot be resolved into finite sets of modes or rays. Proper numerical modeling of such near fields requires sampling at sub-wavelength resolution to avoid aliasing of magnitude and phase information. The goal is to provide a self-consistent model of the mutual coupling of the electrically-small cells comprising the structure.

This chapter reviews the formulation and applications of a candidate numerical modeling approach for this purpose: the finite-difference time-domain (FD-TD) solution of Maxwell's curl equations. FD-TD is very simple in concept and execution. However, it is remarkably robust, providing highly accurate modeling predictions for a wide variety of electromagnetic wave interaction problems. FD-TD is analogous to existing finite-difference solutions of scalar wave propagation and fluid-flow problems in that the numerical model is based upon a direct, time-domain solution of the governing partial differential equation. Yet, FD-TD is a non-traditional approach to numerical electromagnetics for engineering applications where frequency-domain integral equation approaches have dominated for 25 years.

One of the goals of this chapter is to demonstrate that recent advances in FD-TD modeling concepts and software implementation, combined with advances in computer technology, have expanded the scope, accuracy, and speed of FD-TD modeling to the point where it may be the preferred choice for complex electromagnetic wave penetration, scattering, guiding, and inverse scattering problems. With this in mind, this chapter will succinctly review the following FD-TD modeling validations and examples:

1. Electromagnetic wave scattering, two dimensions
   a. Square metal cylinder, TM polarization
   b. Circular muscle-fat layered cylinder, TE polarization
   c. Homogeneous, anisotropic, square material cylinder
   d. Circular metal cylinder, conformally modeled
   e. Flanged metal open cavity
   f. Relativistically vibrating mirror, oblique incidence
2. Electromagnetic wave scattering, three dimensions
   a. Metal cube, broadside incidence
   b. Flat conducting plate, multiple monostatic looks
   c. T-shaped conducting target, multiple monostatic looks
3. Electromagnetic wave penetration and coupling in 2-D and 3-D
   a. Narrow slots and lapped joints in thick screens
   b. Wires and wire bundles in free space and in a metal cavity
4. Very complex three-dimensional structures
   a. Missile seeker section
   b. Inhomogeneous tissue model of the entire human body
5. Microstrip and microwave circuit models
6. Inverse scattering reconstructions in one and two dimensions

Finally, this chapter will conclude with a discussion of computing resources for FD-TD and the potential impact of massively concurrent machines.

8.2   General Characteristics of FD-TD

As stated, FD-TD is a direct solution of Maxwell's time-dependent curl equations. It employs no potential. Instead, it applies simple, second-order accurate central-difference approximations [1] for the space and time derivatives of the electric and magnetic fields directly to the respective differential operators of the curl equations. This achieves a sampled-data reduction of the continuous electromagnetic field in a volume of space, over a period of time. Space and time discretizations are selected to bound errors in the sampling process, and to insure numerical stability of the algorithm [2]. Electric and magnetic field components are interleaved in space to permit a natural satisfaction of tangential field continuity conditions at media interfaces. Overall, FD-TD is a marching-in-time procedure which simulates the continuous actual waves by sampled-data numerical analogs propagating in a data space stored in a computer. At each time step, the system of equations to update the field components is fully explicit, so that there is no need to set up or solve a set of linear equations, and the required computer storage and running time is proportional to the electrical size of the volume modeled.

Figure 1(a) illustrates the time-domain wave tracking concept of the FD-TD method. A region of space within the dashed lines is selected for field sampling in space and time. At time = 0, it is assumed that all fields within the numerical sampling region are identically zero. An incident plane wave is assumed to enter the sampling region at this point. Propagation of the incident wave is modeled by the commencement of time-stepping, which is simply the implementation of the finite-difference analog of the curl equations. Time-stepping continues as the numerical analog of the incident wave strikes the modeled target embedded within the sampling region. All outgoing scattered wave analogs ideally propagate through the lattice truncation planes with negligible reflection to exit the sampling region. Phenomena such as induction of surface currents, scattering and multiple scattering, penetration through apertures, and cavity excitation are modeled time-step by time-step by the action of the curl equations analog. Self-consistency of these modeled phenomena is generally assured if their spatial and temporal variations are well resolved by the space and time sampling process.

Time-stepping is continued until the desired late-time pulse response or steady-state behavior is observed. An important example of

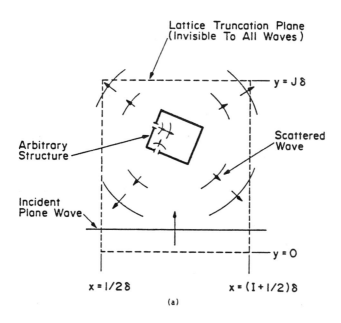

(a)

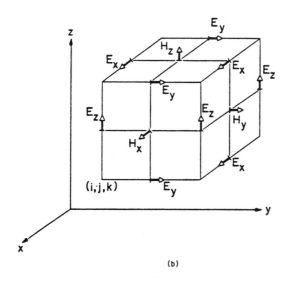

(b)

Figure 1 Basic elements of the FD-TD space lattice: (a) Time-domain wave tracking concept; (b) Lattice unit cell in Cartesian coordinates [1].

the latter is the sinusoidal steady state, wherein the incident wave is assumed to have a sinusoidal dependence, and time-stepping is continued until all fields in the sampling region exhibit sinusoidal repetition. This is a consequence of the limiting amplitude principle [3]. Extensive numerical experimentation with FD-TD has shown that the number of complete cycles of the incident wave required to be time-stepped to achieve the sinusoidal steady state is approximately equal to the Q factor of the structure or phenomenon being modeled.

Figure 1(b) illustrates the positions of the electric and magnetic field components about a unit cell of the FD-TD lattice in Cartesian coordinates [1]. Note that each magnetic field vector component is surrounded by four circulating electric field vector components, and vice versa. This arrangement permits not only a centered-difference analog to the space derivatives of the curl equations, but also a natural geometry for implementing the integral form of Faraday's law and Ampere's Law at the space-cell level. This integral interpretation permits a simple but effective modeling of the physics of thin-slot coupling, thin-wire coupling, and smoothly curved target surfaces, as will be seen later.

Figure 2 illustrates how an arbitrary three-dimensional scatterer is embedded in an FD-TD space lattice comprised of the unit cells of Fig. 1(b). Simply, the desired values of electrical permittivity and conductivity are assigned to each electric field component of the lattice. Correspondingly, desired values of magnetic permeability and equivalent conductivity are assigned to each magnetic field component of the lattice. The media parameters are interpreted by the FD-TD program as local coefficients for the time-stepping algorithm. Specification of media properties in this component-by-component manner results in a stepped-edge, or staircase approximation of curved surfaces. Continuity of tangential fields is assured at the interface of dissimilar media with this procedure. There is no need for special field matching at media interface points. Stepped-edge approximation of curved surfaces has been found to be adequate in the FD-TD modeling problems studied in the 1970's and early 1980's, including wave interactions with biological tissues [4], penetration into cavities [5,6], and electromagnetic pulse (EMP) interactions with complex structures [7–9]. However, recent interest in wide dynamic range models of scattering by curved targets has prompted the development of surface-conforming FD-TD approaches which eliminate staircasing. These will be summarized later in this chapter.

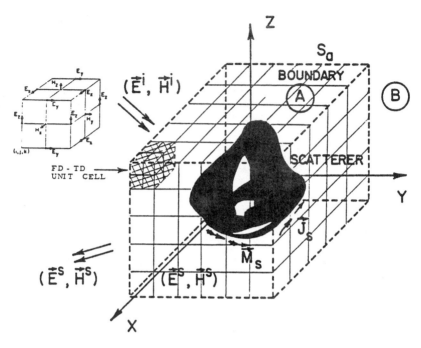

Figure 2 Arbitrary 3-D scatterer embedded in a FD-TD lattice.

8.3 Basic FD-TD Algorithm Details

a. Maxwell's Curl Equations

Consider a region of space which is source-free and has constitutive electrical parameters that are independent of time. Then, using the MKS system of units, Maxwell's curl equations are given by

$$\frac{\partial \overline{H}}{\partial t} = -\frac{1}{\mu} \nabla \times \overline{E} - \frac{\rho'}{\mu}\overline{H} \tag{1}$$

$$\frac{\partial \overline{E}}{\partial t} = \frac{1}{\epsilon} \nabla \times \overline{H} - \frac{\sigma}{\epsilon}\overline{E} \tag{2}$$

where $\overline{E}$ is the electric field in volts/meter; $\overline{H}$ is the magnetic field in amperes/meter; ϵ is the electrical permittivity in farads/meter; σ is the electrical conductivity in mhos/meter (siemens/meter); μ is the magnetic permeability in henrys/meter; and ρ' is an equivalent magnetic resistivity in ohms/meter. (The magnetic resistivity term is provided to yield symmetric curl equations, and allow for the possibility of a magnetic field loss mechanism.) Assuming that ϵ, σ, μ, and ρ' are isotropic, the following system of scalar equations is equivalent to Maxwell's curl equations in the rectangular coordinate system (x, y, z)

$$\frac{\partial H_x}{\partial t} = \frac{1}{\mu}\left(\frac{\partial E_y}{\partial z} - \frac{\partial E_z}{\partial y} - \rho' H_x\right) \tag{3a}$$

$$\frac{\partial H_y}{\partial t} = \frac{1}{\mu}\left(\frac{\partial E_z}{\partial x} - \frac{\partial E_x}{\partial z} - \rho' H_y\right) \tag{3b}$$

$$\frac{\partial H_z}{\partial t} = \frac{1}{\mu}\left(\frac{\partial E_x}{\partial y} - \frac{\partial E_y}{\partial x} - \rho' H_z\right) \tag{3c}$$

$$\frac{\partial E_x}{\partial t} = \frac{1}{\epsilon}\left(\frac{\partial H_z}{\partial y} - \frac{\partial H_y}{\partial z} - \sigma E_x\right) \tag{4a}$$

$$\frac{\partial E_y}{\partial t} = \frac{1}{\epsilon}\left(\frac{\partial H_x}{\partial z} - \frac{\partial H_z}{\partial x} - \sigma E_y\right) \tag{4b}$$

$$\frac{\partial E_z}{\partial t} = \frac{1}{\epsilon}\left(\frac{\partial H_y}{\partial x} - \frac{\partial H_x}{\partial y} - \sigma E_z\right) \tag{4c}$$

The system of six coupled partial differential equations of (3) and (4) forms the basis of the FD–TD algorithm for electromagnetic wave interactions with general three-dimensional objects. Before proceeding with the details of the algorithm, it is informative to consider one important simplification of the full three-dimensional case. Namely, if we assume that neither the incident plane wave excitation nor the modeled geometry has any variation in the z-direction (i.e., all partial derivatives with respect to z equal zero), Maxwell's curl equations reduce to two decoupled sets of scalar equations. These decoupled sets, termed the transverse magnetic (TM) mode and the transverse electric (TE) mode, describe two-dimensional wave interactions with objects. The relevant equations for each case follow

TM case $(E_z, H_x,$ and H_y field components only)

$$\frac{\partial H_x}{\partial t} = -\frac{1}{\mu}\left(\frac{\partial E_z}{\partial y} + \rho' H_x\right) \tag{5a}$$

$$\frac{\partial H_y}{\partial t} = \frac{1}{\mu}\left(\frac{\partial E_z}{\partial x} - \rho' H_y\right) \tag{5b}$$

$$\frac{\partial E_z}{\partial t} = \frac{1}{\epsilon}\left(\frac{\partial H_y}{\partial x} - \frac{\partial H_x}{\partial y} - \sigma E_z\right) \tag{5c}$$

TE case (H_z, E_x, and E_y field components only)

$$\frac{\partial E_x}{\partial t} = \frac{1}{\epsilon}\left(\frac{\partial H_z}{\partial y} - \sigma E_x\right) \tag{6a}$$

$$\frac{\partial E_y}{\partial t} = -\frac{1}{\epsilon}\left(\frac{\partial H_z}{\partial x} + \sigma E_y\right) \tag{6b}$$

$$\frac{\partial H_z}{\partial t} = \frac{1}{\mu}\left(\frac{\partial E_x}{\partial y} - \frac{\partial E_y}{\partial x} - \rho' H_z\right) \tag{6c}$$

b. The Yee Algorithm

In 1966, Yee [1] introduced a set of finite-difference equations for the system of (3) and (4). Following Yee's notation, we denote a space point in a rectangular lattice as

$$(i, j, k) = (i\Delta x, j\Delta y, k\Delta z) \tag{7a}$$

and any function of space and time as

$$F^n(i, j, k) = F(i\Delta x, j\Delta y, k\Delta z, n\Delta t) \tag{7b}$$

where $\Delta x, \Delta y$, and Δz are, respectively, the lattice space increments in the x, y, and z coordinate directions; Δt is the time increment; and i, j, k, and n are integers. Yee used centered finite-difference expressions for the space and time derivatives that are both simply programmed and second-order accurate in the space and time increments, respectively:

$$\frac{\partial F^n(i, j, k)}{\partial x} = \frac{F^n(i + \frac{1}{2}, j, k) - F^n(i - \frac{1}{2}, j, k)}{\Delta x} + O(\Delta x^2) \tag{8a}$$

$$\frac{\partial F^n(i, j, k)}{\partial t} = \frac{F^{n+\frac{1}{2}}(i, j, k) - F^{n-\frac{1}{2}}(i, j, k)}{\Delta t} + O(\Delta t^2) \tag{8b}$$

To achieve the accuracy of (8a), and to realize all of the required space derivatives of the system of (3) and (4), Yee positioned the components of $\overline{E}$ and $\overline{H}$ about a unit cell of the lattice as shown in Fig. 1(b). To achieve the accuracy of (8b), he evaluated $\overline{E}$ and $\overline{H}$ at alternate half time steps. The following are sample finite-difference time-stepping expressions for a magnetic and an electric field component resulting from these assumptions

$$H_x^{n+\frac{1}{2}}(i, j + \tfrac{1}{2}, k + \tfrac{1}{2}) =$$

$$\frac{1 - \frac{\rho'(i,j+1/2,k+1/2)\Delta t}{2\mu(i,j+1/2,k+1/2)}}{1 + \frac{\rho'(i,j+1/2,k+1/2)\Delta t}{2\mu(i,j+1/2,k+1/2)}} \cdot H_x^{n-\frac{1}{2}}(i, j + \tfrac{1}{2}, k + \tfrac{1}{2})$$

$$+ \frac{\Delta t}{\mu(i, j + \frac{1}{2}, k + \frac{1}{2})} \cdot \frac{1}{1 + \frac{\rho'(i,j+1/2,k+1/2)\Delta t}{2\mu(i,j+1/2,k+1/2)}} \cdot \qquad (9)$$

$$\left\{ \begin{array}{l} [E_y^n(i, j + \tfrac{1}{2}, k + 1) - E_y^n(i, j + \tfrac{1}{2}, k)]/\Delta z + \\[2mm] [E_z^n(i, j, k + \tfrac{1}{2}) - E_z^n(i, j + 1, k + \tfrac{1}{2})]/\Delta y \end{array} \right\}$$

$$E_z^{n+1}(i, j, k + \tfrac{1}{2}) = \frac{1 - \frac{\sigma(i,j,k+\frac{1}{2})\Delta t}{2\epsilon(i,j,k+1/2)}}{1 + \frac{\sigma(i,j,k+1/2)\Delta t}{2\epsilon(i,j,k+1/2)}} \cdot E_z^n(i, j, k + \tfrac{1}{2})$$

$$+ \frac{\Delta t}{\epsilon(i, j, k + \frac{1}{2})} \cdot \frac{1}{1 + \frac{\sigma(i,j,k+1/2)\Delta t}{2\epsilon(i,j,k+1/2)}} \cdot \qquad (10)$$

$$\left\{ \begin{array}{l} [H_y^{n+\frac{1}{2}}(i + \tfrac{1}{2}, j, k + \tfrac{1}{2}) - H_y^{n+\frac{1}{2}}(i - \tfrac{1}{2}, j, k + \tfrac{1}{2})]/\Delta x + \\[2mm] [H_x^{n+\frac{1}{2}}(i, j - \tfrac{1}{2}, k + \tfrac{1}{2}) - H_x^{n+\frac{1}{2}}(i, j + \tfrac{1}{2}, k + \tfrac{1}{2})]/\Delta y \end{array} \right\}$$

With the system of finite-difference equations represented by (9) and (10), the new value of a field vector component at any lattice point depends only on its previous value and on the previous values of the components of the other field vector at adjacent points. Therefore, at any given time step, the computation of a field vector can proceed either one point at a time; or, if p parallel processors are employed concurrently, p points at a time.

c. Numerical Stability

To insure the stability of the time-stepping algorithm exemplified by (9) and (10), Δt is chosen to satisfy the inequality [2,10]

$$\Delta t \leq \frac{1}{c_{\max} \left\{ \frac{1}{\Delta x^2} + \frac{1}{\Delta y^2} + \frac{1}{\Delta z^2} \right\}^{\frac{1}{2}}} \tag{11}$$

where c_{max} is the maximum electromagnetic wave phase velocity within the media being modeled. Note that the corresponding numerical stability criterion set forth in Eqs. (7) and (8) of Reference [1] is incorrect [2]. For the TM and TE two-dimensional modeling cases, it can be shown [10] that the modified time-step limit for numerical stability is obtained from (11) simply by setting $\Delta z = \infty$.

d. Numerical Dispersion

The numerical algorithm for Maxwell's curl equations represented by (9) and (10) causes dispersion of the simulated wave modes in the computational lattice. That is, the phase velocity of numerical modes in the FD-TD lattice can vary with modal wavelength, direction of propagation, and lattice discretization. This numerical dispersion can lead to non-physical results such as pulse distortion, artificial anisotropy, and pseudo-refraction. Numerical dispersion is a factor in FD-TD modeling that must be accounted to understand the operation of the algorithm and its accuracy limits.

Following the analysis in [10], it can be shown that the numerical dispersion relation for the three-dimensional case represented by (9) and (10) is given by

$$\left(\frac{1}{c\Delta t}\right)^2 \sin^2\left(\frac{\omega\Delta t}{2}\right) = \frac{1}{\Delta x^2} \sin^2\left(\frac{k_x\Delta x}{2}\right) + \frac{1}{\Delta y^2} \sin^2\left(\frac{k_y\Delta y}{2}\right)$$

$$+ \frac{1}{\Delta z^2} \sin^2\left(\frac{k_z\Delta z}{2}\right) \tag{12}$$

where k_x, k_y, and k_z are, respectively, the x, y, and z components of the wavevector; ω is the wave angular frequency; and c is the speed of light in the homogeneous material being modeled.

In contrast to the numerical dispersion relation, the analytical dispersion relation for a plane wave in a continuous, lossless medium is just

$$\omega^2/c^2 = k_x^2 + k_y^2 + k_z^2 \tag{13}$$

for the three-dimensional case. Although, at first glance, (12) bears little resemblance to the ideal case of (13), we can easily show that (12) reduces to (13) in the limit as $\Delta t, \Delta x, \Delta y$, and Δx all go to zero. Qualitatively, this suggests that numerical dispersion can be reduced to any degree that is desired if we only use a fine-enough FD-TD gridding.

To quantitatively illustrate the dependence of numerical dispersion upon FD-TD grid discretization, we shall take as an example the two-dimensional TM case ($\Delta z = \infty$), assuming for simplicity square unit cells ($\Delta x = \Delta y = \delta$) and wave propagation at an angle α with respect to the positive x-axis ($k_x = k \cos \alpha$; $k_y = \sin \alpha$). Then, dispersion relation (12) simplifies to

$$\left(\frac{\delta}{c\Delta t}\right)^2 \sin^2\left(\frac{\omega\Delta t}{2}\right) = \sin^2\left(\frac{k\delta \cos \alpha}{2}\right) + \sin^2\left(\frac{k\delta \sin \alpha}{2}\right) \tag{14}$$

(14) can be conveniently solved for the wavevector magnitude, k, by applying Newton's method. This process is especially convenient if δ is normalized to the free-space wavelength.

Figure 3a provides results using this procedure which illustrate the variation of numerical phase velocity with wave propagation angle in the FD-TD grid [10]. Three different grid resolutions of the propagating wave are examined: coarse ($\lambda_0/5$); normal ($\lambda_0/10$); and fine ($\lambda_0/20$). For each resolution, the relation $c\Delta t = \delta/2$ was maintained. This relation is commonly used in two- and three-dimensional FD-TD codes to satisfy the numerical stability criterion of (11) with ample safety margin. From Fig. 3a, it is seen that the numerical phase velocity is maximum at 45° (oblique incidence), and minimum at 0° and 90° (incidence along either Cartesian grid axis) for all grid resolutions. This represents a numerical anisotropy that is inherent in the Yee algorithm. However, the velocity error relative to the ideal case diminishes by approximately a 4:1 factor each time that the grid cell size is halved,

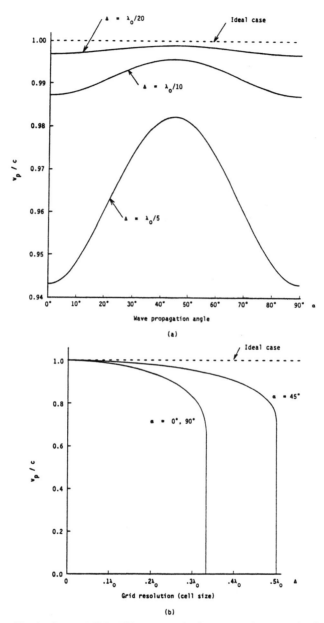

Figure 3 Variation of FD-TD numerical wave phase velocity (dispersion): (a) with wave propagation angle in the grid for three different grid discretizations; (b) with grid resolution for three different wave propagation angles [10].

so that the worst-case velocity error for the normal resolution case is only -1.3%, and only -0.31% for the fine resolution case.

Figure 3(b) graphs the variation of numerical phase velocity with grid resolution at the fixed incidence angles, $45°$ and $0°(90°)$. Again, the relation $c\Delta t = \delta/2$ was maintained for each resolution. Here, it is seen that the numerical phase velocity at each angle of incidence diminishes as the propagating wave is more coarsely resolved, eventually reaching a sharp threshold where the numerical phase velocity goes to zero and the wave can no longer propagate in the FD-TD grid. This represents a numerical low-pass filtering effect that is inherent in the Yee algorithm, wherein the wavelength of propagating numerical modes has a lower bound of 2 to 3 space cells, depending upon the propagation direction. As a result, FD-TD modeling of pulses having finite duration (and thus, infinite bandwidth) can result in progressive pulse distortion as higher spatial frequency components propagate more slowly than lower spatial frequency components, and very high spatial frequency components with wavelengths less than 2 to 3 cells are rejected. This numerical dispersion causes broadening of finite-duration pulses, and leaves a residue of high-frequency ringing on the trailing edges due to the relatively slowly propagating high-frequency components. From Figs. 3(a) and 3(b), we see that pulse distortion can be bounded by obtaining the Fourier spatial frequency spectrum of the desired pulse, and selecting a grid cell size so that the principal spectral components are resolved with at least 10 cells per wavelength. This would limit the spread of numerical phase velocities of the principal spectral components to less than 1%, regardless of wave propagation angle in the grid.

In addition to numerical phase velocity anisotropy and pulse distortion effects, numerical dispersion can lead to pseudo-refraction of propagating modes if the grid cell size is a function of position in the grid. Such variable-cell gridding would also vary the grid resolution of propagating numerical modes, and thereby perturb the modal phase velocity distribution. This would lead to non-physical reflection and refraction of numerical modes at interfaces of grid regions having different cell sizes (even if these interfaces were located in free space), just as physical waves undergo reflection and refraction at interfaces of dielectric media having different indices of refraction. The degree of non-physical refraction is dependent upon the magnitude and abruptness of the change of the modal phase velocity distribution, and can be estimated by using conventional theory for wave refraction at dielectric interfaces.

We have stated that, in the limit of infinitesimal Δt and δ, (12) reduces to (13), the ideal dispersion case. This reduction also occurs if Δt, δ, and the direction of propagation are suitably chosen. For example, in a three-dimensional cubic lattice, reduction to the ideal dispersion case can be demonstrated for wave propagation along a lattice diagonal ($k_x = k_y = k_z = k/\sqrt{3}$) and $\Delta t = \delta/(c\sqrt{3})$ (exactly the limit set by numerical stability). Similarly, in a two-dimensional square grid, the ideal dispersion case can be demonstrated for wave propagation along a grid diagonal ($k_x = k_y = k/\sqrt{2}$) and $\Delta t = \delta/(c\sqrt{2})$ (again the limit set by numerical stability). Finally, in one dimension, the ideal case is obtained for $\Delta t = \delta/c$ (again the limit set by numerical stability) for all propagating modes.

e. Lattice Zoning and Plane Wave Source Condition

The numerical algorithm for Maxwell's curl equations defined by the finite-difference system reviewed above has a linear dependence upon the components of the electromagnetic field vectors. Therefore, this system can be applied with equal validity to either the incident-field vector components, the scattered-field vector components, or the total-field vector components (the sum of incident plus scattered). Present FD-TD codes utilize this property to zone the numerical space lattice into two distinct regions, as shown in Fig. 4(a), separated by a rectangular virtual surface which serves to connect the fields in each region [11,12].

Region 1, the inner region of the FD-TD lattice, is denoted as the total- field region. Here, it is assumed that the finite-difference system for the curl equations operates on total-field vector components. The interacting structure of interest is embedded within this region.

Region 2, the outer region of the FD-TD lattice, is denoted as the scattered-field region. Here, it is assumed that the finite-difference system for the curl equations operates only on scattered-field vector components. This implies that there is no incident wave in Region 2. The outer lattice planes bounding Region 2, called the lattice truncation planes, serve to implement the free-space radiation condition (discussed in the next section) which simulates the field sampling space extending to infinity.

The total-field/scattered-field lattice zoning illustrated in Fig. 4(a) provides a number of key features which enhance the computational

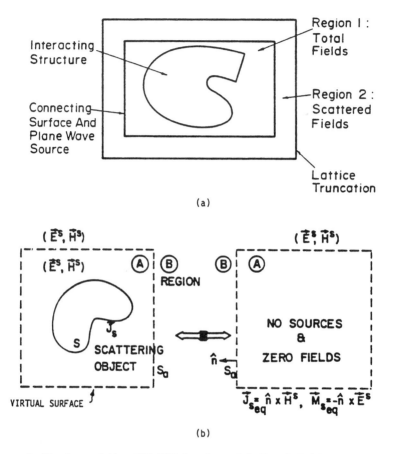

(a)

(b)

Figure 4 **Zoning of the FD-TD lattice:** (a) **Total field and scattered field regions [11,12]; (b) Near-to-far field integration surface located in the scattered field region [12].**

flexibility and dynamic range of the FD-TD method:

Arbitrary incident wave. The connecting condition provided at the interface of the inner and outer regions, which assures consistency of the numerical space derivative operations across the interface, simultaneously generates an arbitrary incident plane wave in Region 1 having a user-specified time waveform, angle of incidence, and angle of polarization. This connecting condition, discussed in detail in [10], almost completely confines the incident wave to Region 1 and yet is transparent to outgoing scattered wave modes which are free to enter Region 2.

Simple programming of inhomogeneous structures. The required continuity of total tangential E and H fields across the interface of dissimilar
media is automatically provided by the original Yee algorithm if the
media are located in a zone (such as Region 1) where total fields are
time-marched. This avoids the problems inherent in a pure scattered-
field code where enforcement of the continuity of total tangential fields
is a separate process requiring the incident field to be computed at all
interfaces of dissimilar media, and then added to the values of the time-
marched scattered fields at the interfaces. Clearly, computation of the
incident field at numerous points along possibly complex, structure-
specific loci is likely to be much more involved than computation of
the incident field only along the simple connecting surface between
Regions 1 and 2 (needed to implement the total-field/scattered-field
zoning). The latter surface has a fixed locus that is independent of the
shape or complexity of the interaction structure that is embedded in
Region 1.

Wide computational dynamic range. Low levels of the total field in
deep shadow regions or cavities of the interaction structure are computed directly by time-marching total fields in Region 1. In a pure
scattered-field code, however, the low levels of total field are obtained
by computing the incident field at each desired point, and then adding
to the values of the time-marched scattered fields. Thus, it is seen that
a pure scattered-field code relies upon near cancellation of the incident
and scattered field components of the total field to obtain accurate results in deep shadow regions and cavities. An undesirable hallmark of
this cancellation is contamination of the resultant low total-field levels
by subtraction noise, wherein slight percentage errors in calculating
the scattered fields result in possibly very large percentage errors in
the residual total fields. By time-marching total fields directly, the
zoned FD-TD code avoids subtraction noise in Region 1 and achieves
a computational dynamic range more than 30 dB greater than that for
a pure scattered-field code.

Far-field response. The provision of a well-defined scattered-field region in the FD-TD lattice permits the near-to-far field transformation
illustrated in Fig. 4(b) [12]. The dashed virtual surface shown in Fig.
4(b) can be located along convenient lattice planes in the scattered-
field region of Fig. 4(a). Tangential scattered E and H fields computed
via FD-TD at this virtual surface can then be weighted by the free-
space Green's function and then integrated (summed) to provide the

far-field response and radar cross section (full bistatic response for the assumed illumination angle) [12–14]. The near-field integration surface has a fixed rectangular shape, and thus is independent of the shape or composition of the enclosed structure being modeled.

8.4   Contour Path Interpretation

a. Usefulness

The Yee algorithm for FD-TD was originally interpreted as a direct approximation of the pointwise derivatives of Maxwell's time-dependent curl equations by using numerical central differences [1]. Although this interpretation is useful for understanding how FD-TD models wave propagation away from material surfaces, it sheds little light on what algorithm modifications are needed to properly model the physics of fine geometrical features such as wires, slots, and curved surfaces requiring sub-cell spatial resolution. Modeling of such features has become increasingly important as confidence in the basic predictive powers of FD-TD has grown.

Recent work has indicated that extension of FD-TD modeling to wires, slots, and curved surfaces can be achieved by departing from Yee's original pointwise derivative interpretation. As shown in Fig. 5, the new idea involves starting with a more macroscopic (but still local) combined-field description based upon Ampere's Law and Faraday's Law in *integral* form, implemented on an array of electrically small, spatially orthogonal contours. These contours mesh (intersect) in the manner of links in a chain, providing a geometrical interpretation of the coupling of Ampere's Law and Faraday's Law. This meshing results in the filling of the FD-TD modeled space by a three-dimensional chain-link array of intersecting, orthogonal contours. The presence of wires, slots, and curved surfaces can be accounted by incorporating appropriate field behavior into the contour and surface integrals implementing Ampere's Law and Faraday's Law at selected meshes, and by deforming contour paths as required to conform with surface curvature.

b. Equivalence to the Yee Algorithm in Free Space

We shall first demonstrate the equivalence of the Yee and contour path interpretations for the free-space case [15]. For simplicity, FD-TD expressions will be developed for only one field component in Fig. 5(a)

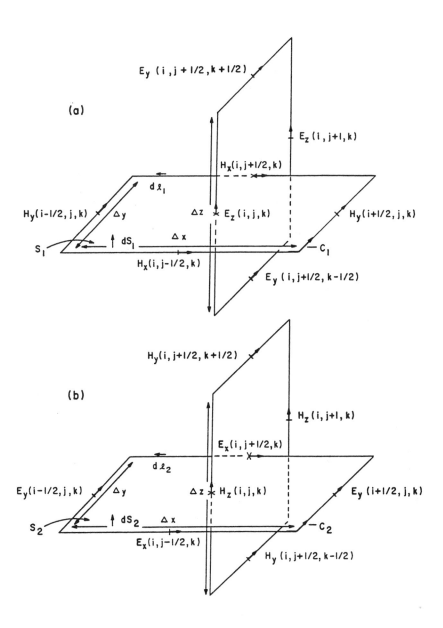

Figure 5 Examples of spatially orthogonal contours in free space: (a) Ampere's Law for E_z; (b) Faraday's Law for H_z [15].

and one field component in Fig. 5(b); extension to all of the rest will be seen to be straightforward.

Applying Ampere's Law along C_1 in Fig. 5(a), and assuming that the field value at a midpoint of one side of the contour equals the average value of that field component along that side, we obtain

$$\frac{\partial}{\partial t} \int_{S_1} \overline{D} \cdot d\overline{S}_1 = \oint_{C_1} \overline{H} \cdot \overline{dl}_1 \tag{15a}$$

$$\frac{\partial}{\partial t} \int_{S_1} \epsilon_0 E_z(i,j,k) dS_1 \simeq H_x(i,j-\tfrac{1}{2},k)\Delta x + H_y(i+\tfrac{1}{2},j,k)\Delta y$$
$$- H_x(i,j+\tfrac{1}{2},k)\Delta x - H_y(i-\tfrac{1}{2},j,k)\Delta y \tag{15b}$$

Now, further assuming that $E_z(i,j,k)$ equals the average value of E_z over the surface, S_1; that $\Delta x = \Delta y = \delta$; and that the time derivative can be numerically realized by using a central-difference expression, (15b) reduces to

$$\epsilon_0 \delta^2 \cdot \left[\frac{E_z^{n+1}(i,j,k) - E_z^n(i,j,k)}{\Delta t} \right] =$$

$$\left[\begin{array}{c} H_x^{n+\frac{1}{2}}(i,j-\tfrac{1}{2},k) - H_x^{n+\frac{1}{2}}(i,j+\tfrac{1}{2},k) + \\ H_y^{n+\frac{1}{2}}(i+\tfrac{1}{2},j,k) - H_y^{n+\frac{1}{2}}(i-\tfrac{1}{2},j,k) \end{array} \right] \cdot \delta \tag{15c}$$

where the superscripts indicate field values at time steps $n, n+\tfrac{1}{2}$, and $n+1$. Isolation of $E_z^{n+1}(i,j,k)$ on the left hand side then yields exactly the Yee time-stepping expression for E_z for the free-space case that was obtained directly from implementing the curl $\overline{H}$ equation.

In an analogous manner, we can apply Faraday's Law along contour C_2 in Fig. 5(b) to obtain:

$$\frac{\partial}{\partial t} \int_{S_2} \overline{B} \cdot d\overline{S}_2 = - \oint_{C_2} \overline{E} \cdot \overline{dl}_2 \tag{16a}$$

$$\frac{\partial}{\partial t} \int_{S_2} \mu_0 H_z(i,j,k) dS_2 \simeq - E_x(i,j-\tfrac{1}{2},k)\Delta x - E_y(i+\tfrac{1}{2},j,k)\Delta y$$
$$+ E_x(i,j+\tfrac{1}{2},k)\Delta x + E_y(i-\tfrac{1}{2},j,k)\Delta y \tag{16b}$$

$$\mu_0 \delta^2 \cdot \left[\frac{H_z^{n+\frac{1}{2}}(i,j,k) - H_z^{n-\frac{1}{2}}(i,j,k)}{\Delta t} \right] =$$

$$\begin{bmatrix} E_x^n(i,j+\frac{1}{2},k) - E_x^n(i,j-\frac{1}{2},k) + \\ E_y(i-\frac{1}{2},j,k) - E_y(i+\frac{1}{2},j,k) \end{bmatrix} \cdot \delta$$

(16c)

Isolation of $H_z^{n+\frac{1}{2}}(i,j,k)$ on the left hand side yields exactly the Yee time-stepping expression for H_z, for the free-space case, that was obtained directly from implementing the curl $\overline{E}$ equation with finite differences.

c. Example 1: Application to the Thin Slot

To illustrate how the contour path interpretation provides the basis for FD-TD modeling of fine geometrical features requiring sub-cell spatial resolution, we first consider the thin slot in a planar, perfectly-conducting screen of finite size and thickness subjected to TE illumination [15]. Figure 6 illustrates the canonical slot geometry studied here, and the Faraday's Law contour paths, C_1, C_2, and C_3, used to derive special FD-TD algorithms for the longitudinal magnetic field components, H_z, located immediately adjacent to the screen.

The following briefly summarizes the assumptions concerning the near-field physics that are incorporated into the Faraday's Law models of Fig. 6. First, for contour C_1 (away from the slot), field components, H_z and E_y, are assumed to have no variation in the y direction (perpendicular to the screen). Evaluated at the x midpoint of contour C_1, H_z, and E_x are assumed to represent the average values of their respective fields over the full x interval. At contour C_2 (at the opening of the slot), H_z is assumed to represent the average value of the magnetic field over the entirety of the free-space part of S_2. Here, E_y is again assumed to have no variation in the y direction, and E_x is again assumed to represent the average value over the full x interval. At contour C_3 (within the slot), H_z is assumed to represent the average value of the magnetic field over the full y interval, and H_z and E_x are assumed to have no variation in the x direction (across the slot gap). Finally, for C_1, C_2, and C_3, the portions of the contours located within the conducting screen are assumed to have zero electric and magnetic

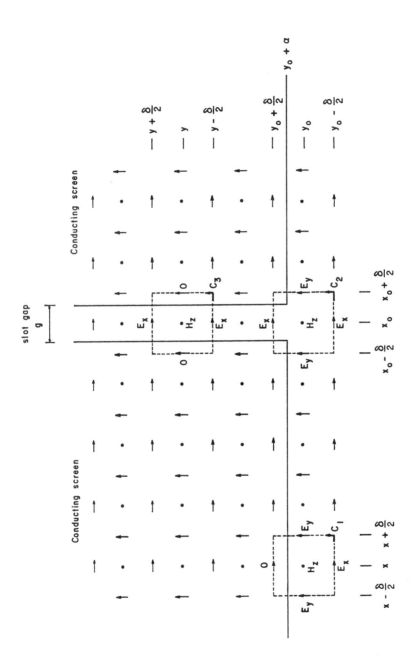

Figure 6   Faraday's Law contour paths for a 2-D planar conducting screen with a thin slot (TE case) [15].

fields.

After applying Faraday's Law of (16a) for the three contours subject to the above assumptions, the following special FD-TD time-stepping relations are obtained for the H_z components immediately adjacent to the screen

Away from the slot (contour C_1)

$$\frac{H_z^{n+\frac{1}{2}}(x, y_0) - H_z^{n-\frac{1}{2}}(x, y_0)}{\Delta t} \simeq$$

$$\frac{[E_y^n(x - \frac{\delta}{2}, y_0) - E_y^n(x + \frac{\delta}{2}, y_0)] \cdot (\frac{\delta}{2} + \alpha) - E_x^n(x, y_0 - \frac{\delta}{2}) \cdot \delta}{\mu_0 \delta(\frac{\delta}{2} + \alpha)}$$

(17a)

At the opening (aperture) of the slot (contour C_2)

$$\frac{H_z^{n+\frac{1}{2}}(x_0, y_0) - H_z^{n-\frac{1}{2}}(x_0, y_0)}{\Delta t} \simeq$$

$$\frac{\left(\begin{array}{c} E_x^n(x_0, y_0 + \frac{\delta}{2}) \cdot g - E_x^n(x_0, y_0 - \frac{\delta}{2}) \cdot \delta + \\ [E_y^n(x_0 - \frac{\delta}{2}, y_0) - E_y^n(x_0 + \frac{\delta}{2}, y_0)] \cdot (\frac{\delta}{2} + \alpha) \end{array} \right)}{\mu_0 \cdot [\delta(\frac{\delta}{2} + \alpha) + g(\frac{\delta}{2} - \alpha)]}$$

(17b)

Within the slot (contour C_3)

$$\frac{H_z^{n+\frac{1}{2}}(x_0, y) - H_z^{n-\frac{1}{2}}(x_0, y)}{\Delta t} \simeq \frac{E_x^n(x_0, y + \frac{\delta}{2}) \cdot g - E_x^n(x_0, y - \frac{\delta}{2}) \cdot g}{\mu_0 g \delta}$$

(17c)

In (17c), we note that the slot gap distance, g, cancels on the right hand side, reducing the time-stepping relation for H_z in the slot to that of a one-dimensional wave ($\pm y$-directed) in free space. For completeness, we also note that no magnetic or electric field components in the FD-TD space grid, other than the H_z components immediately adjacent to the screen, require modified time-stepping relations.

The accuracy of this contour integral model implemented on a coarse FD-TD grid (having $1/10$ wavelength cell size) will be examined in section 8.8a for two cases: (1) a straight slot in a thick conducting screen; and (2) a U-shaped lapped joint in a thick conducting screen, exhibiting resonant transmission and gap-field phenomena. Excellent correspondence with high-resolution method of moments and FD-TD numerical benchmarks will be shown.

d. Example 2: Application to the Thin Wire

A second illustration of how the contour path interpretation permits incorporation of near-field physics (yielding special-purpose time-stepping expressions that were *not* obvious from the previous pure finite-difference perspective) is provided by considering coupling to a sub-cell diameter wire [16]. Figure 7 illustrates the Faraday's Law contour path used to derive the special FD-TD algorithm for the circumferential magnetic fields immediately adjacent to the wire. Although only H_y is shown, the analysis is easily generalized for the other adjacent, looping magnetic field components.

The following briefly summarizes the assumptions concerning the near-field physics that are incorporated into the Faraday's Law model. First, the near scattered circumferential magnetic field components and the near scattered radial electric field components are assumed to vary as $1/r$ near the wire, where r is the distance from the wire center. With r constrained to be less than 0.1 wavelength at any point in C (by FD-TD spatial resolution requirements), the $1/r$ singularity behavior of the scattered H_y and E_x fields is assumed to dominate the respective incident fields, so that the total H_y and E_x fields also take on the $1/r$ singularity. Finally, the near total H_y and the near total E_z fields, evaluated at the z midpoint of the contour, are assumed to represent the average values of their respective fields over the full z interval. These assumptions can be concisely summarized by the following expressions, assumed to apply on and within contour C of Fig. 7

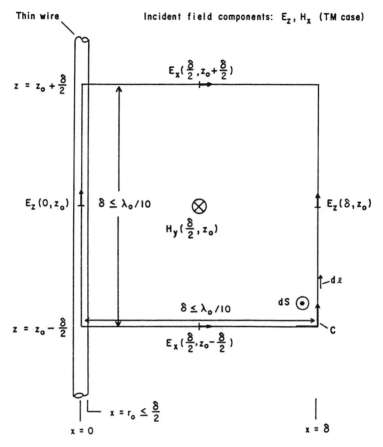

Figure 7 Faraday's Law contour path for thin-wire model [16].

$$H_y(x,z) \simeq H_y(\frac{\delta}{2}, z_0) \cdot \frac{(\frac{\delta}{2})}{x} \cdot [1 + c_1 \cdot (z - z_0)] \qquad (18a)$$

$$E_x(x, z_0 \pm \frac{\delta}{2}) \simeq E_x(\frac{\delta}{2}, z_0 \pm \frac{\delta}{2}) \cdot \frac{(\frac{\delta}{2})}{x} \qquad (18b)$$

$$E_z(0,z) = 0 \qquad (18c)$$

$$E_z(\delta, z) \simeq E_z(\delta, z_0) \cdot [1 + c_2 \cdot (z - z_0)] \qquad (18d)$$

where c_1 and c_2 are arbitrary constants that need not be known.

Using the field expressions of (18a)–(18d), we can now apply Faraday's Law of (16a) along contour C. We find that the $1/x$ variations in H_y and E_x yield natural logarithms. Further, the linear, odd symmetry variation in z assumed for H_y and E_z integrates out. This yields the following expression

$$\frac{H_y^{n+\frac{1}{2}}(\frac{\delta}{2}, z_0) - H_y^{n-\frac{1}{2}}(\frac{\delta}{2}, z_0)}{\Delta t} \cong$$

$$\frac{[E_x^n(\frac{\delta}{2}, z_0 - \frac{\delta}{2}) - E_x^n(\frac{\delta}{2}, z_0 + \frac{\delta}{2})] \cdot \frac{1}{2} \ln\left(\frac{\delta}{r_0}\right) + E_z^n(\delta, z_0)}{\mu_0 \frac{\delta}{2} \ln\left(\frac{\delta}{r_0}\right)} \quad (19)$$

where r_0 (assumed to be less than 0.5 δ) is the wire radius. Isolation of $H_y^{n+\frac{1}{2}}(\frac{\delta}{2}, z_0)$ on the left hand side of (19) yields the required modified time-stepping relation. As stated, the analysis is easily generalized to obtain similar time-stepping relations for the other circumferential magnetic field components immediately adjacent to the wire. It should be noted that *no* other magnetic or electric field components in the FD-TD space lattice require modified time-stepping relations. All other field components are time-stepped by using the ordinary free-space Yee algorithm of section 8.3.

The accuracy of this contour integral model implemented on a coarse FD-TD grid will be examined in section 8.8b for four cases: (1) TM illumination of an infinitely long wire over a very wide range of wire radius; (2) broadside illumination of a two-wavelength long (antiresonant) dipole; (3) broadside illumination of a four-wire bundle where the entire bundle diameter is less than one space cell; and (4) coupling to a single wire and a wire-pair within an aperture-perforated metal cavity exhibiting a moderate-Q (30 to 80) resonant response. Excellent correspondence with either method of moments numerical results or experimental data will be shown.

8.5   Radiation Boundary Conditions

A basic consideration with the FD-TD approach to solve electromagnetic field problems is that most such problems are usually considered to be "open" problems where the domain of the computed field is ideally unbounded. Clearly, no computer can store an unlimited amount of data, and therefore, the field computation zone must be limited in size. The computation zone must be large enough to enclose the structure of interest, and a suitable boundary condition on the outer perimeter of the computation zone must be used to simulate the extension of the computation zone to infinity. This boundary condition suppresses spurious reflections of outward-propagating wave analogs to some acceptable level, permitting the FD-TD solution to remain valid for all time steps (especially after spurious reflected wave analogs return to the vicinity of the modeled structure). Outer lattice boundary conditions of this type have been called either radiation boundary conditions (RBC's), absorbing boundary conditions (ABC's), or lattice truncation conditions.

The radiation condition cannot be directly obtained from the numerical algorithms for Maxwell's curl equations defined by the finite-difference systems reviewed in section 8.3. Principally, this is because these systems employ a central-difference scheme which requires knowledge of the field one-half space cell to each side of an observation point. Central differences cannot be implemented at the outermost lattice plane since, by definition, there is no information concerning the fields at points one-half space cell outside of the outermost lattice plane.

This section will develop the theory and numerical implementation of a very useful radiation condition in Cartesian coordinates. The radiation condition is appropriate for effectively truncating a two- or three-dimensional FD-TD space lattice with an overall level of spurious reflections of 1%–5% for outer lattice planes located 10-20 space cells from a target surface. The radiation condition will be derived using a recent theoretical approach, wave equation factoring. An approach to improvement of the currently used radiation boundary condition will also be summarized.

a. One-Way Wave Equations

A partial differential equation which permits wave propagation only in certain directions is called a "one-way wave equation." Figure 8 shows a finite, two-dimensional Cartesian domain, Ω, on which the time-dependent wave equation is to be simulated. In the interior of Ω, a numerical scheme (such as the algorithms of section 8.3) which models wave propagation in all directions is applied. On $\partial\Omega$, the outer boundary of Ω, only numerical wave motion that is outward from Ω is permitted. The boundary must permit outward propagating numerical

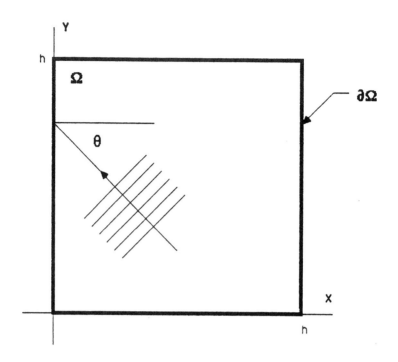

Figure 8 Numerical plane-wave analog incident upon left grid boundary of a 2-D Cartesian computational domain.

wave analogs to exit Ω just as if the simulation were performed on a computational domain of infinite extent. A scheme which enacts a one-way wave equation on $\partial\Omega$ for this purpose is called a radiation boundary condition (RBC).

b. Derivation by Wave Equation Factoring

The derivation of an RBC whose purpose is to absorb numerical waves incident upon the outer boundary of a finite-difference grid can be explained in terms of operator factoring. For example, consider the two-dimensional wave equation in Cartesian coordinates

$$U_{xx} + U_{yy} - \frac{1}{c^2}U_{tt} = 0 \tag{20}$$

where U is a scalar field component; the subscripts xx, yy, and tt denote second partial derivatives with respect to x, y, and t, respectively; and

c is the wave phase velocity. The partial differential operator here is

$$L \equiv D_x^2 + D_y^2 - \frac{1}{c^2} D_t^2 \qquad (21a)$$

which uses the notation

$$D_x^2 \equiv \frac{\partial^2}{\partial x^2}; \ D_y^2 \equiv \frac{\partial^2}{\partial y^2}; \ D_t^2 \equiv \frac{\partial^2}{\partial t^2} \qquad (21b)$$

The wave equation is then compactly written as

$$LU = 0 \qquad (22)$$

The wave operator, L, can be factored in the following manner:

$$LU = L^+ L^- U = 0 \qquad (23a)$$

where L^- is defined as

$$L^- \equiv D_x - \frac{D_t}{c} \sqrt{1 - S^2} \qquad (23b)$$

with

$$S = \frac{D_y}{(D_t/c)} \qquad (23c)$$

The operator, L^+, is similarly defined except for a " + " sign before the radical.

Engquist and Majda [17] showed that at a grid boundary, say at $x = 0$, the application of L^- to the wave function, U, will exactly absorb a plane wave propagating toward the boundary at an arbitrary angle, θ. Thus,

$$L^- U = 0 \qquad (24)$$

applied at $x = 0$ functions as an exact analytical RBC which absorbs wave motion from the interior of the spatial domain, Ω. The operator, L^+, performs the same function for a plane wave propagating at an arbitrary angle toward the other x boundary in Fig. 8 at $x = h$. The presence of the radical in (23b) classifies L^- as a pseudo-differential operator that is non-local in both the space and time variables. This is an undesirable characteristic in that it prohibits the direct numerical implementation of (24) as an RBC.

Approximations of the radical in (23b) produce RBC's that can be implemented numerically and are useful in FD-TD simulations. The numerical implementation of an RBC is not exact in that a small amount of reflection does develop as numerical waves pass through the grid boundary. However, it is possible to design an RBC which minimizes the reflection over a range of incident angles. The Mur RBC, used in current FD-TD electromagnetic wave codes, is simply a two-term Taylor series approximation to the radical in (23b), given by [11]

$$\sqrt{1 - S^2} \simeq 1 - \frac{1}{2}S^2 \tag{25a}$$

Substituting (25a) into (24), we obtain

$$\left(D_x - \frac{D_t}{c} + \frac{cD_y^2}{2D_t}\right)U = 0 \tag{25b}$$

Multiplying (25b) through by D_t, and identifying the differential operators as partial derivatives, we obtain the following approximate, analytical RBC which can be numerically implemented at the $x = 0$ grid boundary

$$U_{xt} - \frac{1}{c}U_{tt} + \frac{c}{2}U_{yy} = 0 \tag{26}$$

Equation (26) is a very good approximation to the exact RBC of (24) for relatively small values of $S = cD_y/D_t$ which satisfy the Taylor series approximation of (25a). This is equivalent to saying that (26) presents a nearly reflectionless grid truncation for numerical plane wave modes which strike the $x = 0$ grid boundary at small values of the incident angle, θ. Analogous approximate, analytical RBC's can be derived for the other grid boundaries

$$U_{xt} + \frac{1}{c}U_{tt} - \frac{c}{2}U_{yy} = 0, \quad x = h \text{ boundary} \tag{27a}$$

$$U_{yt} - \frac{1}{c}U_{tt} + \frac{c}{2}U_{xx} = 0, \quad y = 0 \text{ boundary} \tag{27b}$$

$$U_{yt} + \frac{1}{c}U_{tt} - \frac{c}{2}U_{xx} = 0, \quad y = h \text{ boundary} \tag{27c}$$

For the FD-TD simulation of the vector Maxwell's equations, the RBC's of (26) and (27) are applied to individual Cartesian components of $\overline{E}$ or $\overline{H}$ that are located at, and tangential to, the grid boundaries.

The derivation of RBC's for the three-dimensional case follows the above development closely. The wave equation, given by

$$U_{xx} + U_{yy} + U_{zz} - \frac{1}{c^2}U_{tt} = 0 \tag{28a}$$

has the associated partial differential operator

$$L \equiv D_x^2 + D_y^2 + D_z^2 - \frac{1}{c^2}D_t^2 \tag{28b}$$

L can be factored in the manner of (23a) to provide an exact radiation boundary operator, L^-, having the same form as that of (23b), but with S given by

$$S = \left[\left(\frac{D_y}{D_t/c} \right)^2 + \left(\frac{D_z}{D_t/c} \right)^2 \right]^{\frac{1}{2}} \tag{28c}$$

Again, L^- applied to the scalar wave function, U, at the $x = 0$ grid boundary will exactly absorb a plane wave propagating toward the boundary at an arbitrary angle.

Using the Taylor series approximation of (25a), we obtain an approximate RBC at $x = 0$ in differential-operator form

$$\left(D_x - \frac{D_t}{c} + \frac{cD_y^2}{2D_t} + \frac{cD_z^2}{2D_t} \right)U = 0 \tag{29}$$

Multiplying (29) through by D_t, and identifying the differential operators as partial derivatives, we obtain the corresponding approximate, analytical RBC which can be numerically implemented at the $x = 0$ lattice boundary

$$U_{xt} - \frac{1}{c}U_{tt} + \frac{c}{2}U_{yy} + \frac{c}{2}U_{zz} = 0 \tag{30}$$

Equation (30) is a very good approximation of the exact RBC of (24) for relatively small values of S given by (28c). This is equivalent to saying that (30) presents a nearly reflectionless lattice truncation for numerical plane wave modes which strike the $x = 0$ lattice boundary close to broadside. Analogous approximate, analytical RBC's can be derived for the other lattice boundaries:

$$U_{xt} + \frac{1}{c}U_{tt} - \frac{c}{2}U_{yy} - \frac{c}{2}U_{zz} = 0, \quad x = h \text{ boundary} \qquad (31a)$$

$$U_{yt} - \frac{1}{c}U_{tt} + \frac{c}{2}U_{xx} + \frac{c}{2}U_{zz} = 0, \quad y = 0 \text{ boundary} \qquad (31b)$$

$$U_{yt} + \frac{1}{c}U_{tt} - \frac{c}{2}U_{xx} - \frac{c}{2}U_{zz} = 0, \quad y = h \text{ boundary} \qquad (31c)$$

$$U_{zt} - \frac{1}{c}U_{tt} + \frac{c}{2}U_{xx} + \frac{c}{2}U_{yy} = 0, \quad z = 0 \text{ boundary} \qquad (31d)$$

$$U_{zt} + \frac{1}{c}U_{tt} - \frac{c}{2}U_{xx} - \frac{c}{2}U_{yy} = 0, \quad z = h \text{ boundary} \qquad (31e)$$

For the FD-TD simulation of the vector Maxwell's equations, the RBC's of (30) and (31) are applied to individual Cartesian components of $\overline{E}$ or $\overline{H}$ that are located at, and tangential to, the lattice boundaries.

Equations (26) and (27), representing approximate RBC's for a two-dimensional grid, and (30) and (31), representing approximate RBC's for a three-dimensional lattice, have been found to be very effective when implemented using the differencing scheme proposed by Mur (discussed below). These RBC's truncate an FD-TD space grid or lattice with an overall level of spurious reflections of only 1%–5% for arbitrary targets, if the outer grid or lattice planes are located 10–20 space cells from the target surface. This level of suppression of spurious reflections has been found sufficient to permit highly accurate computational modeling of scattering. For example, the radar cross section of three-dimensional targets spanning 9 wavelengths (96 space cells) has been modeled with an accuracy of 1 dB over a 40-dB dynamic range using an FD-TD space lattice having outer planes located only 0.75 wavelength (8 cells) from the target surface, as is shown in section 8.7.

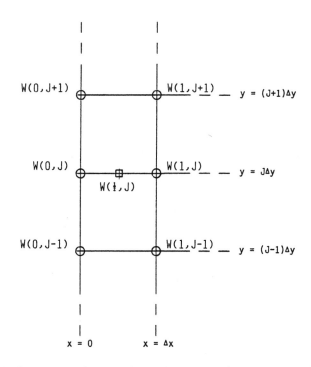

Figure 9   Points near the $x=0$ boundary used in the Mur differencing scheme.

c. Mur Differencing Scheme

A simple and successful finite-difference scheme for the two-term Taylor series RBC's of (26), (27) and (30), (31) was introduced by Mur [11]. For clarity, this scheme is illustrated for the two-dimensional grid case at the $x = 0$ grid boundary. Referring to Fig. 9, $W^n(i,j)$ represents an individual Cartesian component of $\overline{E}$ or $\overline{H}$ that is located at, and tangential to, the grid boundary at $x = 0$. The Mur scheme involves implementing the partial derivatives of (26) as numerical central differences expanded about the auxiliary W component, $W^n(\frac{1}{2},j)$, located one-half space cell from the grid boundary at $(0,j)$. In the first step of the derivation of the Mur scheme, the mixed partial x and t derivatives on the left hand side of (26) are written out using central differences

$$W_{xt}\Big|_{(\frac{1}{2},j,n)} = \frac{\frac{\partial W^{n+1}}{\partial x}\left(\frac{1}{2},j\right) - \frac{\partial W^{n-1}}{\partial x}\left(\frac{1}{2},j\right)}{2\Delta t} \tag{32a}$$

$$= \frac{\left[\frac{W^{n+1}(1,j)-W^{n+1}(0,j)}{\Delta x}\right] - \left[\frac{W^{n-1}(1,j)-W^{n-1}(0,j)}{\Delta x}\right]}{2\Delta t}$$

Next, the partial t derivative on the left hand side of (26) is written out as an average of time derivatives at the adjacent points $(0,j)$ and $(1,j)$

$$W_{tt}\Big|_{(\frac{1}{2},j,n)} = \frac{1}{2}\left[\frac{\partial^2 W}{\partial t^2}^n (0,j) + \frac{\partial^2 W}{\partial t^2}^n (1,j)\right]$$

$$= \frac{1}{2}\left[\frac{W^{n+1}(0,j) - 2W^n(0,j) + W^{n-1}(0,j)}{\Delta t^2}\right. \tag{32b}$$

$$+ \left.\frac{W^{n+1}(i,j) - 2W^n(1,j) + W^{n-1}(1,j)}{\Delta t^2}\right]$$

And, the partial y derivative on the left hand side of (26) is written out as an average of y derivatives at the adjacent points $(0,j)$ and $(1,j)$

$$W_{yy}\Big|_{(\frac{1}{2},j,n)} = \frac{1}{2}\left[\frac{\partial^2 W^n}{\partial y^2}(0,j) + \frac{\partial^2 W^n}{\partial y^2}(1,j)\right]$$

$$= \frac{1}{2}\left[\frac{W^n(0,j+1) - 2W^n(0,j) + W^n(0,j-1)}{\Delta y^2}\right. \tag{32c}$$

$$+ \left.\frac{W^n(1,j+1) - 2W^n(1,j) + W^n(1,j-1)}{\Delta y^2}\right]$$

Substituting the finite-difference expressions of (32) into (26) and solving for $W^{n+1}(0,j)$, we obtain the following time-stepping algorithm for components of W along the $x = 0$ grid boundary which implements the Taylor series RBC of (26)

$$W^{n+1}(0,j) = -W^{n-1}(1,j) + \frac{c\Delta t - \Delta x}{c\Delta t + \Delta x}[W^{n+1}(1,j) + W^{n-1}(0,j)]$$

$$+ \frac{2\Delta x}{c\Delta t + \Delta x}[W^n(0,j) + W^n(1,j)]$$

$$+ \frac{(c\Delta t)^2 \Delta x}{2\Delta y^2(c\Delta t + \Delta x)}[W^n(0,j+1) - 2W^n(0,j) + W^n(0,j-1)$$

$$+ W^n(1,j+1) - 2W^n(1,j) + W^n(1,j-1)]$$

$$(33)$$

For a square grid, $\Delta x = \Delta y = \delta$, and the Mur RBC at x = 0 can be written as

$$W^{n+1}(0,j) = -W^{n-1}(1,j) + \frac{c\Delta t - \delta}{c\Delta t + \delta}[W^{n+1}(1,j) + W^{n-1}(0,j)]$$

$$+ \frac{2\delta}{c\Delta t + \delta}[W^n(0,j) + W^n(1,j)]$$

$$+ \frac{(c\Delta t)^2}{2\delta(c\Delta t + \delta)}[W^n(0,j+1) - 2W^n(0,j) + W^n(0,j-1)$$

$$+ W^n(1,j+1) - 2W^n(1,j) + W^n(1,j-1)]$$

$$(34)$$

Analogous finite-difference expressions for the Mur RBC at each of the other grid boundaries, $x = h, y = 0$, and $y = h$, can be derived by substituting into (27a), (27b), and (27c), respectively, in the same manner. More simply, these Mur RBC's can be obtained by inspection from (33) and (34) using coordinate symmetry arguments.

The derivation of Mur finite-difference expressions for the radiation boundary condition in three dimensions follows the above development closely. For clarity, the Mur scheme is again illustrated at the $x = 0$ lattice boundary, with Fig. 9 now representing individual Cartesian components of $\overline{E}$ or $\overline{H}$ located in lattice plane $z = k\Delta z$. Here, the Mur scheme involves implementing the partial derivatives of (30) as numerical central differences expanded about the auxiliary W component, $W^n(\frac{1}{2}, j, k)$, located one-half space cell from the grid boundary at $(0, j, k)$. The partial derivatives, W_{xt}, W_{tt}, and W_{yy} are identical in form to (32a), (32b), and (32c), respectively, and are evaluated in lattice plane $z = k\Delta z$. The partial derivative, W_{zz}, is expressed as an average of z derivatives at the adjacent points $(0, j, k)$ and $(1, j, k)$

$$
\begin{aligned}
W_{zz}\Big|_{(\frac{1}{2}, j, k, n)} &= \frac{1}{2}\left[\frac{\partial^2 W^n}{\partial z^2}(0, j, k) + \frac{\partial^2 W^n}{\partial z^2}(1, j, k)\right] \\
&= \frac{1}{2}\left[\frac{W^n(0, j, k+1) - 2W^n(0, j, k) + W^n(0, j, k-1)}{\Delta z^2}\right. \\
&\quad + \left.\frac{W^n(1, j, k+1) - 2W^n(1, j, k) + W^n(1, j, k-1)}{\Delta z^2}\right]
\end{aligned}
\tag{35}
$$

Substituting these finite-difference expressions into (30) and solving for $W^{n+1}(0, j, k)$, we obtain the following time-stepping algorithm for components of W along the $x = 0$ lattice boundary which implements the Taylor series RBC of (30)

$$W^{n+1}(0,j,k) = -W^{n-1}(1,j,k) + \frac{c\Delta t - \Delta x}{c\Delta t + \Delta x}[W^{n+1}(1,j,k)$$

$$+ W^{n-1}(0,j,k)] + \frac{2\Delta x}{c\Delta t + \Delta x}[W^n(0,j,k) + W^n(1,j,k)]$$

$$+ \frac{(c\Delta t)^2 \Delta x}{2\Delta y^2(c\Delta t + \Delta x)}[W^n(0,j+1,k) - 2W^n(0,j,k) + W^n(0,j-1,k)$$

$$+ W^n(1,j+1,k) - 2W^n(1,j,k) + W^n(1,j-1,k)]$$

$$+ \frac{(c\Delta t)^2 \Delta x}{2\Delta z^2(c\Delta t + \Delta x)}[W^n(0,j,k+1) - 2W^n(0,j,k) + W^n(0,j,k-1)$$

$$+ W^n(1,j,k+1) - 2W^n(1,j,k) + W^n(1,j,k-1)]$$

$$(36)$$

For a cubic lattice, $\Delta x = \Delta y = \Delta z = \delta$, and the Mur RBC at $x = 0$ can be written as

$$W^{n+1}(0,j,k) = -W^{n-1}(1,j,k) + \frac{c\Delta t - \delta}{c\Delta t + \delta}[W^{n+1}(1,j,k)$$

$$+ W^{n-1}(0,j,k)] + \frac{2\delta}{c\Delta t + \delta}[W^n(0,j,k) + W^n(1,j,k)]$$

$$+ \frac{(c\Delta t)^2}{2\delta(c\Delta t + \delta)}[W^n(0,j+1,k) - 4W^n(0,j,k) + W^n(0,j-1,k)$$

$$+ W^n(1,j+1,k) - 4W^n(1,j,k) + W^n(1,j-1,k) + W^n(0,j,k+1)$$

$$+ W^n(0,j,k-1) + W^n(1,j,k+1) + W^n(1,j,k-1)]$$

$$(37)$$

Analogous finite-difference expressions for the Mur RBC at each of the other lattice boundaries, $x = h, y = 0, y = h, z = 0$, and $z = h$, can

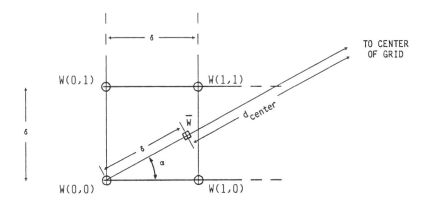

Figure 10 Points near the $x = 0$, $y = 0$ grid corner used in the special corner radiation boundary condition (square grid case).

be derived by substituting into (31a)–(31e), respectively, in the same manner. More simply, these Mur RBC's can be obtained by inspection from (36) and (37) using coordinate symmetry arguments.

d. Special Corner RBC

Upon inspecting (33) and (36), it is clear that the Mur finite-difference scheme for the two-term Taylor series RBC's cannot be implemented for field components located at grid corners, since some of the necessary field data used in the Mur expressions at these points is outside of the grid and not available. It is necessary to implement a special corner radiation boundary condition at these points which: (1) utilizes available field data in the grid; (2) yields acceptably low levels of reflection of outgoing numerical wave modes; and (3) is numerically stable.

Figure 10 illustrates the two-dimensional grid geometry for a simple and stable special corner RBC used successfully since 1982 for a wide variety of two- and three-dimensional FD-TD simulations beginning with that of [12]. The special corner RBC uses a first-order accurate propagation argument wherein the value of a corner field component, for example $W(0,0)$, is taken to be just the time-retarded value of an interior field, $\overline{W}$, located along a radial line connecting the corner point to the center of the grid. This propagation argument assumes that each scattered numerical wave mode is radially outgoing at the corner point. For simplicity, we further assume that the relation $c\Delta t = \delta/2$ is maintained, so that if $\overline{W}$ is located exactly one cell-width, δ, inward along the radial line, the time retardation of the outgoing numerical wave in propagating from $\overline{W}$ to $W(0,0)$ is exactly two time steps. Overall, the special corner RBC is given by

$$W^{n+1}(0,0) = f_{\text{radial}} \cdot \overline{W}^{n-1} \tag{38}$$

where f_{radial} is the attenuation factor for the radially outgoing wave. In two dimensions, we have from Fig. 10

$$f_{\text{radial}} = \left(\frac{d_{\text{center}}}{d_{\text{center}} + 1}\right)^{\frac{1}{2}} \tag{39a}$$

$$\begin{aligned}
\overline{W}^{n-1} &= (1 - \sin\alpha)(1 - \cos\alpha)\, W^{n-1}(0,0) \\
&+ (1 - \sin\alpha)\cos\alpha\, W^{n-1}(1,0) \\
&+ \sin\alpha(1 - \cos\alpha)\, W^{n-1}(0,1) \\
&+ \sin\alpha\,\cos\alpha\, W^{n-1}(1,1)
\end{aligned} \tag{39b}$$

where d_{center} is the radial distance, in cell-widths, from $\overline{W}$ to the center of the grid, and α is the azimuth angle of the radial line at $W(0,0)$. Note that the value of $\overline{W}^{n-1}$ is determined by simple linear interpolation of the four surrounding field values, including $W(0,0)$, at time step $n - 1$. Extension to three dimensions is straightforward, yielding for $W^{n+1}(0,0,k)$

$$f_{\text{radial}} = \left(\frac{d_{\text{center}}}{d_{\text{center}} + 1}\right) \tag{40a}$$

$$\overline{W}^{n-1} = (1 - \sin\beta)(1 - \cos\beta\,\sin\alpha)(1 - \cos\beta\,\cos\alpha)\,\overline{W}^{n-1}(0,0,k)$$
$$+ (1 - \sin\beta)(1 - \cos\beta\,\sin\alpha)\cos\beta\,\cos\alpha\,\overline{W}^{n-1}(1,0,k)$$
$$+ (1 - \sin\beta)\cos\beta\,\sin\alpha\,(1 - \cos\beta\,\cos\alpha)\,\overline{W}^{n-1}(0,1,k)$$
$$+ (1 - \sin\beta)\cos^2\beta\,\sin\alpha\,\cos\alpha\,\overline{W}^{n-1}(1,1,k)$$
$$+ \sin\beta(1 - \cos\beta\,\sin\alpha)(1 - \cos\beta\,\cos\alpha)\,\overline{W}^{n-1}(0,0,k+1)$$
$$+ \sin\beta(1 - \cos\beta\,\sin\alpha)\cos\beta\,\cos\alpha\,\overline{W}^{n-1}(1,0,k+1)$$
$$+ \sin\beta\,\cos\beta\,\sin\alpha\,(1 - \cos\beta\,\cos\alpha)\,\overline{W}^{n-1}(0,1,k+1)$$
$$+ \sin\beta\,\cos^2\beta\,\sin\alpha\,\cos\alpha\,\overline{W}^{n-1}(1,1,k+1)$$

$$\tag{40b}$$

where β is the elevation angle of the radial line at $W(0,0,k)$. Here, note that the value of $\overline{W}^{n-1}$ is determined by simple linear interpolation of the eight surrounding field values, including $W(0,0,k)$, at time step $n-1$. Special RBC's for field components along the other corners of a three-dimensional lattice can be obtained by inspection from (40) using coordinate symmetry arguments, and properly defining angles α and β.

e. Generalized and Higher-Order RBC's

Trefethen and Halpern [18] proposed a generalization of the two-term Taylor series approximation to the radical in (23b), considering the use of the rational function approximation

$$\sqrt{1 - S^2} \simeq r(S) = \frac{p_m(S)}{q_n(S)} \tag{41}$$

on the interval $[-1,1]$, where p_m and q_n are polynomials in S of degree m and n, respectively; and $r(S)$ is said to be of type (m,n). With $S = cD_y/D_t$, the $[-1,1]$ approximation interval on S is equivalent to approximation of the exact one-way wave equation of (24) along the $x = 0$ grid boundary for the range of incident wave angles $\theta = -90°$ to $\theta = +90°$.

For example, by specifying $r(S)$ as a general $(2,0)$ approximant, the radical is approximated by an interpolating polynomial of the form

$$\sqrt{1 - S^2} \simeq p_0 + p_2 S^2 \tag{42a}$$

resulting in the general second-order, approximate, analytical RBC,

$$U_{xt} - \frac{p_0}{c}U_{tt} - p_2 c\, U_{yy} = 0 \qquad (42b)$$

The choice of the coefficients, p_0 and p_2, is determined by the method of interpolation that is used. Standard techniques such as Padé, least-square, or Chebyshev approximation are applied with the goal of interpolating the radical optimally over the $[-1, 1]$ range of S, thereby producing an approximate RBC whose performance is good over a wide range of incident wave angles. Mur's two-term Taylor series approximation of (25a) is now seen in a more general sense as a Padé $(2,0)$ interpolant, i.e., with coefficients $p_0 = +1$ and $p_2 = -\frac{1}{2}$ in (42b).

Higher-order rational function approximations to the $\sqrt{1 - S^2}$ term were proposed in [18] as a means to derive an approximate RBC having good accuracy over a wider range of incident wave angles than that possible with (42). For example, the use of the general type $(2,2)$ rational function

$$\sqrt{1 - S^2} \simeq \frac{p_0 + p_2 S^2}{q_0 + q_2 S^2} \qquad (43a)$$

gives the general third-order, approximate, analytical RBC

$$q_0\, U_{xtt} + q_2 c^2\, U_{xyy} - \frac{p_0}{c}\, U_{ttt} - p_2 c\, U_{tyy} = 0 \qquad (43b)$$

Appropriate selection of the p and q coefficients in (43) produces various families of RBC's, as suggested in [18]. For example, $q_0 = p_0 = 1, p_2 = -\frac{3}{4}$, and $q_2 = -\frac{1}{4}$ gives a Padé $(2,2)$ approximation in (43a) with the resulting RBC functioning better than (26) for numerical waves impacting the $x = 0$ grid boundary at all angles. Figure 11 depicts two ways of quantifying the improved performance of the Padé $(2,2)$ RBC relative to Mur's Padé $(2,0)$ condition [19,20]. In Fig. 11(a), the theoretical numerical wave reflection coefficient is plotted as a function of angle of incidence for the two Padé RBC's. In Fig. 11(b), the total squared-error in a test grid due to imperfect RBC's (generated by a smooth, finite-duration, cylindrical outgoing pulse centered in the grid) is plotted as a function of time-step number for the two RBC's. We see that the theoretical improvement of reflection coefficient for the Padé $(2,2)$ RBC (most pronounced near normal incidence, $0°$) translates to about a 10:1 actual reduction of total error energy in the test grid as the outgoing pulse propagates radially through the Cartesian grid

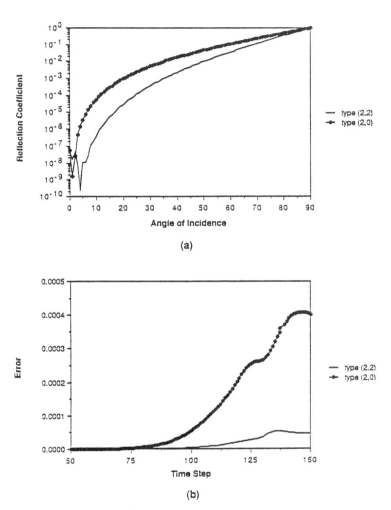

(a)

(b)

Figure 11 Improved performance of the Padé (2,2) RBC relative to the
Mur condition: (a) Theoretical reflection coefficient; (b) Total squared-
error in a test grid [19,20].

boundaries. This reduction in grid noise is worthwhile, permitting in
principle extension of FD-TD modeling to targets having correspondingly reduced radar cross section. As a consequence, the Padé (2,2)
RBC and similar higher-order conditions are currently being studied
as potential replacements for the long-used Mur RBC.

8.6   FD-TD Modeling Validations in 2-D

Analytical and code-to-code validations have been obtained relative to FD-TD modeling of electromagnetic wave scattering for a wide variety of canonical two-dimensional structures. Both convex and re-entrant (cavity- type) shapes have been studied; and structure material compositions have included perfect conductors, homogeneous and inhomogeneous lossy dielectrics, and anisotropic dielectric and permeable media. Selected validations will be reviewed here.

a. Square Metal Cylinder, TM Polarization

Here, we consider the scattering of a TM-polarized plane wave obliquely incident upon a square metal cylinder of electrical size $k_0 s = 2$, where s is the side width of the cylinder [12]. The square FD-TD grid cell size is set equal to $s/20$, and the grid truncation (radiation boundary) is located at a uniform distance of 20 cells from the cylinder surface.

Figure 12 compares the magnitude and phase of the cylinder surface electric current distribution computed using FD-TD to that computed using a benchmark code which solves the frequency-domain surface electric field integral equation (EFIE) via the method of moments (MOM). The MOM code assumes target symmetry and discretizes one-half of the cylinder surface with 84 divisions. The FD-TD computed surface current is taken as $\widehat{n} \times \overline{H}_{tan}$, where $\widehat{n}$ is the unit normal vector at the cylinder surface, and $\overline{H}_{tan}$ is the FD-TD value of the magnetic field vector component in free space immediately adjacent to the cylinder surface. From Fig. 12, we see that the magnitude of the FD-TD computed surface current agrees with the MOM solution to better than $\pm 1\%$ (± 0.09 dB) at all comparison points more than 2 FD-TD cells from the cylinder corners (current singularities). The phase of the FD-TD solution agrees with the MOM solution to within $\pm 3°$ at virtually every comparison point, including the shadow region.

b. Circular Muscle-Fat Layered Cylinder, TE Polarization

Here, we consider the penetration of a TE-polarized plane wave into a simulated biological tissue structure represented by a 15 cm radius muscle-fat layered cylinder [21]. The inner layer (radius = 7.9 cm) is assumed to be comprised of muscle having a relative permittivity of 72 and conductivity of 0.9 S/m. The outer layer is assumed to be

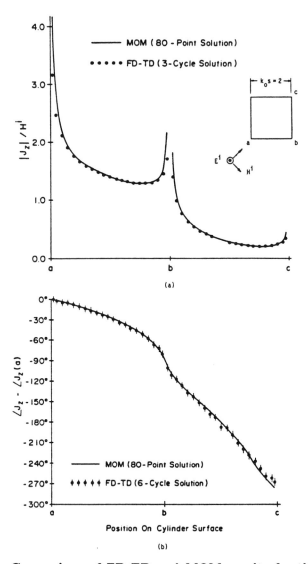

Figure 12 Comparison of FD-TD and MOM results for the cylinder surface electric current distribution: (a) Magnitude; (b) Phase, [12].

comprised of fat having a relative permittivity of 7.5 and conductivity of 0.048 S/m. An illumination frequency of 100 MHz is modeled, with the FD-TD grid cell size set equal to 1.5 cm (approximately 1/24 wavelength within the muscle). A stepped-edge (staircase) approximation of the circular layer boundaries is used.

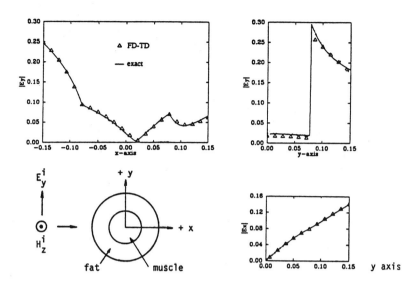

Figure 13 **Comparison of FD-TD and exact solution for penetrating electric field vector components within a circular muscle-fat layered cylinder, TE polarization, 100 MHz [21].**

Figure 13, taken from [21], shows the analytical validation results for the magnitude of the penetrating electric field vector components along two cuts through the muscle-fat cylinder, one parallel to the direction of propagation of the incident wave, and one parallel to the incident electric field vector. The exact solution is obtained by summing sufficient terms of the eigenfunction expansion to assure convergence of the sum. Excellent agreement of the FD-TD and exact solutions is noted, even at jump discontinuities of the field (and at jump discontinuities of the slope of the field distribution) that occur at the layer boundaries. This fine agreement is observed despite the stepped-edge approximation of the circular layer boundaries.

c. Homogeneous, Anisotropic, Square Material Cylinder

The ability to independently specify electrical permittivity and conductivity for each $\overline{E}$ vector component in the FD-TD lattice, and magnetic permeability and equivalent loss for each $\overline{H}$ vector component, leads immediately to the possibility of using FD-TD to model material structures having diagonalizable tensor electric and magnetic properties [22]. No alteration of the basic FD-TD algorithm is required. The more complicated behavior associated with off-diagonal tensor components can also be modeled, in principle, with some algorithm complications [23].

Recent development of coupled surface combined-field integral equation (CFIE) theory for modeling electromagnetic wave scattering by arbitrary-shaped, two-dimensional anisotropic material structures [22] has permitted detailed code-to-code validation studies of FD-TD anisotropic models. Figure 14 illustrates one such study. Here, the magnitude of the equivalent surface electric current induced by TM illumination of a square anisotropic cylinder is graphed as a function of position along the cylinder surface for both the FD-TD and CFIE models. The incident wave propagates in the $+y$-direction and has a $+z$-directed electric field. The cylinder has an electrical size $k_0 s = 5$, permittivity $\epsilon_{zz} = 2$, and diagonal permeability tensor $\mu_{xx} = 2$ and $\mu_{yy} = 4$. For the case shown, the FD-TD grid cell size is set equal to $s/50$, and the radiation boundary is located at a uniform distance of 20 cells from cylinder surface.

From Fig. 14, we see that the FD-TD and CFIE results agree very well almost everywhere on the cylinder surface, despite the presence of a complicated series of peaks and nulls. Disagreement is noted at the cylinder corners where CFIE predicts sharp local peaks, but FD-TD predicts local nulls. Studies are continuing to resolve this corner physics issue.

d. Circular Metal Cylinder, Conformally Modeled

A key flaw in previous FD-TD models of conducting structures with smooth curved surfaces has been the need to use stepped-edge (staircase) approximations of the actual structure surface. Although not a serious problem for modeling wave penetration and scattering for low-Q metal cavities, recent FD-TD studies have shown that stepped approximations of curved walls and aperture surfaces can shift center frequencies of resonant responses by 1% to 2% for Q factors of 30 to 80, and can possibly introduce spurious nulls [16]. In the area of scattering, the use of stepped surfaces has limited application of FD-TD for modeling the important class of targets where surface roughness, exact curvature, and dielectric or permeable loading is important in determining the radar cross section.

Recently, a number of FD-TD conformal surface models have been proposed for two-dimensional problems. These fall into two principal

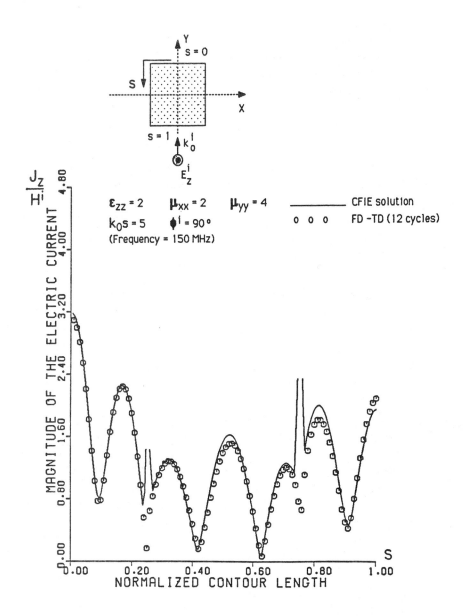

Figure 14 Comparison of FD-TD and CFIE solutions for longitudinal surface electric current on a $k_0 s = 5$ square anisotropic cylinder, TM case [22].

groups:

1. *Locally-stretched grid models.* These preserve the basic Cartesian grid arrangement of field components at all space cells except those adjacent to the structure surface. Space cells adjacent to the surface are deformed to conform with the surface locus. Only field components in these cells are provided with a modified time-stepping algorithm. Examples of this approach include Faraday's Law contour path models [24] and the mixed-polygonal modified finite volume method [25].

2. *Globally-stretched grid models.* These employ available numerical mesh generation schemes to construct non-Cartesian grids which are continuously and globally stretched to conform with structure surfaces. Examples of this approach include Cartesian algorithms adapted for the curvilinear grid case [26], control region algorithms [27], and tangential flux conservation schemes [28].

Research is ongoing for each of these types of conformal surface models. Key questions include: ease of mesh generation; suppression of numerical artifacts such as instability, dispersion, pseudo-refraction, and subtraction noise limitation of computational dynamic range; coding complexity; and computer execution time.

The accuracy of the Faraday's Law contour path models for smoothly curved structures subjected to TE and TM illumination is illustrated in Figs. 15a and 15b, respectively. Here, a moderate-resolution Cartesian FD-TD grid (having 1/20 wavelength cell size) is used to compute the azimuthal or longitudinal electric current distribution on the surface of a $ka = 5$ circular metal cylinder. For both polarizations, the contour path FD-TD model achieves an accuracy of 1.5% or better at most surface points relative to the exact series solution. Running time for the conformal FD-TD model is essentially the same as for the old staircase FD-TD model since only a few H components immediately adjacent to the target surface require a slightly modified time-stepping relation.

e. Flanged Metal Open Cavity

Here, we consider the interactions of a TM-polarized plane wave obliquely incident upon a flanged metal open cavity [29]. The open cavity is formed by a flanged parallel-plate waveguide having a plate spacing, a, of 1m, short-circuited by a terminating plate located at a

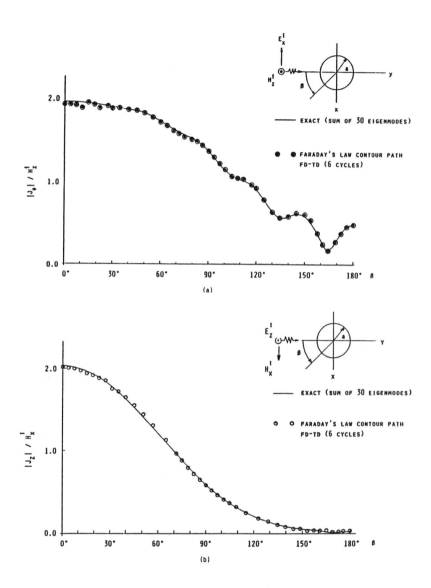

Figure 15 Comparison of FD-TD and exact solution for surface electric current distribution on a $ka = 5$ circular conducting cylinder (conformal FD-TD model used, 0.05 wavelength grid cell size): (a) TE case, azimuthal current; (b) TM case, longitudinal current [24].

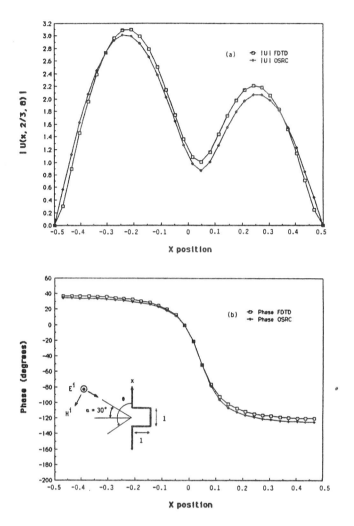

Figure 16 Comparison of FD-TD and modal/OSRC approximate solution for the penetrating electric field distribution 2/3 m within the flanged open cavity: (a) Magnitude; (b) Phase, [29].

distance, d, of 1m from the aperture. At the assumed illumination frequency of 382 MHz, $ka = kd = 8$, and only the first two TE waveguide modes propagate within the open cavity. An oblique angle of incidence, $\alpha = 30°$, is assumed for this case.

Figure 16 compares the magnitude and phase of the penetrating electric field within the cavity 2/3 m from the aperture computed using

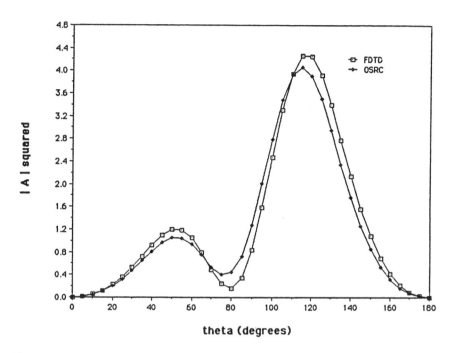

Figure 17 **Comparison of FD-TD and modal/OSRC approximate solu-tion for the bistatic radar cross section due to the induced aperture field distribution of the flanged open cavity [29].**

FD-TD to that computed using a cavity modal expansion and OSRC [29]. Good agreement is seen. Figure 17 shows a similar comparison for the bistatic radar cross section due to the induced aperture field distribution. Again, good agreement is noted.[†]

f. Relativistically Vibrating Mirror, Oblique Incidence

Analytical validations have been recently obtained for FD-TD models of reflection of a monochromatic plane wave by a perfectly conducting surface either moving at a uniform relativistic velocity or vibrating at a frequency and amplitude large enough so that the sur-

---

[†] It should be noted that the results obtained using the cavity modal expansion and OSRC represent a good approximation, but not a rigorous solution.

face attains relativistic speeds [30,31]. This FD-TD approach is novel in that it does not require a system transformation where the conducting surface is at rest. Instead, the FD-TD grid is at rest in the laboratory frame, and the computed field solution is given directly in the laboratory frame. This is accomplished by implementing the proper relativistic boundary conditions for the fields at the surface of the moving conductor.

Figure 18 shows results for one of the more interesting problems of this type modeled so far, that of oblique plane wave incidence on an infinite vibrating mirror. This case is much more complicated than the normal incidence case in that it has no closed-form solution. An analysis presented in the literature [32] writes the solution in an infinite-series form using plane-wave expansions, where the unknown coefficients in the series are solved numerically. This analysis serves as the basis of comparison for the FD-TD model results for the time variation of the scattered field envelope at points near the mirror.

Since it is difficult to model exactly an infinite plane mirror in a finite two-dimensional grid, a long, thin, rectangular perfectly conducting slab is used as the mirror model, as shown in Fig. 18a. Relativistic boundary conditions for the fields are implemented on the front and back sides of the slab. The other two sides, parallel to the velocity vector, are insensitive to the motion of the slab, and therefore no relativistic boundary conditions are required there. To minimize the effect of edge diffraction, the slab length is carefully selected so that the slab appears to be infinite in extent at observation point, P, during a well-defined early-time response when the edge effect has not yet propagated to P. Since the TM case does not provide appreciably different results than the TE case [32], only the TE case is considered. From Fig. 18b, we see good agreement between the FD-TD and analytical results obtained from [32] for the envelope of the scattered E field vs. time for an incident angle of 30°, peak mirror speed 20% that of light, and observation points $z/d = -5$ and $z/d = -50$, where $kd = 1$ [30]. Similar agreement is shown in [31] for the major propagating sidebands of the reflected field spectrum (at oblique incidence angles up to 50°). This agreement is satisfying since the action of the relativistically vibrating mirror is so complicated, generating a reflected wave having a spread both in frequency and spatial reflection angle, as well as evanescent modes.

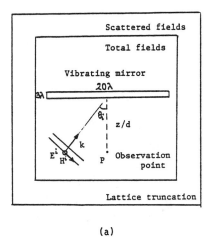

(a)

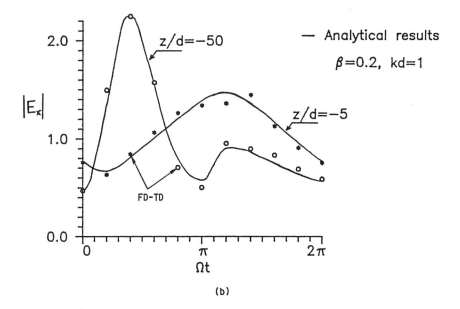

(b)

Figure 18 Comparison of FD-TD and analytical results for the envelope of the scattered E field vs. time for a monochromatic plane wave
illuminating a vibrating mirror at 30° [30].

8.7   FD-TD Modeling Validations in 3-D

Analytical, code-to-code, and experimental validations have been obtained relative to FD-TD modeling of electromagnetic wave scattering for a wide variety of canonical three-dimensional structures, including cubes, flat plates, and crossed plates. Selected validations will be reviewed here.

a. Metal Cube, Broadside Incidence

Results are now shown for the FD-TD computed surface electric current distribution on a metal cube subject to plane-wave illumination at broadside incidence [13]. The electric current distribution is compared to that computed by solving a frequency-domain surface EFIE using a standard triangular surface-patching MOM code [13]. It is shown that a very high degree of correspondence exists between the two sets of predictive data.

The detailed surface current study involves a cube of electrical size $k_0 s = 2$, where s is the size width of the cube. For the FD-TD model, each face of the cube is spanned by 400 square cells (20 × 20), and the radiation boundary is located at a uniform distance of 15 cells from the cube surface. For the MOM model, each face of the cube is spanned by either 18 triangular patches or 32 triangular patches (to test the convergence of the MOM model). Comparative results for surface current are graphed along two straight-line loci along the cube: $\overline{abcd}$, which is in the plane of the incident magnetic field; and $\overline{ab'c'd}$, which is in the plane of the incident electric field.

Figure 19 compares the FD-TD and MOM results for the magnitude and phase of the surface current along $\overline{ab'c'd}$. The FD-TD values agree with the high-resolution MOM data to better than ±2.5% (± 0.2 dB) at all comparison points. Phase agreement for the same sets of data is better than ±1°. (The low-resolution MOM data has a phase anomaly in the shadow region.) In Fig. 20, comparably excellent agreement is obtained along $\overline{abcd}$, but only after incorporation of an edge-correction term in the MOM code [33] to enable it to properly model the current singularities at the cube corners, b and c.

b. Flat Conducting Plate, Multiple Monostatic Looks

We next consider a 30 cm × 10 cm × 0.65 cm flat conducting plate target [14], [23]. At 1 GHz, where the plate spans 1 wavelength,

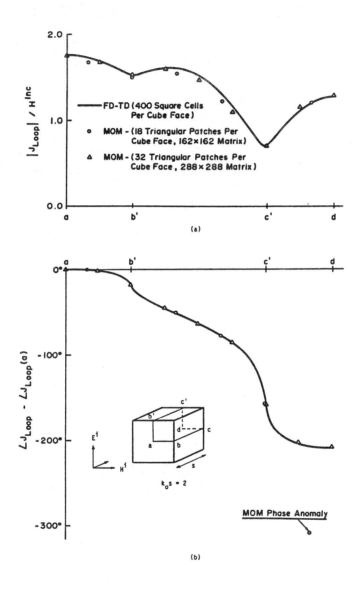

Figure 19 Comparison of FD-TD and MOM results for the cube sur-
face electric current distribution along the E-plane locus, $\overline{ab'c'd}$: (a)
Magnitude; (b) Phase, [13].

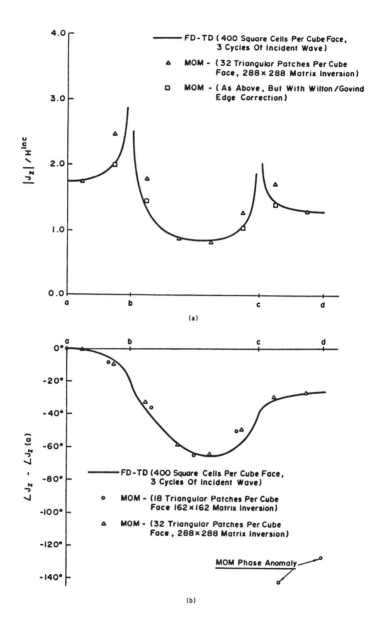

Figure 20 Comparison of FD-TD and MOM results for the cube surface electric current distribution along the n-plane locus, $\overline{abcd}$: (a) Magnitude; (b) Phase.

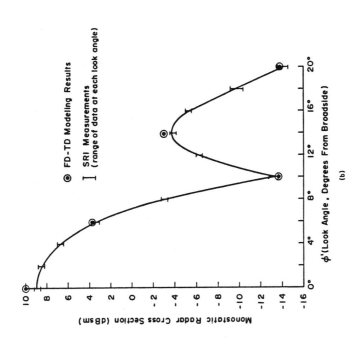

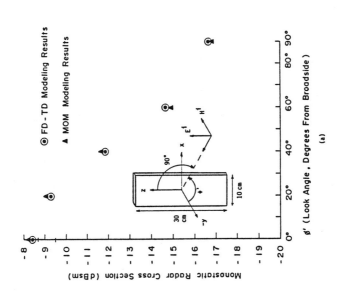

Figure 21 Validation of FD-TD results for the monostatic RCS of a flat conducting plate: (a) Versus MOM at 1 GHz (plate size = 1 λ_0); (b) Versus SRI measurements at 9 GHz (plate size = 9 λ_0) [14,23].

a comparison is made between FD-TD and MOM results for the monostatic radar cross section (RCS) vs look-angle azimuth (keeping a fixed elevation angle), as shown in Fig. 21(a). Here, the FD-TD model uses a uniform cell size of 0.625 cm ($\lambda_0/48$), forming the plate by 48 × 16 × 1 cells. The radiation boundary is located at a uniform distance of only 8 cells from the plate surface. From the MOM model, study of the convergence of the computed broadside RCS indicates that the plate thickness must be accounted by using narrow side patches, and the space resolution of each surface patch should be finer than approximately 0.2 wavelength. As a result, the MOM model forms the plate by 10 × 3 × 1 divisions, yielding a total of 172 triangular surface patches. Figure 21(a) shows excellent agreement between the two models (within about ±0.2 dB).

At 9 GHz, the plate spans 9 wavelengths, and the use of the MOM model is virtually precluded. If we follow the convergence guidelines discussed above, the plate would require approximately 50 × 15 × 1 divisions to properly converge, yielding a total of 3,260 triangular surface patches, and requiring the generation and inversion of a 4,890 × 4,890 complex-valued system matrix. On the other hand, FD-TD remains feasible for the plate at 9 GHz. Choosing a uniform cell size of 0.3125 cm ($\lambda_0/$ 10.667), the plate is formed by 96 × 32 × 2 cells. With the radiation boundary again located only 8 cells from the plate surface, the overall lattice size is 112 × 48 × 18, containing 580,608 unknown field components (real numbers). Figure 21b shows excellent agreement between the FD-TD results and measurements of the monostatic RCS vs. look angle performed in the anechoic chamber facility operated by SRI International. The observed agreement is within about 1 dB and 1° of look angle. As will be seen next, this level of agreement is maintained for more complicated targets having corner reflector properties.

c. T-shaped Conducting Target, Multiple Monostatic Looks

We last consider the monostatic RCS pattern of a T-shaped target comprised of two flat conducting plates electrically bonded together [14,23]. The main plate has the dimensions 30 cm × 10 cm × 0.33 cm, and the bisecting fin is 10 cm × 10 cm × 0.33 cm. [†] The illumination

---

[†] The center line of the "bisecting" fin is actually positioned 0.37 cm to the right of the center line of the main plate. This is accounted for in the FD-TD model.

is a 9.0-GHz plane wave at 0° elevation angle and TE polarization relative to the main plate. Thus, the main plate spans 9.0 wavelengths. Note that look-angle azimuths between 90° and 180° provide substantial corner reflector physics, in addition to the edge diffraction, corner diffraction, and other effects found for an isolated flat plate.

For this target, the FD-TD model uses a uniform cell size of 0.3125 cm ($\lambda_0/10.667$), forming the main plate by 32 × 96 × 1 cells and the bisecting fin by 32 × 32 × 1 cells. With the radiation boundary again located only 8 cells from the target's maximum surface extensions, the overall lattice size is 48 × 112 × 48, containing 1,548,288 unknown field components (212.6 cubic wavelengths). Starting with zero-field initial conditions, 661 time steps are used, equivalent to 31 cycles of the incident wave at 9.0 GHz.

Figure 22 compares the FD-TD predicted monostatic RCS values at 32 key look angles between 0° and 180° with measurements performed by SRI International. These look angles are selected to define the major peaks and nulls of the monostatic RCS pattern. It is seen that the agreement is again excellent: in amplitude, within about 1 dB over a total RCS-pattern dynamic range of 40 dB; and in azimuth, within 1° in locating the peaks and nulls of the RCS pattern. Note especially the fine agreement for look-angle azimuths greater than 90°, where there is a pronounced corner reflector effect.

8.8   Penetration and Coupling in 2-D and 3-D

a. Penetration Models for Narrow Slots and Lapped Joints

The physics of electromagnetic wave transmission through narrow slots and lapped joints in shielded enclosures must be accurately understood to permit good engineering design of equipment to meet specifications for performance concerning electromagnetic pulse, lightning, high-power microwaves, electromagnetic interference and compatibility, undesired radiated signals, and RCS. In many cases, slots and joints can have very narrow gaps filled by air, oxidation films, or layers of anodization. Joints can be simple (say, two metal sheets butted together); more complex (a lapped or "furniture" joint); or even more complex (a threaded screw-type connection with random points of metal-to-metal contact, depending upon the tightening). Extra complications arise from the possibility of electromagnetic resonances within the joint, either in the transverse or longitudinal (depth) direction.

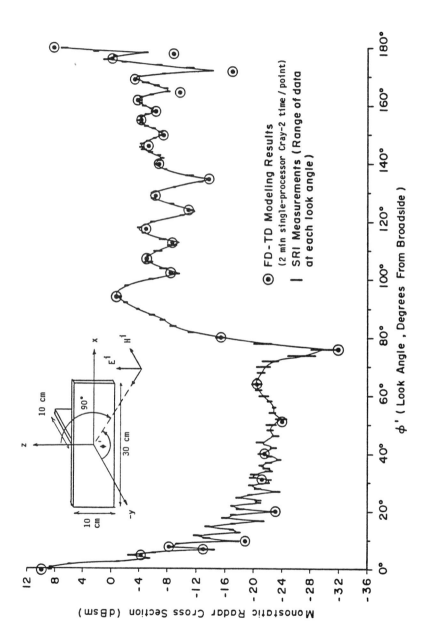

Figure 22 Comparison of FD-TD modeling predictions with SRI measurements of monostatic RCS for the crossed-plate scatterer at 9 GHz (maximum scatterer size = $9\,\lambda_0$) [14,23].

Clearly, to make any headway with this complicated group of problems using the FD-TD approach, it is necessary to develop and validate FD-TD models which can simulate the geometric features of generic slots and joints. Since a key geometric feature is likely to be the narrow gap of the slot or joint relative to one FD-TD space cell, it is important to understand how sub-cell gaps can be efficiently modeled.

Three different types of FD-TD sub-cell models have been proposed and examined for modeling narrow slots and joints:

1. *Equivalent slot loading* [34]. Here, rules are set to define an equivalent permittivity and permeability in a slot formed by a single-cell gap to effectively narrow the gap to the desired degree.

2. *Subgridding* [35]. Here, the region within the slot or joint is provided with a sufficiently fine grid. This grid is properly connected to the coarser grid outside of the slot.

3. *Faraday's Law contour path model* [15]. Here, as discussed in section 8.4c, special FD-TD time-stepping relations (based on Faraday's Law in integral form) are implemented for the longitudinal magnetic field components located immediately adjacent to the screen.

The accuracy of the Faraday's Law contour path model for narrow slots and joints is illustrated in Figs. 23–25 by direct comparison of the computed gap electric field distribution against high-resolution numerical benchmarks [15]. Figure 23 models a 0.1 wavelength thick conducting screen which extends 0.5 wavelength to each side of a straight slot which has a gap of 0.025 wavelength. Broadside TE illumination is assumed. Three types of predictive data are compared: (1) The low-resolution ($0.1 \lambda_0$) FD-TD model using the contour path approach to treat the slot as a 1/4-cell gap; (2) A high-resolution ($0.025 \lambda_0$) FD-TD model treating the slot as a 1-cell gap; and (3) A very-high-resolution frequency-domain EFIE model, solved via MOM (having $0.0025 \lambda_0$ sampling in the slot) which treats the slotted screen as a pure scattering geometry. From Fig. 23, we see that there is excellent agreement between all three sets of predictive data in both magnitude and phase. Of particular interest is the ability of the low-resolution FD-TD model, using the contour path approach, to accurately compute the peak electric field in the slot.

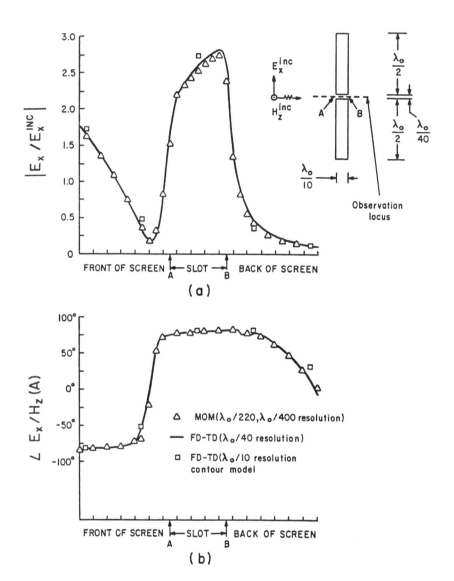

Figure 23   Comparison of FD-TD and MOM solutions for the GAP electric field distribution, straight slot case: (a) Magnitude; (b) Phase.

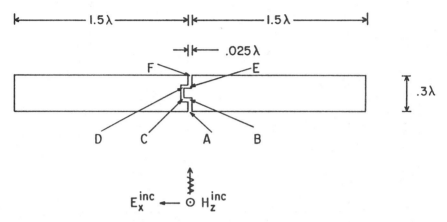

Figure 24 **Geometry of U-shaped lapped joint for TE illumination,** shown to scale [15].

Figure 24 shows the geometry of a U-shaped lapped joint which was selected for detailed study of path-length (depth) power transmission resonances. The U shape of the joint permits adjustment of the overall joint path length without disturbing the positions of the input and output ports at A and F. A uniform gap of 0.025 wavelength is assumed, as is a screen thickness of 0.3 wavelength and width of 3 wavelengths. Figure 25 compares the gap electric field distribution within the joint as computed by : (1) A low-resolution ($0.09 \lambda_0$) contour path FD-TD model treating the gap as 0.28 cell; and (2) A high resolution ($0.025 \lambda_0$) FD-TD model treating the gap as 1 cell. The total path length $ABCDEF$ within the lapped joint is adjusted to equal 0.45 wavelength, which provides a sharp power transmission peak to the shadow side of the screen. From Fig. 25, we see a very good agreement between the low- and high-resolution FD-TD models, even though this is a numerically stressful resonant penetration case.

An implication of these results is that coarse ($0.1 \lambda_0$) FD-TD gridding can be effectively used to model the fine-grained physics of wave penetration through sub-cell slots and joints if simple algorithm modifications are made in accordance with the contour path approach. This can substantially reduce computer resource requirements and coding complexity for FD-TD models of complex structures, without sacrificing appreciable accuracy in the results.

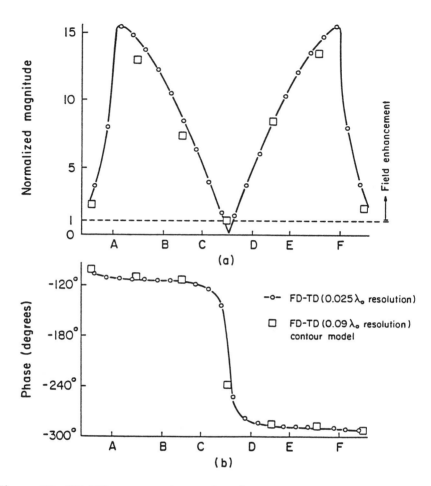

Figure 25 FD-TD computed gap electric field distribution within the lapped joint at the first transmission resonance: (a) $|E_{gap}/E_{inc}|$; (b) $\angle E_{gap}/H_z(A)$ [15].

b. Coupling Models for Wires and Wire Bundles

In equipment design for threats represented by electromagnetic pulse, high-power microwaves, and electromagnetic interference, understanding electromagnetic wave coupling to wires and cable bundles located within shielding enclosures is a problem that is complementary to that of wave penetration through apertures of the shield (such as narrow slots and joints). Similar to the narrow slot problem, a key dimension of the interacting structure, in this case the wire or bundle diameter, may be small relative to one FD-TD space cell. Thus, it is important to understand how thin sub-cell wires and bundles can be efficiently modeled if FD-TD is to have much application to coupling problems.

Two different types of FD-TD sub-cell models have been proposed and examined for modeling thin wires:

1. *Equivalent inductance* [36]. Here, an equivalent inductance is defined for a wire within a space cell, permitting a lumped-circuit model of the wire to be set up and computed in parallel with the field solution.

2. *Faraday's Law contour path model* [16]. Here, as discussed in section 8.4d, special FD-TD time-stepping relations (based on Faraday's Law in integral form) are implemented for the azimuthal magnetic field components located immediately adjacent to the wire. These relations incorporate assumed $1/r$ singularities of the scattered azimuthal magnetic field and radial electric field adjacent to the wire.

The accuracy of the Faraday's Law contour path model for thin wires in free space is illustrated in Fig. 26 [16]. Figure 26a graphs the scattered azimuthal magnetic field at a fixed distance of 1/20 wavelength from the center of an infinitely long wire having a radius ranging between 1/30,000 and 1/30 wavelength. TM illumination is assumed. We see that there is excellent agreement between the exact series solution and the low-resolution ($0.1 \lambda_0$) FD-TD contour path model over the entire 3-decade range of wire radius. Figure 26b graphs the scattered azimuthal magnetic field distribution along a 2.0-wavelength (antiresonant) wire of radius 1/300 wavelength. Broadside TM illumination is assumed, and the field is observed at a fixed distance of 1/20 wavelength from the wire center. We see that there is excellent agreement between a frequency-domain EFIE (MOM) solution sampling the wire current at 1/60 wavelength increments, and the low-resolution ($0.1 \lambda_0$) FD-TD contour path model.

The FD-TD contour path model can be extended to treat thin wire bundles, as well as single wires. Figure 27 shows the code-to-code validation results for the induced currents on a bundle comprised of 4 wires, where 3 are of equal length. Here, a wire of length 60 cm (2.0 wavelengths) is assumed to be at the center of the bundle, and three parallel wires of length 30 cm (1.0 wavelength) are assumed to be located at 120° angular separations on a concentric circle of radius

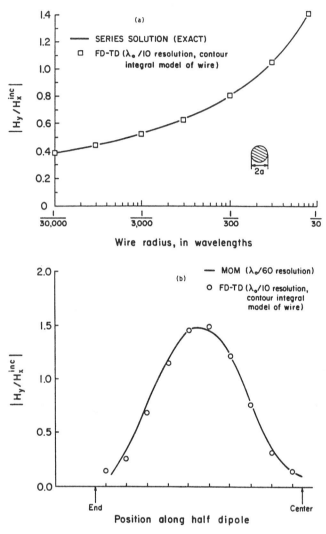

Figure 26 Validation studies for the FD-TD Faraday's Law contour path model for thin wires in free space: (a) Comparison of FD-TD and exact solutions for scattered circumferential magnetic field at point 1/20 wavelength from center of infinite wire; (b) Comparison of FD-TD and MOM solutions for scattered circumferential magnetic field distribution along 2.0-wavelength (antiresonant) wire of radius 1/300 wavelength (broadside TM illumination).

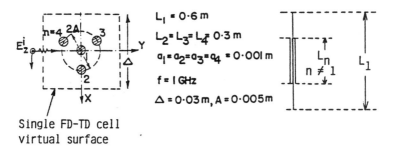

$L_1 = 0.6$ m

$L_2 = L_3 = L_4 = 0.3$ m

$a_1 = a_2 = a_3 = a_4 = 0.001$ m

$f = 1$ GHz

$\Delta = 0.03$ m, $A = 0.005$ m

Single FD-TD cell
virtual surface

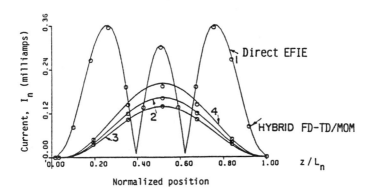

Figure 27 Comparison of hybrid FD-TD/MOM modeling predictions with direct EFIE for induced currents on a wire bundle illuminated broadside by a plane wave in free space [16].

5 mm (1/60 wavelength). The radii of all wires in the bundle are equal and set to 1 mm (1/300 wavelength). The assumed excitation is in free space, provided by a 1-GHz broadside TM plane wave. Following the technique of [16], the bundle is replaced by a single wire having varying equivalent radius corresponding to the three sections along the bundle axis. The physics of the single wire of varying equivalent radius is incorporated in a low-resolution ($0.1\,\lambda_0$) FD-TD contour path model, as discussed above. The FD-TD model is then run to obtain the tangential E and H fields at a virtual surface conveniently located at the cell boundary containing the equivalent wire (shown as a dashed line in Fig. 27). These fields are then utilized as excitation to obtain the currents induced on the individual wires of the original bundle. This last step is performed by setting up an EFIE and solving via MOM.

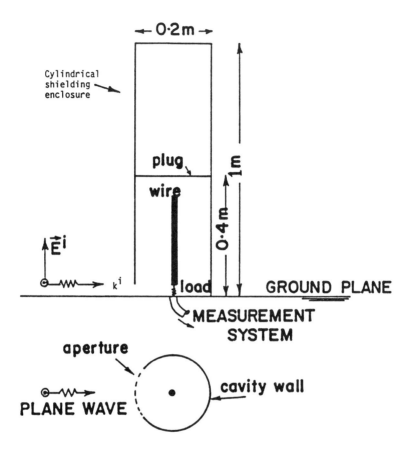

Figure 28 Geometry of the cylindrical shielding enclosure and internal wire or wire-pair [16].

Figure 27 shows an excellent correspondence between the results of the hybrid FD-TD/MOM procedure described above and the usual direct EFIE (MOM) solution for the induced current distribution on each wire of the bundle.

The hybrid FD-TD/MOM procedure for modeling thin wire bundles is most useful when the bundle is located within a shielding enclosure. Figures 28 and 29 show the geometry and test results for such a model involving the variation of induced load current with illumination frequency for a single wire and a wire-pair located at the center

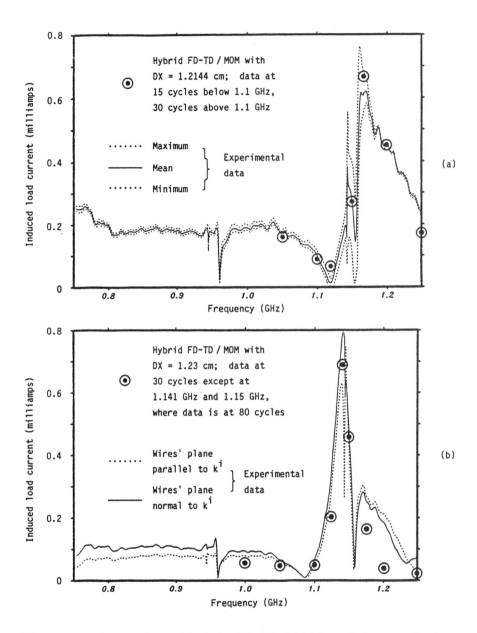

Figure 29 Comparison of hybrid FD-TD/MOM modeling predictions with experimental data for induced load current: (a) Single wire in shielding enclosure; (b) Wire-pair in shielding enclosure [16].

of a cylindrical metal enclosure [16]. The enclosure is 1.0 m high, 0.2 m in diameter, and referenced to a large metal ground plane. Approximate plane wave illumination is provided by an electrically-large conical monopole referenced to the same ground plane. Wave penetration into the interior of the enclosure is through a circumferential slot aperture (12.5 cm arc length, 1.25 cm gap) at the ground plane. For the cases studied, an internal shorting plug is located 40 cm above the ground plane. For the single-wire test, a wire of length 30 cm and radius 0.495 mm is centered within the interior and connected to the ground plane with a lumped 50-ohm load. For the wire-pair test, parallel wires of these dimensions are located 1 cm apart, with one wire shorted to the ground plane and the other connected to the ground plane with a lumped 50-ohm load. All results are normalized to a 1 volt/m incident wave electric field.

From Fig. 29, we see that there is a good correspondence between the measured and numerically modeled wire load current for both test cases. The two-wire test proved to be especially challenging since the observed Q factor of the coupling response (center frequency divided by the half-power bandwidth) is quite high, about 75. Indeed, it is found that the FD-TD code has to be stepped through as many as 80 cycles to approximately reach the sinusoidal steady state for illumination frequencies near the resonant peak [16]. However, substantially fewer cycles of time-stepping are needed away from the resonance, as indicated in the figure.

8.9 Modeling Very Complex 3-D Structures

Two characteristics of FD-TD make it very promising for numerical modeling of electromagnetic wave interactions with very complex objects. First, dielectric and permeable media can be specified independently for each electric and magnetic field vector component in the three-dimensional volume being modeled. Since there may be tens of millions of such vector components in large FD-TD models, inhomogeneous media of enormous complexity can be specified in principle. Second, the required computer resources for this type of detailed volumetric modeling are dimensionally low, only of order N, where N is the number of space cells in the FD-TD lattice.

The emergence of supercomputers has recently permitted FD-TD to be seriously applied to a number of very complex electromagnetic wave interaction problems. Two of these will now be briefly reviewed.

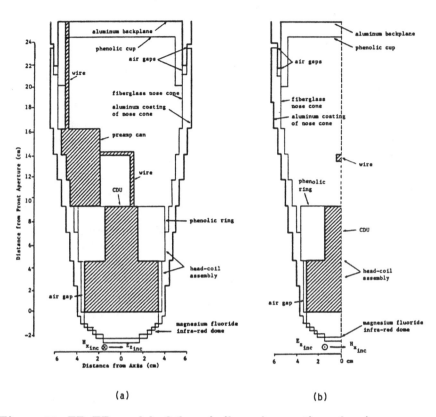

Figure 30 FD-TD model of the missile seeker section, showing component materials: (a) At the vertical symmetry plane; (b) At the horizontal observation plane [6, 37].

a. UHF Wave Penetration into a Missile Seeker Section

Here, FD-TD is applied to model the penetration of an axially incident 300-MHz plane wave into a metal-coated missile guidance section [6,37]. The FD-TD model, shown in Fig. 30, contains the following elements: 1. magnesium fluoride infrared dome; 2. circular nose aperture; 3. circumferential sleeve-fitting aperture 23 cm aft (loaded with Fiberglas); 4. head coil assembly; 5. cooled detector unit with enclosing phenolic ring; 6. pre-amp can; 7. wire bundle connecting the detector unit to the pre-amp can; 8. wire bundle connecting the pre-amp can to the metal backplane; and 9. longitudinal metal support rods. The Fiberglas structure of the nose cone and its metalization are approximated in a stepped-surface manner, as is the infrared dome.

For this structure, the FD-TD model uses a uniform cell size of 1/3 cm ($\lambda_0/300$), with an overall lattice size of 24 × 100 × 48 cells containing 690,000 unknown field components. (A single symmetry plane is used, giving an effective lattice size of 48 × 100 × 48). The model is run for 1800 time steps, equivalent to 3.0 cycles of the incident wave at 300 MHz.

Figure 31 plots contour maps of the FD-TD computed field vector components at the symmetry plane of the model. An important observation is that the simulated wire bundles connecting the cooled detector unit, pre-amp can, and metal backplane are paralleled by high-level magnetic field contours (Fig. 31b). This is indicative of substantial uniform current flow along each bundle. Such current flow would generate locally a magnetic field looping around the wire bundle which, when "cut" by the symmetry plane, shows up as parallel field contours spaced equally on each side of the bundle. By using a simple Ampere's Law argument, the common-mode bundle currents can be calculated, thus obtaining a key transfer function between free-field incident UHF plane wave power density and coupled wire currents [37]. As stated earlier, this information is useful for studies of vulnerability of electronic systems to upset due to both natural and man-made electromagnetic phenomena.

Although this missile seeker model was composed to demonstrate the capability of FD-TD to map fields penetrating into a complex structure having multiple apertures and realistic internal engineering details, it should be understood that the full bistatic radar cross section pattern of the structure is available as a by-product with virtually no additional effort. Further, with the 1/3 cm space resolution used, the FD-TD radar cross section model would be useful up to 9 GHz.

b. *Whole-Body Human Dosimetry at VHF and UHF Frequencies*

Here, FD-TD is applied to model the penetration of plane waves at VHF and UHF frequencies into the entire human body [38,39]. Directly exploiting the ability of FD-TD to model media inhomogeneities down to the space-cell level, highly realistic three-dimensional FD-TD tissue models of the complete body have been constructed. Specific electrical parameters are assigned to each of the electric field vector components at the 16,000 to 40,000 space cells comprising the body model. Assignments are based upon detailed cross-section tissue maps

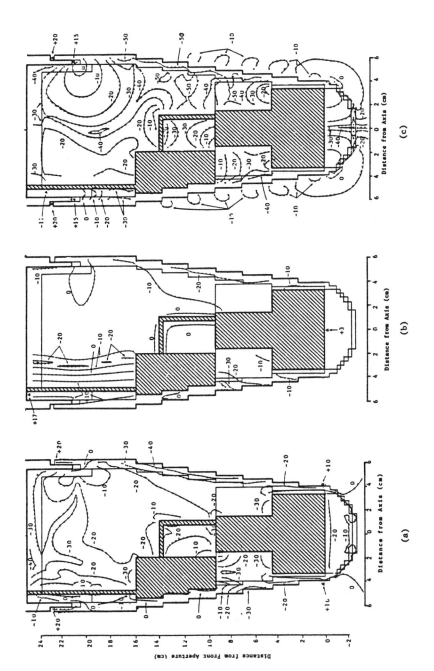

Figure 31 FD-TD computed contour maps of the penetrating fields in the vertical symmetry plane of the missile seeker section: (a) E_z; (b) H_x; (c) E_y [6,37].

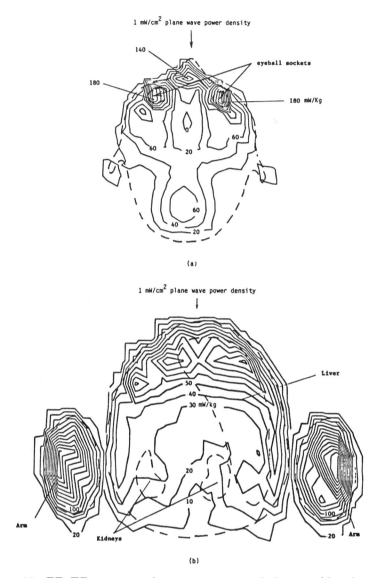

Figure 32 FD-TD computed contour maps of the specific absorption rate due to penetrating electromagnetic fields within a highly-realistic model of the entire human body: (a) Along a horizontal cut through the head at 350 MHz; (b) Along a horizontal cut through the liver at 100 MHz [39].

of the body (as obtained via cadaver studies available in the medical literature), and cataloged measurements of tissue dielectric properties. Uniform FD-TD space resolutions as fine as 1.3 cm throughout the entire human body have proven feasible with the Cray-2.

Figure 32, taken from [39], shows the FD-TD computed contour maps of the specific absorption rate (SAR) distribution along horizontal cuts through the head and liver of the three-dimensional inhomogeneous man model. In Fig. 32a, the incident wave has a power density of 1 mW/cm^2 at 350 MHz, while in Fig. 32b, the incident wave has the same power density but is at 100 MHz. These contour maps illustrate the high level of detail of local features of the SAR distribution that is possible via FD-TD modeling for highly realistic tissue models.

8.10 Microstrip and Microwave Circuits

Recently, FD-TD modeling has been extended to provide detailed characterizations of microstrips, resonators, finlines, and two-dimensional microwave circuits. In [40], FD-TD is used to calculate the dispersive characteristics of a typical microstrip on a gallium arsenide substrate. A Gaussian pulse excitation is used, and the effective dielectric constant and characteristic impedance vs. frequency is efficiently obtained over a broad frequency range via Fourier transform of the time-domain field response.

In [41], FD-TD is first used to obtain resonant frequencies of several three-dimensional cavities loaded by dielectric blocks. Next, the resonant frequency of a finline cavity is computed. Last, the resonant frequencies of a microstrip cavity on anisotropic substrate are obtained, and the dispersion characteristics of the microstrip used in the cavity are calculated. FD-TD modeling results are compared primarily to those obtained using the transmission line matrix (TLM) approach, and the two methods are found to give practically the same results.

In [42], a modified version of FD-TD is presented which provides central-difference time-stepping expressions for distributions of voltage and surface current density along arbitrary-shaped two-dimensional microwave circuits. This approach is quite different from that of [40] and [41], which utilizes the original volumetric field sampling concept for FD-TD. As a result, the method of [42] requires fewer unknowns to be solved, and avoids the need for a radiation boundary condition. However, an auxiliary condition is required to describe the loading effects of the fringing fields at the edges of the microstrip conducting

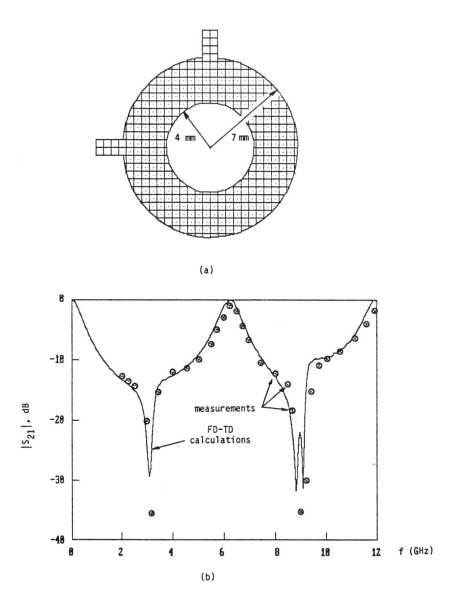

(a)

(b)

Figure 33 Comparison of FD-TD modeling predictions with measure-
ments of $|S_{21}|$ for a two-port microstrip ring circuit: (a) Geometry and
gridding of microstrip circuit; (b) Comparative results over 2–12 GHz
[42].

paths. Figure 33, taken from [42], shows the FD-TD computed S parameter, $|S_{21}|$, as a function of frequency for a two-port microstrip ring circuit. The ring circuit, gridded as shown in the figure, has an inner radius of 4 mm, outer radius of 7 mm, substrate relative permittivity of 10 and relative permeability of 0.93 (simulating duroid), and is connected to two 50-ohm lines making a 90° angle. The broadband response of the circuit is obtained using a single FD-TD run for an appropriate pulse excitation, followed by Fourier transformation of the desired response time-domain waveform. From Fig. 33, we see good agreement of the predicted and measured circuit response over the 2–12 GHz frequency band and a dynamic range of about 30 dB. [42] concludes that the application of its FD-TD approach to arbitrarily-shaped microstrip circuits is encouraging, but more work is needed to determine the modeling limitations, especially at higher frequencies where media dispersion can become important.

8.11   Inverse Scattering Reconstructions

Initial work has demonstrated the possibility of accurately reconstructing one-dimensional profiles of permittivity and conductivity [43], and the shape and dielectric compositions of two-dimensional targets [44,45] from minimal scattered field pulse response data. The general approach involves setting up a numerical feedback loop which uses a one- or two-dimensional FD-TD code as a forward-scattering element, and a specially constructed non-linear optimization code as the feedback element. FD-TD generates a test pulse response for a trial layering or target shape/composition. The test pulse is compared to the measured pulse, and an error signal is developed. Working on this error signal, the non-linear optimization element perturbs the trial layering or target shape/composition in a manner to drive down the error. Upon repeated iterations, the proposed layering or target ideally converges to the actual one, a strategy similar to that of [46].

The advantage of working in the time domain is that a layered medium or target shape can be reconstructed sequentially in time as the wavefront of the incident pulse sweeps through, taking advantage of causality. This reduces the complexity of reconstruction since only a portion of the layering or target shape is being generated at each iteration. Advanced strategies for reconstruction in the presence of additive noise may involve the use of prediction/correction, where the trial layer or target shape is considered to be a predictor of the actual

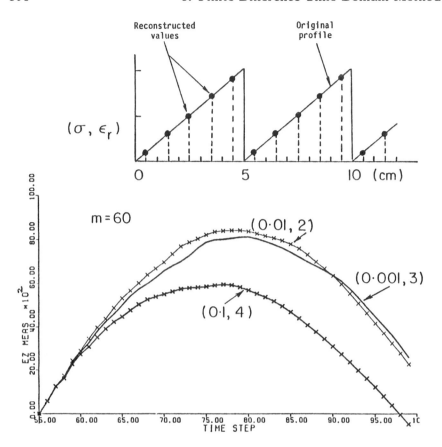

Figure 34 Application of the FD-TD/feedback strategy to reconstruct a 1-D sawtooth variation of electrical permittivity and conductivity in the absence of noise [43].

case, which is subsequently corrected by optimization of the entire layered medium or target shape using the complete scattered pulse waveform.

Figure 34 shows the application of the basic FD-TD feedback strategy to a one-dimensional layered medium in the absence of noise. Both the electrical permittivity and conductivity of the medium vary in a "sawtooth" manner with depth. The curves show simulated measured data for the reflected pulse for three cases defined by the peak values of the conductivity (0.001 S/m, 0.01 S/m, and 0.1 S/m) and the corresponding spatially coincident peak values of relative permittivity (3, 2, and 4) of the medium. In each case, the incident pulse is

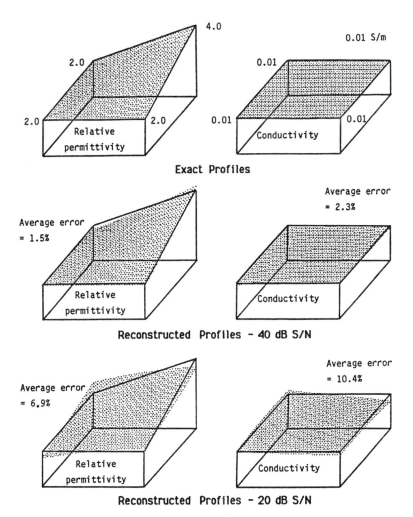

Figure 35 Application of the FD-TD/feedback strategy to reconstruct a 2-D lossy dielectric target in the presence of noise [45].

assumed to be a half-sinusoid spanning 50 cm between zero crossings. Noting that the dark dots superimposed on the "sawtooth" represent the reconstructed values of permittivity and conductivity, we see that the basic FD-TD feedback strategy is quite successful in the absence of noise [43].

Figure 35 shows the application of the FD-TD feedback strategy to reconstruct a two-dimensional lossy dielectric target. The target is a 30 cm × 30 cm square cylinder having a uniform conductivity of 0.01

S/m, and a tent-like relative permittivity profile which starts at 2.0 at the front and left sides and increases linearly to a peak value of 4.0 at the back corner on the right side. These profiles are illustrated in a perspective manner at the top of Fig. 35. The target is assumed to be illuminated by a TM polarized plane wave that is directed toward the front of the target (as visualized at the top of the figure). The incident waveform is a 3-cycle sinusoidal tone burst having a 60-MHz carrier frequency. For the reconstruction, the only data set utilized is the time-domain waveform of the scattered electric field, as observed at two points. These points are located 1 m from the front of the target, and are positioned 15 cm to either side of the target center line. To simulate measured data, the FD-TD computed scattered field waveforms are contaminated with additive Gaussian noise. In all of the reconstructions, the target shape and location are assumed to be known.

From Fig. 35, we see that for a signal/noise ratio of 40 dB, the average error in the reconstructed permittivity and conductivity profiles is 1.5% and 2.3%, respectively. If the signal/noise ratio is reduced to 20 dB, the average errors increase to 6.9% and 10.4%, respectively [45]. Research is ongoing to determine means of improving the noise performance, especially using predictor/corrector techniques briefly discussed earlier. Given the relatively small amount of scattered field data utilized, the FD-TD feedback strategy appears promising for future development.

8.12   Very Large-Scale Software

The FD-TD method is naturally suited for large-scale processing by state-of-the-art vector supercomputers and concurrent processors. This is because essentially all of the arithmetic operations involved in a typical FD-TD run can be vectorized or cast into a highly concurrent format. Further, the $O(N)$ demand for computer memory and clock cycles (where N is the number of lattice space cells) is dimensionally low. This permits three-dimensional FD-TD models of structures spanning 50–100 λ_0 to be anticipated in the early 1990's.

Let us now consider computation times of present FD-TD codes. Table 1 lists computation times (derived either from benchmark runs or based on analysts' estimates) for modeling one illumination angle of a 10-λ_0 three-dimensional structure using the present FD-TD code. Note that the fourth computing system listed in the table is a hypothetical next-generation machine operating at an average rate of 10 Gflops. This capability is generally expected to be available in the early 1990's.

Table 1. Computation Times

Machine	Time †
VAX 11/780 (no floating point accelerator)	40 hours
Cray-2 (single processor, using VAX Fortran)	12 min
Cray-2 (single processor, with optimization)	2 min
Cray-2 (four processors, with optimization)	30 sec (est.)
True 10 Gflop machine	2 sec (est.)

From Table 1, it is fairly clear that steadily advancing super-computer technology will permit routine engineering usage of FD-TD for modeling electromagnetic wave interactions with electrically-large structures by 1995.

An interesting prospect that has recently arisen is the reduction of the $O(N)$ computational burden of FD-TD to $O(N^{1/3})$. This possibility is a consequence of the appearance of the Connection Machine (CM), which has tens of thousands of simple processors and associated memories arranged in a highly efficient manner for processor-to-processor communication. With the CM, a single processor could be assigned to store and time-step a single row of vector field components in a three-dimensional FD-TD space lattice. For example, $1.5 \cdot 10^6$ processors would be sufficient to store the 6 Cartesian components of E and H for each of the 500×500 rows of a cubic lattice spanning $50\lambda_0$ (assuming 10 cells/λ_0 resolution). FD-TD time-stepping would be performed via row operations mapped onto the individual CM processors. These row operations would be performed concurrently. Thus, for a fixed number of time steps, the total running time would be proportional to the time needed to perform a single row operation, which

---

† Computation times are for the 9-wavelength T-shaped target using the present FD-TD code. There are 1.55×10^6 unknown field vector components and 661 time steps. The complete bistatic RCS pattern is obtained for a single illumination angle at a single frequency. Times are increased by 50%-100% if an impulsive illumination / Fourier transform is used to obtain the bistatic RCS pattern at a multiplicity of frequencies within the spectrum of the impulsive illumination.

in turn would be proportional to the number of field vector components in the row, or $O(N^{1/3})$.

For the 50-λ_0 cubic lattice noted above, this would imply a dimensional reduction of the computational burden from $O(500^3)$ to $O(500)$, a tremendous benefit. As a result, it is conceivable that a suitably scaled CM could model one illumination angle of a 50-λ_0 three-dimensional structure in only a few seconds, achieving effective floating-point rates in the order of 100 Gflops. For this reason, FD-TD software development for the CM is a promising area of research for developing ultra-large numerical models of electromagnetic wave interactions with complex structures.

8.13   Conclusion

This chapter has reviewed the basic formulation of the FD-TD numerical modeling approach for Maxwell's equations. A number of two- and three-dimensional examples of FD-TD modeling of electromagnetic wave interactions with structures were provided to indicate the accuracy and breadth of FD-TD applications. The objects modeled range in nature from simple geometric shapes to extremely complex aerospace and biological systems. In all cases studied to date where rigorous analytical, code-to-code, or experimental validations were possible, FD-TD predictive data for penetrating and scattered near fields as well as radar cross section were in excellent agreement with benchmark data. It was also shown that opportunities are arising in applying FD-TD to model rapidly time-varying systems, microwave circuits, and inverse scattering. With continuing advances in FD-TD modeling theory, as well as continuing advances in vector and concurrent supercomputer technology, there is a strong possibility that FD-TD numerical modeling will occupy an important place in high-frequency engineering electromagnetics as we move into the 1990's.

Acknowledgements

The authors wish to acknowledge the research contributions of their colleague, Prof. Gregory A. Kriegsmann of Northwestern University, Department of Engineering Science and Applied Mathematics. Contributions of graduate students at Northwestern and the University of Illinois at Chicago, especially Mr. Ben Beker, Mr. Jeffrey Blaschak,

Mr. Fady Harfoush, Mr. Thomas Jurgens, Mr. Thomas Moore, and Mr. Mark Strickel are also gratefully acknowledged.

The authors also wish to acknowledge the support of their sponsors, past and present, including the U.S. Air Force Rome Air Development Center (Contracts F30602-77-C-0163, F30602-79-C-0039, F30602-80-C-0302, and F19628-82-C-0140); Lawrence Livermore National Laboratory (Contract 6599805); NASA Lewis Research Center (Grant NAG 3-635); National Science Foundation (Grants ECS-8515777 and ASC-8811273); Office of Naval Research (Contract N00014-88-K-0475); General Dynamics (PO-4059045); and Cray Research Inc.

References

[1] Yee, K. S., "Numerical solution of initial boundary value problems involving Maxwell's equations in isotropic media," *IEEE Trans. Antennas Propagat.*, **AP-14**, 302–307, 1966.

[2] Taflove, A., and M. E. Brodwin. "Numerical solution of steady-state electromagnetic scattering problems using the time-dependent Maxwell's equations," *IEEE Trans. Microwave Theory Tech.*, **MTT-23**, 623–630, 1975.

[3] Kriegsmann, G. A., "Exploiting the limiting amplitude principle to numerically solve scattering problems," *Wave Motion*, 4, 371–380, 1982.

[4] Taflove, A., and M. E. Brodwin. "Computation of the electromagnetic fields and induced temperatures within a model of the microwave-irradiated human eye," *IEEE Trans. Microwave Theory Tech.*, **MTT-23**, 888–896, 1975.

[5] Taflove, A., "Application of the finite-difference time-domain method to sinusoidal steady state electromagnetic penetration problems," *IEEE Trans. Electromagn. Compat.*, **EMC-22**, 191–202, 1980.

[6] Taflove, A., and K. R. Umashankar, "A hybrid moment method/finite-difference time-domain approach to electromagnetic coupling and aperture penetration into complex geometries," *IEEE Trans. Antennas Propagat.*, **AP-30**, 617–627, 1982.

[7] Holland, R., "Threde: A free-field EMP coupling and scattering code," *IEEE Trans. Nuclear Sci.*, **NS-24**, 2416–2421, 1977.

[8] Kunz, K. S., and K. M. Lee, "A three-dimensional finite-difference solution of the external response of an aircraft to a complex transient EM environment: Part I, The method and its implementation," *IEEE Trans. Electromagn. Compat.*, **EMC-20**, 328–333, 1978.

[9] Merewether, D. E., R. Fisher, and F. W. Smith, "On implementing a numeric Huygens' source scheme in a finite-difference program to illuminate scattering bodies," *IEEE Trans. Nuclear Sci.*, **NS-27**, 1819–1833, 1980.

[10] Taflove, A., and K. R. Umashankar, "Advanced numerical modeling of microwave penetration and coupling for complex structures," Final Rept. No. UCRL-15960, Contract 6599805, Lawrence Livermore Nat. Lab., 1987.

[11] Mur, G., "Absorbing boundary conditions for the finite- difference approximation of the time-domain electromagnetic field equations," *IEEE Trans. Electromagn. Compat.*, **EMC-23**, 377–382, 1981.

[12] Umashankar, K. R., and A. Taflove, "A novel method to analyze electromagnetic scattering of complex objects," *IEEE Trans. Electromagn. Compat.*, **EMC-24**, 397–405, 1982.

[13] Taflove, A., and K. R. Umashankar, "Radar cross section of general three-dimensional scatterers," *IEEE Trans. Electromagn. Compat.*, **EMC-25**, 433–440, 1983.

[14] Taflove, A., K. R. Umashankar, and T. G. Jurgens, "Validation of FD-TD modeling of the radar cross section of three-dimensional structures spanning up to nine wavelengths," *IEEE Trans. Antennas Propagat.*, **AP-33**, 662–666, 1985.

[15] Taflove, A., K. R. Umashankar, B. Beker, F. Harfoush, and K. S. Yee, "Detailed FD-TD analysis of electromagnetic fields penetrating narrow slots and lapped joints in thick conducting screens," *IEEE Trans. Antennas Propagat.*, **AP-36**, 247–257, 1988.

[16] Umashankar, K. R., A. Taflove, and B. Beker, "Calculation and experimental validation of induced currents on coupled wires in an arbitrary shaped cavity," *IEEE Trans. Antennas Propagat.*, **AP-35**, 1248–1257, 1987.

[17] Engquist, B., and A. Majda, "Absorbing boundary conditions for the numerical simulation of waves," *Math. Comp.*, **31**, 629–651, 1977.

[18] Trefethen, L. N., and L. Halpern, "Well-posedness of one-way wave equations and absorbing boundary conditions," *Inst. Comput. Appl. Sci. and Engrg.* (ICASE), NASA Langley Res. Ctr., Hampton, VA, Rept. 85-30, 1985.

[19] Moore, T. G., J. G. Blaschak, A. Taflove, and G. A. Kriegsmann, "Theory and application of radiation boundary operators," *IEEE Trans. Antennas Propagat.*, **AP-36**, 1988 (in press).

[20] Blaschak, J. G., and G. A. Kriegsmann, "A comparative study of absorbing boundary conditions," *J. Computational Physics*, **77**, 109–139, 1988.

[21] Borup, D. T., D. M. Sullivan, and O. P. Gandhi, "Comparison of the FFT conjugate gradient method and the finite-difference time-domain method for the 2-D absorption problem," *IEEE Trans. Microwave Theory Tech.*, **MTT-35**, 383–395, 1987.

[22] Beker, B., K. R. Umashankar, and A. Taflove, "Numerical analysis and validation of the combined-field surface integral equations for electromagnetic scattering by arbitrary shaped two-dimensional anisotropic objects," *IEEE Trans. Antennas Propagat.*, **AP-37**, 1989.

[23] Taflove, A., and K. R. Umashankar, "Analytical models for electromagnetic scattering," Final Rept. RADC-TR-85-87, Contract F19628-82-C-0140, Electromagn. Sci. Div., Rome Air Dev. Center., Hanscom AFB, Mass., 1985.

[24] Jurgens, T. G., A. Taflove, and K. R. Umashankar, "FD-TD conformal modeling of smooth curved surfaces," presented at URSI Radio Science Meeting, Blacksburg, Virginia, June, 1987.

[25] Madsen, N. K., and R. W. Ziolkowski, "Numerical solution of Maxwell's equations in the time domain using irregular nonorthogonal grids," *Wave Motion*, **10**, 1988 (in press).

[26] Fusco, M., "FD-TD algorithm in curvilinear coordinates," *IEEE Trans. Antennas Propagat.*, submitted.

[27] McCartin, B., L. J. Bahrmasel, and G. Meltz, "Application of the control region approximation to two-dimensional electromagnetic scattering," Chap. 5 in this text.

[28] Shankar, V., and W. Hall, "A time-domain differential solver for electromagnetic scattering problems," *Proc. IEEE*, **77**, 1989 (in press).

[29] Blaschak, J. G., G. A. Kriegsmann, and A. Taflove, "A study of wave interactions with flanged waveguides and cavities using the

on-surface radiation condition method," *Wave Motion*, **19**, 1989 (in press).

[30] Harfoush, F., A. Taflove, and G. A. Kriegsmann, "A numerical technique for analyzing electromagnetic wave scattering from moving surfaces in one and two dimensions," *IEEE Trans. Antennas Propagat.*, **AP-37**, 1989 (in press).

[31] Harfoush, F., A. Taflove, and G. A. Kriegsmann, "Numerical implementation of relativistic electromagnetic field boundary conditions in a laboratory-frame grid," *J. Computational Physics*, accepted for publication.

[32] De Zutter, D., "Reflections from linearly vibrating objects: plane mirror at oblique incidence," *IEEE Trans. Antennas Propagat.*, **AP-30**, 898–903, 1982.

[33] Wilton, D. R., and S. Govind, "Incorporation of edge conditions in moment method solutions," *IEEE Trans. Antennas Propagat.*, **AP-25**, 845–850, 1977.

[34] Gilbert, J., and R. Holland, "Implementation of the thin-slot formalism in the finite-difference EMP code THREDII," *IEEE Trans. Nuclear Sci.*, **NS-28**, 4269–4274, 1981.

[35] Yee, K. S., "A numerical method of solving Maxwell's equations with a coarse grid bordering a fine grid," SGEMP Note #9, Document D-DV-86-0008, D Division, Lawrence Livermore Nat. Lab., 1986.

[36] Holland, R., and L. Simpson, "Finite-difference analysis of EMP coupling to thin struts and wires," *IEEE Trans. Electromagn. Compat.*, **EMC-23**, 88–97, 1981.

[37] Taflove, A., and K. R. Umashankar, "Evaluation of time-domain electromagnetic coupling techniques. Vol. I: Theory and numerical results," Final Rept. RADC-TR-80-251, Contract F30602-79-C-0039, Rome Air Dev. Center, Griffiss AFB, NY, 1980.

[38] Sullivan, D. M., D. T. Borup, and O. P. Gandhi, "Use of the finite-difference time-domain method in calculating EM absorption in human tissues," *IEEE Trans. Biomed. Engr.*, **BME-34**, 148–157, 1987.

[39] Sullivan, D. M., O. P. Gandhi, and A. Taflove, "Use of the finite-difference time-domain method for calculating EM absorption in man models," *IEEE Trans. Biomed. Eng.*, **35**, 179–186, 1988.

[40] Zhang, X., J. Fang, K. K. Mei, and Y. Liu, "Calculations of the dispersive characteristics of microstrips by the time-domain finite-

difference method," *IEEE Trans. Microwave Theory Tech.*, **MTT-36**, 263–267, 1988.

[41] Choi, D. H., and W. J. Hoefer, "The finite-difference time-domain method and its application to eigenvalue problems," *IEEE Trans. Microwave Theory Tech.*, **MTT-34**, 1464–1470, 1986.

[42] Gwarek, W. K., "Analysis of arbitrarily-shaped two-dimensional microwave circuits by the finite-difference time-domain method," *IEEE Trans. Microwave Theory Tech.*, **MTT-36**, 738–744, 1988.

[43] Umashankar, K. R., S. K., Chaudhuri, and A. Taflove, "Finite-difference time-domain formulation of an inverse scattering scheme for remote sensing of inhomogeneous lossy layered media," *IEEE Trans. Antennas Propagat.*, submitted.

[44] Strickel, M. A., A. Taflove, and K. R. Umashankar, "Accurate reconstruction of two-dimensional conducting and homogeneous dielectric target shapes from a single-point TM scattered field pulse response," *IEEE Trans. Antennas Propagat.*, submitted.

[45] Strickel, M. A., and A. Taflove, "Reconstruction of one- and two-dimensional inhomogeneous dielectric targets using the FD-TD/ feedback method," *IEEE Trans. Antennas Propagat.*, submitted.

[46] Bennett, C. L., and G. F. Ross, "Time-domain electromagnetics and its applications," *Proc. IEEE*, **66**, 299–318, 1978.

INDEX